★★★ THE ★★★
CIVIL WAR
PAINTINGS OF
MORT KÜNSTLER

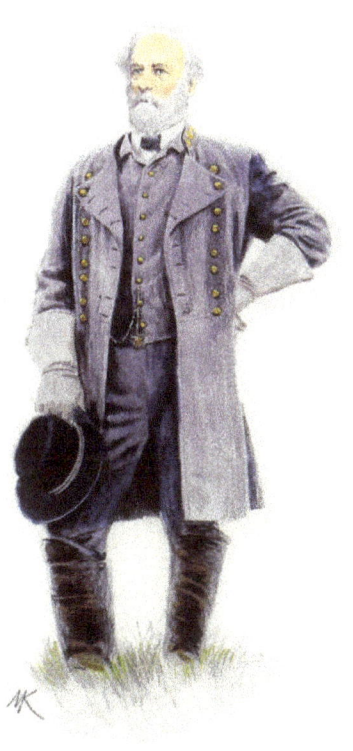

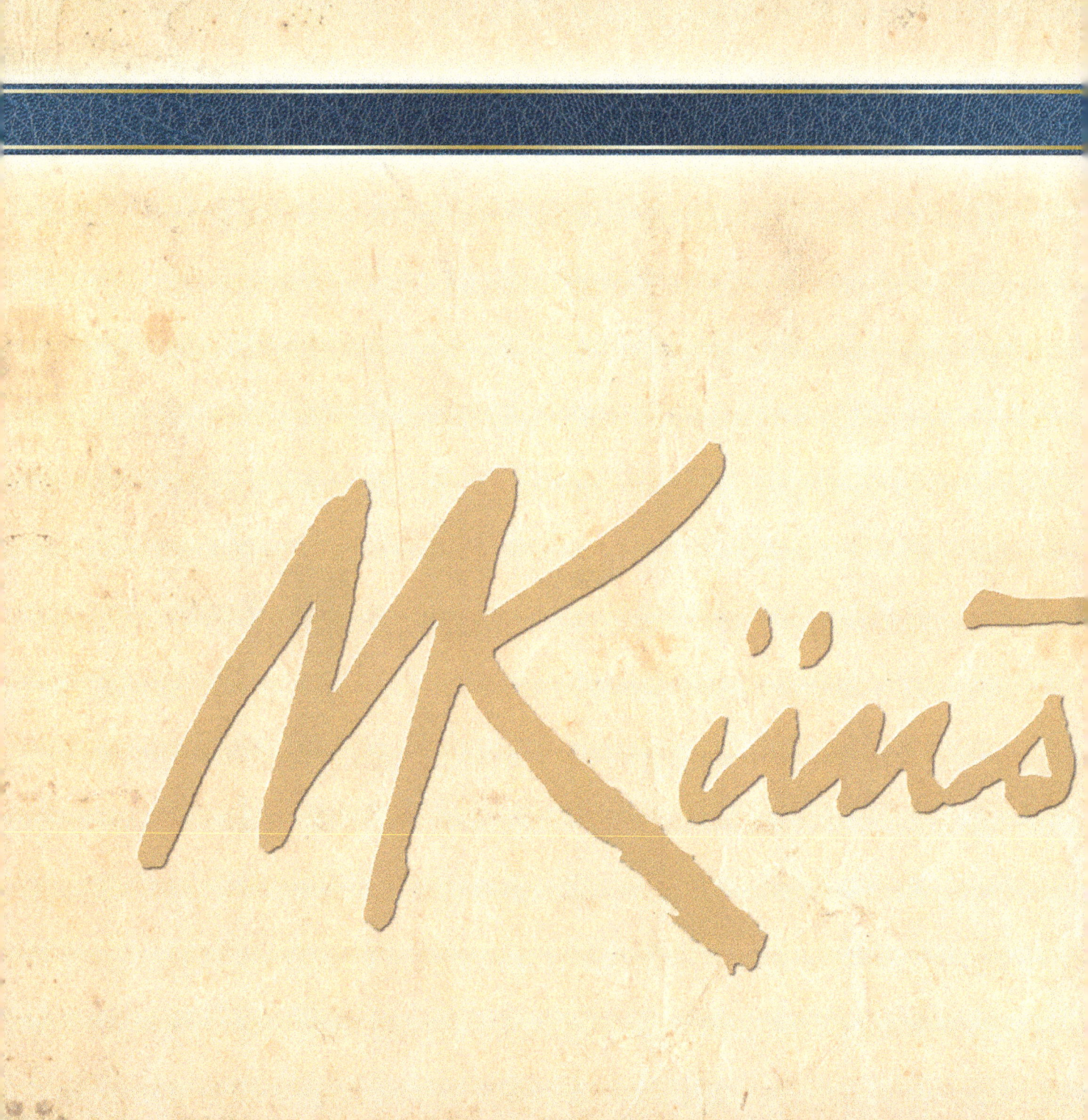

★★★ THE ★★★ CIVIL WAR PAINTINGS OF MORT KÜNSTLER

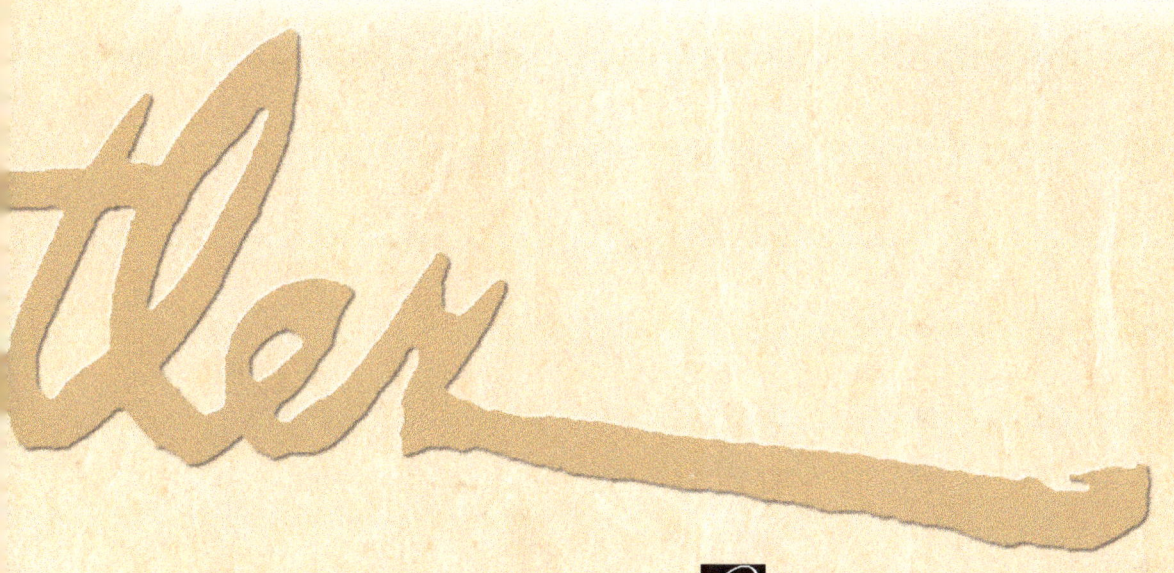

CUMBERLAND HOUSE
NASHVILLE, TENNESSEE

THE CIVIL WAR PAINTINGS OF MORT KÜNSTLER
VOLUME 4: FROM GETTYSBURG TO APPOMATTOX
PUBLISHED BY CUMBERLAND HOUSE PUBLISHING, INC.
431 Harding Industrial Drive
Nashville, Tennessee 37211

Text based on the writings of Rod Gragg, Mort Künstler, James M. McPherson, and James I. Robertson Jr. All art dimensions are presented height x width in inches.

Cover design by Gore Studio, Inc., Nashville, Tennessee

Library of Congress Cataloging-in-Publication Data
Künstler, Mort.
  The Civil War paintings of Mort Künstler / Mort Künstler.
      v. cm.
    Contents: v. 4. From Gettysburg to Appomattox
    ISBN-13: 978-1-58182-559-6 (hardcover : alk. paper)
    ISBN-13: 978-1-68442-927-1 (hardcover)
    1. United States—History—Civil War, 1861–1865—Pictorial works—Catalogs. 2. United States—History—Civil War, 1861–1865—Art and the war—Catalogs. 3. Künstler, Mort—Catalogs. I. Title.
  E468.7.K844 2006
  759.13—dc22   2006015631

Jacket Design: *Gore Studio, Inc. | www.GoreStudio.com*

Printed in the United States of America

To Florence and the late Louis Goldberg—
with much love and appreciation for allowing your
daughter to marry a starving artist

CONTENTS

FOREWORD

Defeats at Gettysburg and Vicksburg the first week of July 1863 were crippling but not fatal for the South. Virginia still stood defiant, and in mid-July a Confederate cavalry raid by John Hunt Morgan through southern Indiana and Ohio created near panic.

While Robert E. Lee spent the next eight months poised to lash out at the main Federal army, the South lost its foothold in Tennessee. Two days of intense fighting in September at Chickamauga brought the Confederacy an empty victory because Gen. Braxton Bragg failed to exploit his success. The contest for control of Chattanooga remained undecided until November 24, when Northern infantry fought its way up the steep face of Lookout Mountain, south of the city. The following day, Federals stormed and overran Missionary Ridge east of town. The once-proud Confederate Army of Tennessee retreated into nearby Georgia.

Abraham Lincoln named Ulysses S. Grant, the hero of the hour in the North, general in chief of all Union forces. With half a million men in his charge, Grant devised a simple strategy. Union forces would advance everywhere, on the premise that the weak Confederate lines would snap somewhere.

What became the decisive campaign began the first week of May 1864. The navies continued to tighten their hold on the rivers and at sea. The Union's western forces, under Grant's favorite lieutenant, William T. Sherman, advanced from Chattanooga toward the second-most-important supply center left in the Confederacy: Atlanta. Simultaneously, Grant joined the Army of the Potomac for a concerted offensive in Virginia.

It took Sherman more than two months to maneuver the one hundred miles to Atlanta's outskirts. An exasperated Confederate President Jefferson Davis then put the aggressive John B. Hood in command of the Southern forces. Hood promptly made major attacks on July 20 and 22 against Sherman's lines. Both failed, and on September 2, with Union forces about to complete an encirclement, Hood abandoned Atlanta.

This victory went far in ensuring Lincoln's reelection to a second term, which in turn meant a prosecution of the Civil War to a clear Union victory. Sherman further cemented his hold on the Deep South by using part of his army to deliver resounding defeats to the Confederates at Franklin and Nashville, Tennessee.

Meanwhile, Grant's multi-pronged invasions of Virginia had gone bloodily awry A heavy raid in the isolated southwestern quadrant of the state aimed at neutralizing such natural resources as salt works and lead mines. It gained only temporary success. A new Army of the James advanced from the coast to threaten Richmond. That movement floundered under Gen. Benjamin F Butler. The third offensive was in the Shenandoah Valley, aptly known as the "Breadbasket of the Confederacy" Yet it took three different Union generals, five months of effort, and much loss of life before Federals could claim any lasting accomplishment.

The fourth, and major, effort by Grant involved the Army of the Potomac moving directly against Lee. This Overland campaign began May 5–6 when

Lee surprised and pounded Grant's forces while they were wedged in a tangled, wooded mass known as the Wilderness. Unlike prior commanders of the Army of the Potomac, Grant did not retreat afterward. Instead, he shook off the defeat and plowed ahead in pursuit of Lee.

Desperate fighting came at Spotsylvania, North Anna, and Cold Harbor. Grant then moved his army across the James River and sought to strike Richmond from its supposedly soft underbelly. Lee arrived at nearby Petersburg in time to stave off disaster. By mid-June, Grant had suffered sixty thousand casualties—more men than Lee had when the campaign began—and he was farther away from the Southern capital than George B. McClellan had been two years earlier. Yet Grant had the hard-pressed Southern army trapped in the earthworks east and south of Richmond. Grant thereupon resorted to siege tactics, which had served him well at Vicksburg.

In Georgia, in the autumn, Sherman embarked on a daring movement that broke the back of the Confederacy. Some sixty thousand Federals left Atlanta in flames and marched unmolested 285 miles to the Atlantic coast. Having cut the South in two, Sherman turned north in February 1865 and advanced through the Carolinas.

Grant spent that winter strengthening and extending his lines in preparation for the spring offensive. His heavy April 2 attacks snapped the thin Confederate defenses. Lee limped westward in search of rations and refuge. Federals pursued his army like wolves tracking a wounded animal.

The end came on Palm Sunday, April 9, at Appomattox Court House. Lee vetoed a suggestion that he resort to guerrilla warfare. Such a course, Lee stated, would destroy the South and be the death of any future union of states. Honorably he had fought; honorably he surrendered.

That is why Appomattox will always be an end as well as a beginning. Four years of war decided an uncertain present and opened the door to a brighter future.

No artist is more aware of the Civil War's human emotions than Mort Künstler. The sheer volume of his paintings is staggering, but the quality of each rendition far exceeds quantity Künstler has that rare talent of not only capturing on canvas a moment in time; he has an enviable ability to bring a scene alive and give it feeling.

In this volume are several examples of Künstler's mastery of time and thought: Grant's determination to continue advancing south after the Wilderness, the heavy-handed Sherman silhouetted by a burning Atlanta, Lee's despair as his army melts away on the road to Appomattox.

Künstler can even create historical coincidence. Early on the night of February 17, 1864, the crew of the Confederate submarine *H. L. Hunley* left a Charleston pier for an ill-fated attack on the Union blockading fleet. At precisely the same moment, Lee and his staff were riding past a prayer meeting at a Virginia church.

Years of effort and dedication have made the name Mort Künstler the hallmark of Civil War art.

James I. Robertson Jr.

★★★ THE ★★★
CIVIL WAR
PAINTINGS OF
MORT KÜNSTLER

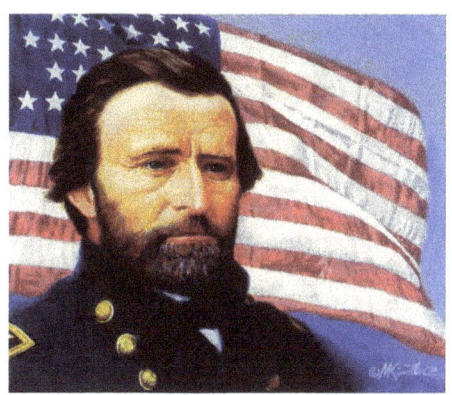
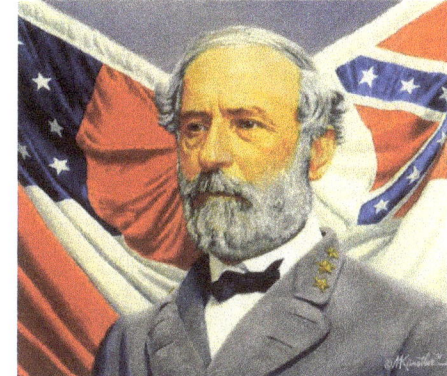

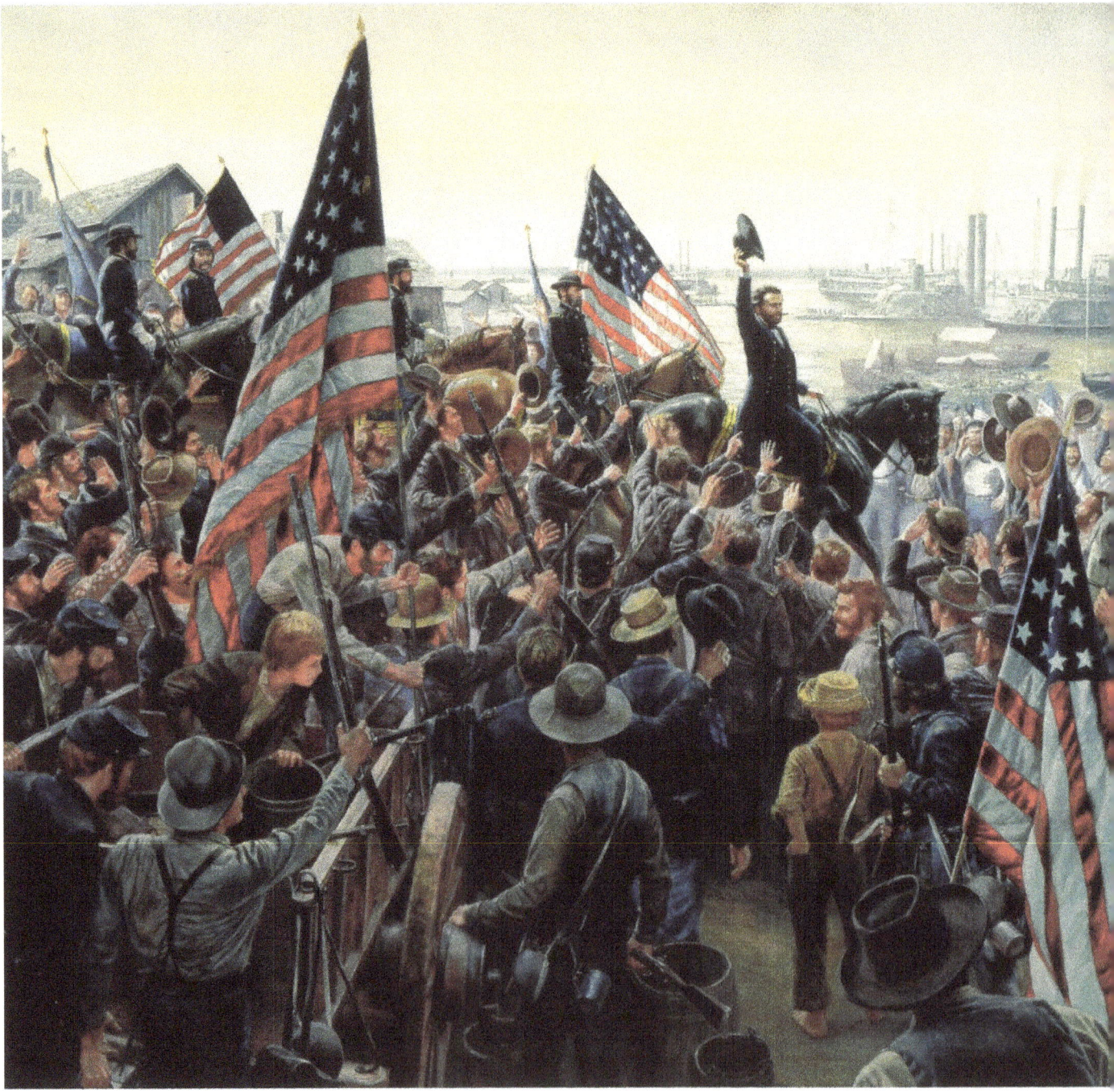

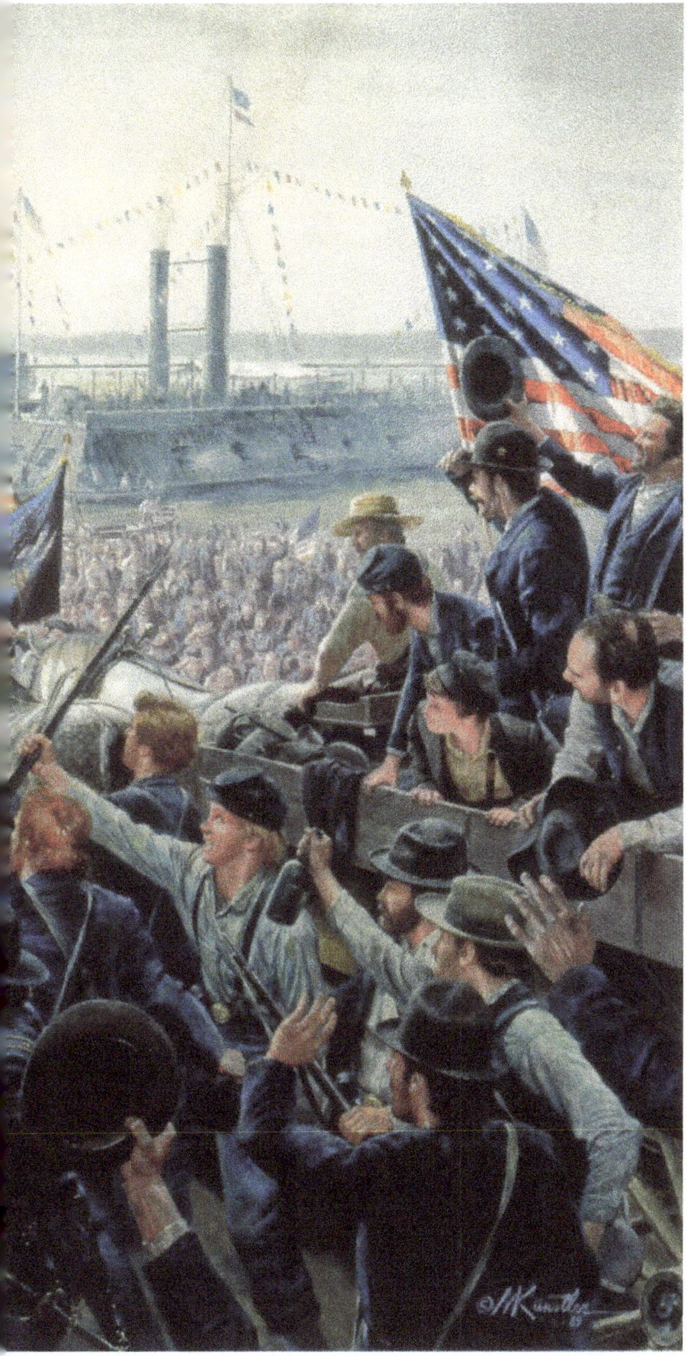

THE GLORIOUS FOURTH

GEN. ULYSSES S. GRANT AT VICKSBURG
JULY 4, 1863

1989, oil, 34 x 56

THE FALL OF VICKSBURG, Mississippi, on July 4, 1863, came one day after the Union victory at Gettysburg. Here Confederate Gen. John C. Pemberton surrendered, in addition to the river stronghold, more than sixty thousand small arms, almost two hundred cannon, and thirty thousand men. With this victory, the North won complete control of the river. Ulysses S. Grant later said, "The fate of the Confederacy was sealed when Vicksburg fell."

When I became familiar with the Vicksburg siege, I felt the celebratory scene was excellent material for a painting. I consulted historians, pored over maps and photographs, reviewed

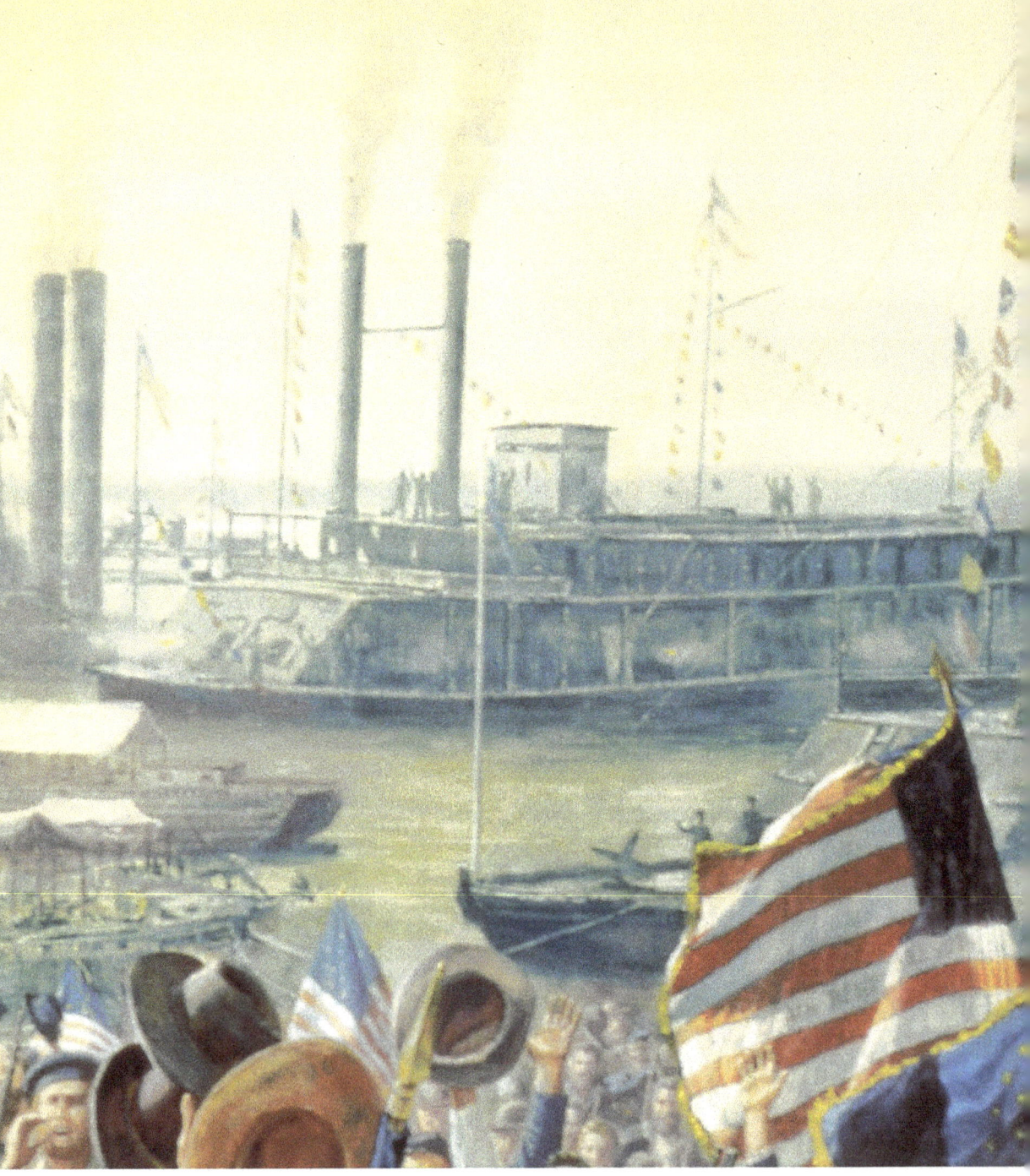

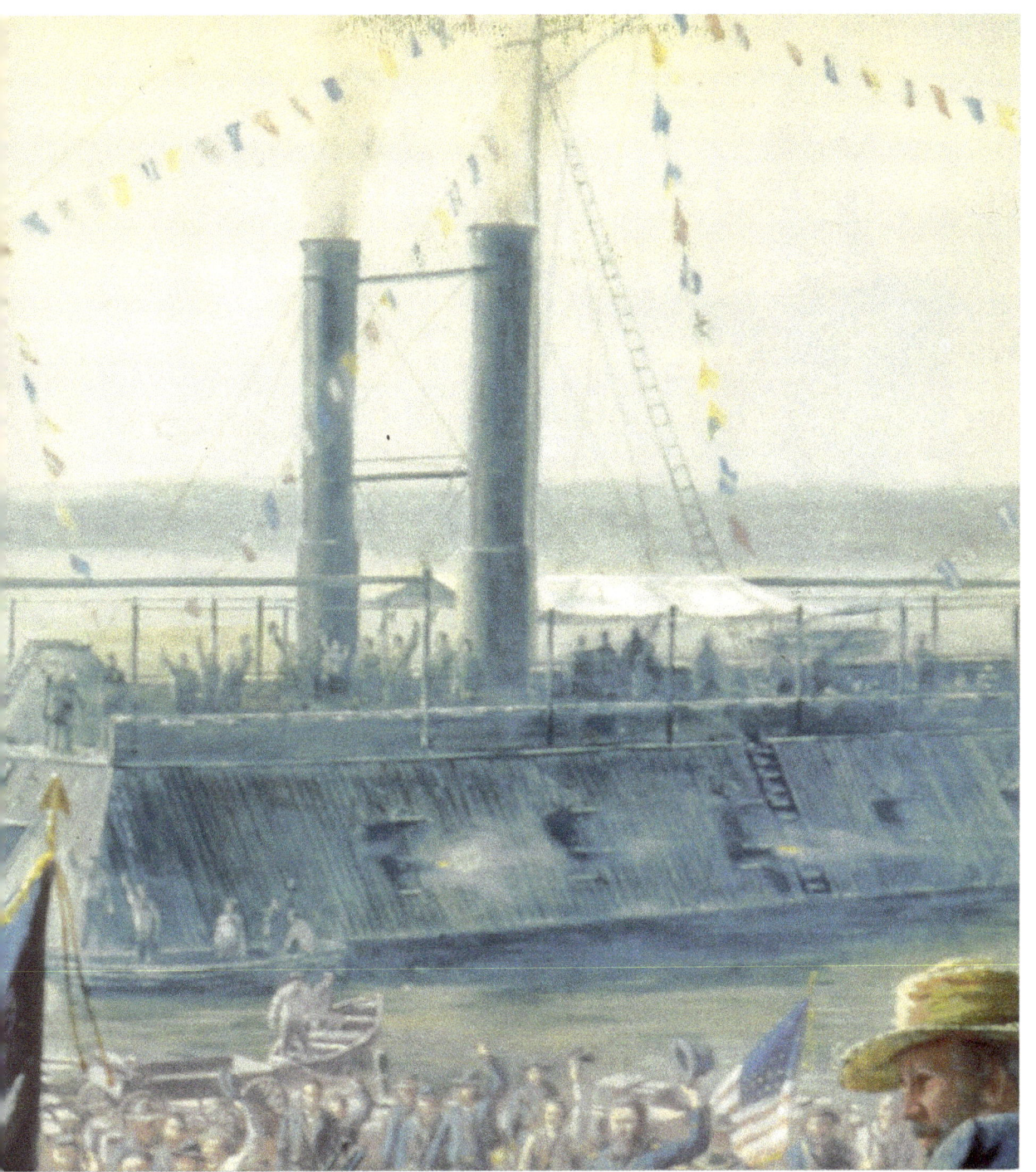

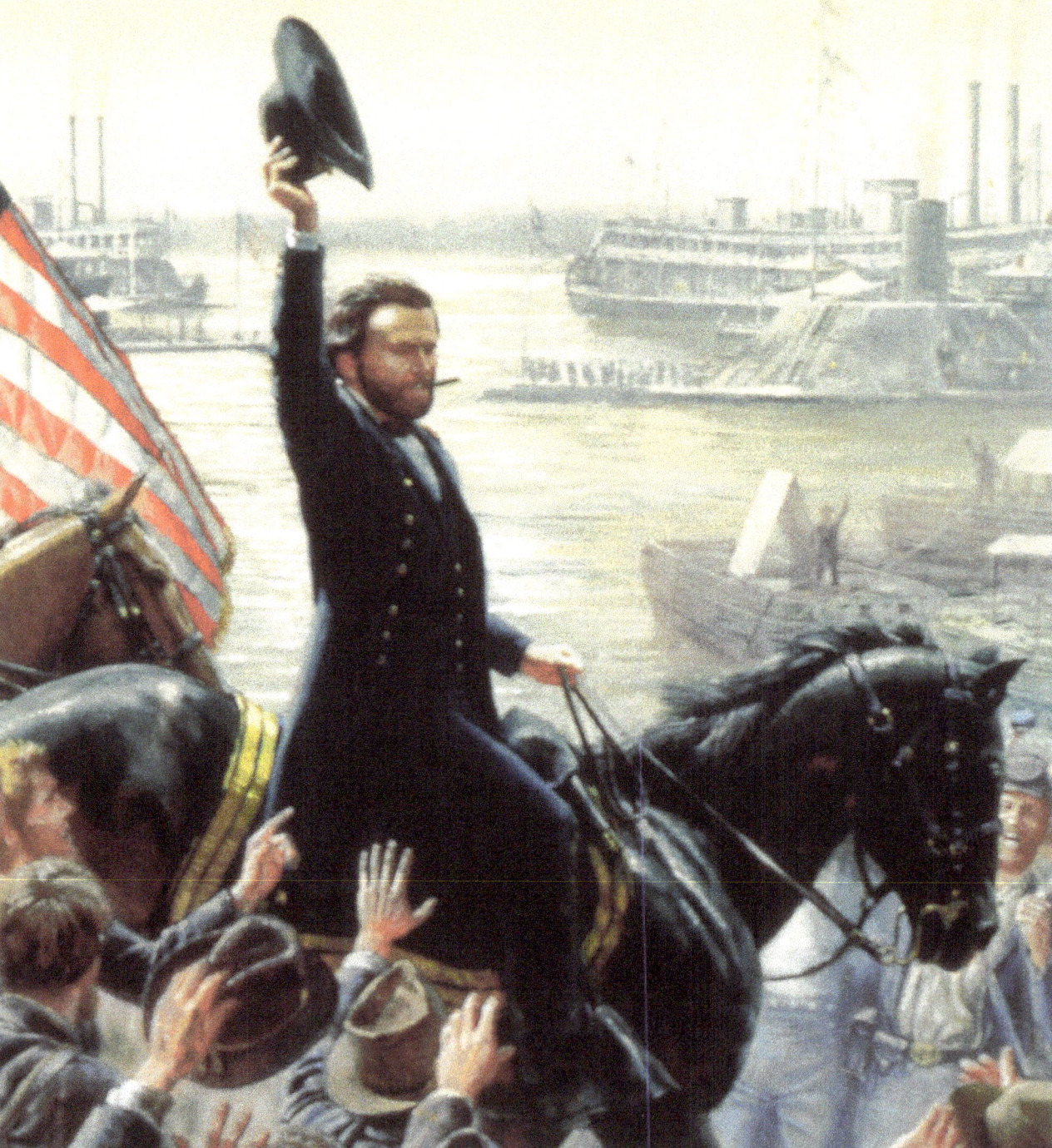

the literature and records of the siege, and visited the U.S. Navy Memorial Museum in Washington, D.C.

After forty-seven days of siege, Pemberton believed that he would obtain generous surrender terms by capitulating on July 4, the anniversary of the signing of the Declaration of Independence. So at 10:00 a.m. he yielded the city to the Federals. Grant and his entourage were en route to a meeting with Adm. David Porter, commander of the river fleet, and passed through a flag-waving, cheering crowd of eight thousand Union troops as they celebrated their Fourth of July victory at the Old Landing.

The painting shows Grant just before his meeting aboard Porter's flagship, the USS *Benton*. The admiral can be seen on the extreme left of the top deck, on the steps of the pilothouse.

The key to a picture this complex is to capture the crowd's enthusiasm and still lead the viewer's eye to Grant. Atop his favorite mount, Cincinnati, the general is in his typical informal dress with no sword belt, acknowledging the cheers of his men. In his party, immediately behind him, are Gens. John D. Stevenson, James B. McPherson, and John C. Logan. These three likenesses were difficult to master because I could not find photographs of any of the three generals in the positions in which they are portrayed here.

I learned that Illinois, Indiana, Minnesota, and Wisconsin regiments were present, and this is indicated by the lettering on the battle flags. The flags of the Forty-fifth Illinois and the Fourth Minnesota, which both claimed to have been the first to enter the city, are shown prominently. The shieldlike symbol on the forage cap of the soldier behind the cart on the extreme left and on the hat of the soldier in the wagon on the far right attest that they are members of the Seventeenth Corps. A few sailors can be seen in the crowd and immediately behind Grant's mount.

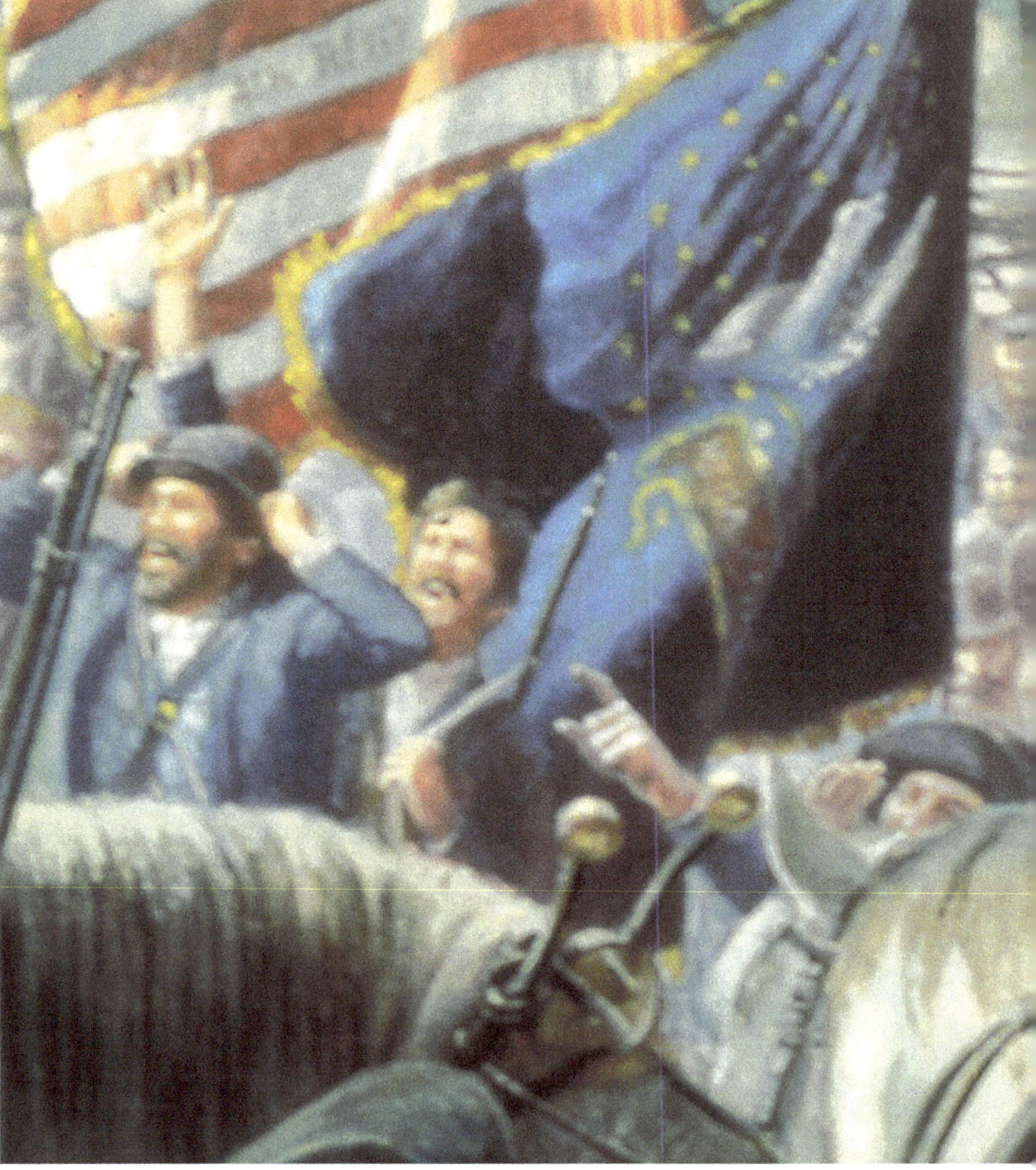

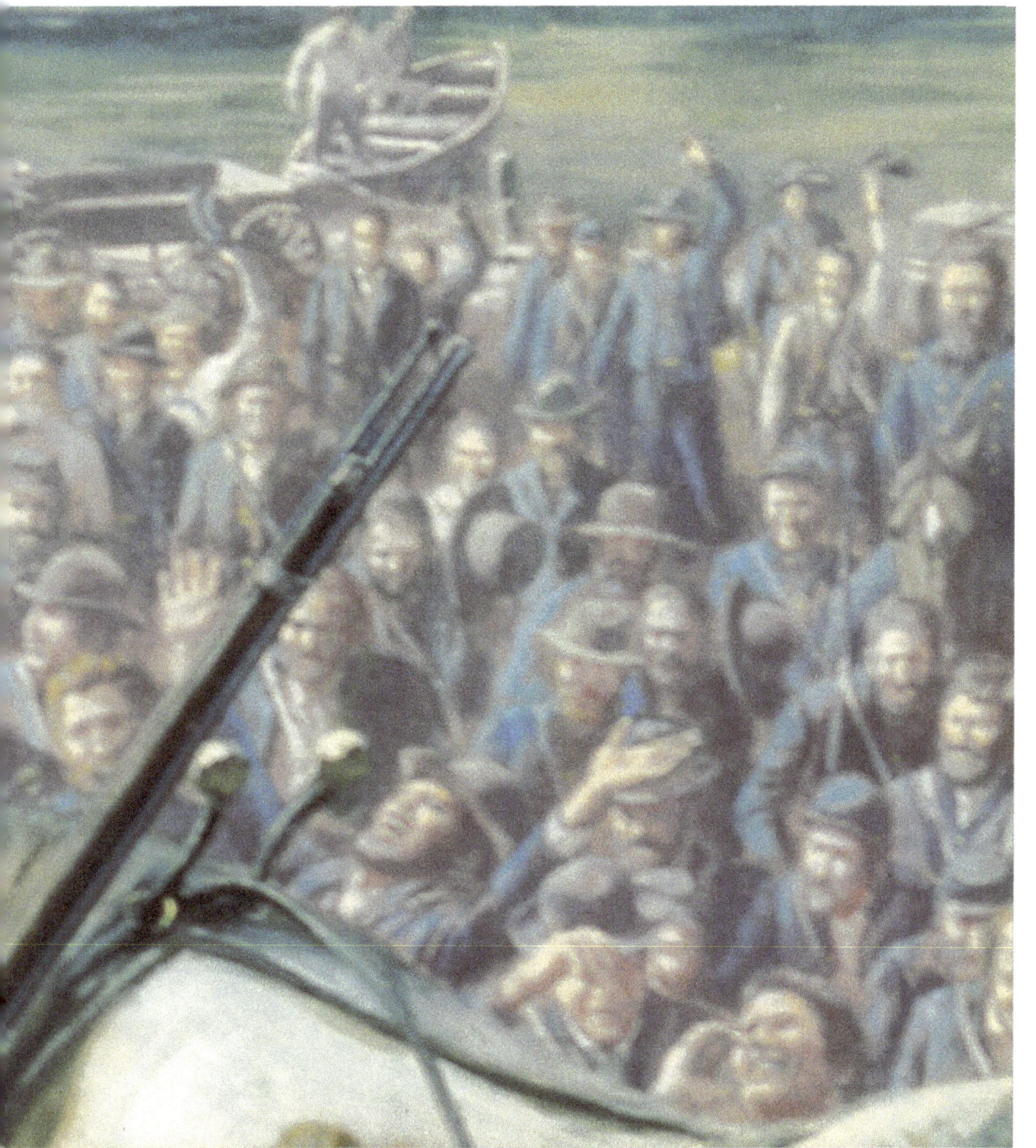

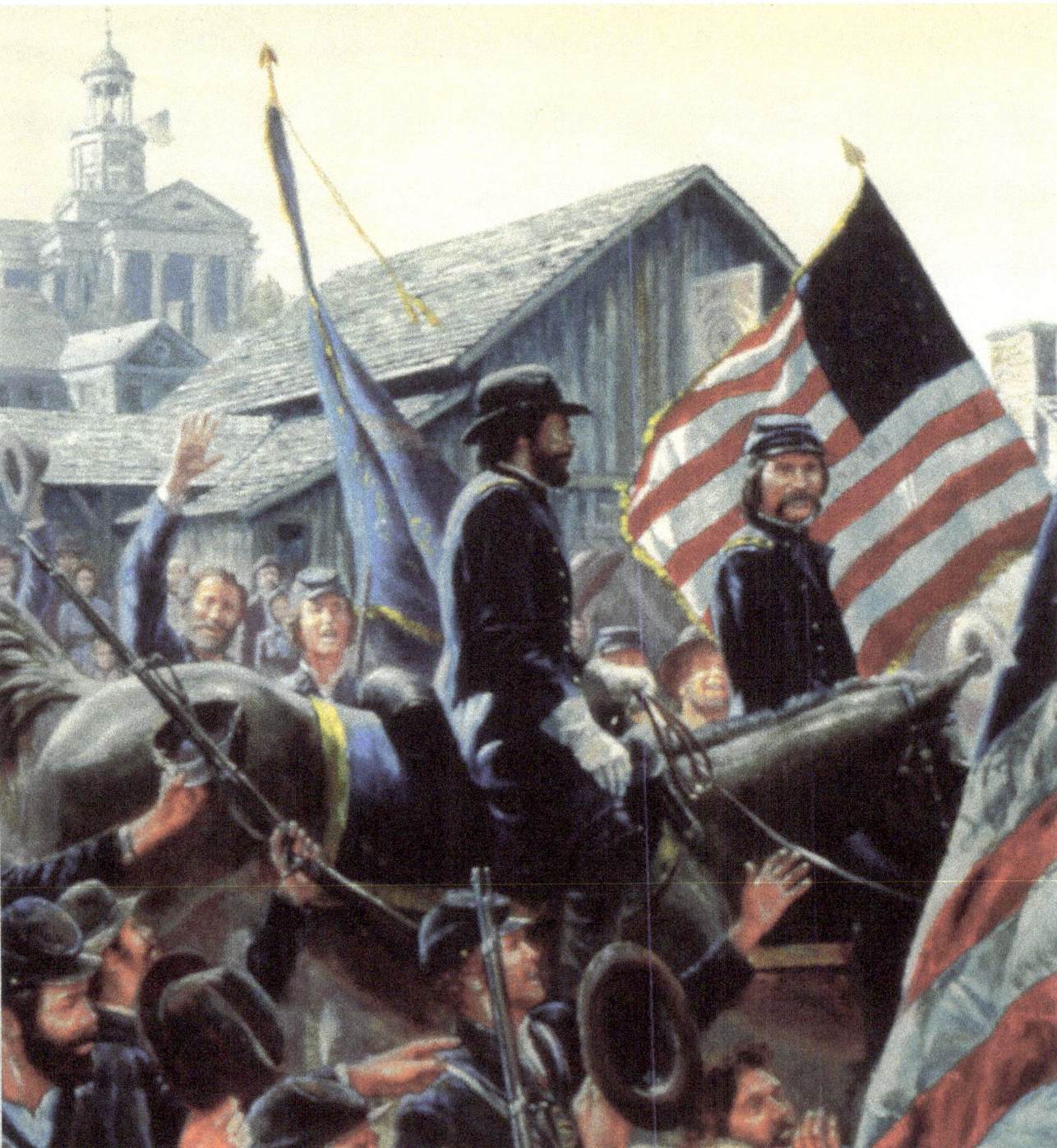

Although Grant's orders called for the Federals to be in full uniform, it was a hot summer day in Mississippi, and many of the soldiers are in shirtsleeves. I recalled the old saying that a Civil War soldier obeyed any reasonable order, not because it was an order, but because it was reasonable.

Empty buckets and barrels in and beside the cart in the foreground are symbolic of the shortages that forced the city to surrender after the seven-week siege. The few civilians present are old men—like the farmer on the wagon—women, and children. A small group can be seen in the extreme left background, sullenly observing the festivities. Behind them in the upper left corner of the picture is the Warren County Courthouse flying a Union flag.

The flagship of the river fleet, the *Benton* is the ship in the forefront on the far right. The topmost flag with the star on the mainmast is a headquarters flag. The red, green, and blue pennant immediately below it is the ship's identification pennant. Signal flags spell out congratulations and greetings and are based on George Preble's *History of the Flag of the United States of America.*

All ships, rams, monitors, and converted riverboats in the background represent the vessels that were present at the ceremony. Directly behind the *Benton* is a riverboat that was converted into a fighting vessel when the war began. The other four major ships in the background, from right to left, are the USS *Choctaw,* a double-turreted Monitor-class gunboat (two of which were at Vicksburg), Gunboat Number 53, and Gunboat Number 54.

An interesting postscript is that I finished the painting on July 4, 1989, exactly 126 years after the event. It was truly a glorious Fourth for me!

VETERANS OF GETTYSBURG

1982, oil, 16 x 20

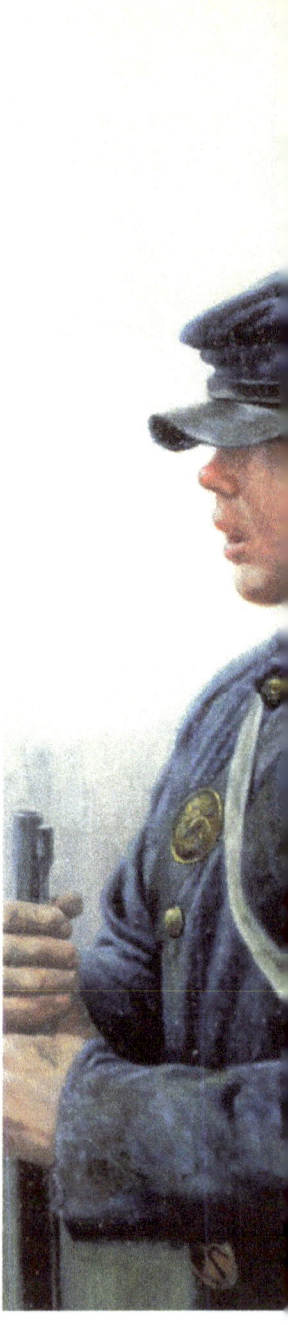

THE WORD *VETERAN* CONJURES up an image of a timeworn person with a host of experiences. In the context of war, we think of grizzled soldiers marked by the hardships of living in the field and surviving the hazards of combat. The idea of this painting is to illustrate the youth of the soldiers in the ranks.

In this painting, four youngsters stand in the calm that followed the battle of Gettysburg. The dirt and scratches on their faces, hands, and uniforms and the battered tree in the background are signs that a battle has just occurred. The boys' eyes reflect a mixture of relief and grief—relieved to be survivors and grieved at the sheer horror they have witnessed for the past three days.

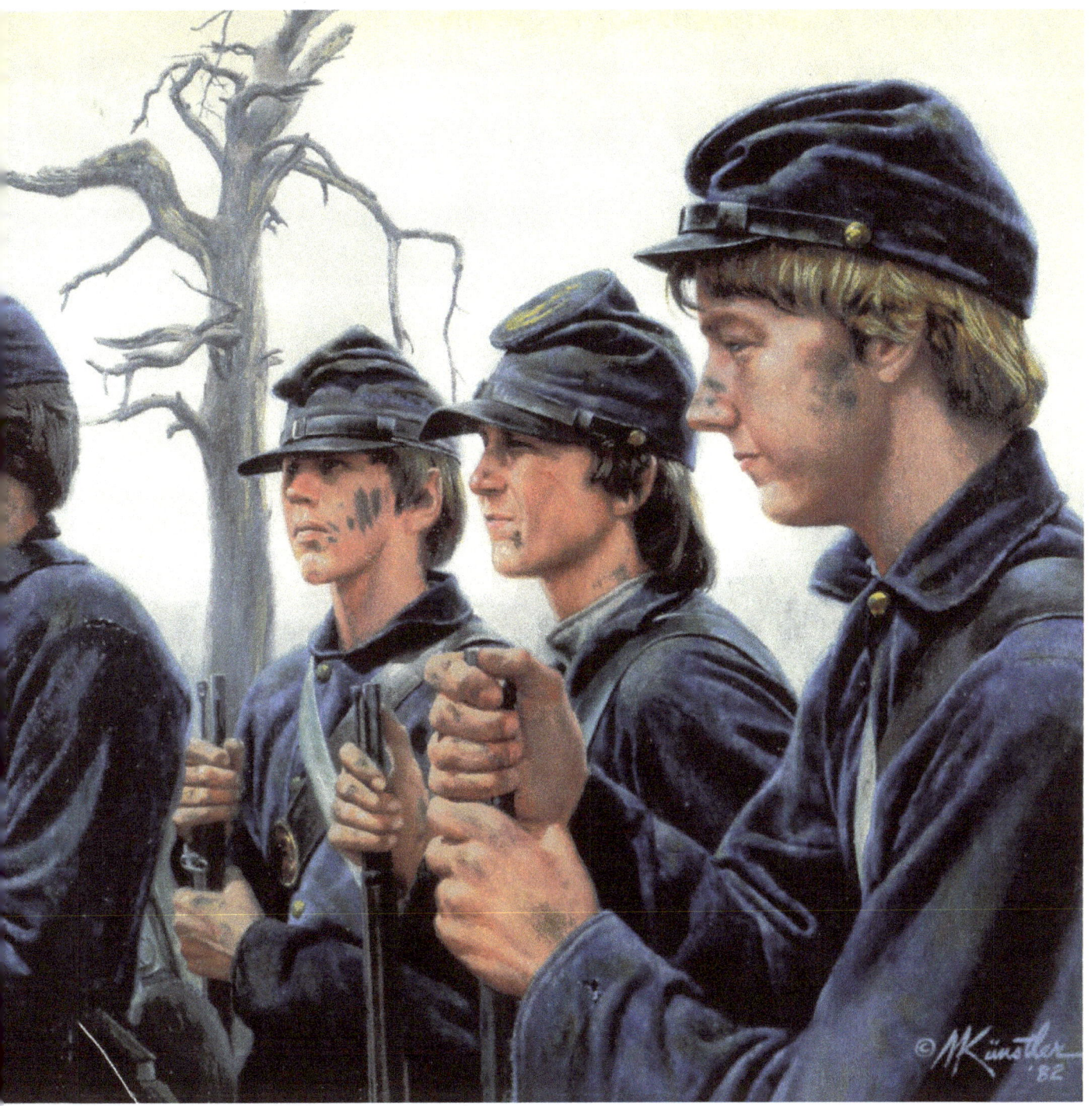

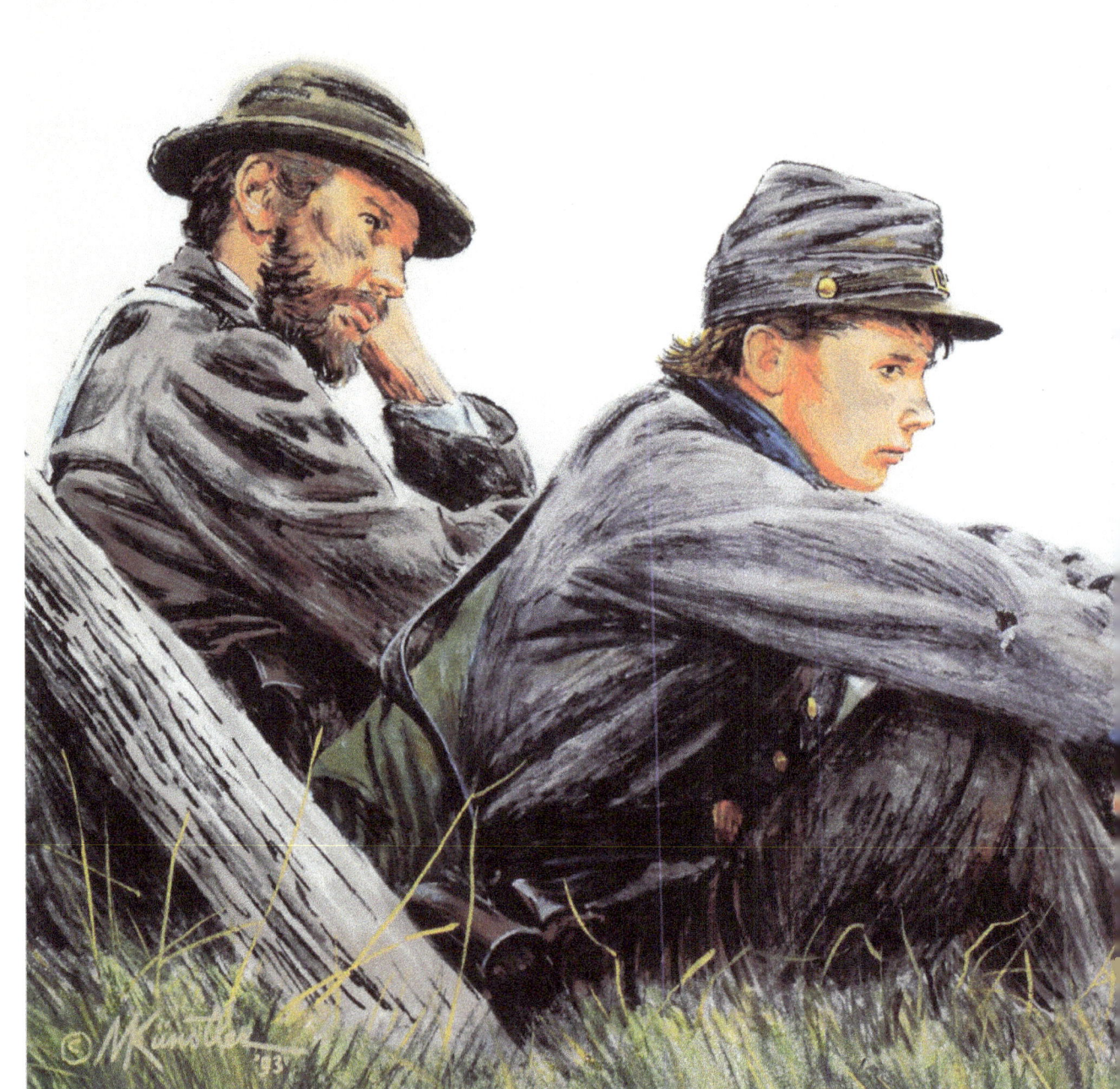

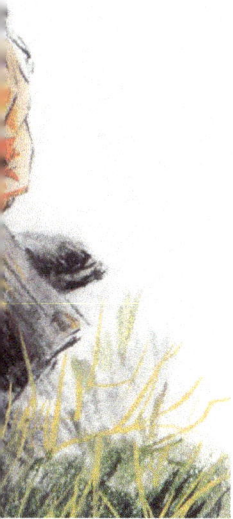

A LONG WAY FROM HOME

1993, mixed media, 9³/₈ x 11

THE CONFEDERATE ARMY SUFFERED an enormous manpower loss at Gettysburg. Five thousand soldiers surrendered to the Federals, more than half of them during the repulse of Pickett's Charge. In addition, nearly seven thousand wounded Southerners were left behind as prisoners.

The Confederacy's hopes for victory and the South's quest for independence were also casualties at Gettysburg. Desertion rates rose sharply in the Army of Northern Virginia. Unprecedented criticism of Lee crept into Southern newspaper accounts of Gettysburg. The general offered his resignation to Jefferson Davis, who refused it, yet commented to a friend, "We are now in the darkest hour of our political existence."

Confederate ordnance chief Josiah Gorgas recorded his thoughts in his diary: "The Confederacy totters to its destruction."

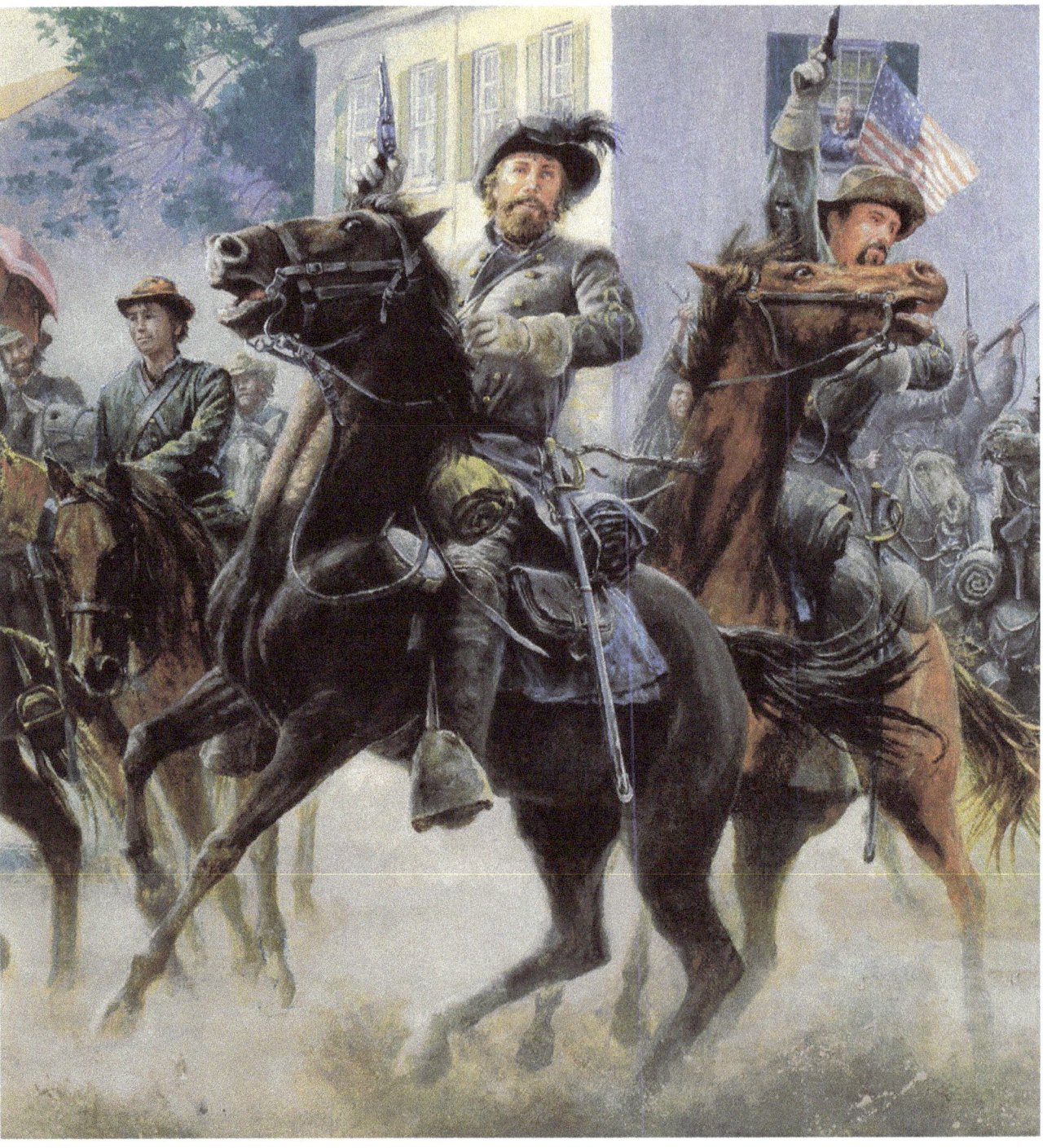

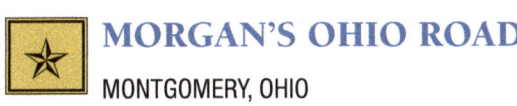

MORGAN'S OHIO ROAD

MONTGOMERY, OHIO

JULY 14, 1863

2003, oil, 22 x 38

FROM JULY 2 to July 26, 1863, Confederate Gen. John Hunt Morgan led twenty-five hundred cavalrymen on a daring three-week raid through Indiana and Ohio—one of the boldest cavalry operations of the war. They captured six thousand Federal soldiers, distracted fourteen thousand soldiers and more than one hundred thousand state militiamen from other responsibilities, destroyed thirty-four bridges, wrecked railroads at more than sixty locations, and damaged property worth hundreds of thousands of dollars.

Morgan's men were relentlessly pursued by determined Federal cavalry and encountered staunch resistance from civilians. In Montgomery, Ohio—a village near Cincinnati—the raiders received a chilly reception from defiant townspeople. Five days later, Union cavalry overtook the raiders at Buffington Island and captured approximately seven hundred Southern horsemen.

The surviving raiders raced northward from there but were cornered in northeastern Ohio. Morgan surrendered his command and was imprisoned in the Ohio Penitentiary. In late November 1863 he daringly escaped from there and returned South to command troops again.

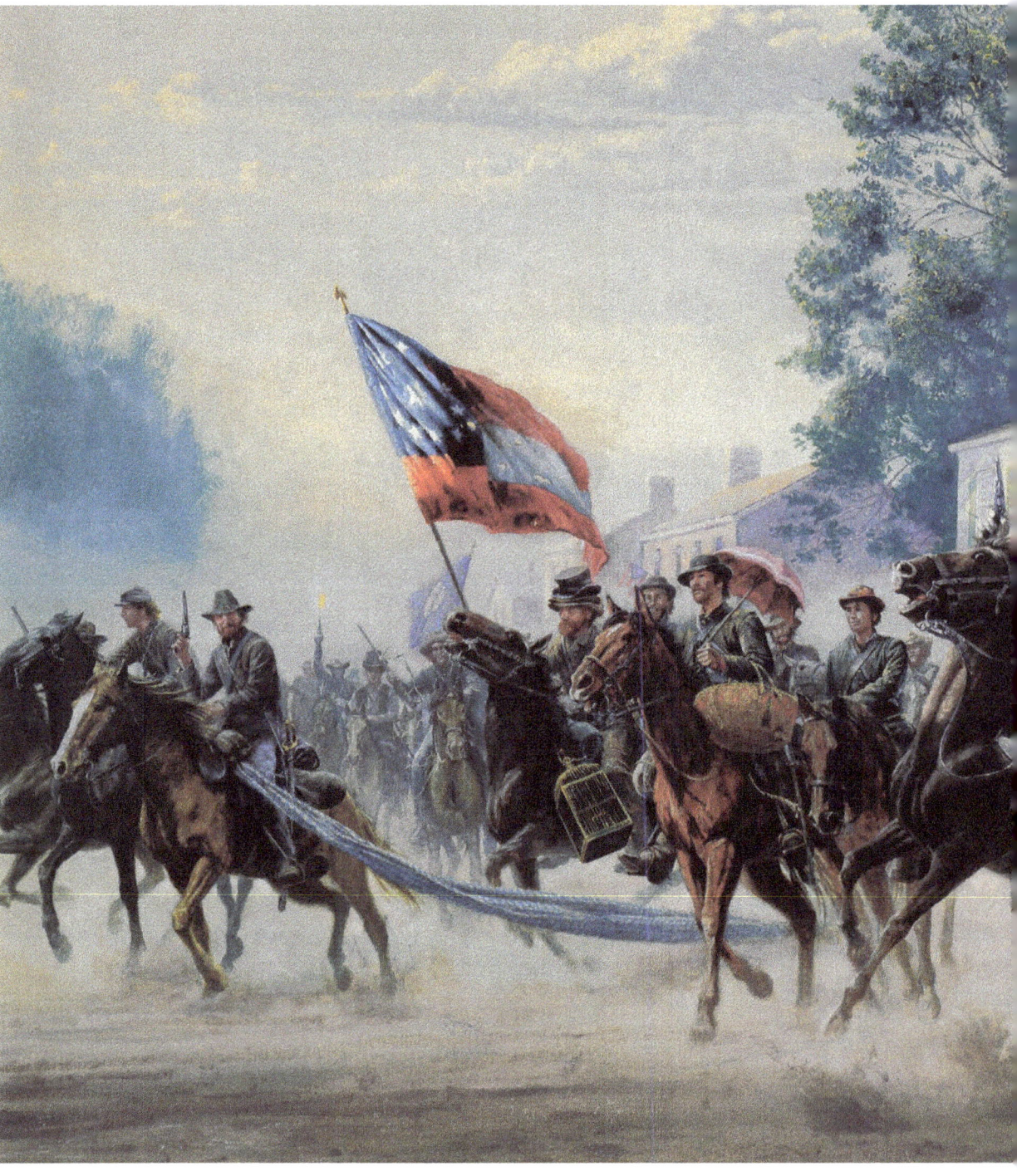

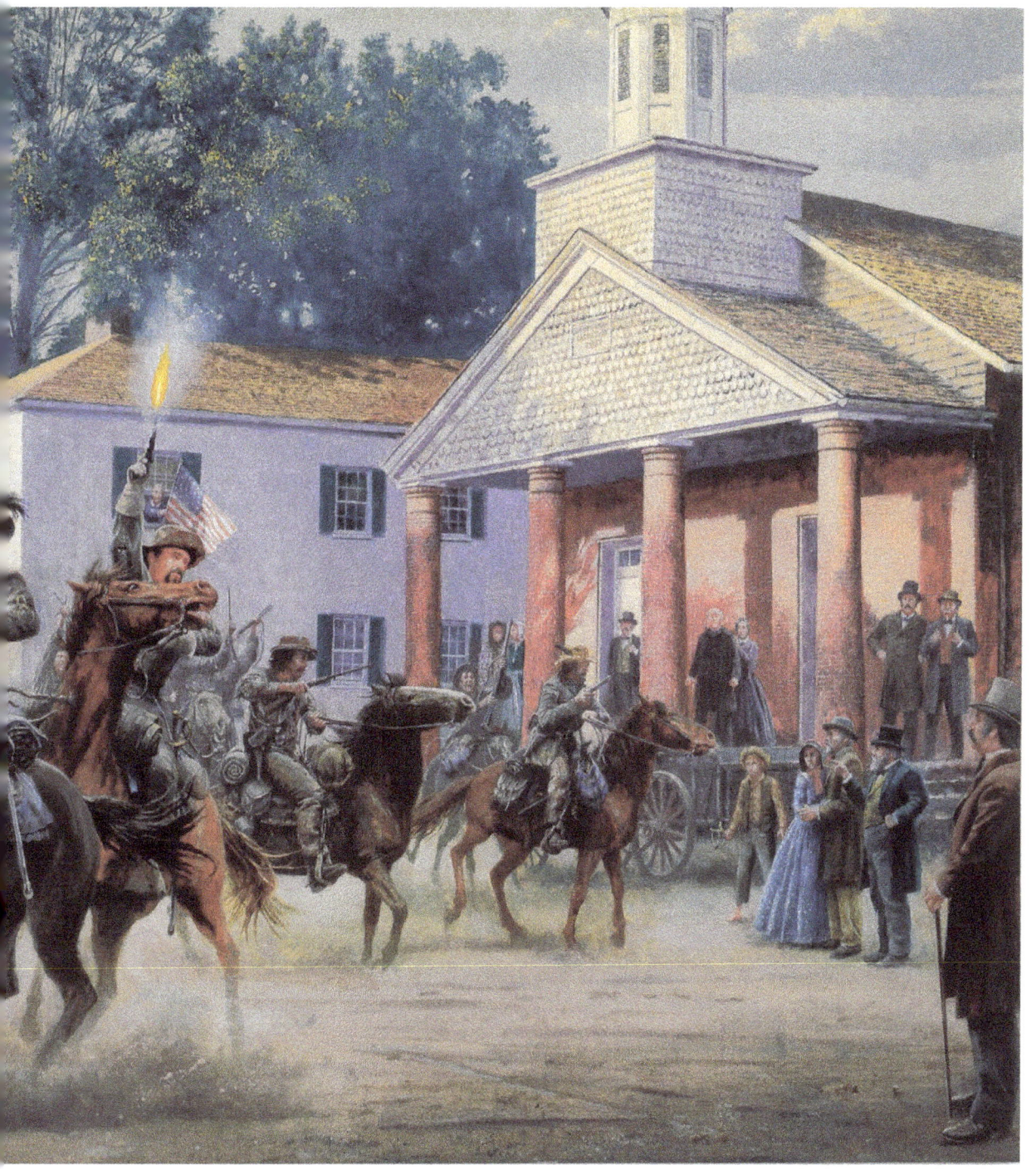

When I toured Montgomery, which is now a suburb of Cincinnati, I was impressed with the charm of the Universalist Church on Montgomery and Remington Roads. I knew I had found the setting for this painting.

All the action depicted here is based on letters, diaries, and newspaper articles. Morgan's men carried the First National Flag of the Confederacy and the Kentucky state flag. An Ohio state flag flies from an open window in the distance, and the Stars and Stripes is defiantly unfurled by a woman in the window of the center building.

Morgan occupies the center of the painting, a revolver in hand and wearing a plumed hat. Directly behind him is his brother-in-law, Col. Basil W. Duke, who is firing in the air to chase a stoic citizen off the roadway The faces of the other Confederates are based on photographs of the men who were eventually imprisoned in the state penitentiary after their capture.

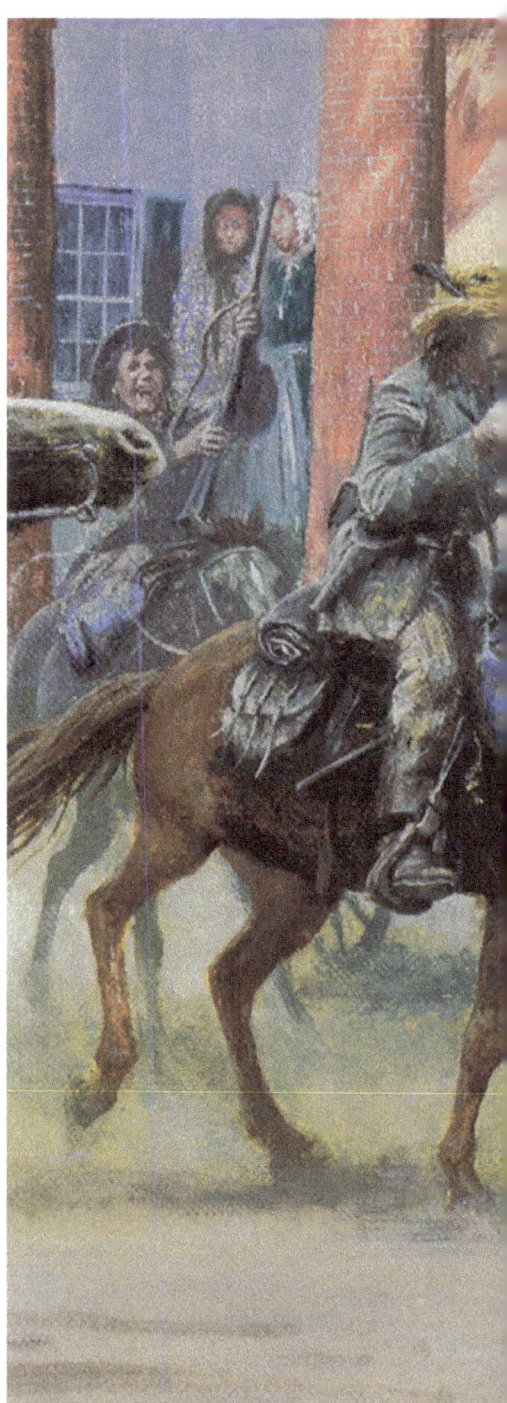

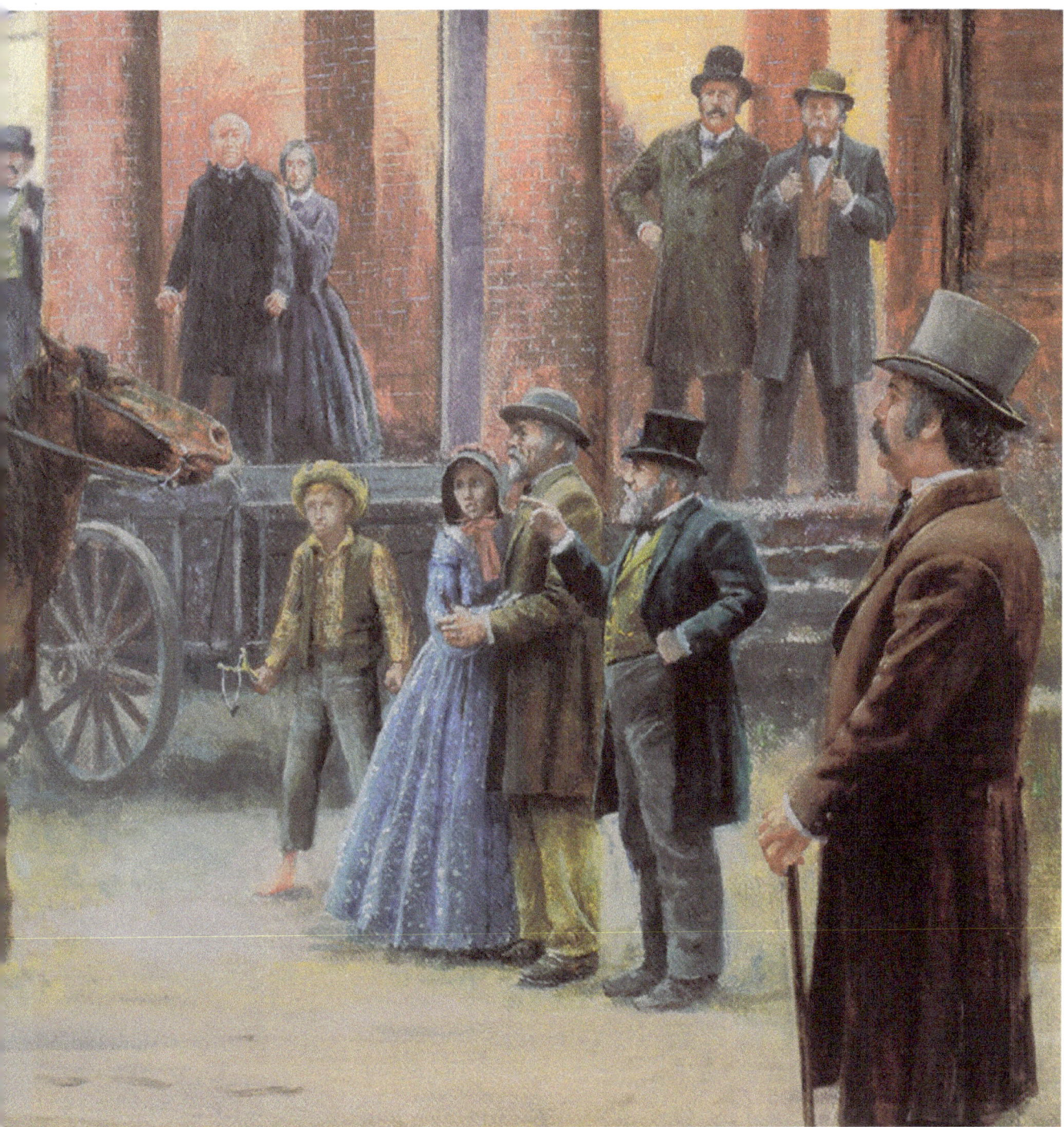

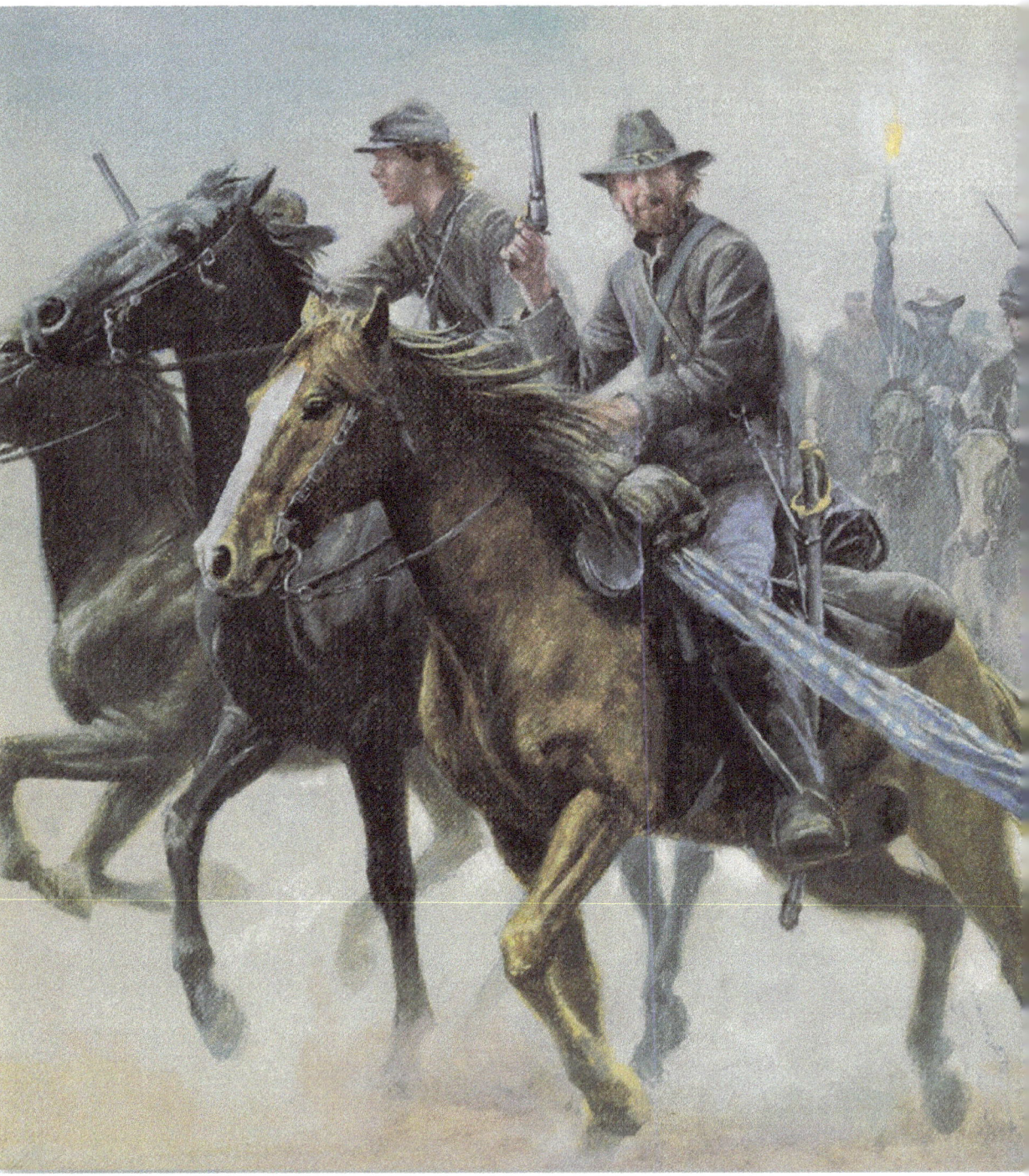

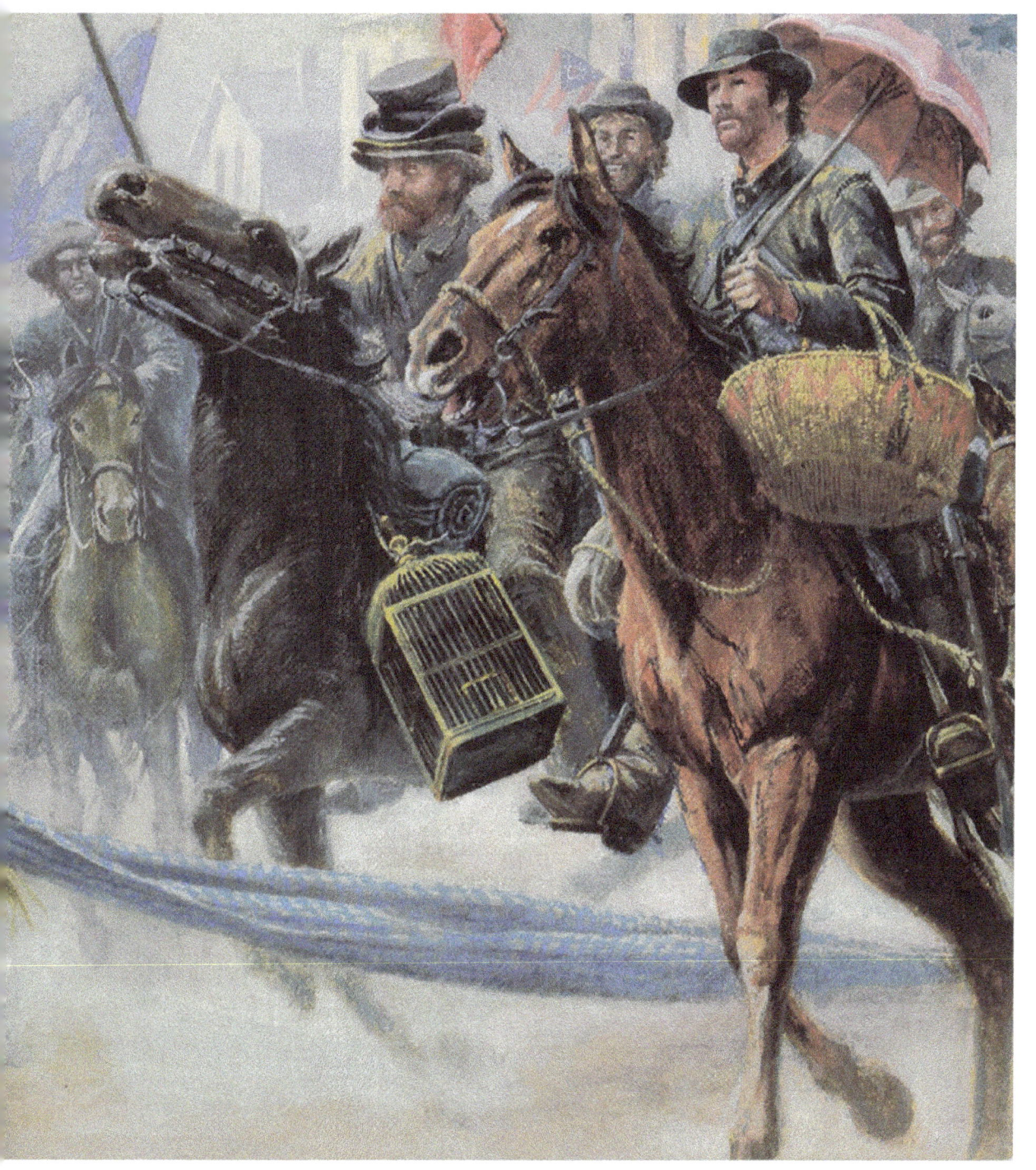

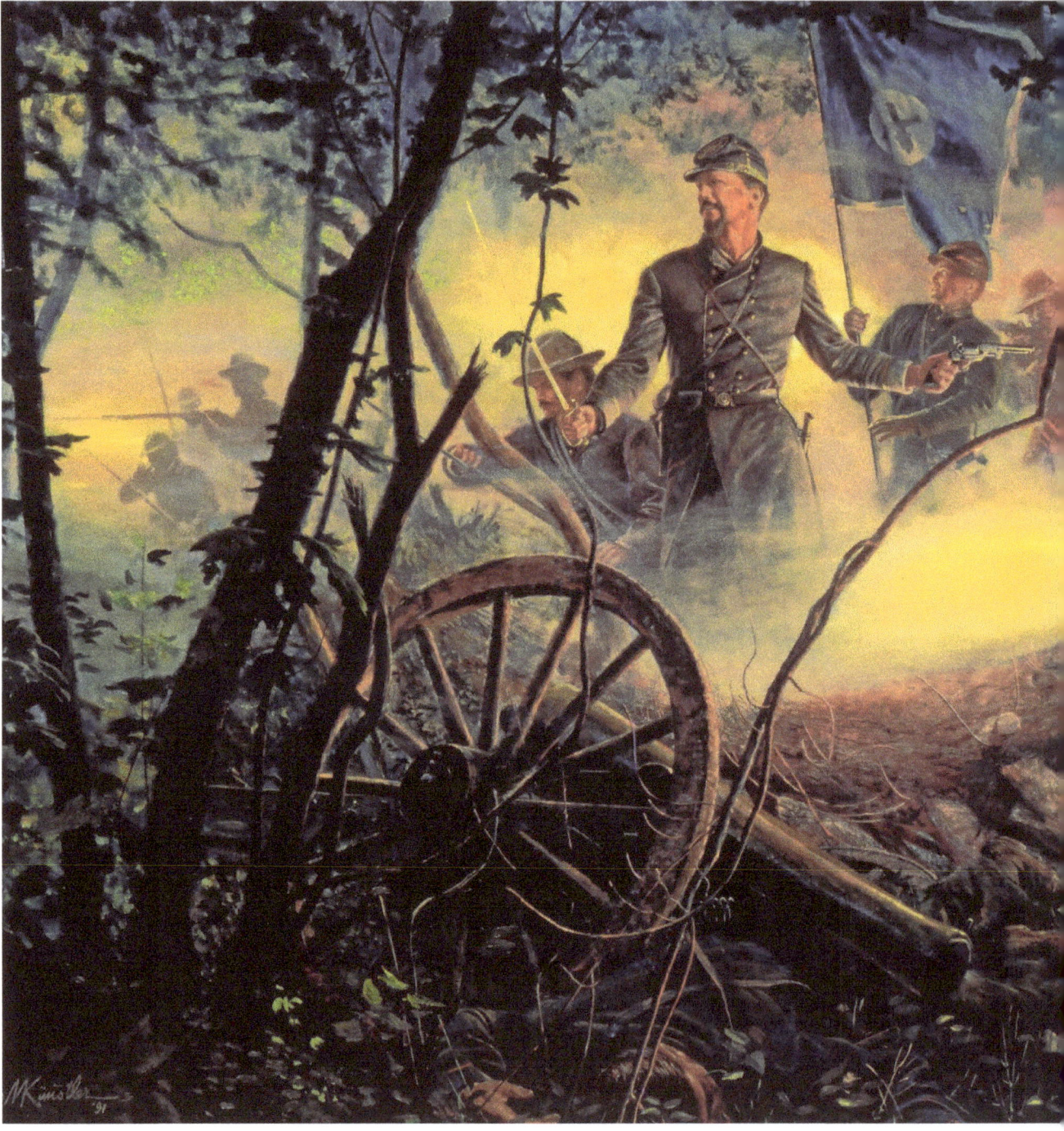

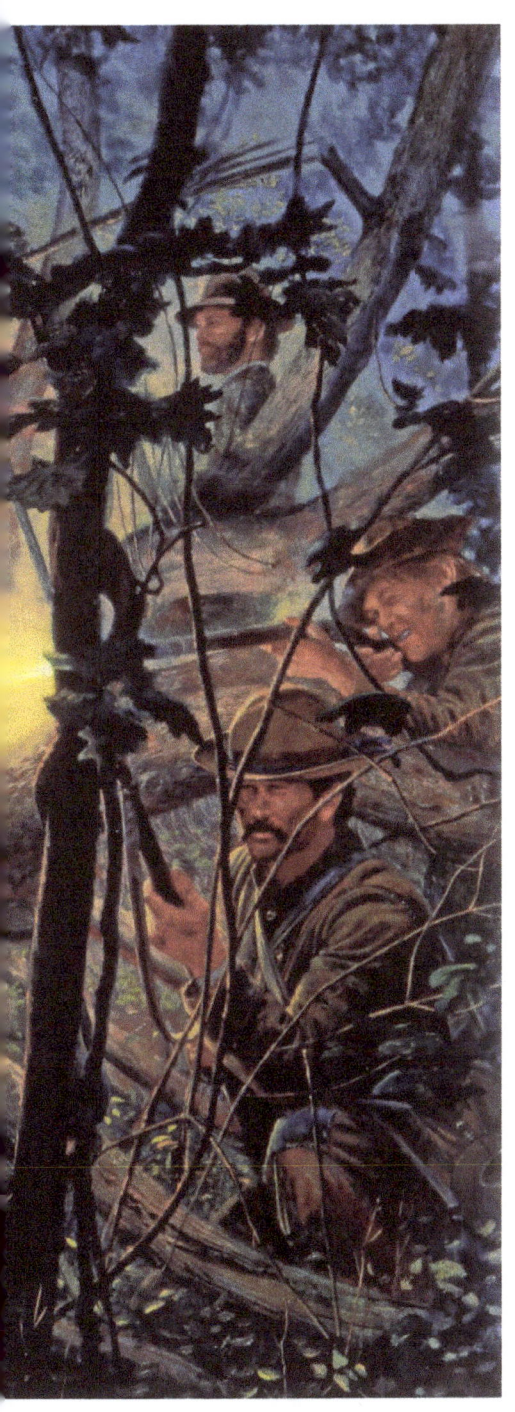

EYE OF THE STORM

PATRICK CLEBURNE AT CHICKAMAUGA
SEPTEMBER 19, 1863

1991, oil, 26 x 35

WHILE RESEARCHING THE BATTLE of Chickamauga, I came across some accounts of Gen. Patrick Cleburne in action during the evening of September 18, 1863. When I read of the fighting that had begun after sunset and found that it never before had been portrayed, I decided to use this setting for a Chickamauga painting. I had never seen a painting of a battle conducted in total darkness, illuminated only by the flash of gunfire, and the concept struck me as something very dramatic and unlike any other Civil War painting I had seen.

Because of the powder smoke, the darkness, and the thickness of the woods around Chickamauga Creek, I decided I would have to portray the men closer than I had in any other battle painting I had done. Cleburne serves as the center of interest, highlighted clearly by the simultaneous flash of two guns. After crossing the Chickamauga, Cleburne's division marched more than four miles through heavy woods to where the fighting took place. The woods were too thick to allow a man to remain on horseback, so I showed Cleburne dismounted.

The flag nearest Cleburne, held by a standard bearer, is the "Full Moon" Hardee flag that was used by the division at Chickamauga. One peculiarity of this flag is the inverted crossed cannons in the center of the white circle. This device was usually painted in black and was on the infantry and artillery flags. Not all of Cleburne's regiments had this device on their flags, but surviving examples from the 1864 issue show that a large number did.

After fighting fiercely in the dark, Cleburne's division overran the Union positions and captured three guns. One of them, a bronze 12-pounder Napoleon, is in the foreground with a dead artillerist pinned beneath it.

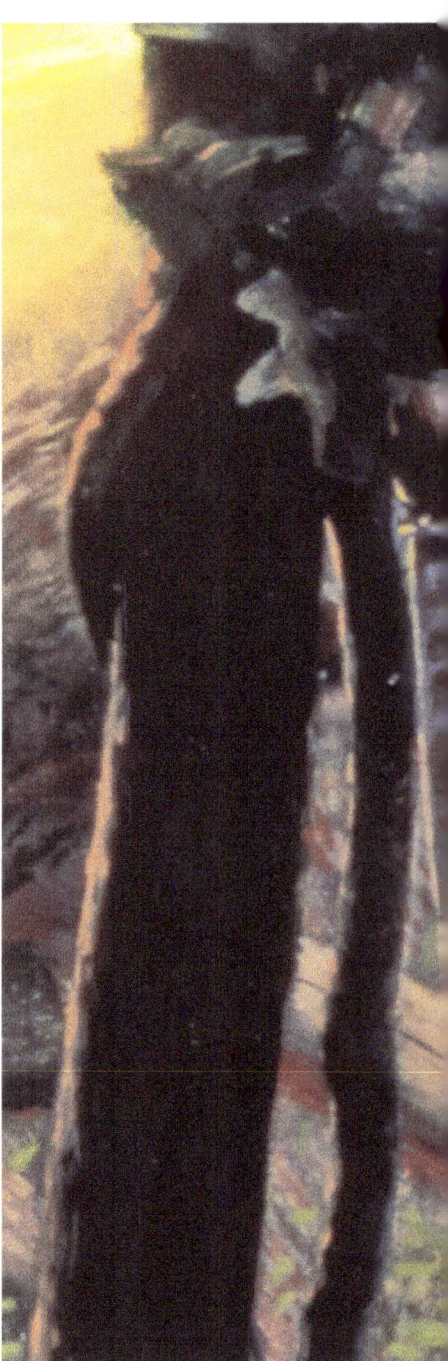

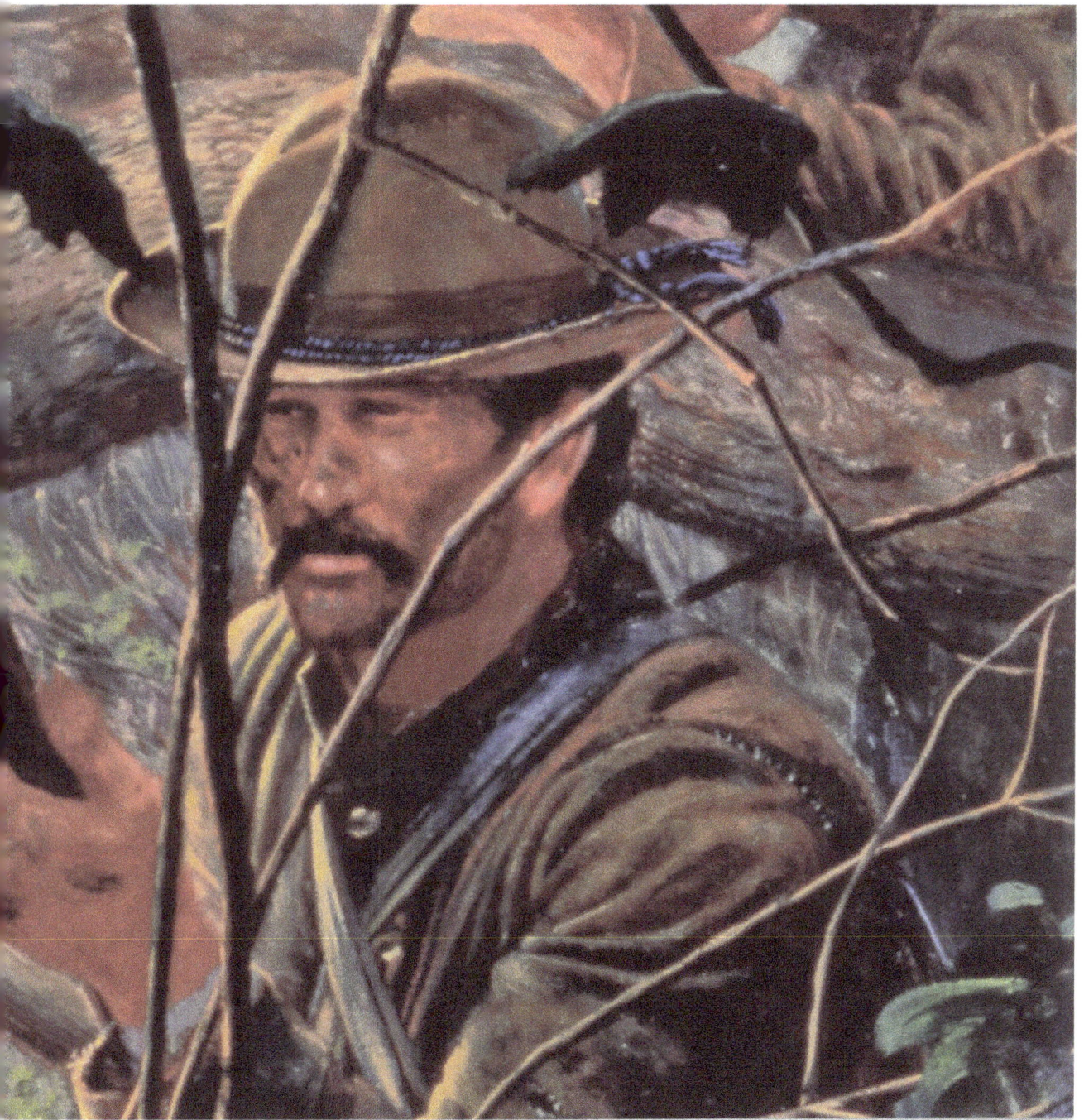

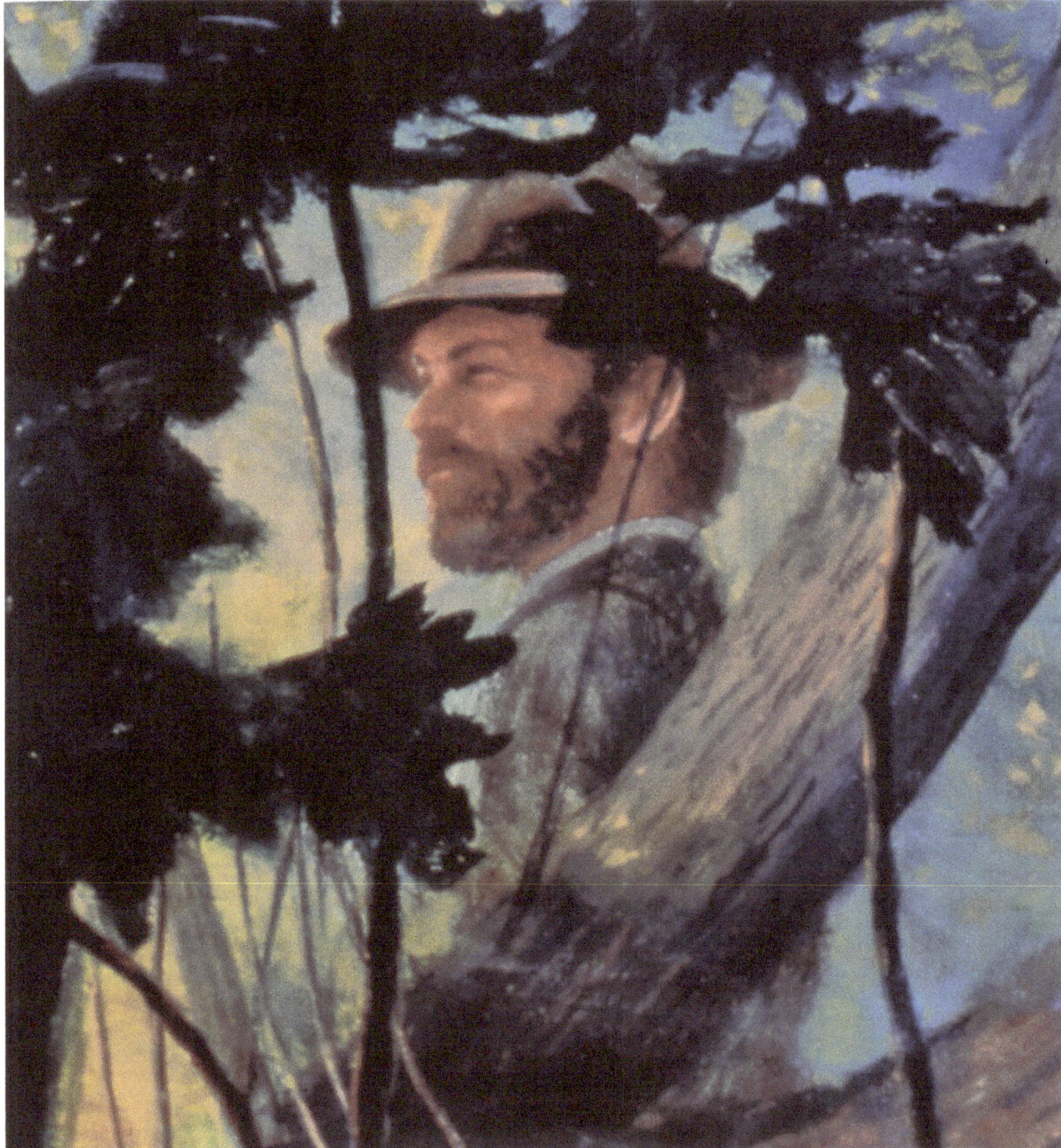

After a time of intense firing, and with neither side able to determine where its opponent was, the men fell exhausted, with the battle lines only yards apart, and slept among the dead and wounded. Only an officer with Cleburne's leadership qualities could demand and get the kind of devotion to duty that was demonstrated on the night of September 18, 1863, along Chickamauga Creek.

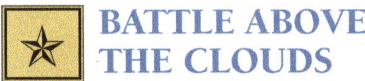

BATTLE ABOVE THE CLOUDS

LOOKOUT MOUNTAIN, TENNESSEE
NOVEMBER 24, 1863

1992, oil, 22 x 35

Gen. Ulysses S. Grant called the legendary Battle Above the Clouds a minor skirmish. But when you realize that Lookout Mountain was the battlefield and the weather conditions consisted of mist and fog, compounded by smoke from the battle, hampering visibility significantly, this is the stuff of which legends are made.

When I learned that no one had painted the battle, I called John Ogden, chief historian for the National Park Service at Chickamauga-Chattanooga National Battlefield, to make arrangements to visit the area at the same time of the year that the battle occurred. He explained the battle while we walked over virtually every

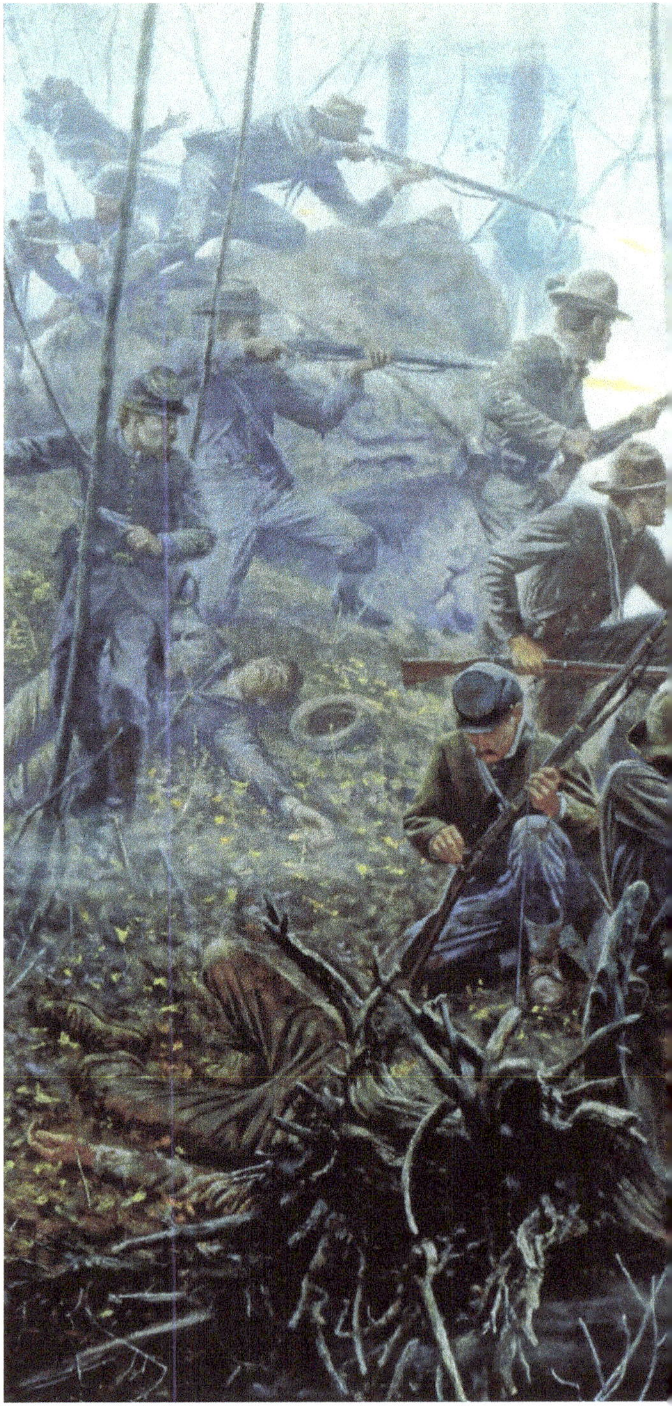

42

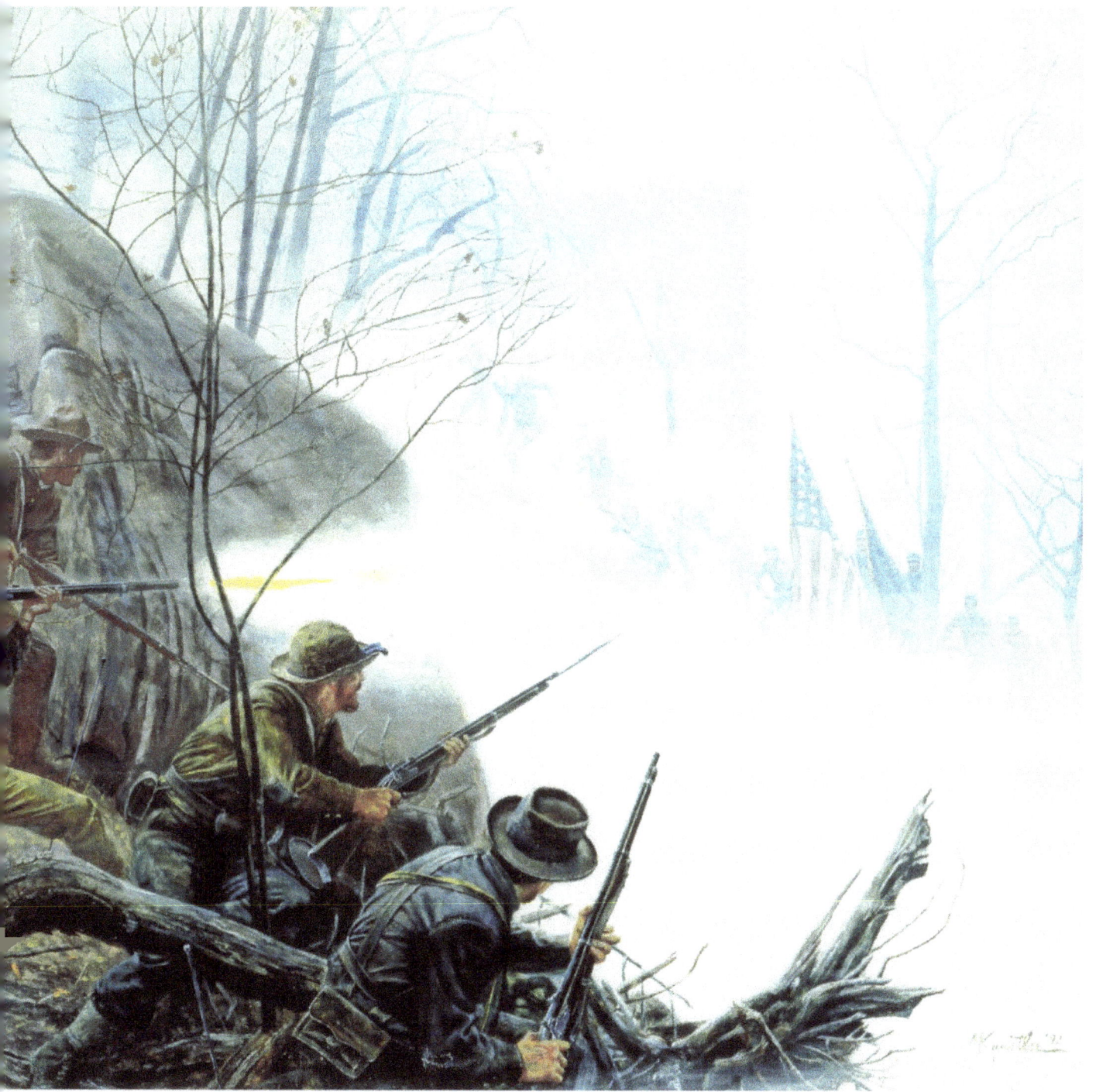

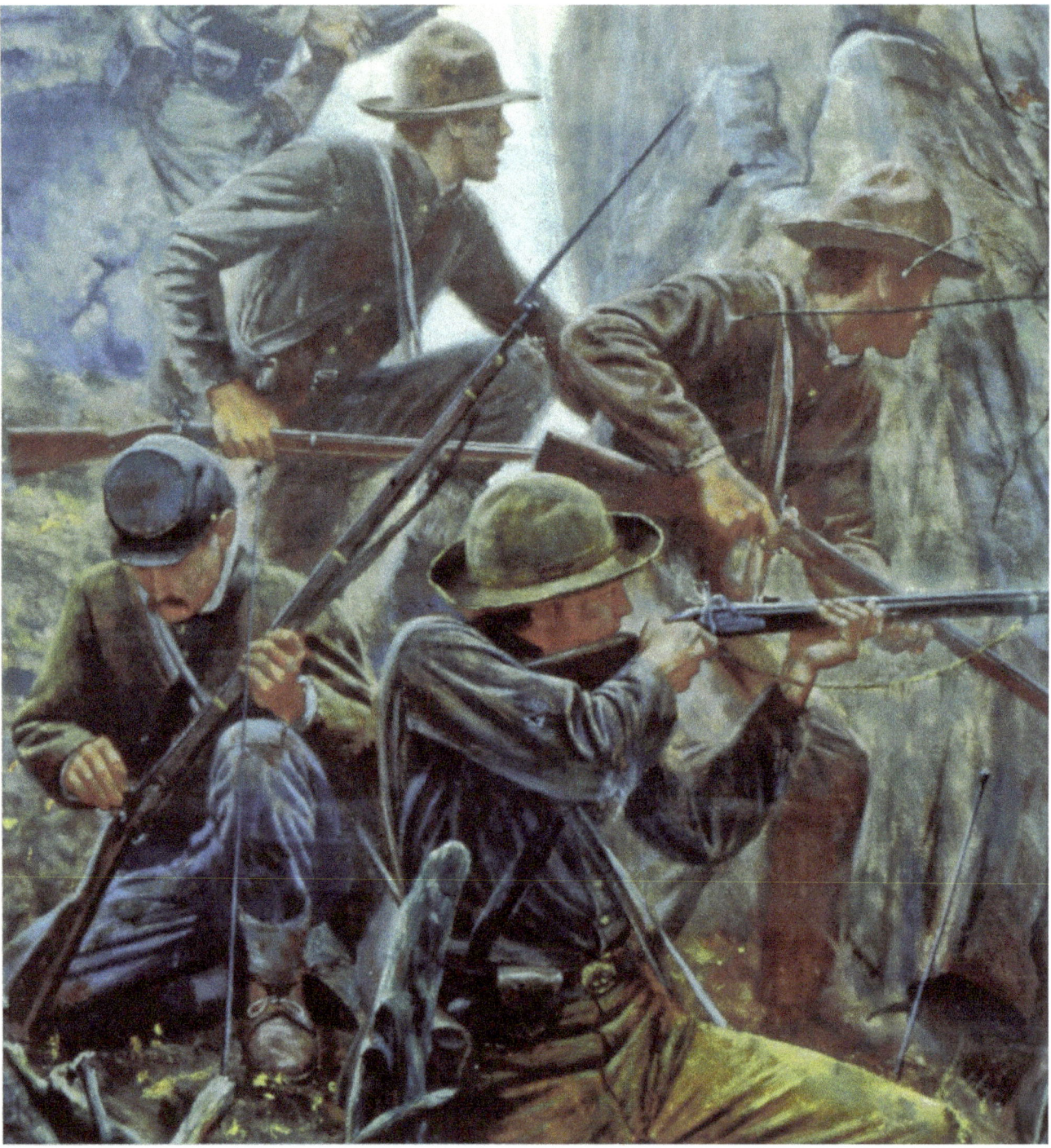

part of Lookout Mountain. My only regret was not having my picture taken on Umbrella Rock, a popular setting for almost every tourist who visited the area in the decades after the war.

In my painting, I wanted to show the palisades at the top of the mountain because they are distinctive and recognizable to anyone familiar with the scene. But it was impossible to see the palisades from the battle site as there were dense woods on the mountainside. Then I learned that the mountain had been heavily logged during the mid-1800s. Since the battle took place on November 24, when most of the trees were barren of leaves, there was no problem in showing the palisades in the painting.

After a great deal of tramping up, down, and around the mountain, I found a distinctive boulder just above the Craven house, where some of the fiercest fighting took place. I could now get the landmark palisades and distinctive boulders in one view! A very dense fog and smoke had encircled the Craven house during the fighting, so this allowed me to place the fog and smoke in the lower part of the painting.

The last obstacle in my composition was to identify the soldiers for the viewer when the men involved in the fighting had trouble doing so under these conditions. I used the Stars and Stripes as the center of interest so that the army in the left foreground could be easily distinguished as the Confederate: all the Confederates look toward this flag, their guns acting as pointers. I also added branches as visual arrows to lead the viewer's eye to the Union flag. The Confederate banner in the background is the Hardee pattern with a white disk on a blue field. Since this does not instantly convey itself as a Confederate flag, I made the Union flag more of a focal point.

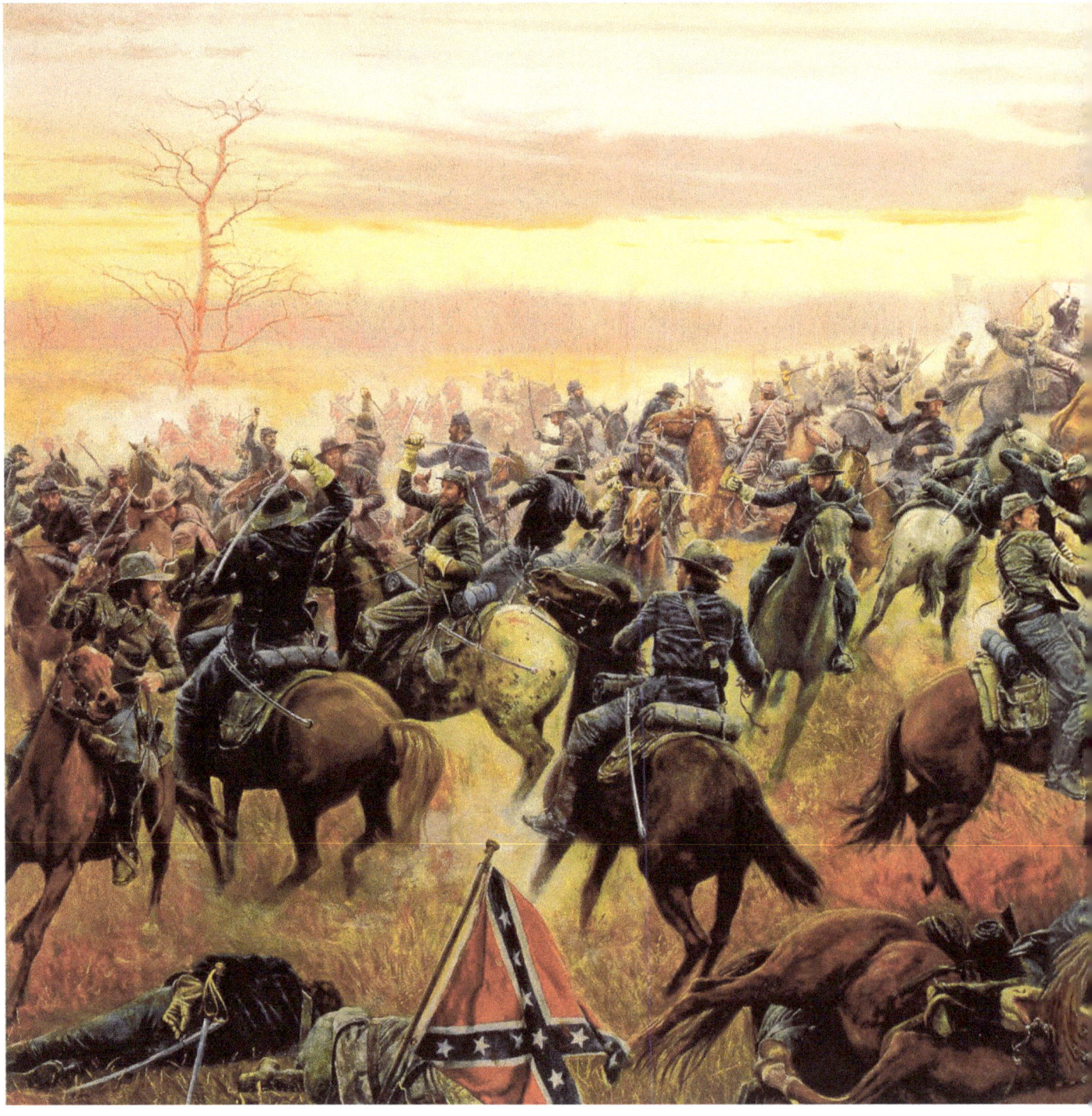

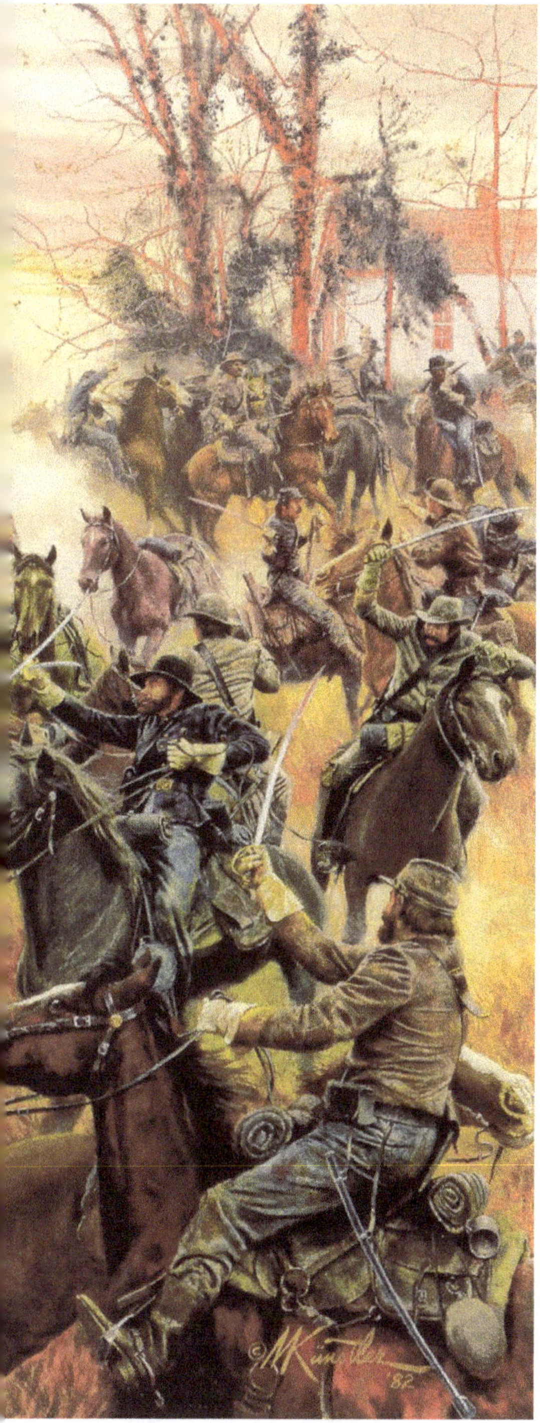

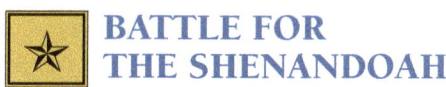

BATTLE FOR
THE SHENANDOAH

1982, oil, 28¼ x 40

THROUGHOUT THE WAR, THE Shenandoah Valley was a thoroughfare for both the
Confederate and Union armies. A nearly
150-mile-long corridor of fertile farms and
numerous mills, it was both a central gra-
nary of the South and a primary invasion
pipeline toward the North. In 1862, Thomas J. "Stonewall" Jackson had defended the
Valley from Union occupation, and in 1863,
Robert E. Lee had utilized it as his invasion
avenue into Maryland and Pennsylvania. In
1864, three separate Union advances were
attempted, with their targets being New
Market and Lynchburg.

At the head of the armies engaged in this
effort were the cavalries that had clashed

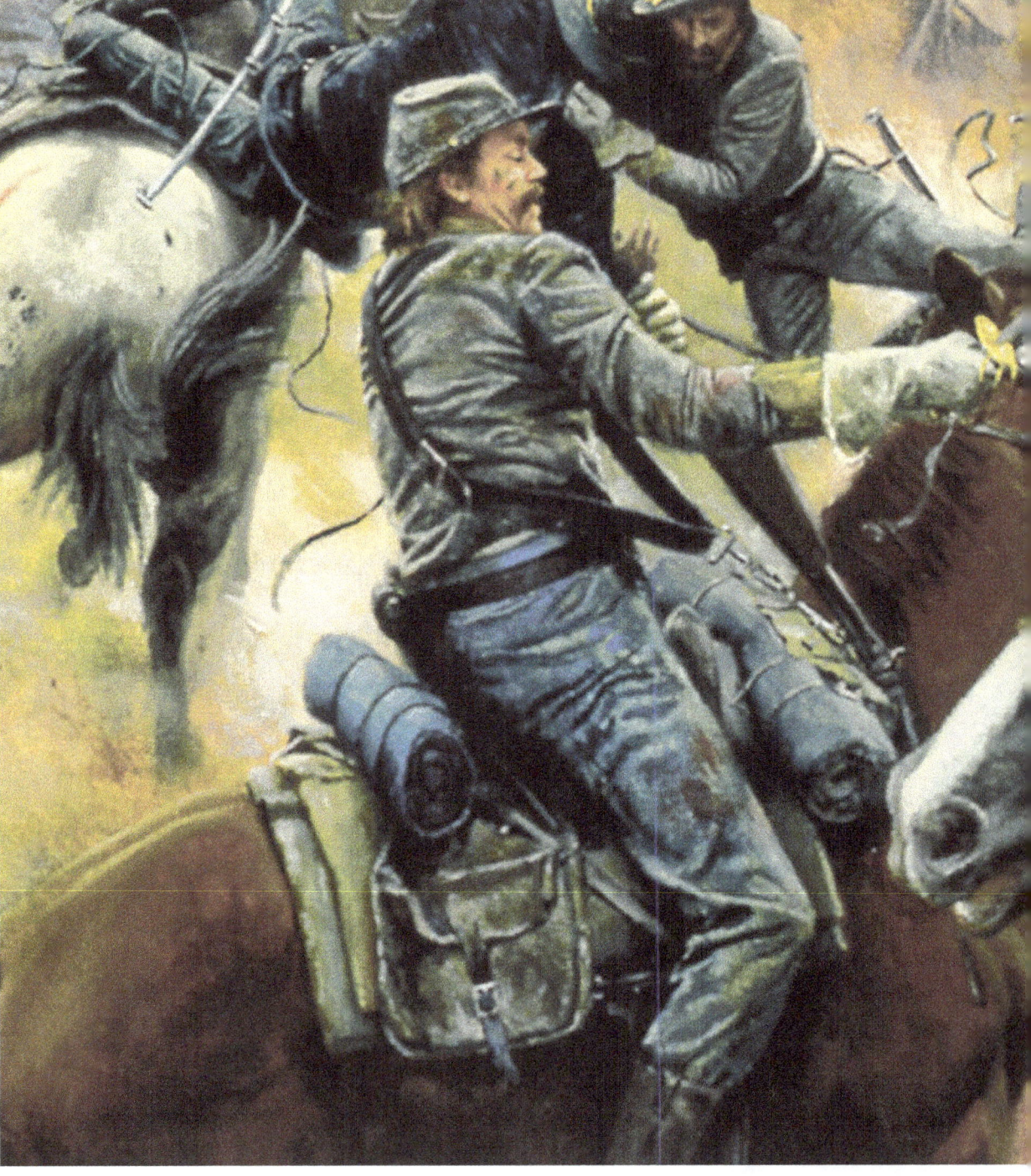

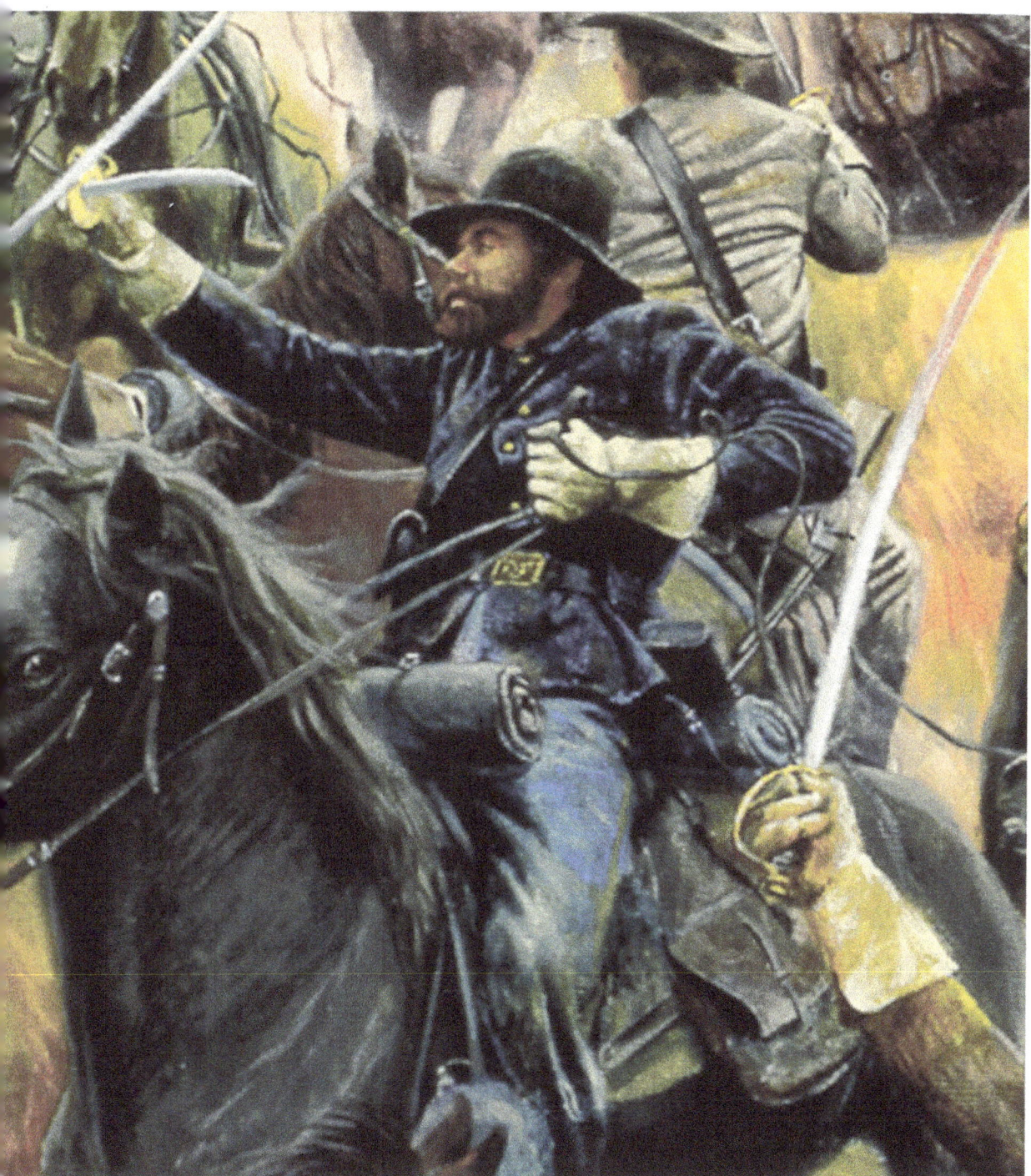

head-on for more than two years. In 1861 the cavalry embodied a spirit of heroism, and hundreds of young men rushed to join what they perceived as the "romantic" branch of the service. Their officers in flashy uniforms inspired them with bold speeches and incredible horsemanship. And as the mounted troops passed the dusty footsore columns of infantry, they would hear the familiar jeer, "Who ever saw a dead cavalryman?" "Not I," "Nor I," the response would echo through the ranks as the troopers rode by. But the romance of the cavalry ended abruptly after the first battles of the war.

For a while, commanders were unsure of what to do with their cavalry. For some they were no more than mounted infantry that rode into battle, dismounted, and fought on foot. Skilled commanders, however, used their horsemen as the eyes and ears of the army. They scouted the enemy and screened their own army's movements with quick clashes when the enemy approached.

For the first two years of the conflict, Union horsemen suffered constant defeat and embarrassment at the hands of their Confederate counterparts. But in mid-1863, after the battle of Brandy Station, the two cavalries reached a level of parity; neither side easily vanquished the other. Cavalry regularly clashed with cavalry, especially when raiding behind enemy lines.

During the first half of 1864, mounted columns in the Shenandoah would encounter each other, and a battle would begin over a river ford or road intersection. Cracking pistols and carbines would join snorting horses and flashing sabers as men became hopelessly intermingled, each man "facing the maelstrom of steel. No order could be heard or obeyed as it was every man for himself." As soon as a fight began, it would end, the participants riding away from the field, leaving behind only the dead and wounded.

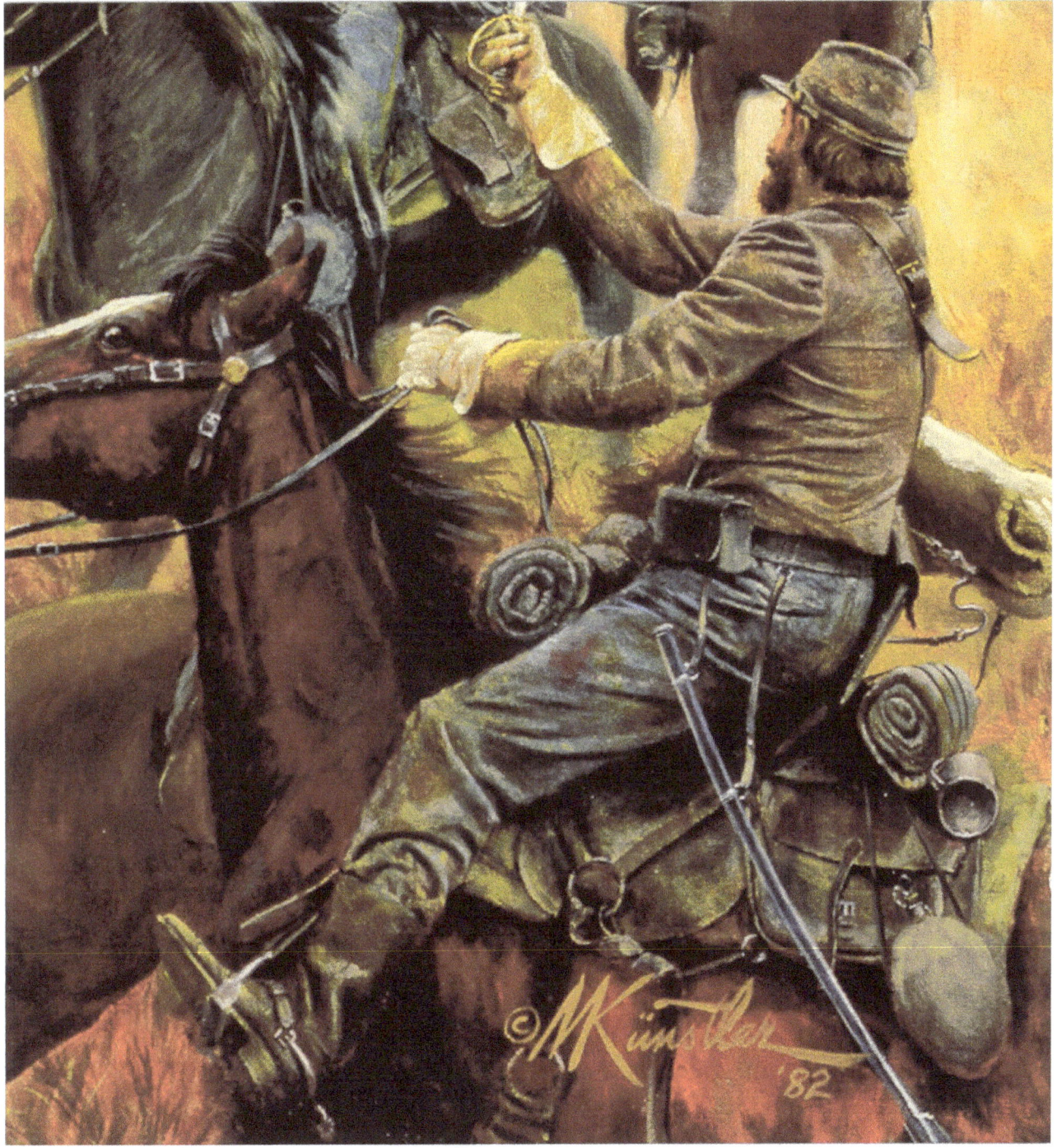

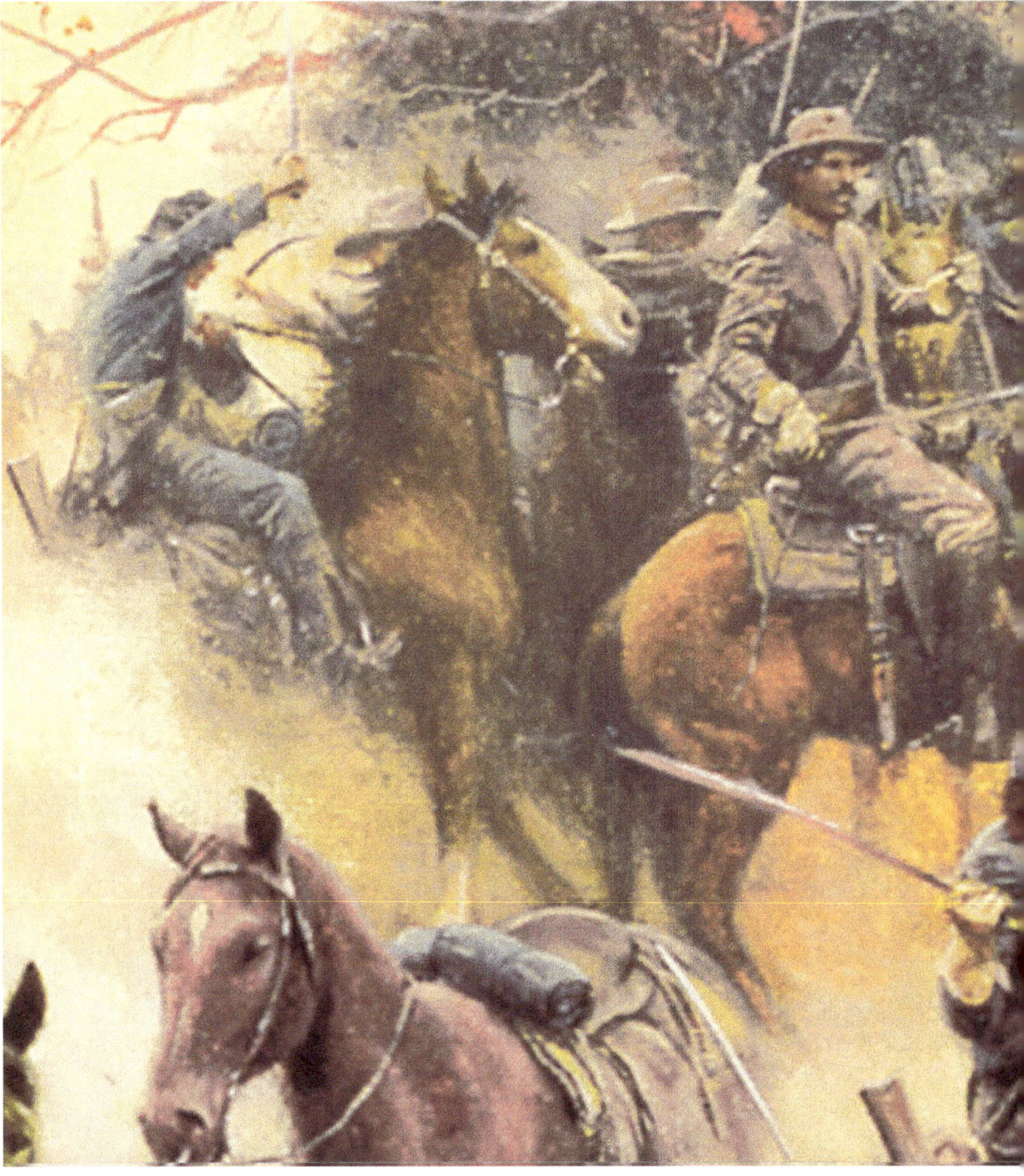

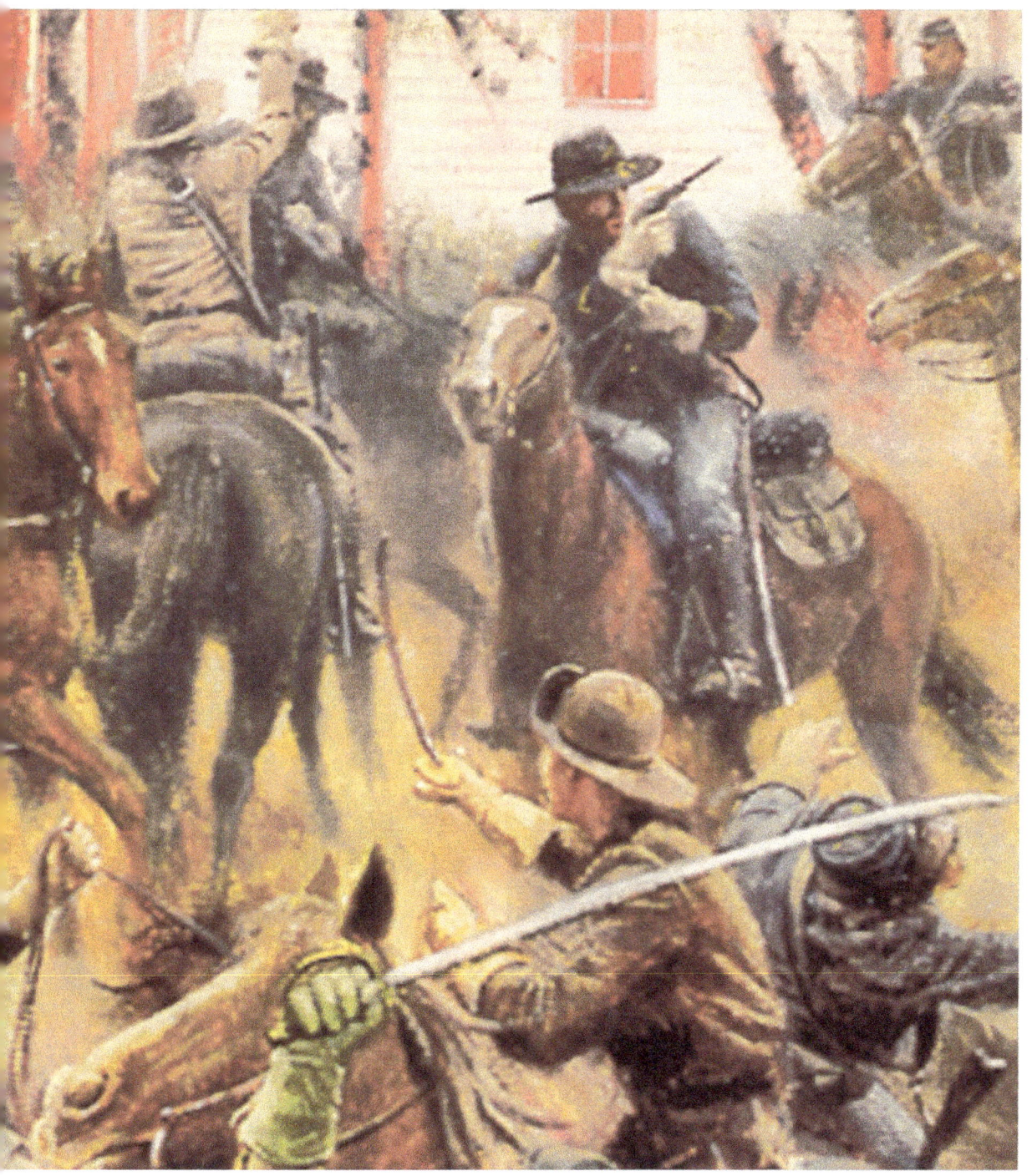

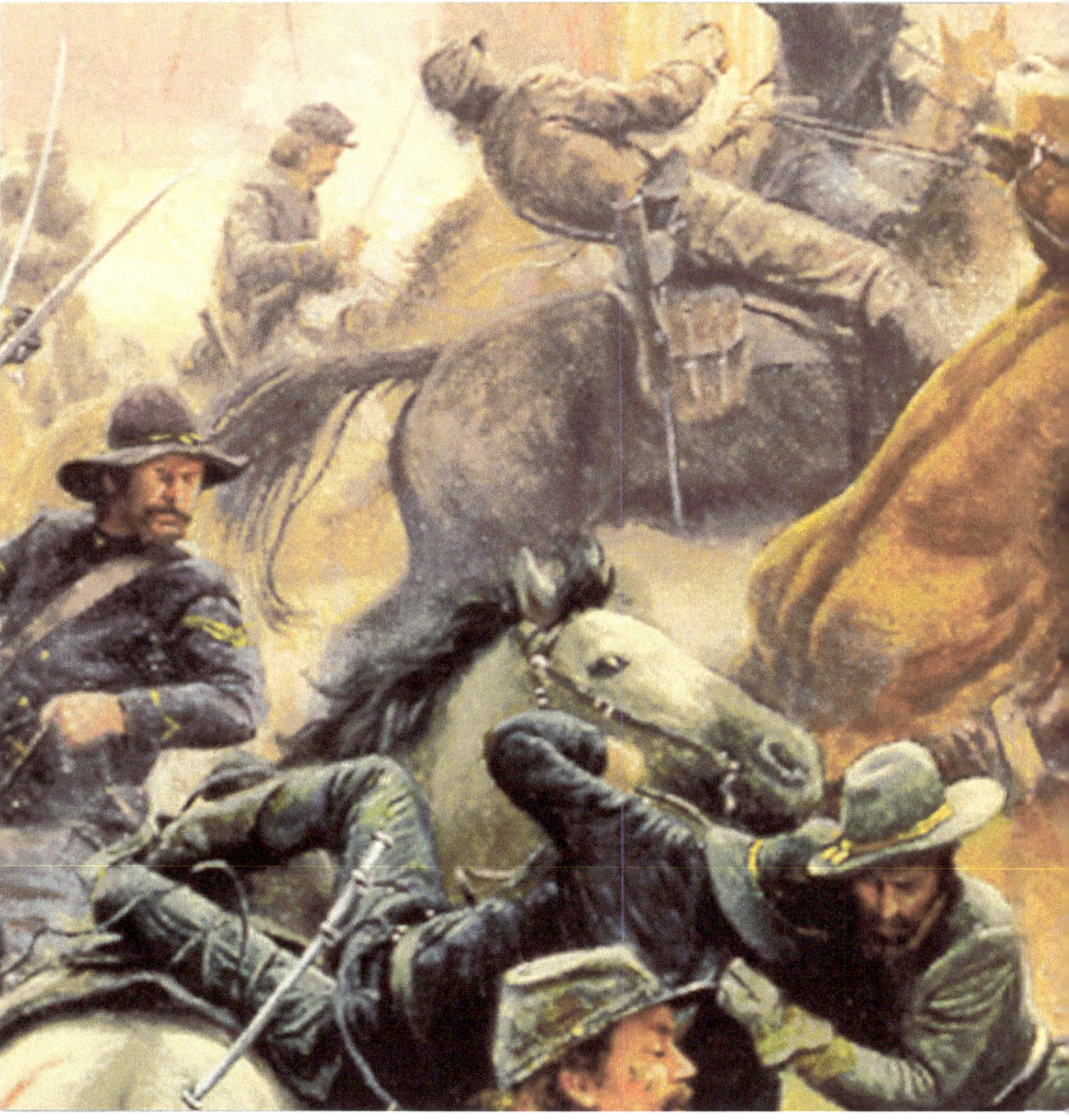

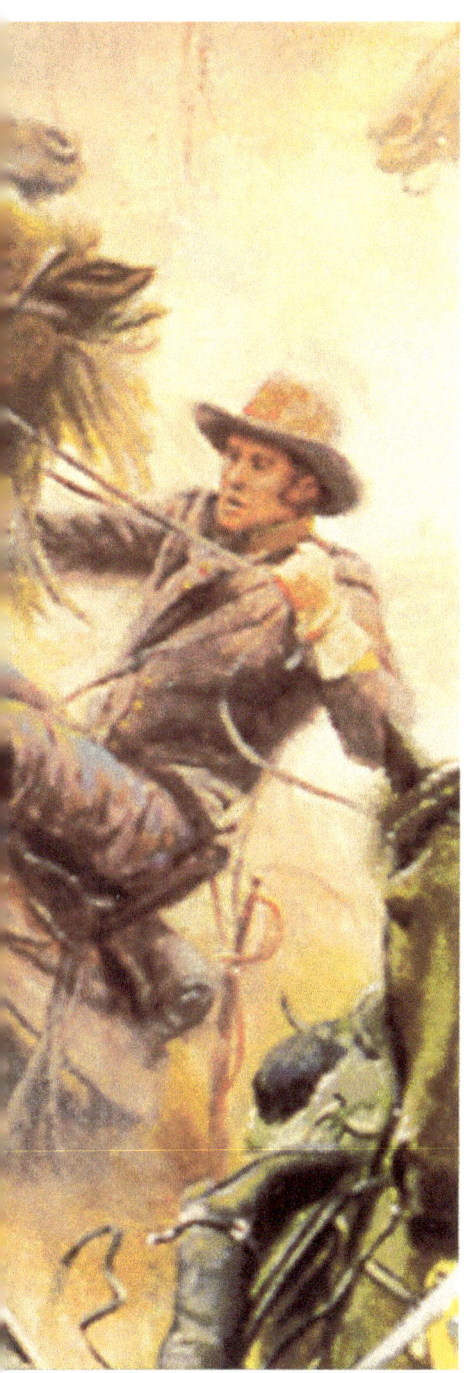

There were countless cavalry skirmishes between the armies, and only the veterans of those clashes knew the violence and horror of those few desperate moments. The early 1864 campaigns in the Shenandoah were filled with such clashes, most occurring on nondescript farms, in lonely lanes, and over vast woodlots. In the wild excitement of battle, there were no battle lines, only the desperate need to win and survive. Such was the spirit of the cavalries of the armies as the 1864 campaigning commenced.

LETTER FROM HOME

2001, oil, 20 x 16

AMONG THE HARDEST BURDENS borne by the troops was separation from their loved ones. Receiving a letter from home was a heart-stirring event for war-weary soldiers. Family news, bits of gossip, words of encouragement, endearing sentiments—all provided welcome diversion from dull duties and battlefield dangers. Poignant reminders of home refreshed tender memories, but they could also kindle the pain of separation. For most soldiers, however, the pleasures afforded by mail far outweighed the pain. Letters were read and read again. In the lull between battles, even amid the ruckus of a bustling nighttime camp, a letter from home was a priceless treasure.

The Army of Northern Virginia was emerging from its winter quarters in 1864. It had retreated from Pennsylvania in the summer of 1863 and reached a tactical standoff at Mine Run at year's end. With the coming of spring, new campaigns were ahead—and the Army of the Potomac would again be targeting Lee's legions. As yet, however, no orders had been issued, and the army waited in its camps. This is the setting for *Letter from Home*.

Many paintings take years to become a finished work. *Letter from Home* is one of these. In 1993 I did a study of three soldiers over a checkerboard.

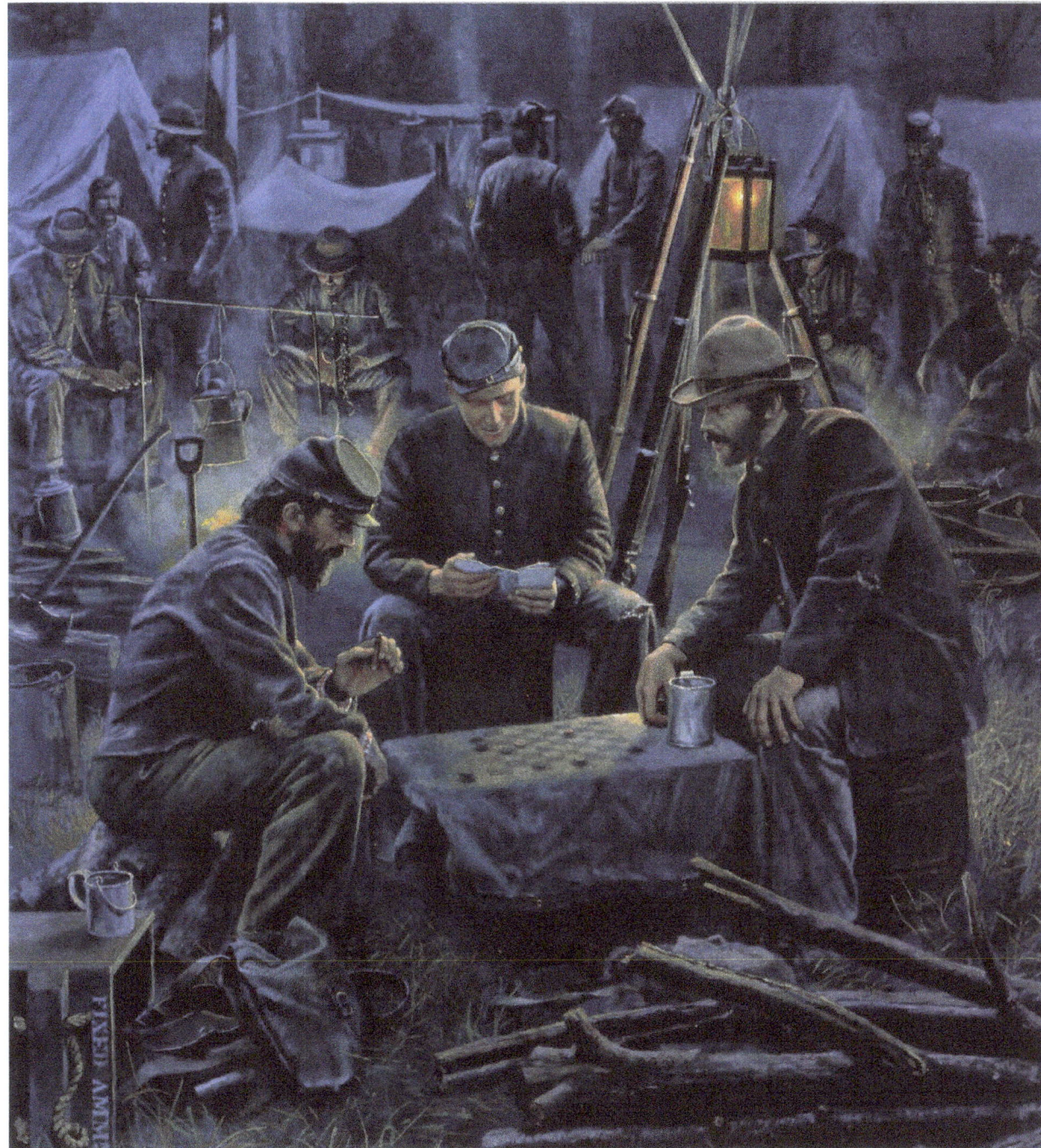

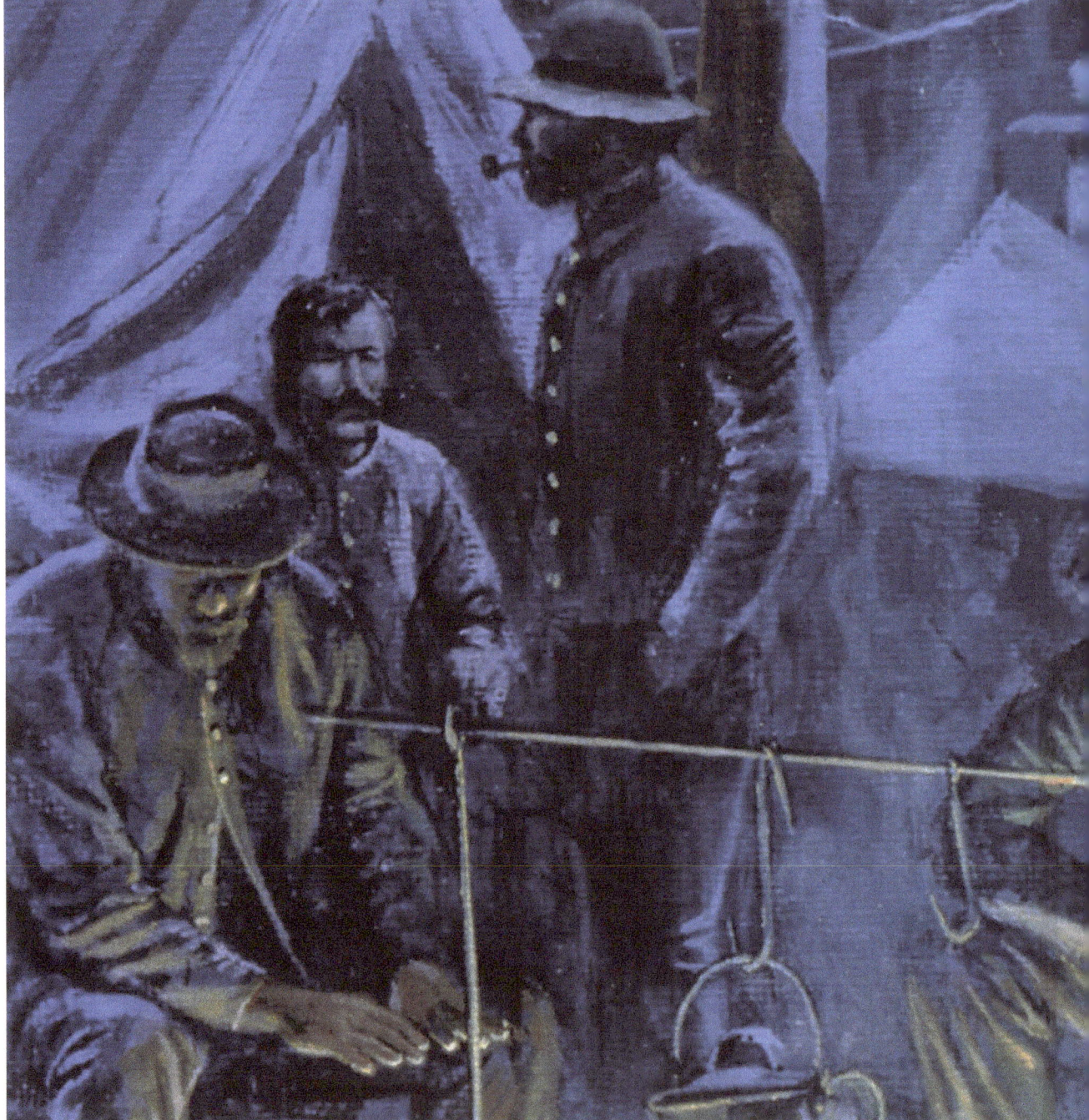

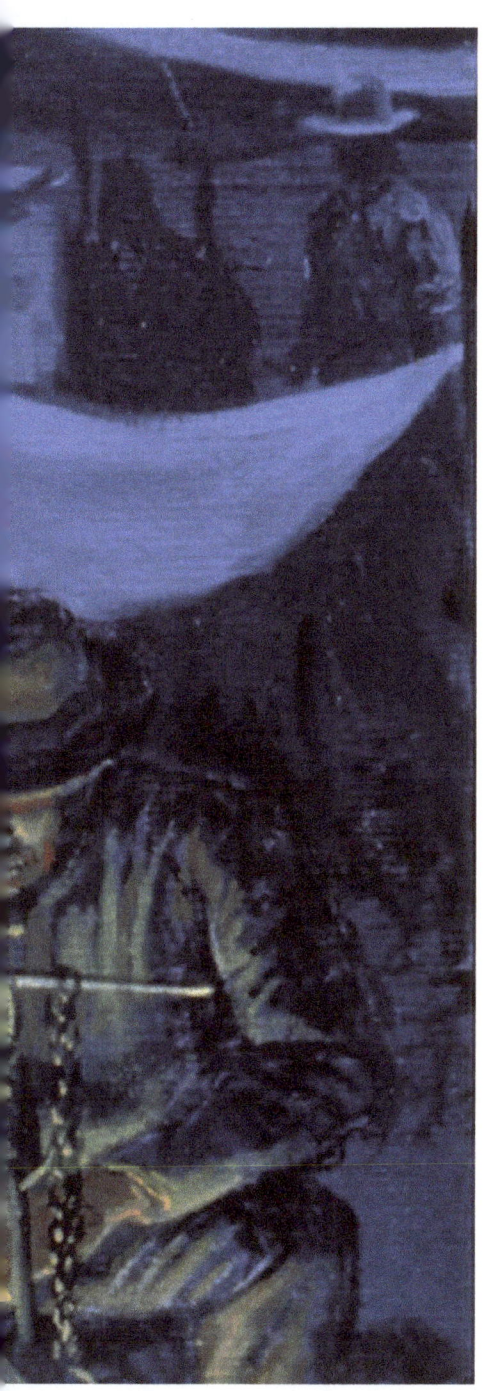

I decided to paint the men as Confederates because of their colorful, ragtag look as opposed to the well-equipped, look-alike uniforms and accoutrements of the Federals. I also decided to set the scene at night because this gave me some interesting lighting effects, such as a lantern hanging from some stacked arms, tripod style.

In the original study, the checker players were the focal point. I kept the players—checkers was a popular game and was often played on a makeshift board painted on the inside of a poncho or blanket. For the painting, however, I painted the letter in the center of the canvas and worked the rest of the scene around that point. I added other camp activities in the background to illustrate what one soldier said about the war being interminable boredom interspersed with moments of sheer terror. Games and duties provided much-needed distractions from the hardships of fighting, but nothing provided more relief than a letter from home.

SOLDIER OF FAITH

GEN. ROBERT E. LEE
ORANGE, VIRGINIA
FEBRUARY 17, 1864

2002, oil, 24 x 32

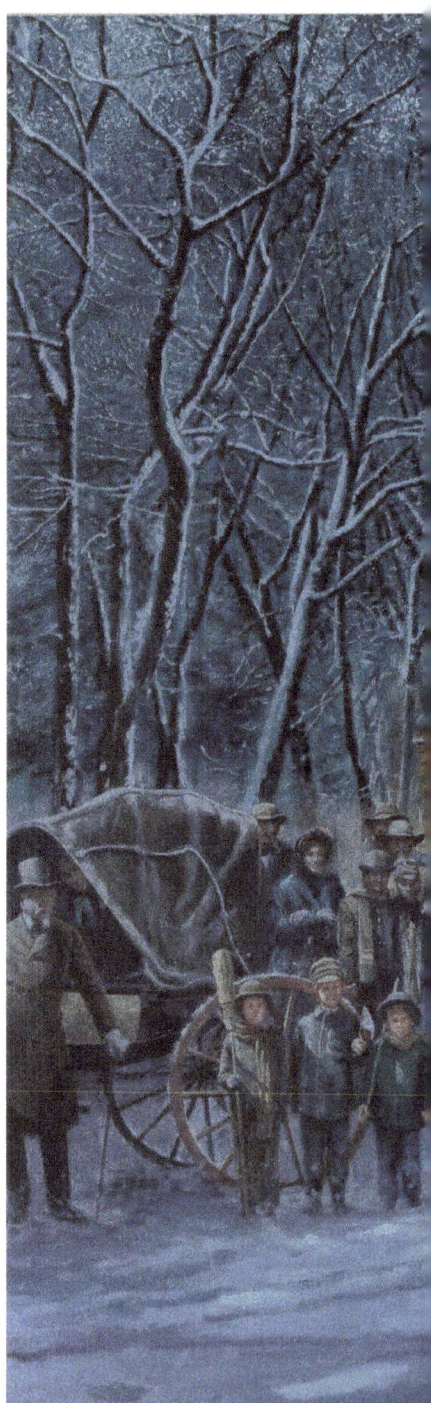

THOSE WHO KNEW Robert E. Lee knew that his faith was his life's foundation. "In sunshine and in storm, in victory and in defeat," observed Gen. John B. Gordon, "his heart turned to God."

In February 1864, while in winter camp near Orange, Virginia, Lee was visited by a delegation of army chaplains. Recalled the Reverend J. William Jones: "As we began to answer his questions about the spiritual interests of the army, and to tell of that great revival which was then extending through the camps . . . he expressed his delight [and] we forgot the great warrior, and only remembered that we were communing with 'a humble, earnest Christian.'" Another observer, one who knew Lee the soldier, noted, "He was a

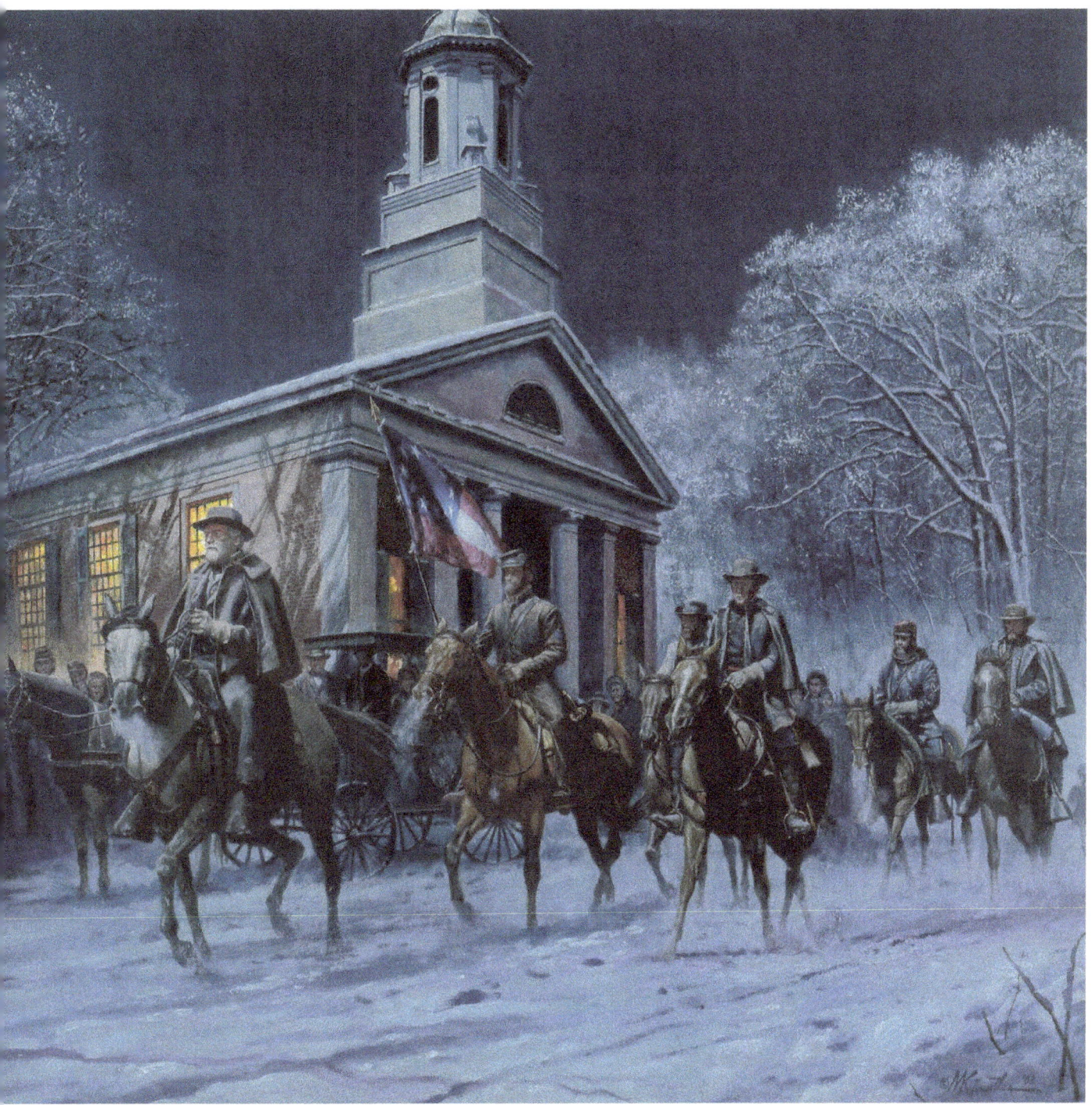

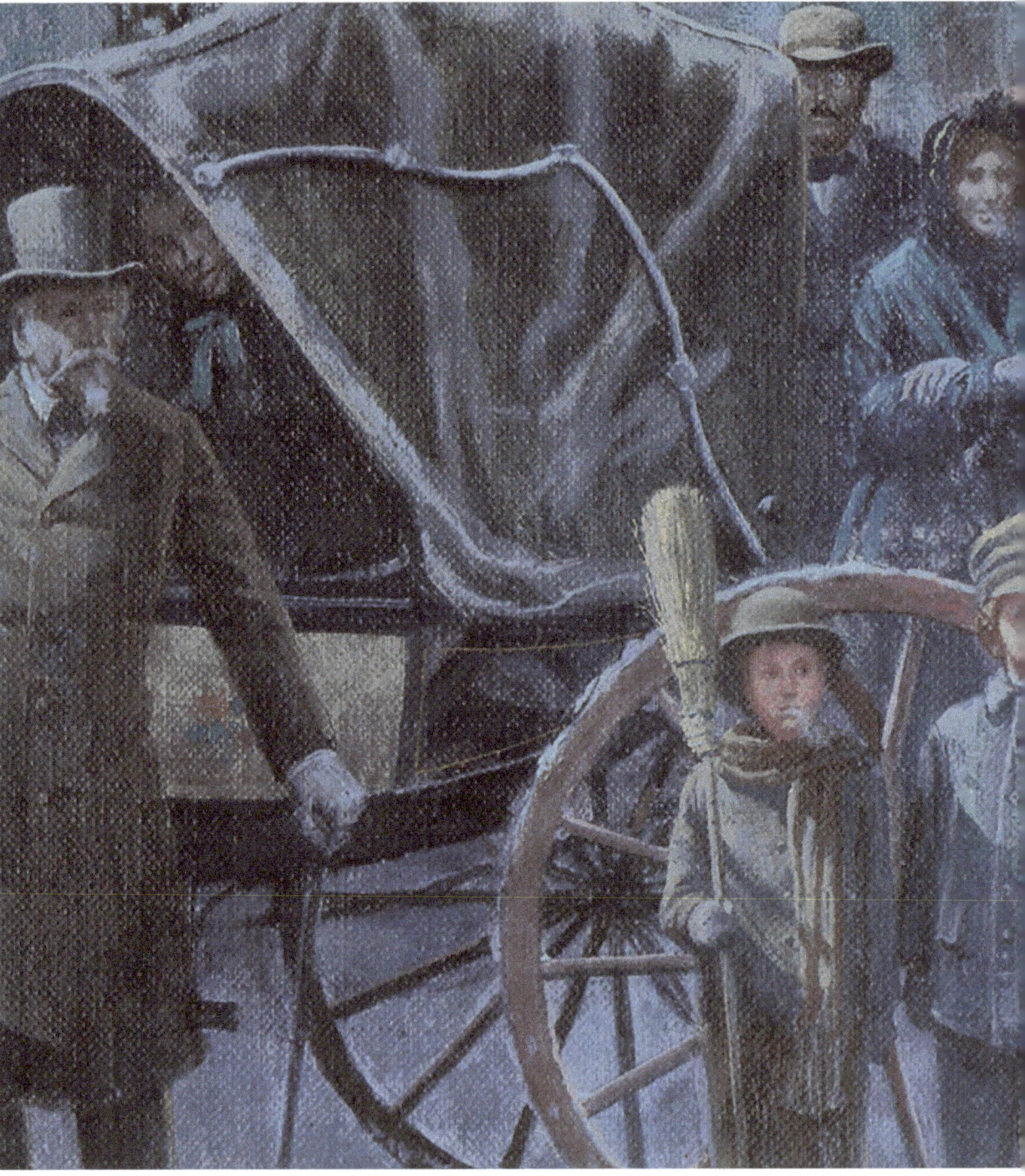

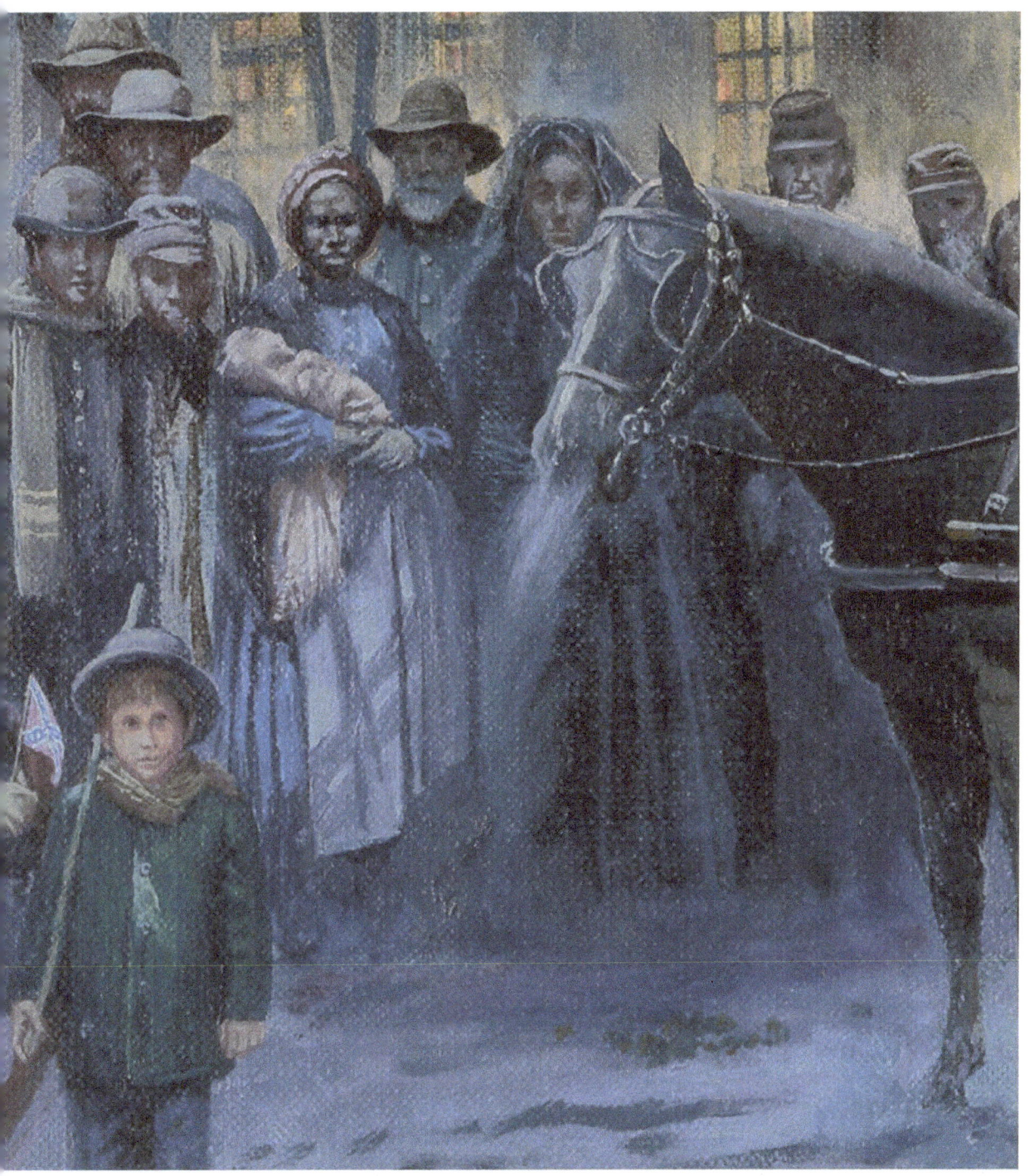

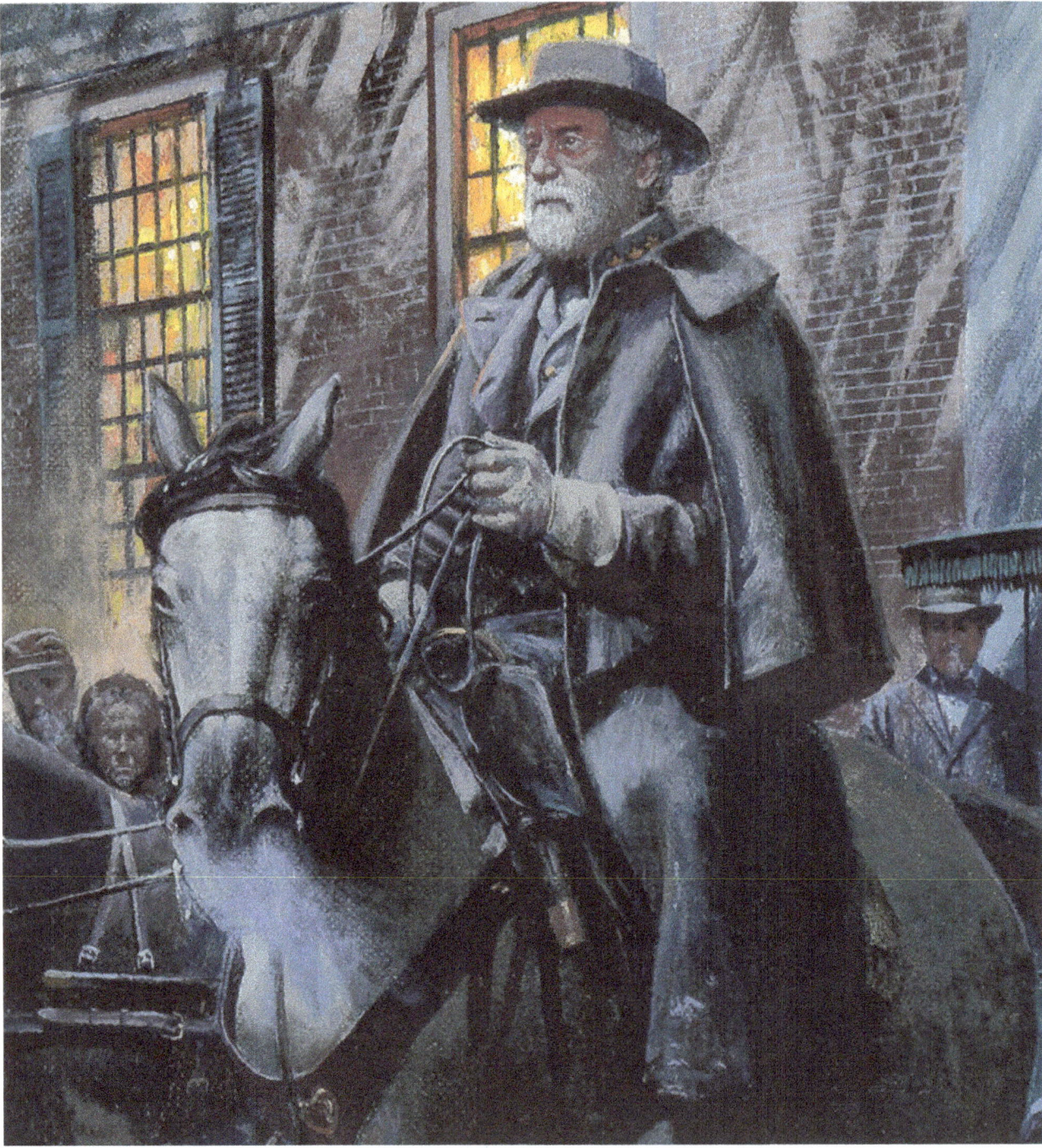

foe without hate, a friend without treachery, a soldier without cruelty, a victim without murmuring . . . and a man without guile."

While I was visiting an art gallery in Virginia, a small group of people from the city of Orange asked me to consider painting a historical scene from their community. Later, as I was working on other paintings, I noticed that the Army of Northern Virginia spent the winter of 1863–64 near Orange. I decided to see for myself what the residents loved so much about their history

In Orange, I discovered a delightful place rich with Civil War history I met with Jay Harrison, executive director of Orange Downtown Alliance Inc., local history expert Frank Walker, and others from the group that had called on me years earlier. I examined historic maps and studied period photographs and became fascinated with several period structures in the town. When I saw St. Thomas Episcopal Church, I realized it would be the perfect setting for a painting with Lee as the central figure.

Lee's army was in winter camp nearby during the winter of 1863–64, and the general prayed at the church regularly. His church pew is preserved and designated by a bronze plaque today, and an ancient locust tree outside had been the "hitching post" for Traveller. I learned from Civil War historian James I. Robertson Jr. that a heavy snow fell on February 15, 1864, so there would have been snow on the ground during Wednesday vespers. I've always admired Lee's character, which was, of course, rooted in his personal faith—as historian Rod Gragg noted in his book *Robert E. Lee: A Commitment to Valor.* So I decided this would be the setting for the painting of Lee in Orange, Virginia.

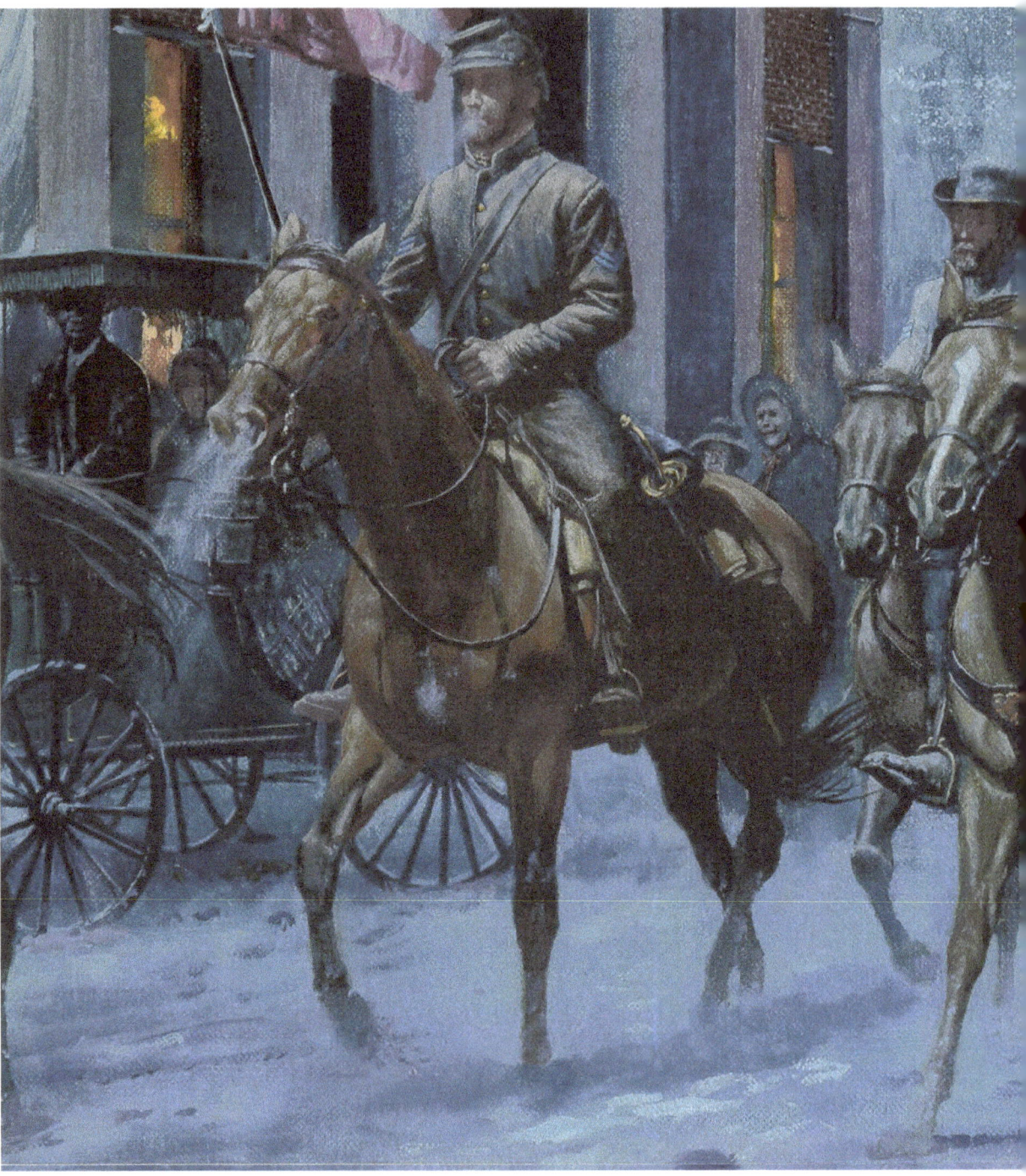

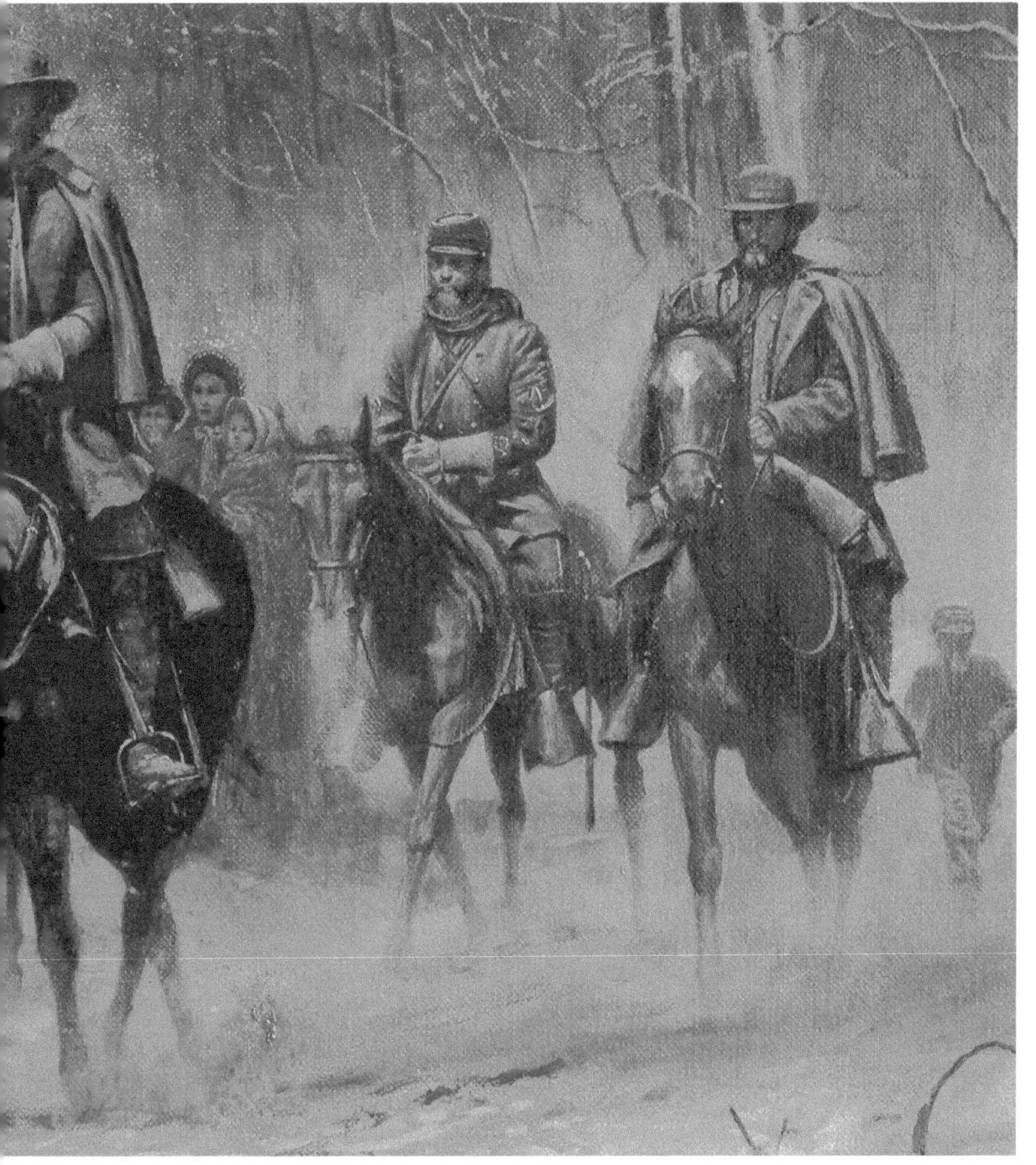

THE FINAL MISSION

H. L. HUNLEY,
CHARLESTON, SOUTH CAROLINA
FEBRUARY 17, 1864

2003, oil, 32 x 48

WHEN THE *H. L. HUNLEY* was recovered from Charleston harbor in 2000, I watched the television coverage with the same fascination that affected most students of the Civil War. The long-lost *Hunley*—the first submarine to sink a ship in warfare-was actually raised from its watery grave! Despite my interest in the salvage of the vessel, I have to admit that I did not think about painting the *Hunley*. I had painted the engagement between the *Monitor* and the *Virginia,* but my primary focus has always been the war between armies, not navies.

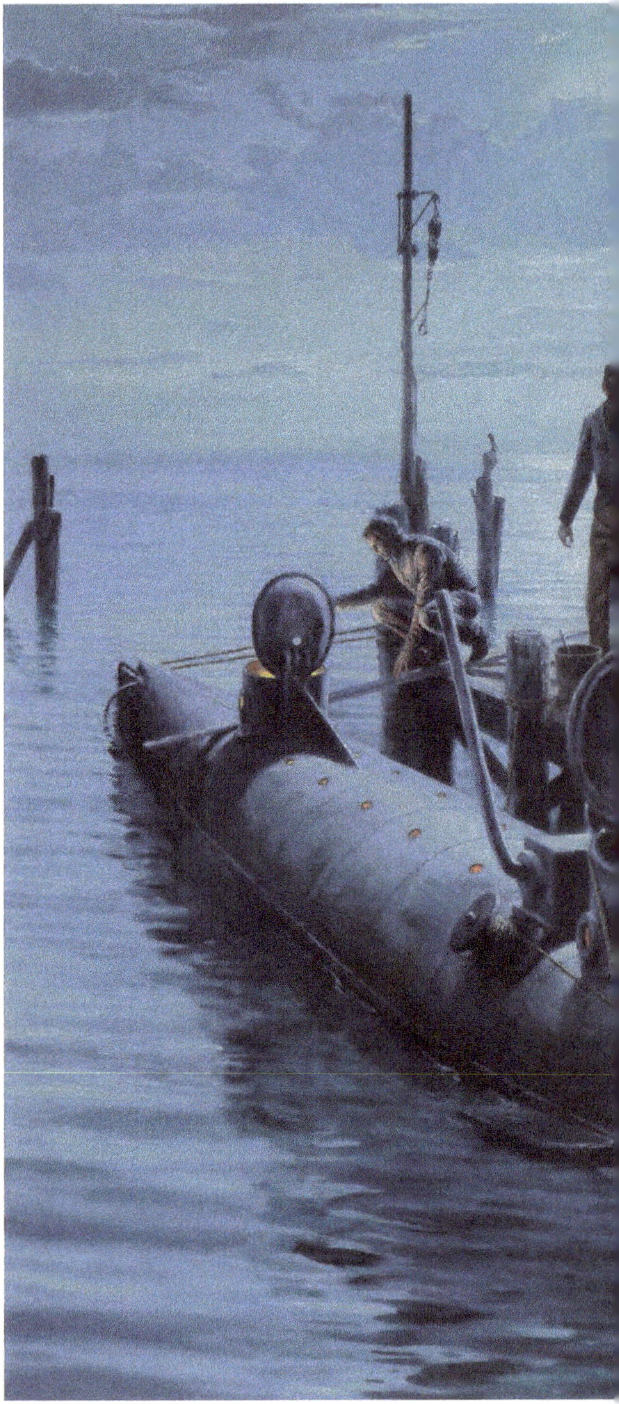

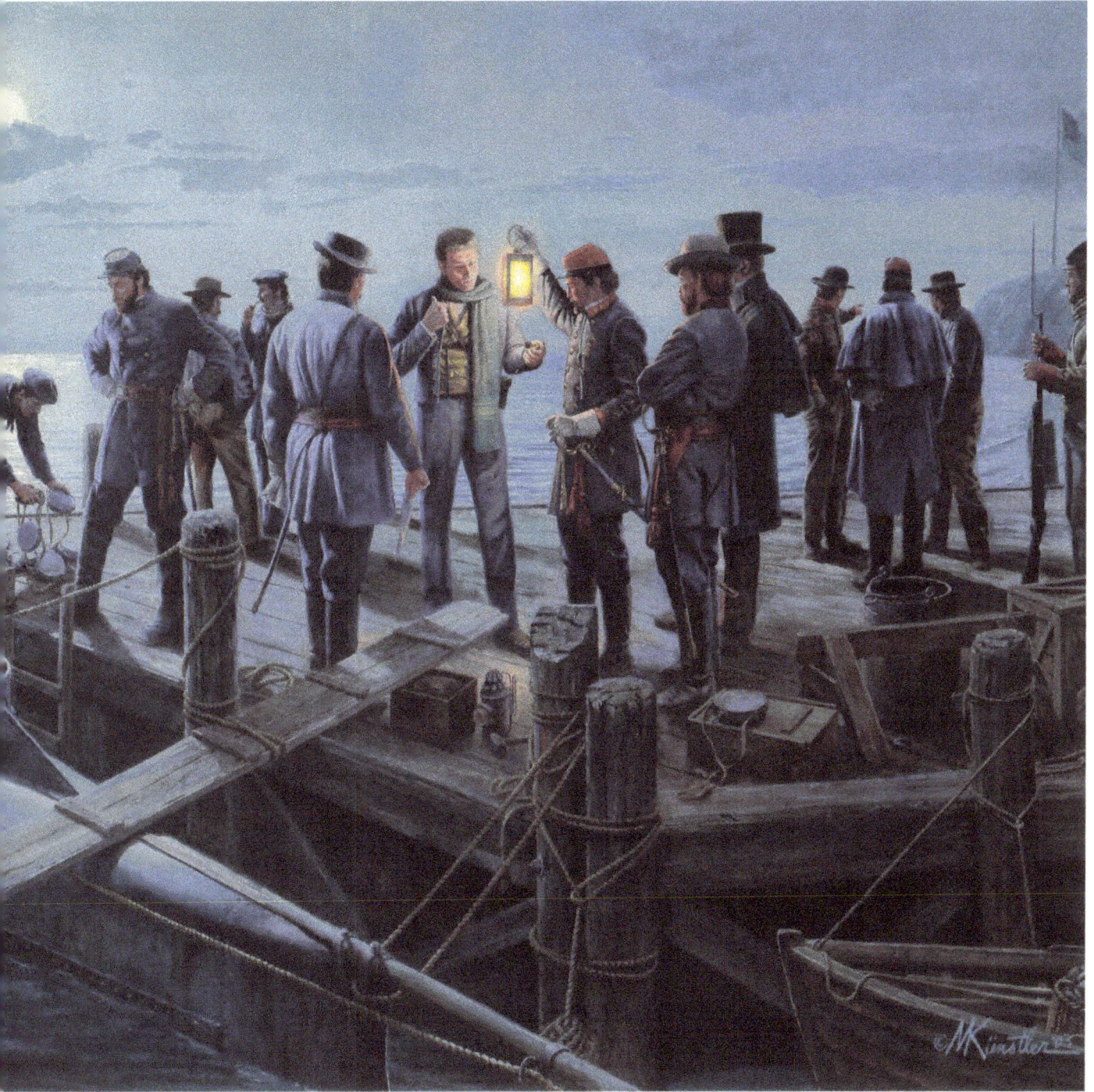

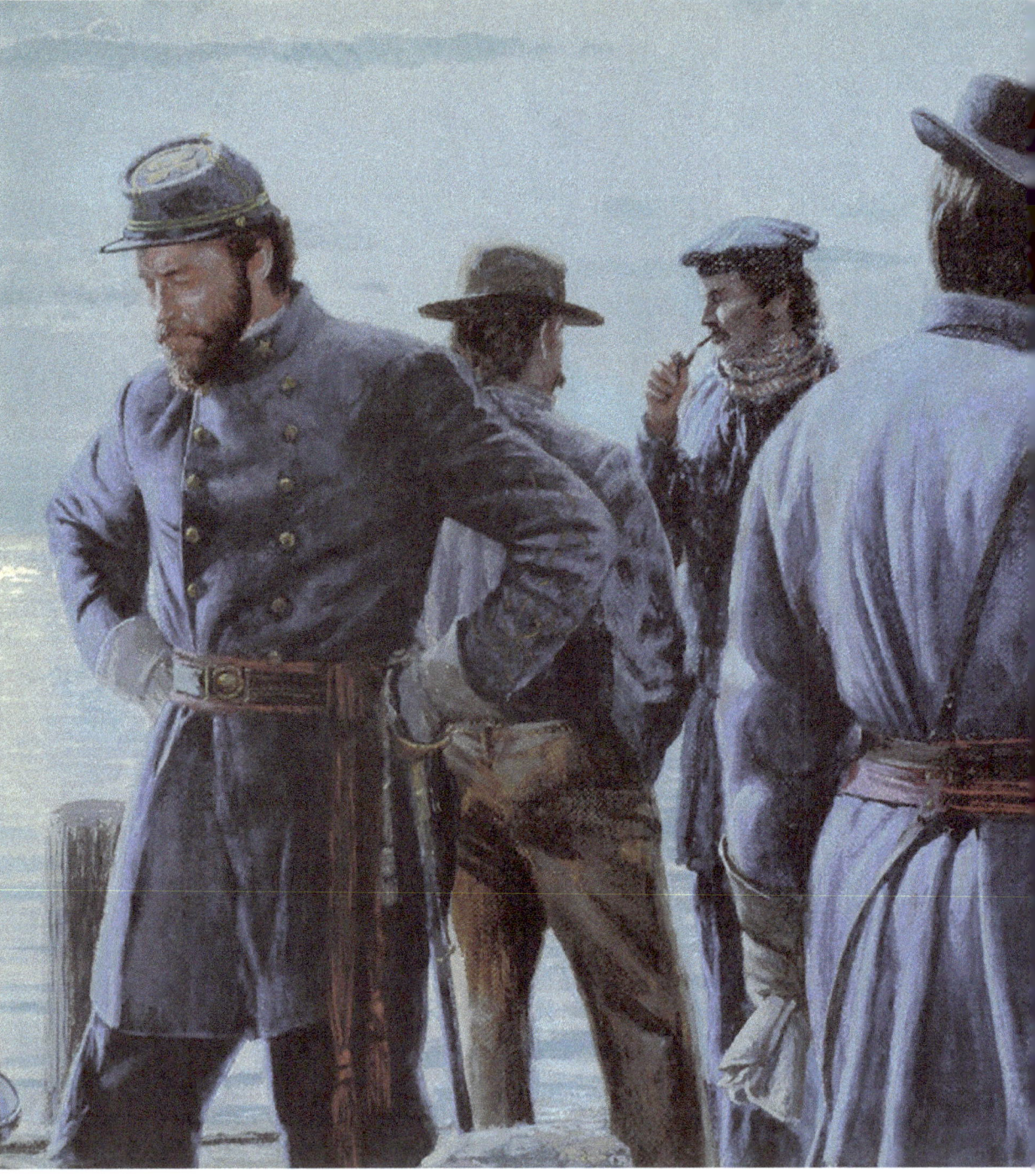

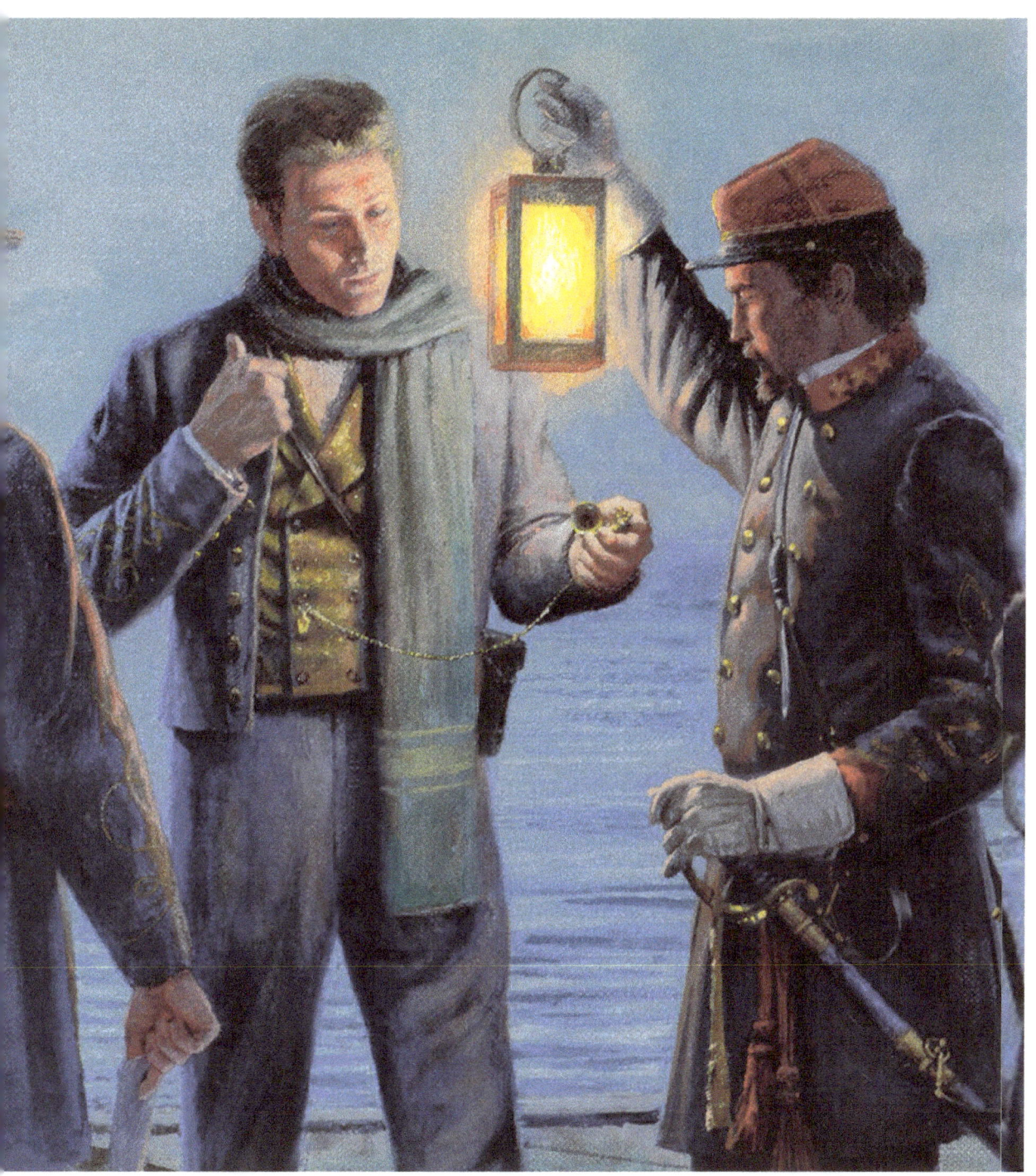

During one of my regular visits to Charleston, the chairman of the Hunley Commission, South Carolina Senator Glenn McConnell, invited me to examine the *Hunley* at the Warren Lasch Conservation Center. I happened to visit the center on the day that senior conservator Paul Mardikian first opened the gold pocket watch carried by the *Hunley's* commander, Lt. George E. Dixon.

The *Hunley* is an extraordinary vessel—sophisticated and advanced for its day. And the crew consisted of exceptionally courageous men. As I stood there, looking down at this famous submarine, I was caught up in the history, tragedy, and adventure associated with the *Hunley*. When the senator asked if I would be interested in serving as an official artist for the *H. L. Hunley*, I immediately accepted. The result is this painting.

While researching the painting, I went out to Sullivan's Island and Breach Inlet, overlooking Charleston harbor, and examined the launch site for the *Hunley's* last mission—the site where this painting is set. The time for the painting is set at approximately 6:30 p.m. on February 17, 1864. High tide has crested, and the tide is shifting seaward again. That, of course, would help the crew propel the *Hunley* through Breach Inlet and toward her target—the USS *Housatonic*.

As the first officially sanctioned image of the *Hunley*, I felt a serious responsibility to faithfully portray the vessel, its crew, and the surroundings in the most authentic manner. It's the first time that Dixon and his crew have been authentically portrayed. I have included many of the major artifacts that were recovered from the *Hunley*: a signal lantern, compass box, canteens, buttons, tobacco pipes, and, of course, Dixon's pocket watch.

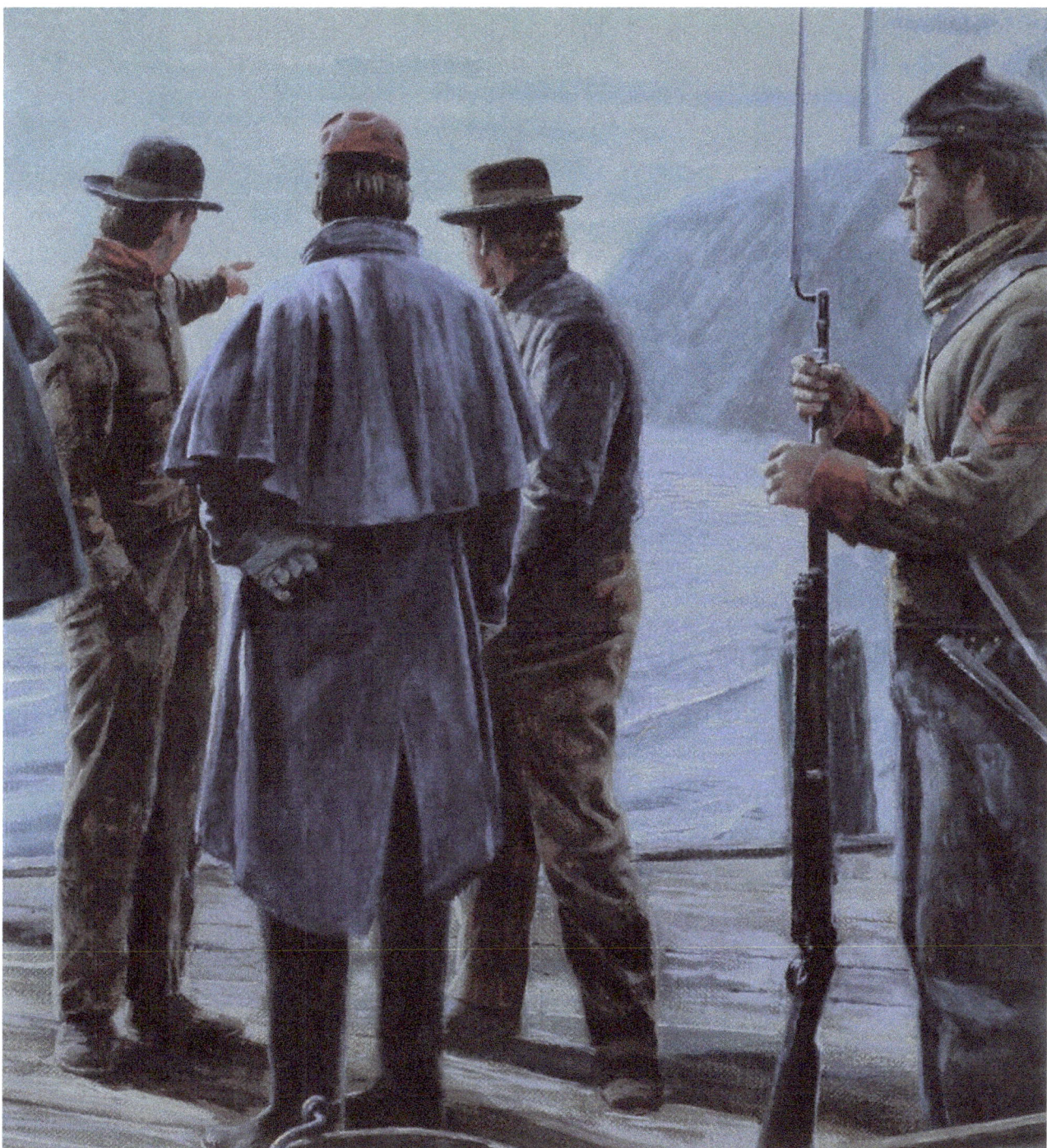

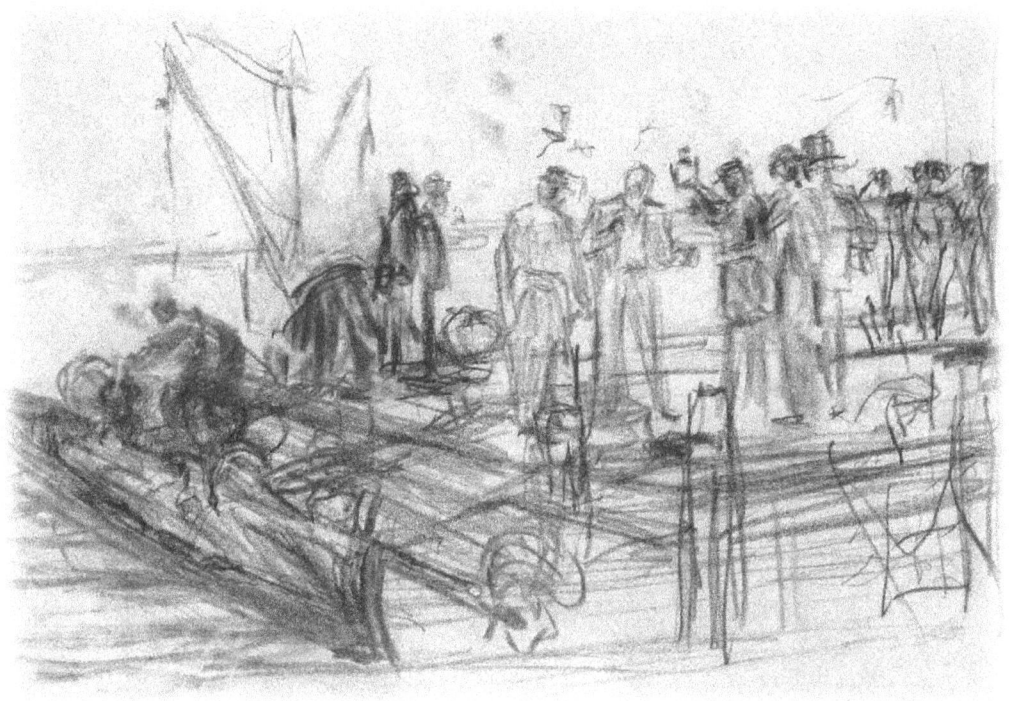

I worked extensively with Dr. Robert Neyland, the *Hunley* project manager, as well as experts at the U.S. Navy Historical Center in Washington, D.C., Senator McConnell, and the conservators at the Lasch lab. I was allowed to review x-rays, site photos, artifact photos, facial reconstructions based on the crewmen's remains, DNA findings, tidal records, weather data, and information on the phases of the moon in February 1863. Also included was a lengthy list of measurements that had to be translated into perspective and put eventually on canvas. Of course, modern Charleston is much different from the wartime city, so I based my reconstruction of Battery Marshall—with the Second National Flag of the Confederacy flying over it—on the period painting by Southern artist Conrad Wise Chapman.

Painting *The Final Mission* was an exhilarating experience. Thanks to the enormous amount of research assistance, I believe the painting will stand the test of time. I hope that generations of Americans will be able to visit the restored *Hunley,* examine the submarine closely—then study this painting and understand what that incredible mission was really like. The *Hunley* deserves to be preserved as a cherished symbol of the innovative spirit, valor, and sacrifice that was so common to Americans of the nineteenth century.

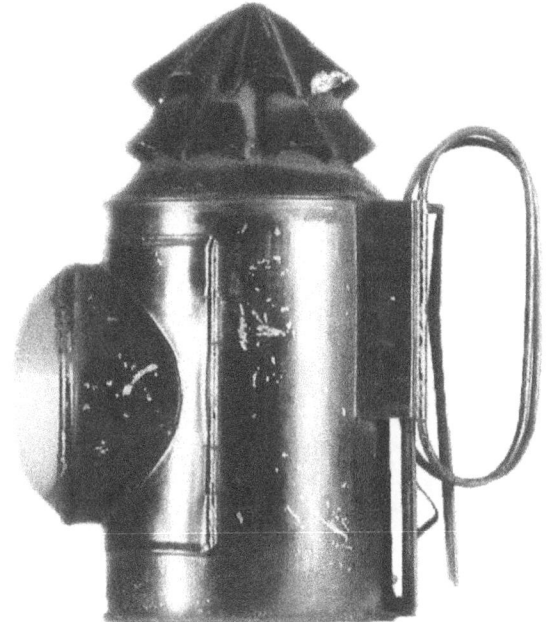

The signal light recovered from the *H. L. Hunley*

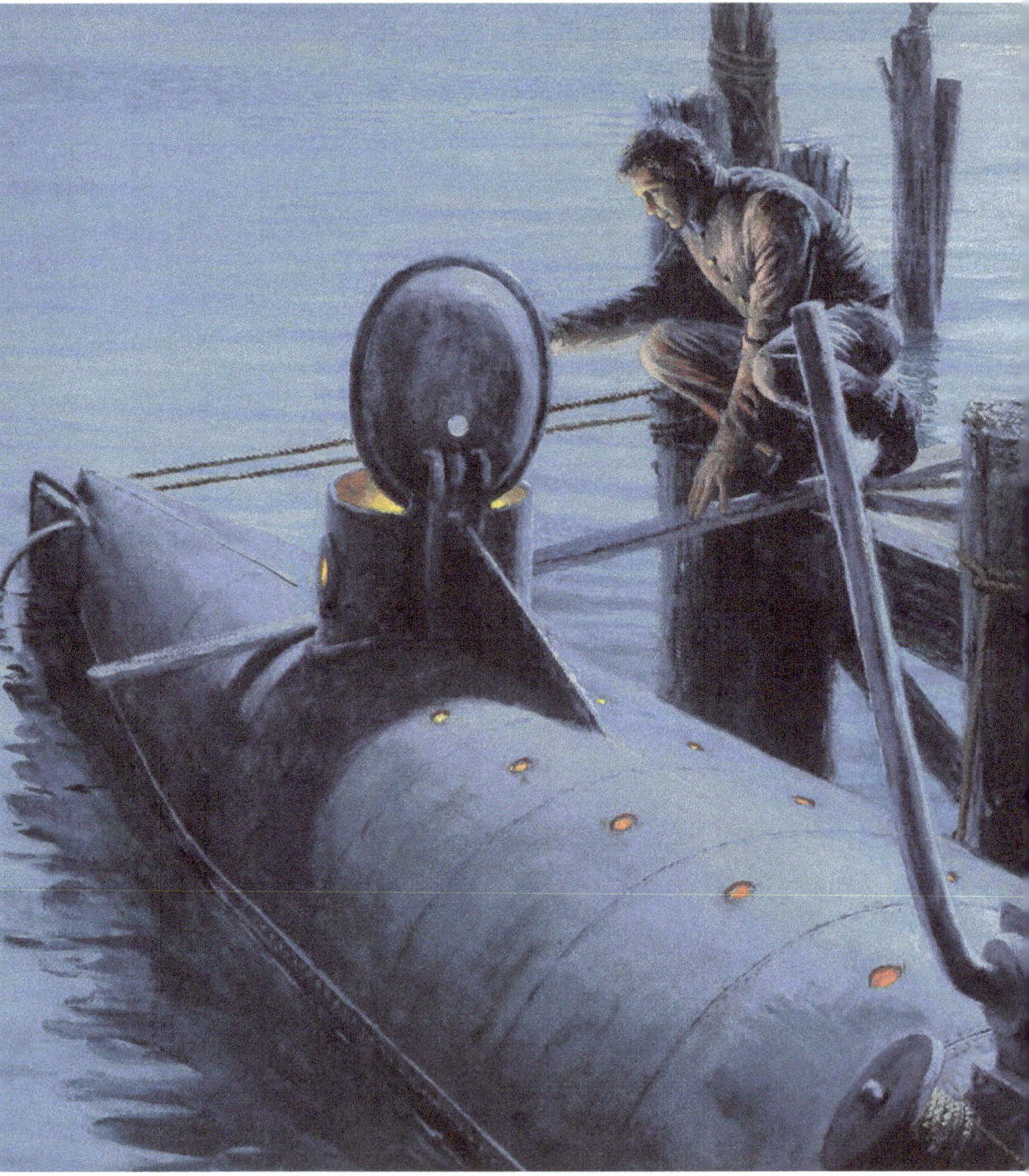

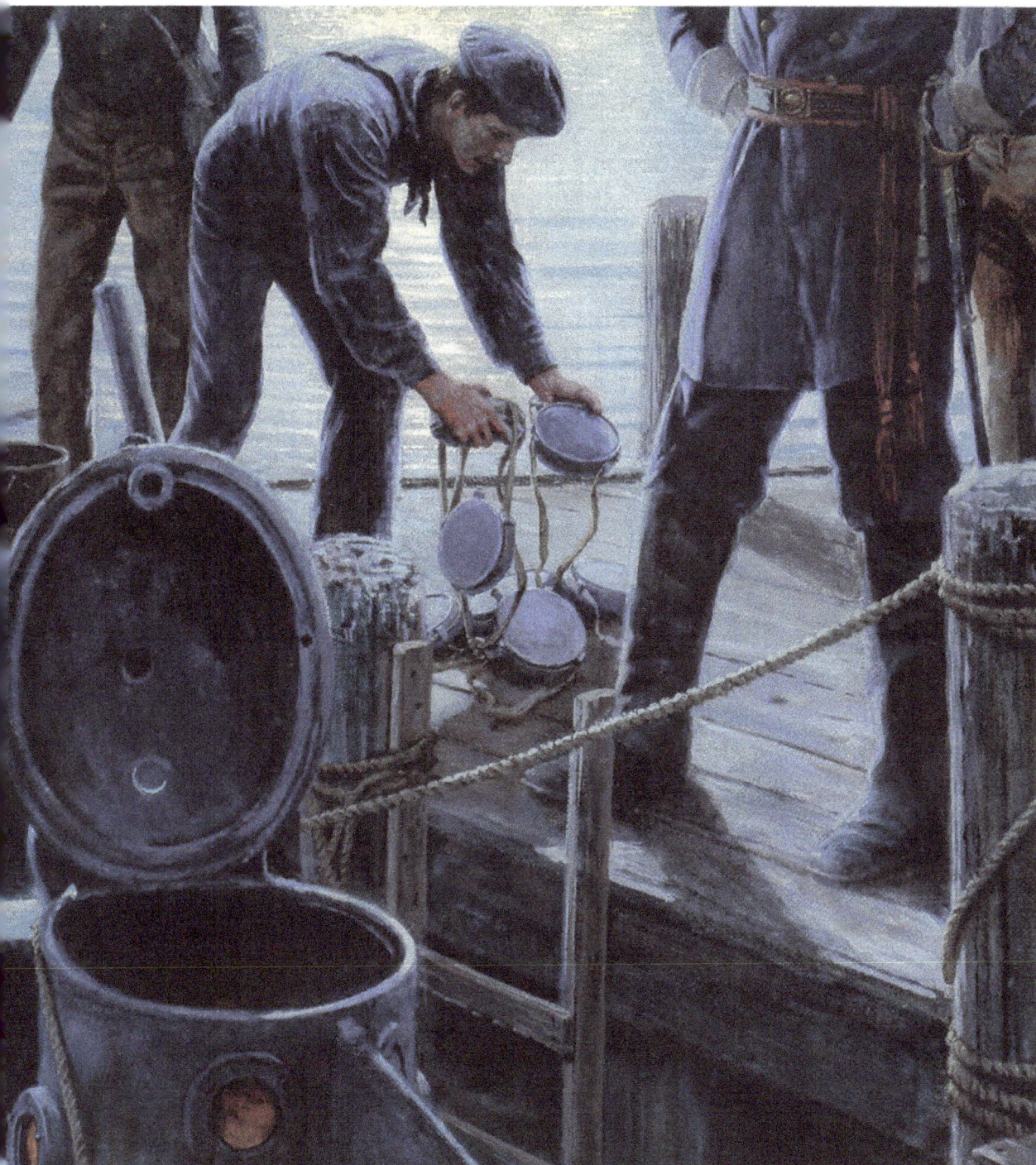

WHITE HOUSE GALA

ULYSSES S. GRANT AT THE WHITE HOUSE

MARCH 8, 1864

1996, oil, 36 x 48

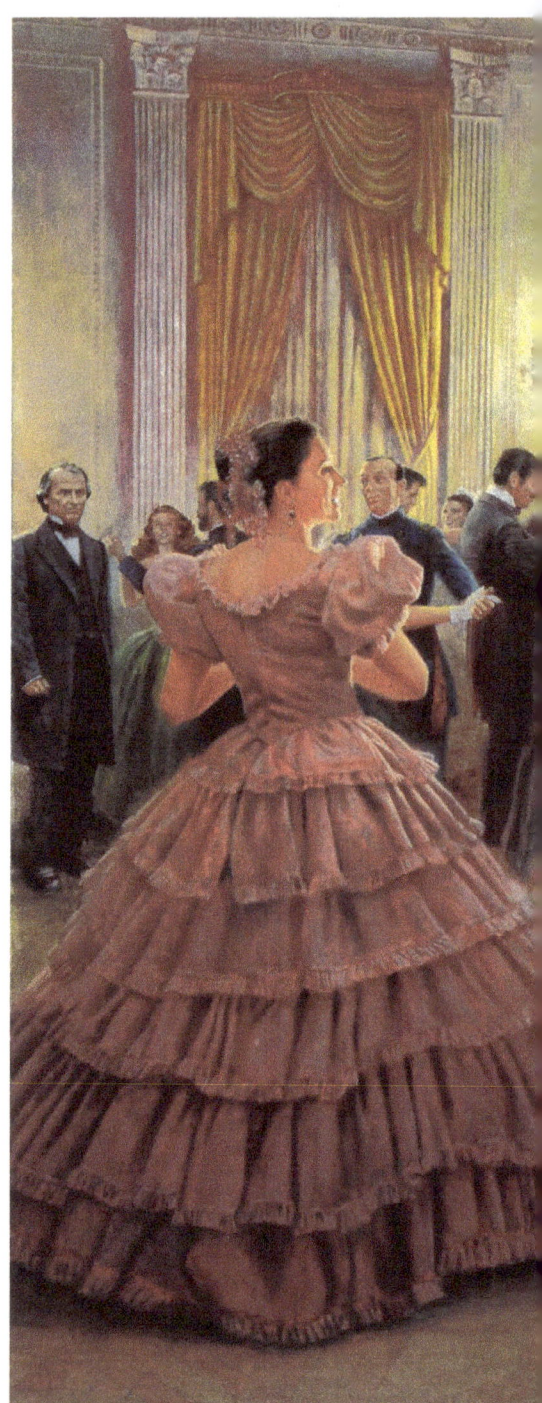

BETWEEN VICKSBURG AND CHATTANOOGA Ulysses S. Grant had accomplished much to secure Union victory in the western theater. In early 1864 Congress revived the rank of lieutenant general, and Lincoln nominated Grant to fill it. The general was then summoned to Washington. He arrived on March 8 and attended a regular evening reception at the White House. The number of attendees was much larger than usual, due to rumors that the hero of Chattanooga would be there.

The painting depicts the general's first appearance at the White House and his initial meeting with Lincoln.

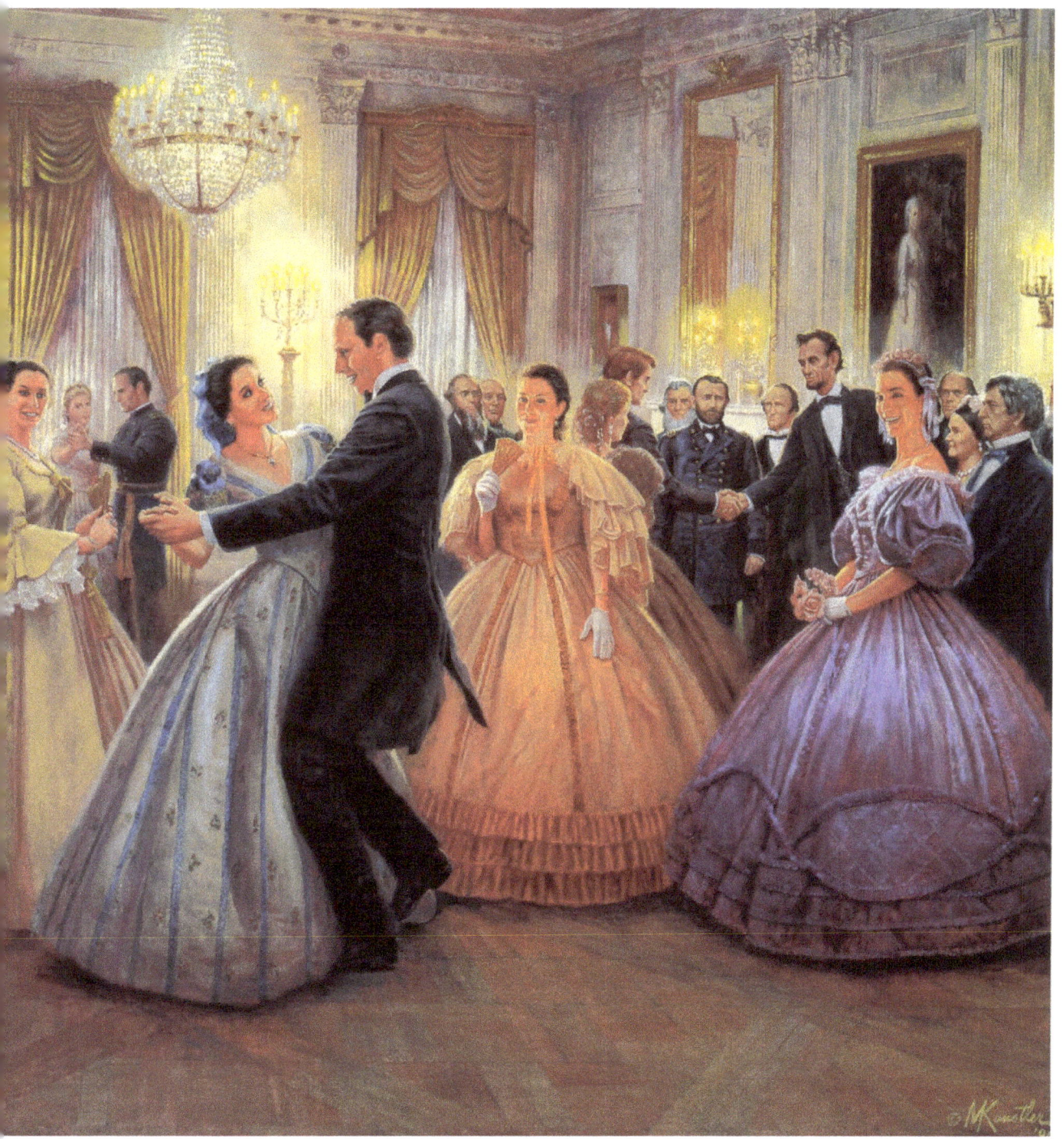

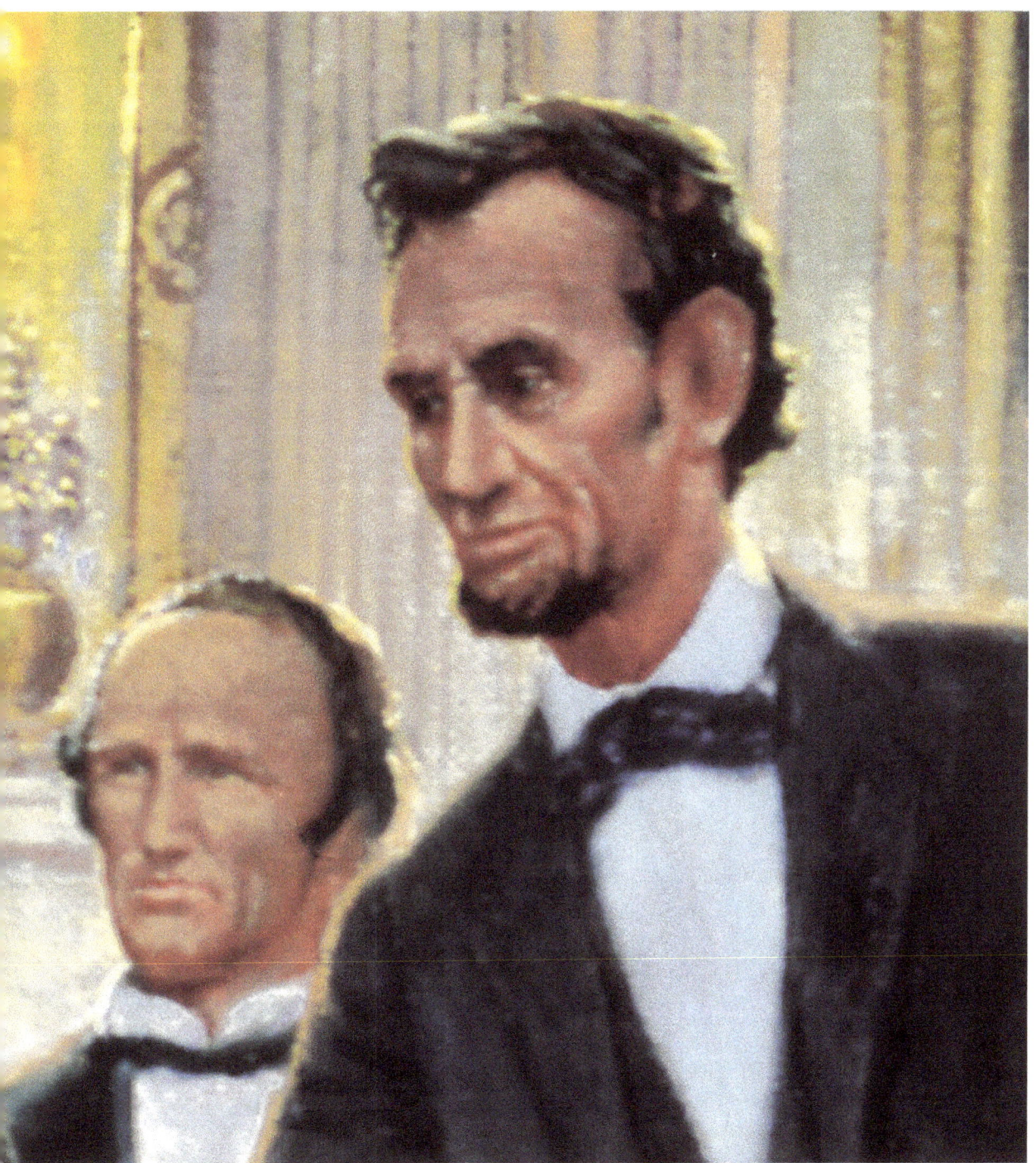

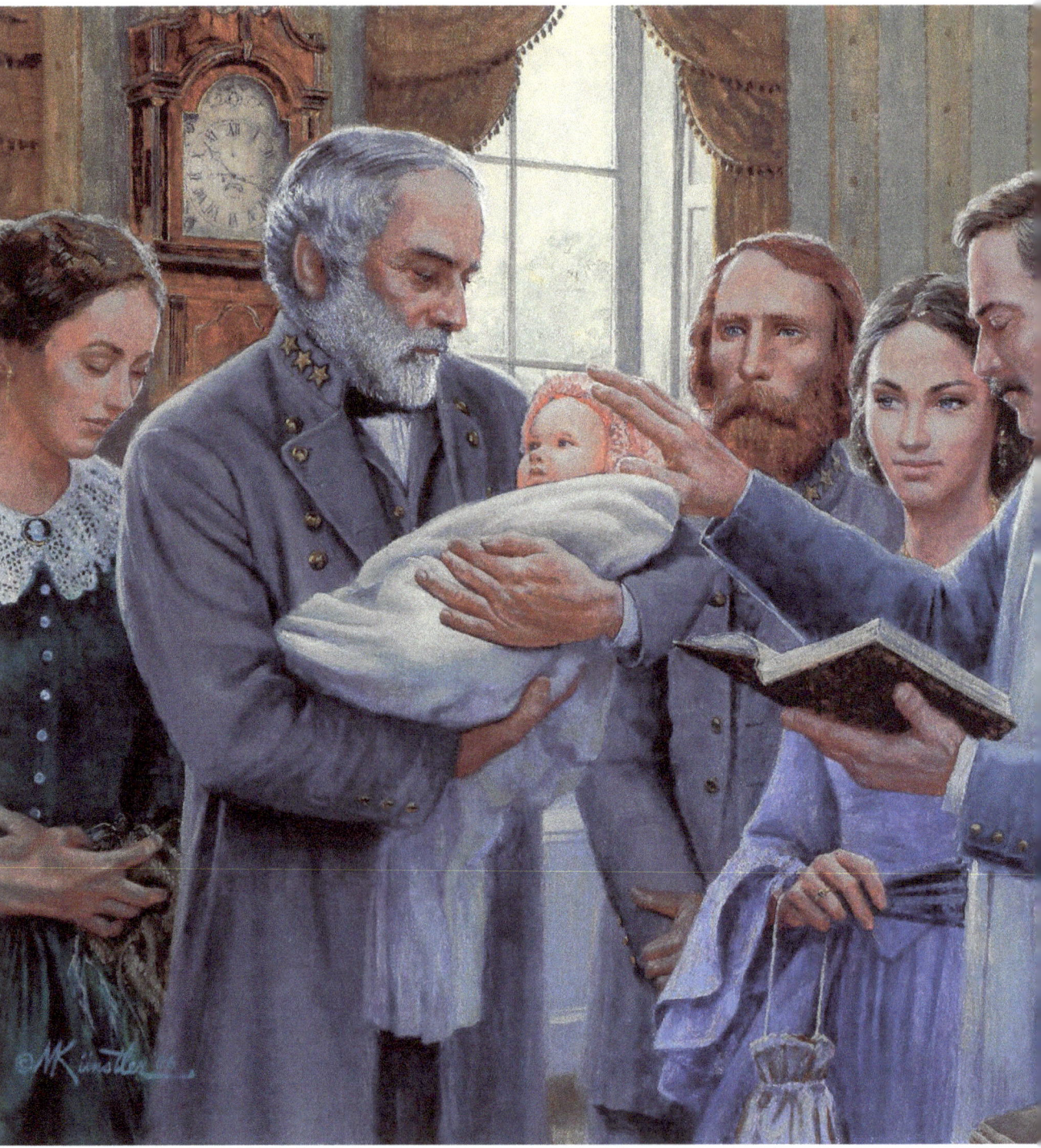

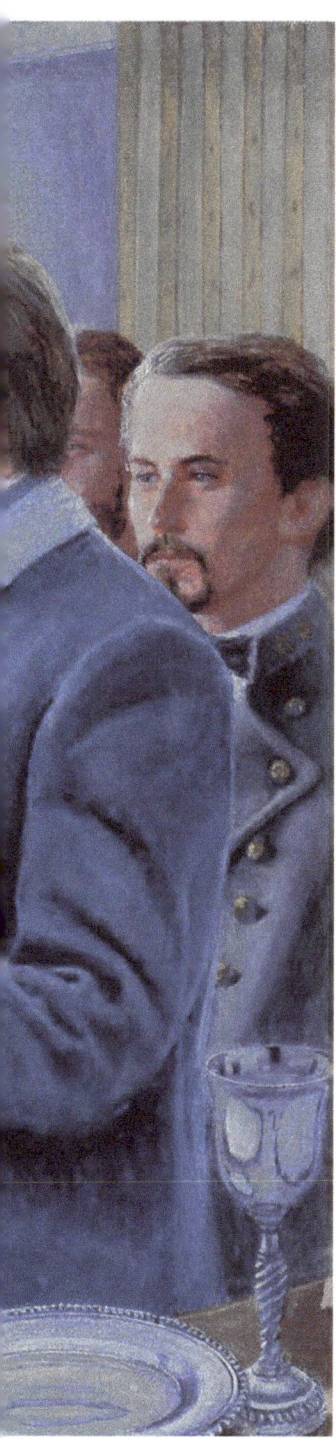

TENDER IS THE HEART

GENS. ROBERT E. LEE AND A. P. HILL
ORANGE, VIRGINIA
MAY 1, 1864

2006, oil, 16 x 20

Aᴍɪᴅ ᴛʜᴇ ʀᴀᴠᴀɢᴇs ᴏꜰ war was a celebration of life. On May 1, 1864, a group of high-ranking officers gathered in Orange, Virginia. Chief among them were Robert E. Lee and corps commander A. P Hill. They were not engaged in strategizing but to witness the baptism of Lucy Lee Hill, the daughter of Hill and his wife, Kitty. The child had been named in honor of the general who agreed to be her godfather. The Reverend Richard Davis of St. Thomas's Episcopal Church officiated.

Throughout the ceremony, Lee gently held the baby. It was undoubtedly a pleasant experience for the general, himself the father of seven children. Although his duties had called him away from home during much of his child-rearing years, Lee doted on his children—and all of them revered him in return.

This was a tender but fleeting moment for Lee, Hill, and the others present that day. Soon, the spring campaigns would draw Lee and his army into a series of savage and bloody contests. Within a year, Hill would fall mortally wounded at the battle of Five Forks, Lee would surrender his tattered and battered army at Appomattox Court House, and Lucy Lee Hill—like countless children in the North and the South—would be fatherless. She would eventually become a revered figure in the South—a symbol of Southern courage and sacrifice—and be known regionally as the "Daughter of the Confederacy."

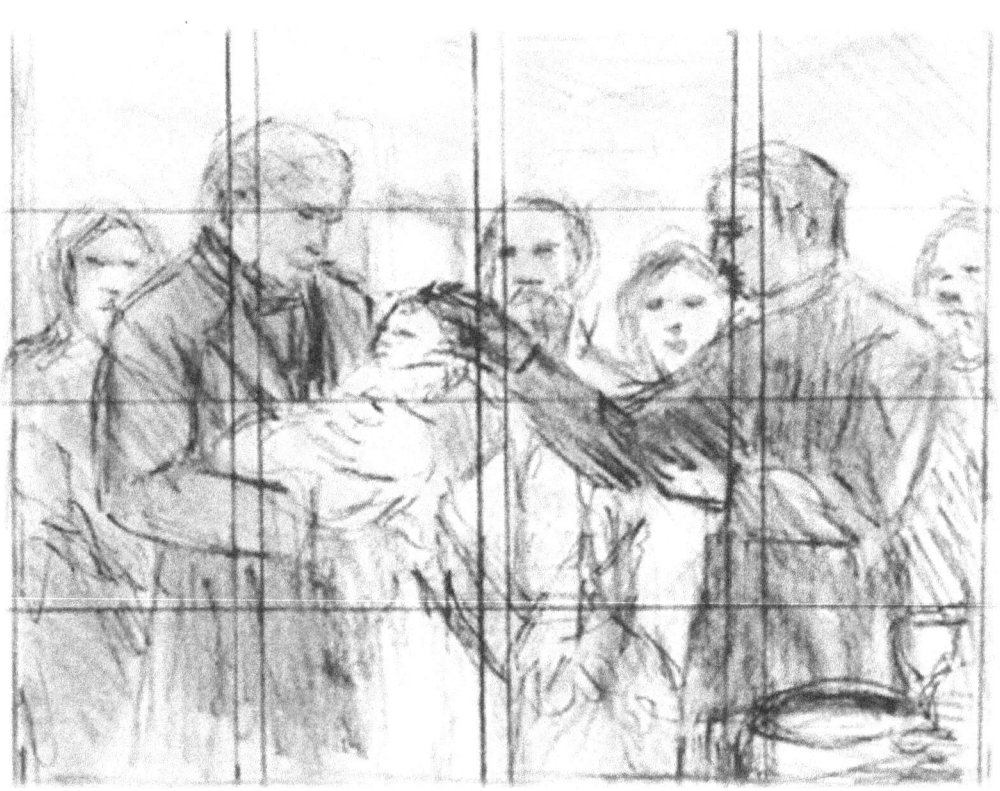

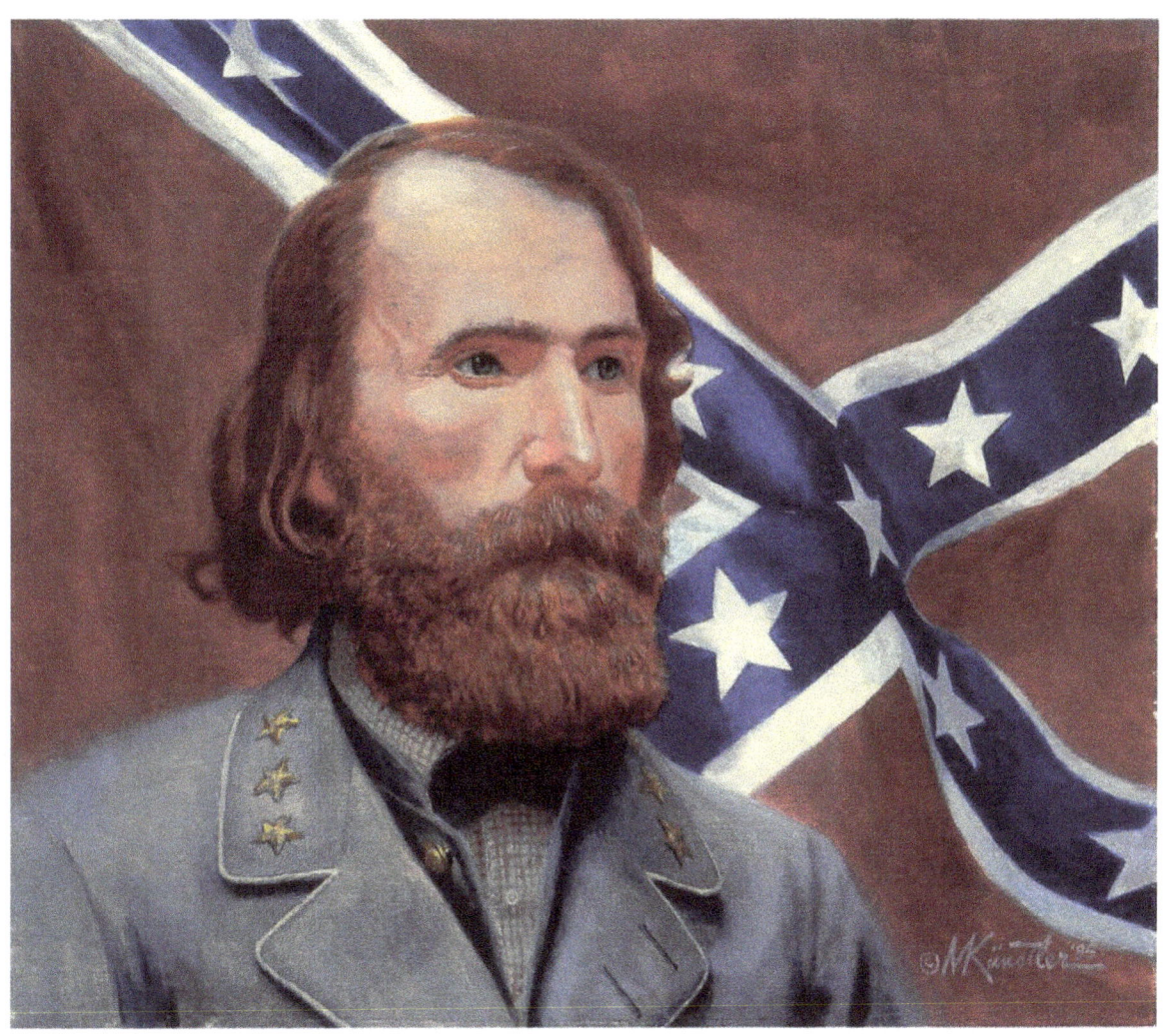

GEN. A. P. HILL

1995, oil, 10 x 11¼

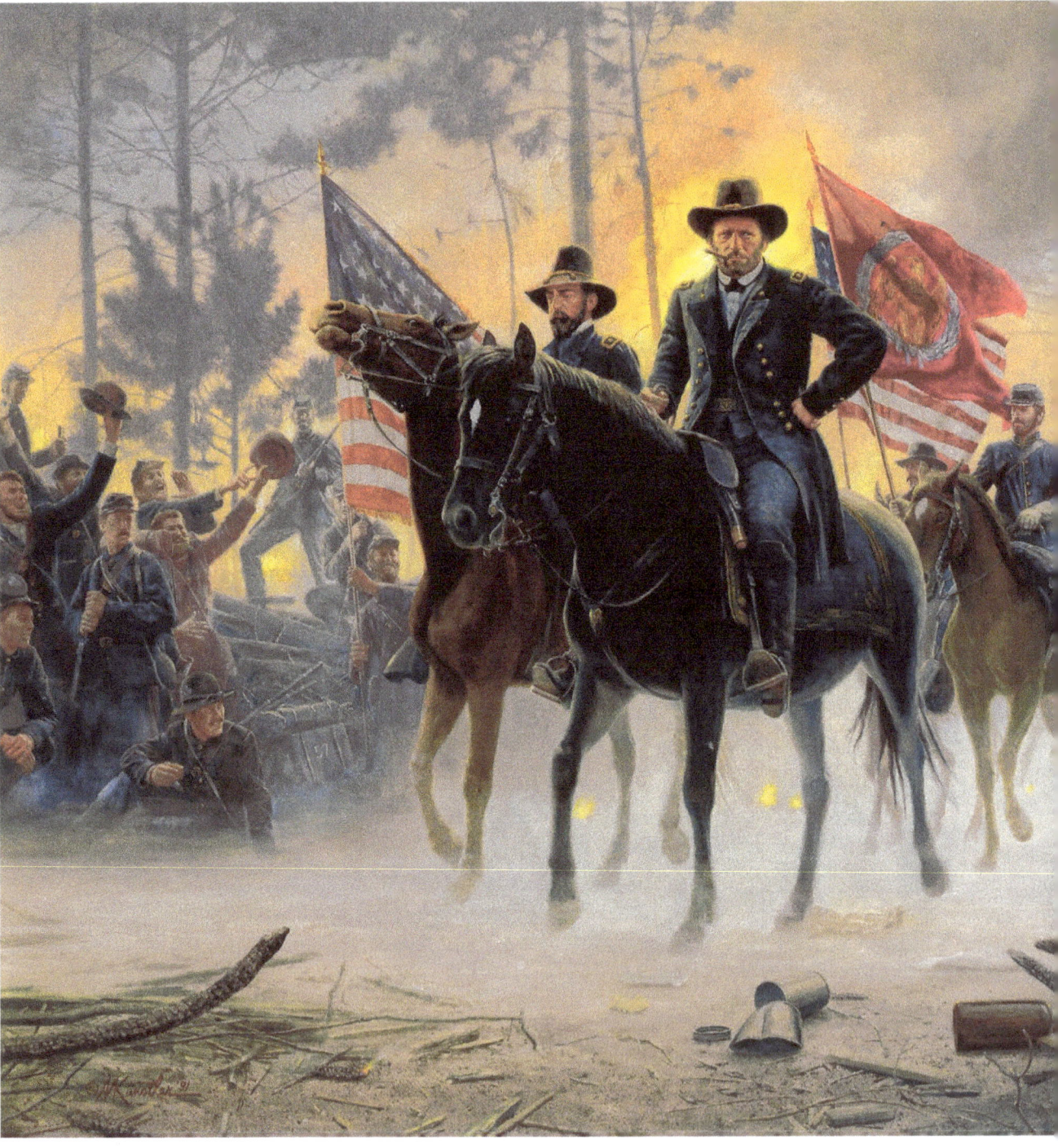

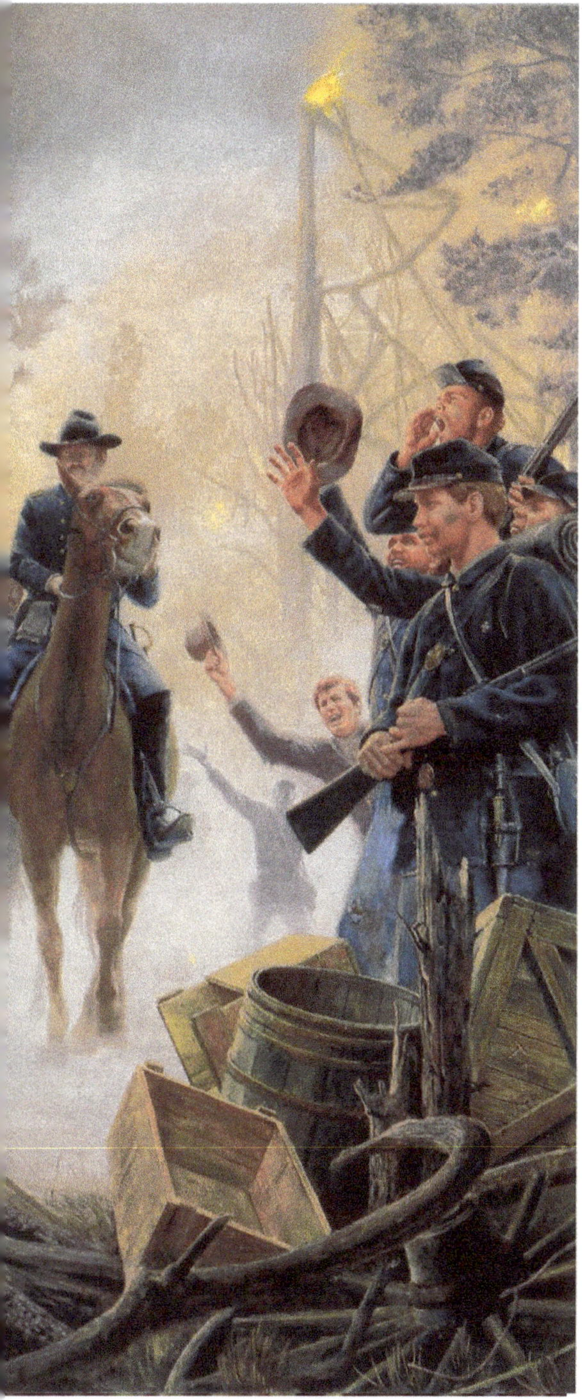

ON TO RICHMOND

GRANT IN THE WILDERNESS
MAY 7, 1864

1991, oil, 30 x 42

THE COMMISSION FOR THIS painting from the U.S. Army War College gave me the opportunity to show Ulysses S. Grant in a moment of great decision. After Grant's victories at Vicksburg and Chattanooga, Abraham Lincoln had made Grant general in chief of all Union armies. As such, he initiated a coordinated strategy for all theaters of the war. To carry out that strategy, he rode with Gen. George Gordon Meade's Army of the Potomac. Robert E. Lee, however, took the initiative and attacked Grant.

On the evening of May 7, 1864, the battle of the Wilderness ended in a draw. The two armies had fought for two days in dense, marshy woods. To the Federal soldiers, it seemed that Lee had again

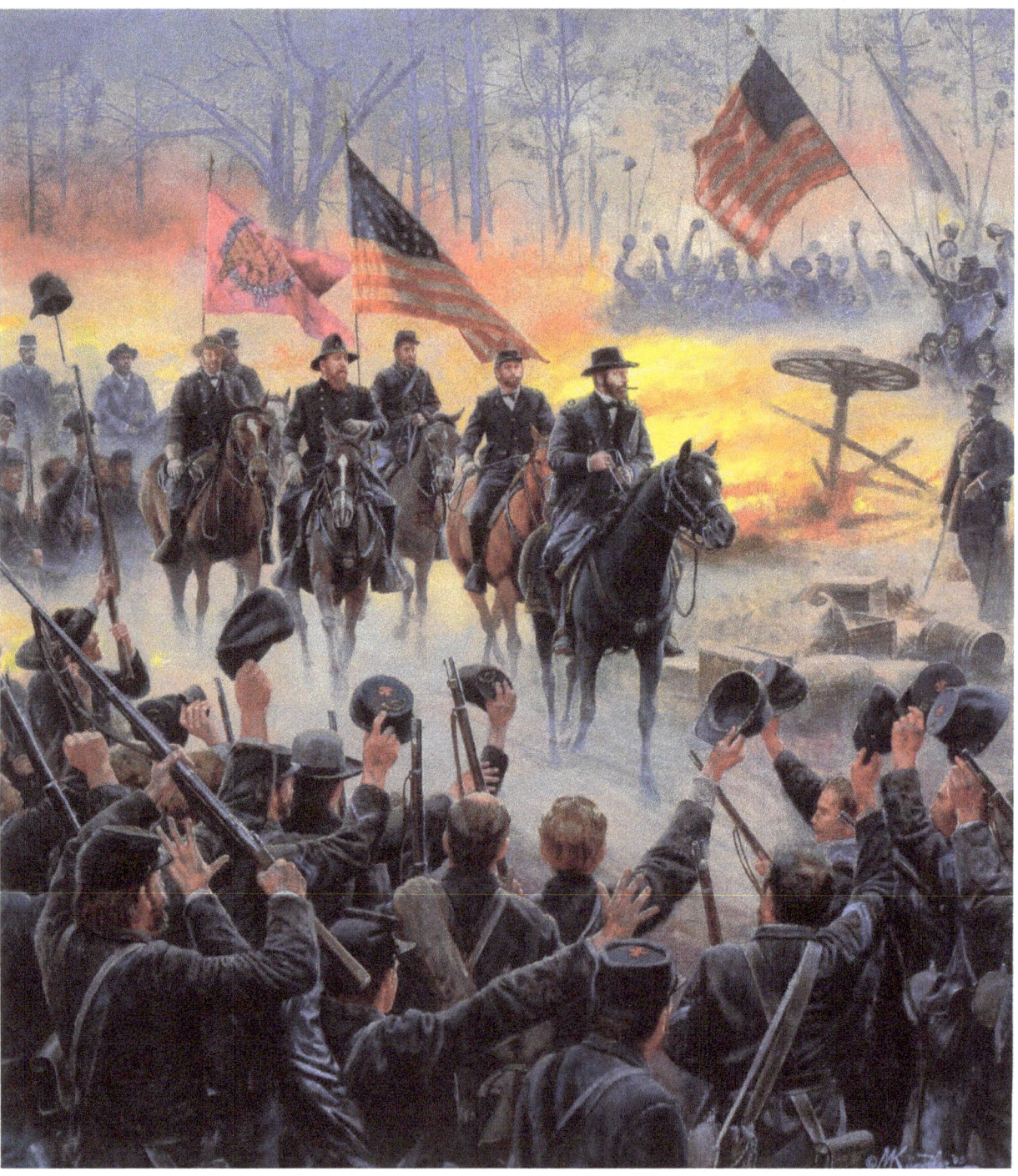

frustrated their commander, and they prepared for yet another retreat toward Washington. Yet Grant had promised Lincoln that there would be no tuning back and ordered his army south to Richmond rather than north in retreat. His men, realizing that their efforts had not been in vain on this battlefield, cheered spontaneously The cycle of defeat and retreat under all their previous commanders had been broken.

Because fire and smoke covered the battlefield that dark night, I heightened the drama by showing Grant close to the foreground. Meade, the hero of Gettysburg, is alongside. The debris of war is everywhere as the soldiers applaud their commanders.

Directly over Grant's left shoulder is Meade's headquarters flag, which is documented in *American Military Equipage.* Its color is described as solferino, which is a vivid, purplish pink, and the design was of a golden eagle encircled with a silver wreath. Grant was said to have remarked on first seeing it, "What's this? Is Imperial Caesar anywhere about here?"

The Fifth Corps troops, marching with knapsacks, give way to the generals and their staffs. The infantryman in the extreme right foreground wears the identity pin of the Fifth Corps on his chest.

FACING

NO TURNING BACK

GRANT IN THE WILDERNESS

MAY 7, 1864

2005, oil, 28 x 24

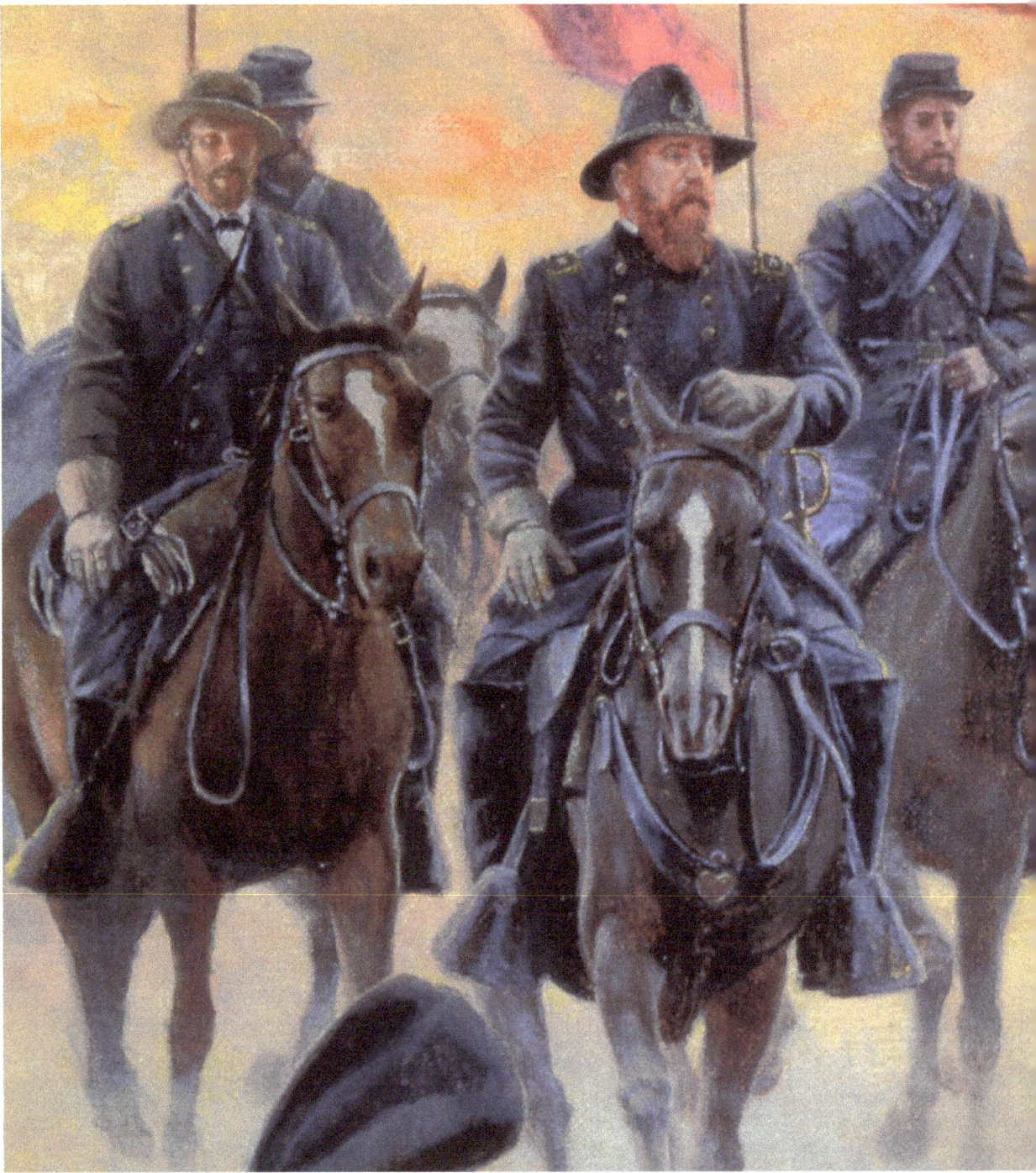

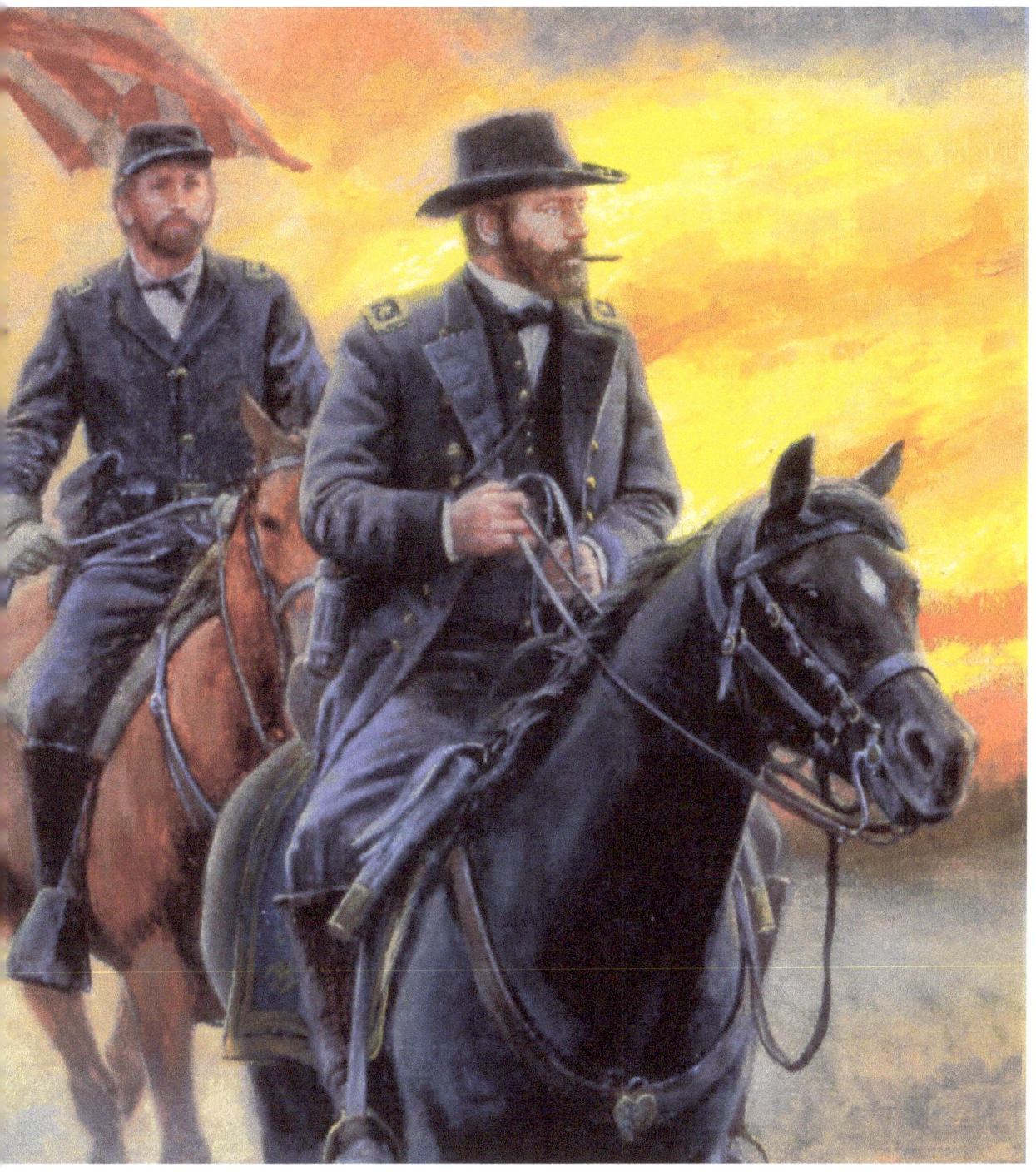

The men dug in behind the barricade are from the Second Corps, which is indicated by the shamrock corps badges on the forage caps of the two men kneeling and sitting in the extreme left front. The blue corps badges on their caps denote the Third Division. A knapsack from the Fifty-seventh Pennsylvania is in the background.

I designed *No Turning Back* as a kind of companion piece to a similar magisterial event for Robert E. Lee, *His Supreme Moment,* which depicted the Confederate commander at Chancellorsville. Also connecting the two pieces is that the actual scenes are separated by only a few miles and depicts events that occurred almost a year to the date of each other.

Although the battle was a statistical draw, the Union's unimpeded movement toward Richmond was a strategic victory. As the Federal army headed south, these soldiers realized there was something different about Grant. After years of being led into retreat by a succession of generals—Irvin McDowell, George B. McClellan, John Pope, Ambrose E. Burnside, and Joseph Hooker—they finally had a commander who would lead them on to Richmond.

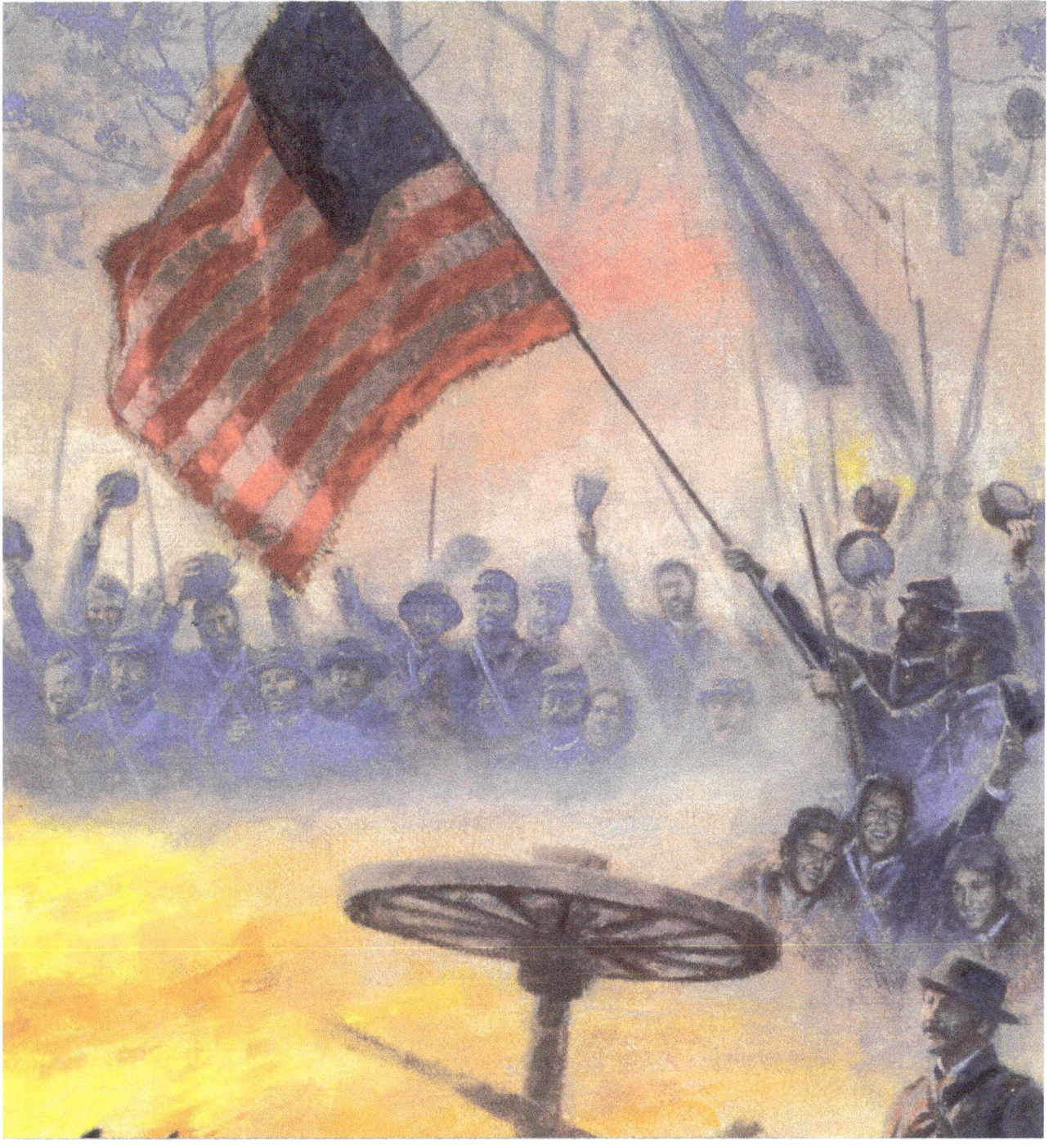

THE BLOODY ANGLE

SPOTSYLVANIA COURT HOUSE, VIRGINIA

MAY 12, 1864

1991, oil, 24 x 36

EIGHTEEN HOURS AT THE Bloody Angle at
Spotsylvania Court House, Virginia, rank
among the legendary actions of the war.
I chose to paint this scene even though I
knew the confusion of hand-to-hand fighting, the closeness of the lines, and the
harshness of the elements—rain, mud, and
fog—would make this scene complex.

   To continue its march on Richmond,
Grant's army had to break through the
Confederate defenses around Spotsylvania
Court House, the strongest and most
elaborate system of trenches and earthworks
seen in the war to that date. Five and a
half feet of earth was piled in front of the

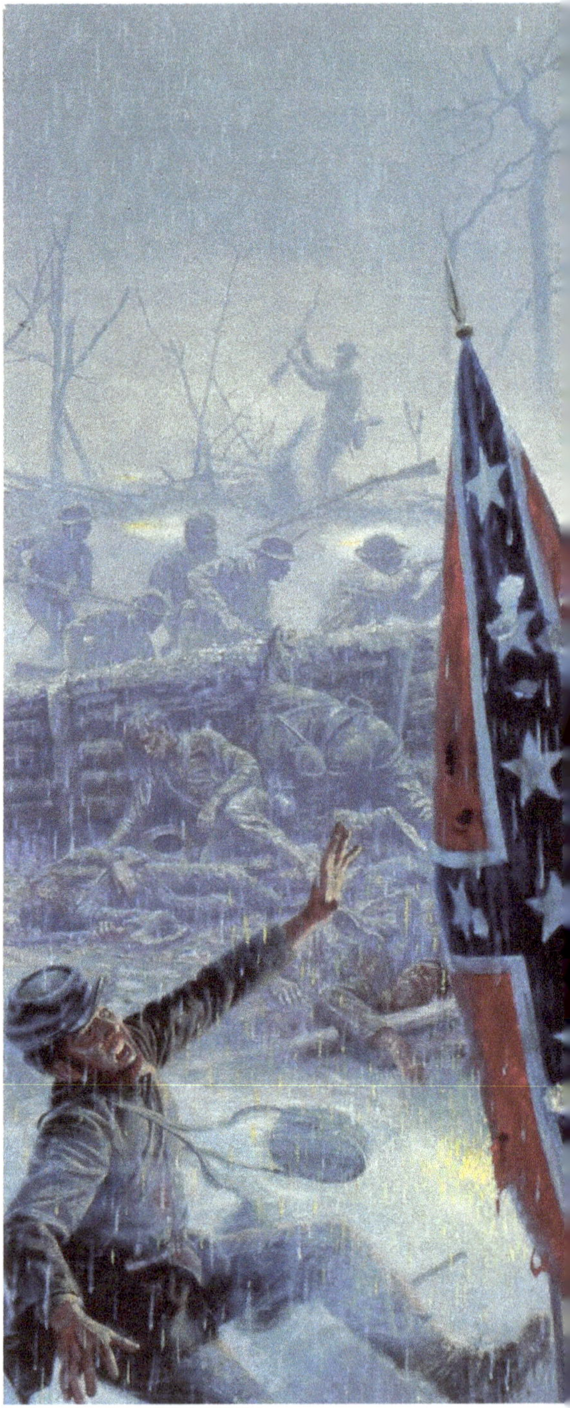

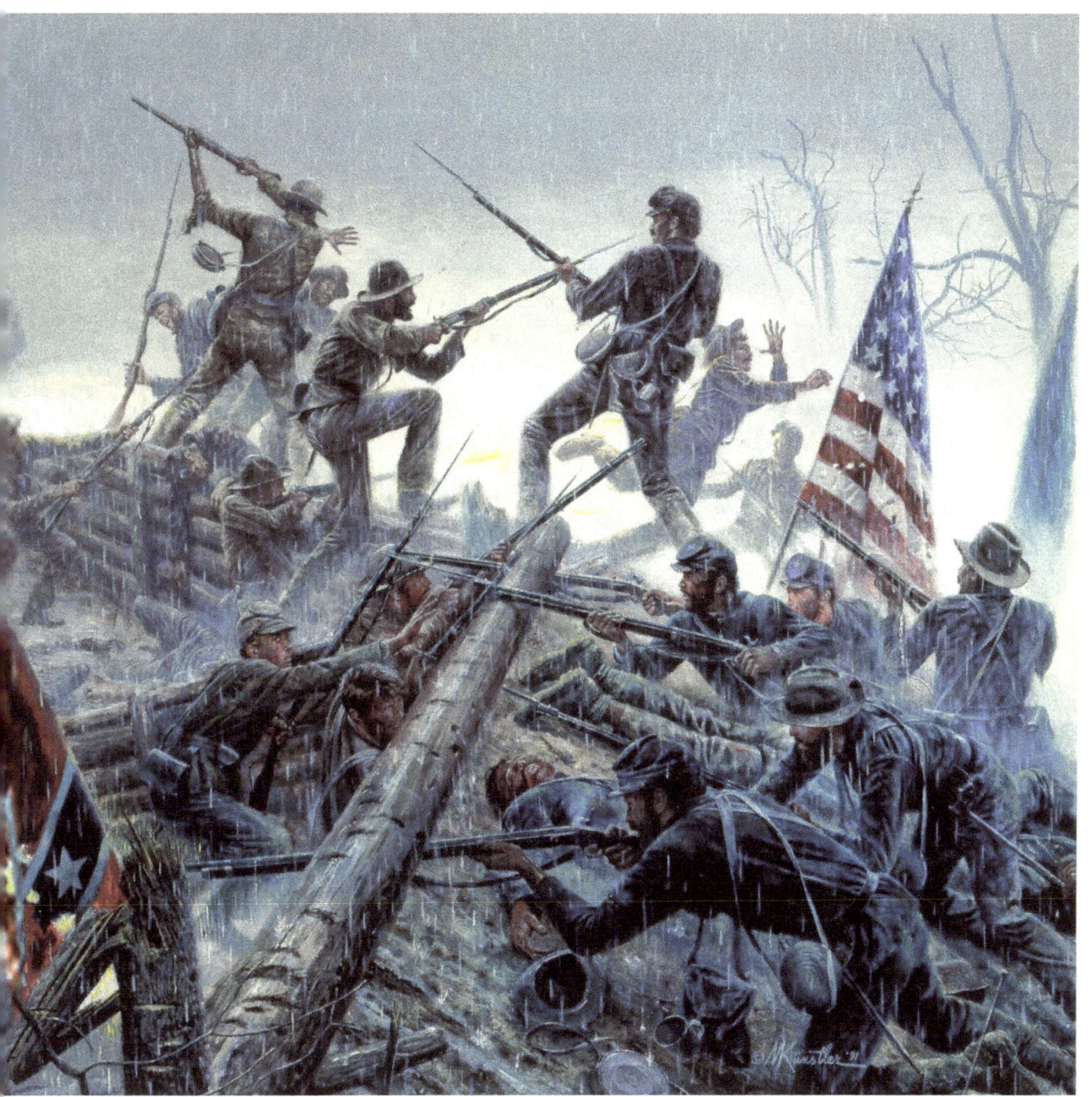

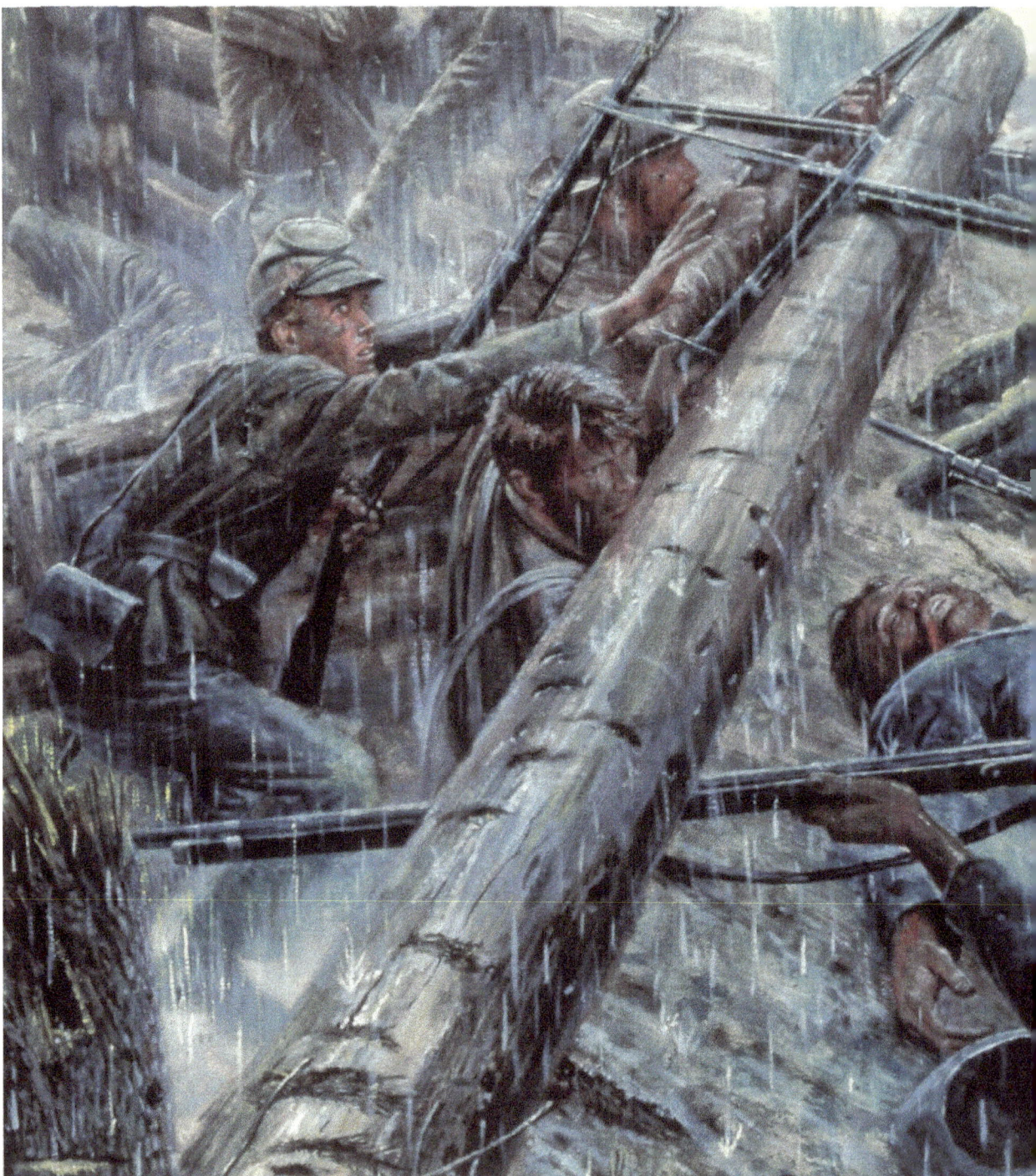

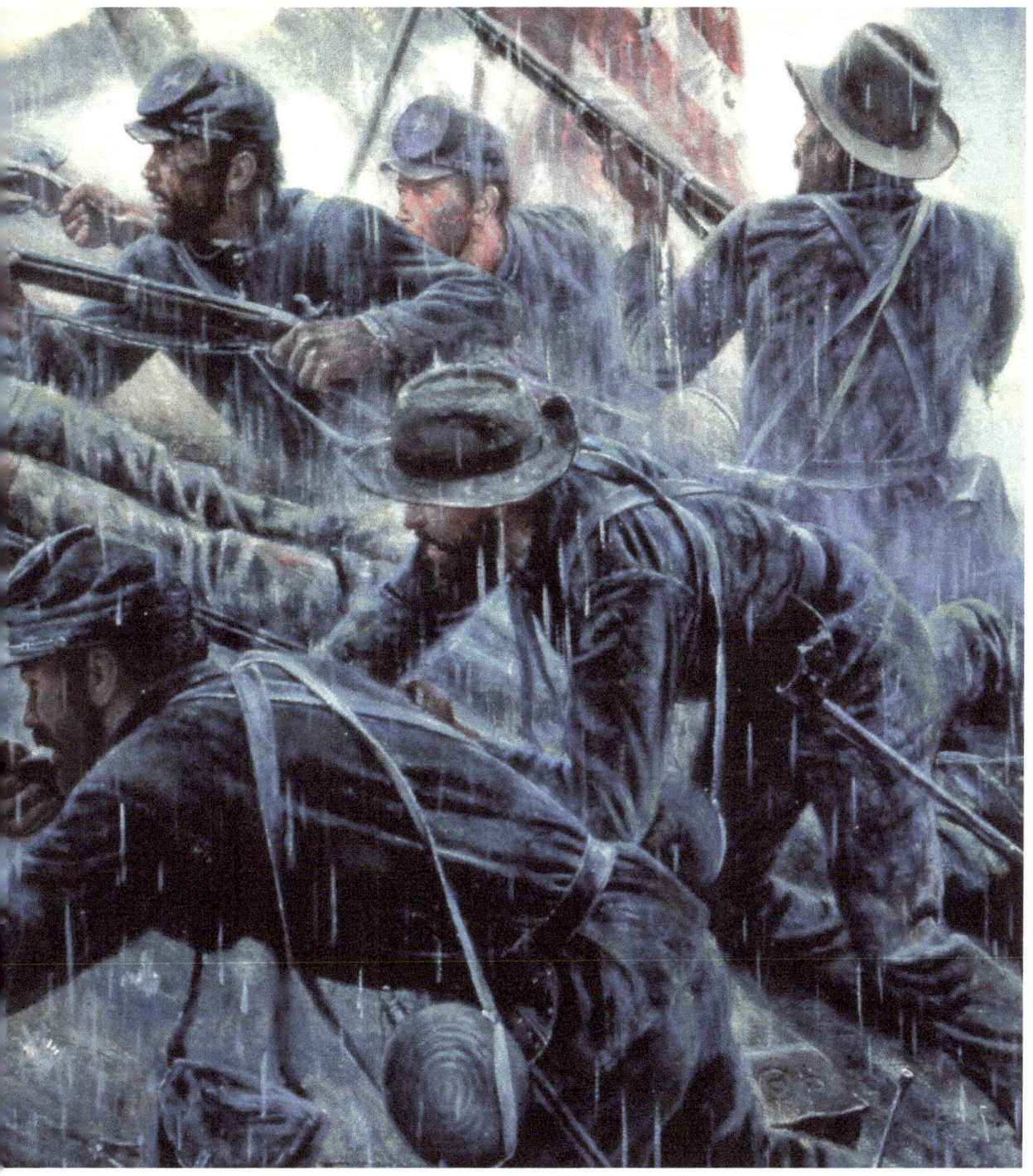

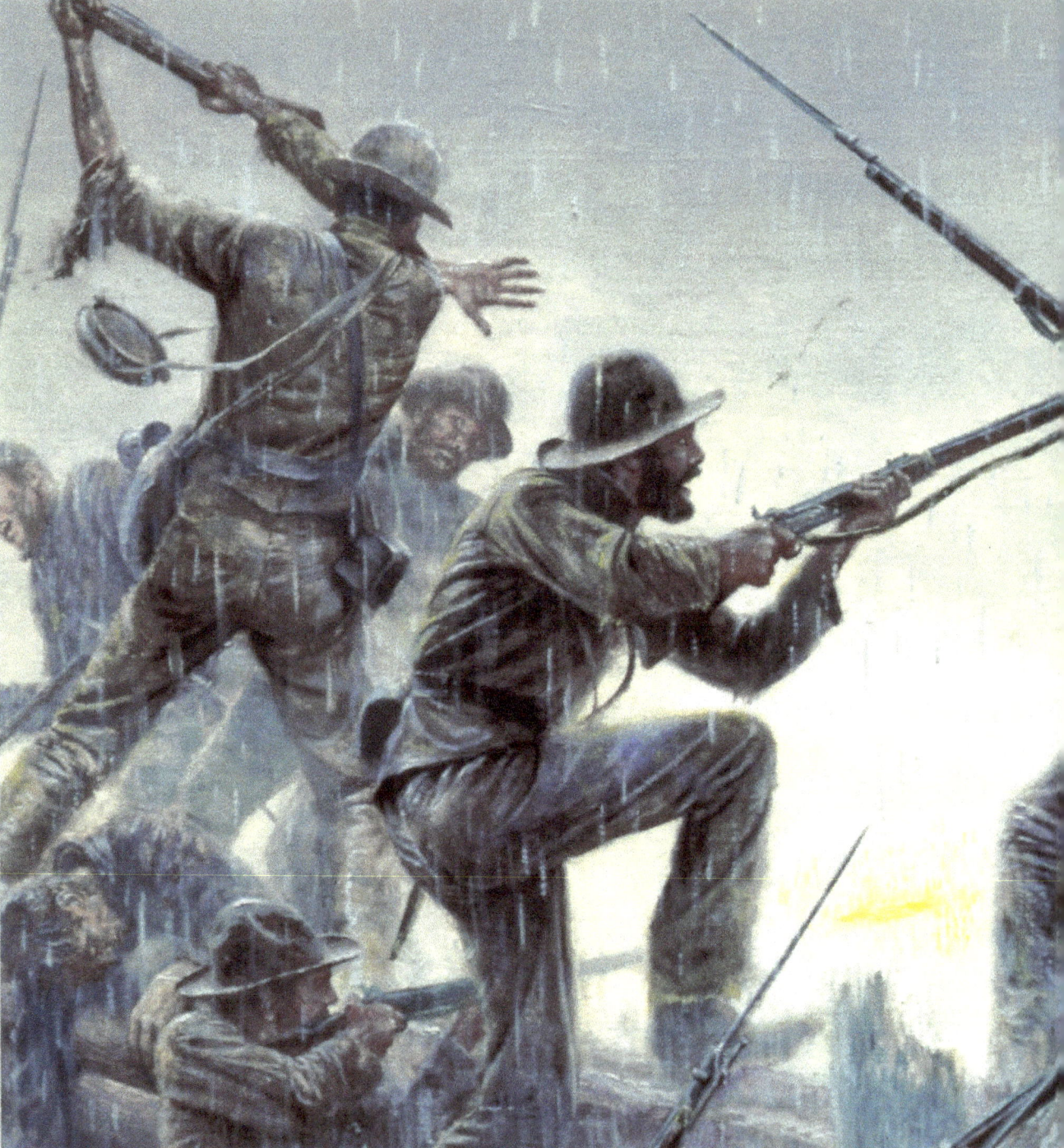

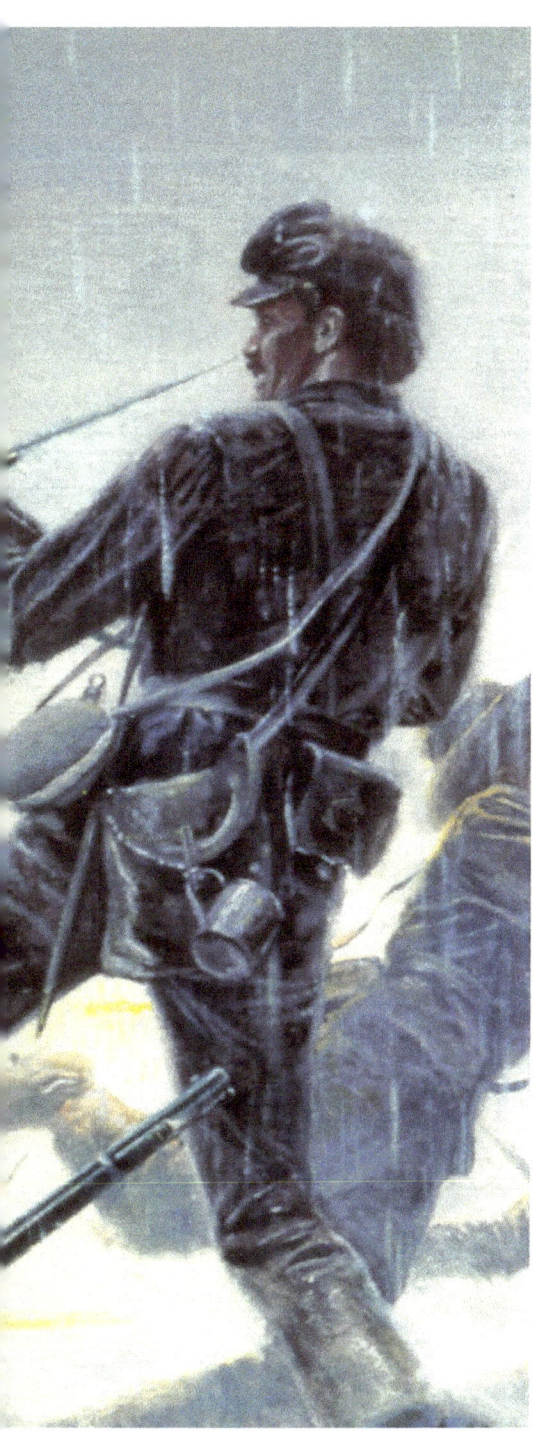

Confederate trenches, which were divided into pens about twelve to eighteen feet wide to prevent enfilading fire if the Federals broke the line.

The worst fighting took place in an angle in the log-and-earthen wall. Called the Bloody Angle, this two-hundred-foot area was littered with bodies, sometimes two or three deep. Wounded men suffocated in the mud and drowned in the flooded trenches. Large oak trees were cut down by the continuous fire, frequently crashing down on the men in the trenches. The mud and blood mixed to turn the trenches into sticky, horrible graves.

In the painting, Union soldiers try to top a fallen log while Confederates fire from behind it. Fog obscures the landscape in the background, and the light is diffused. I can think of no more desperate moment for either Northerner or Southerner than the kill-or-be-killed muddy melee at the Bloody Angle.

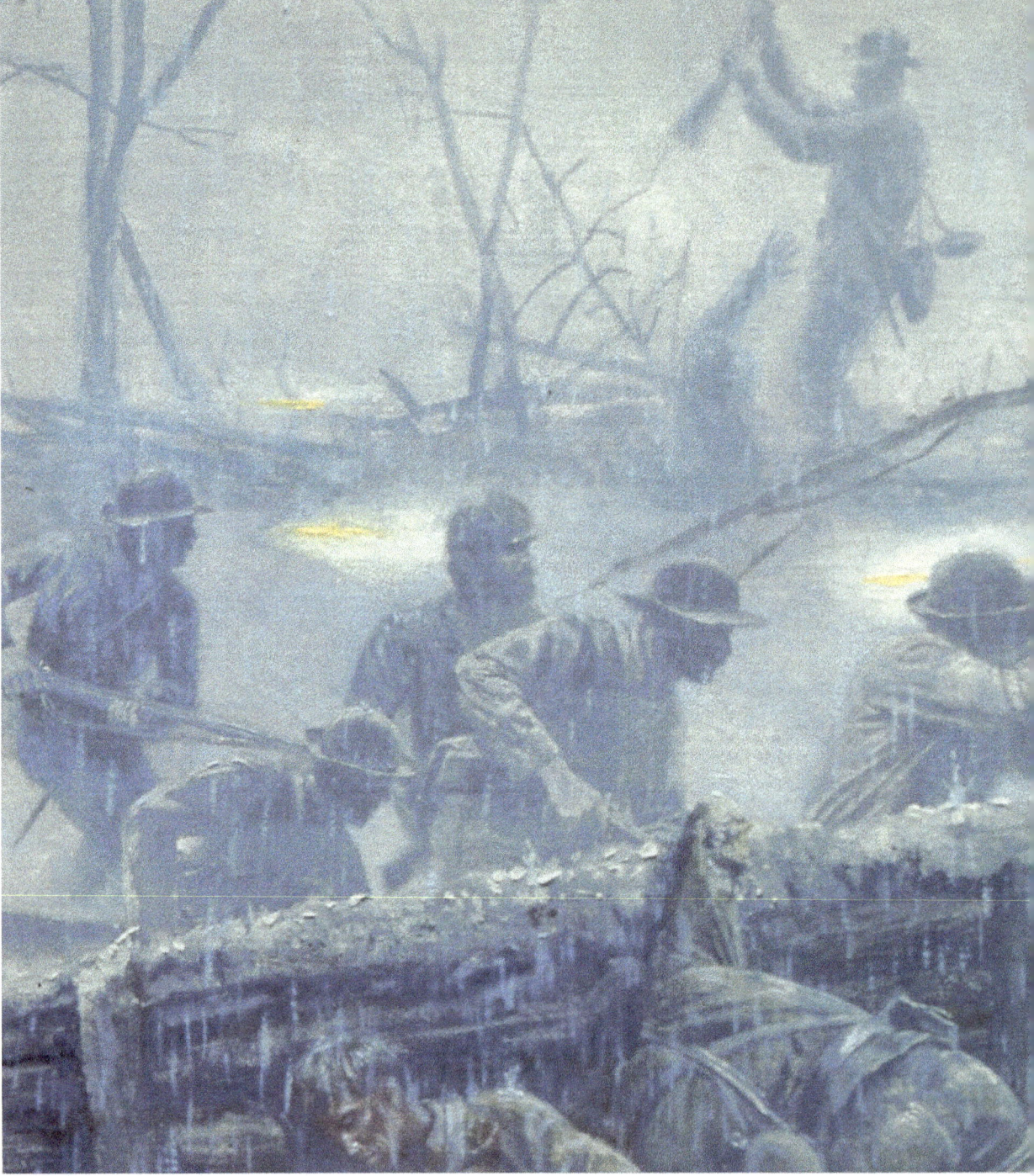

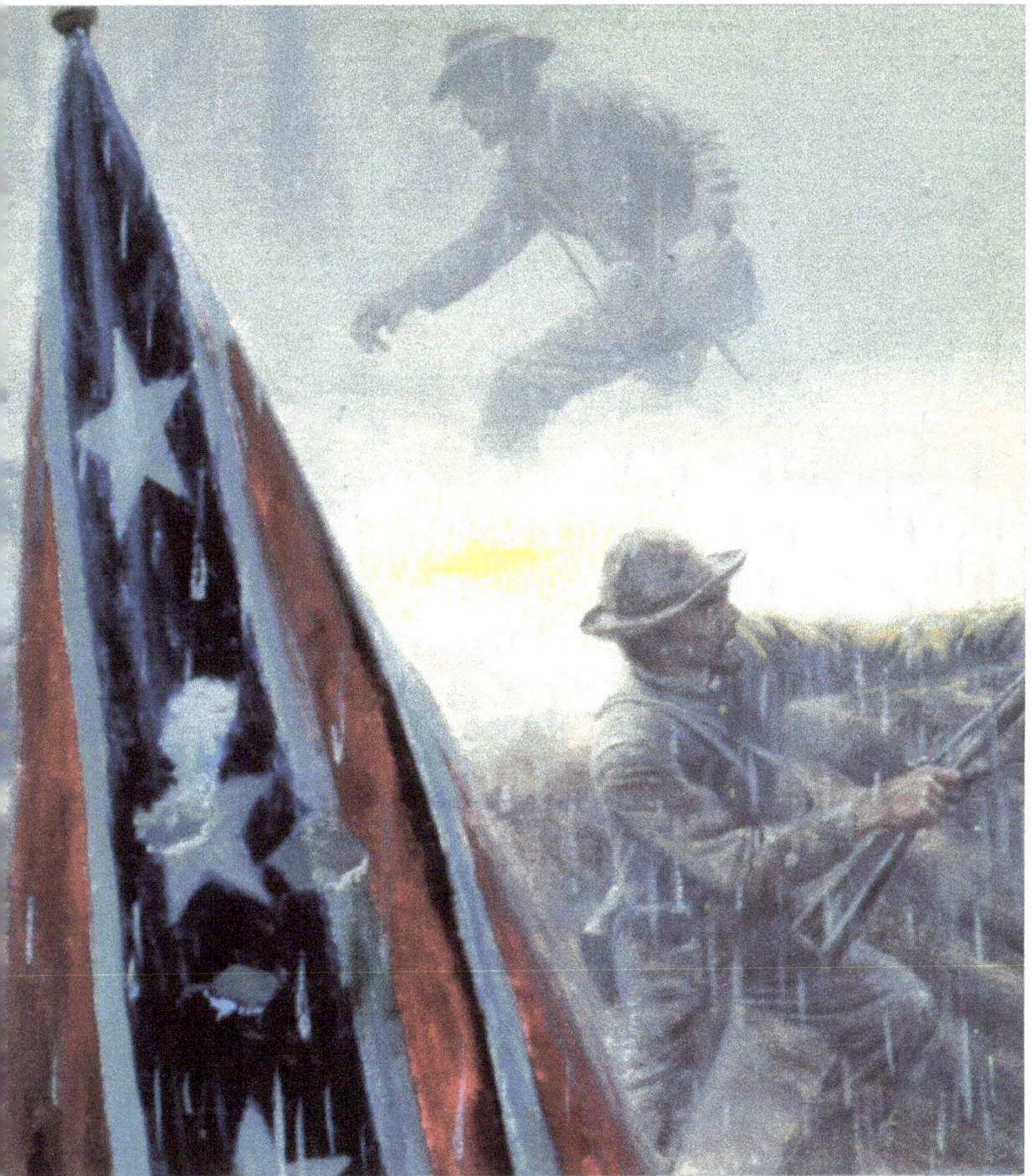

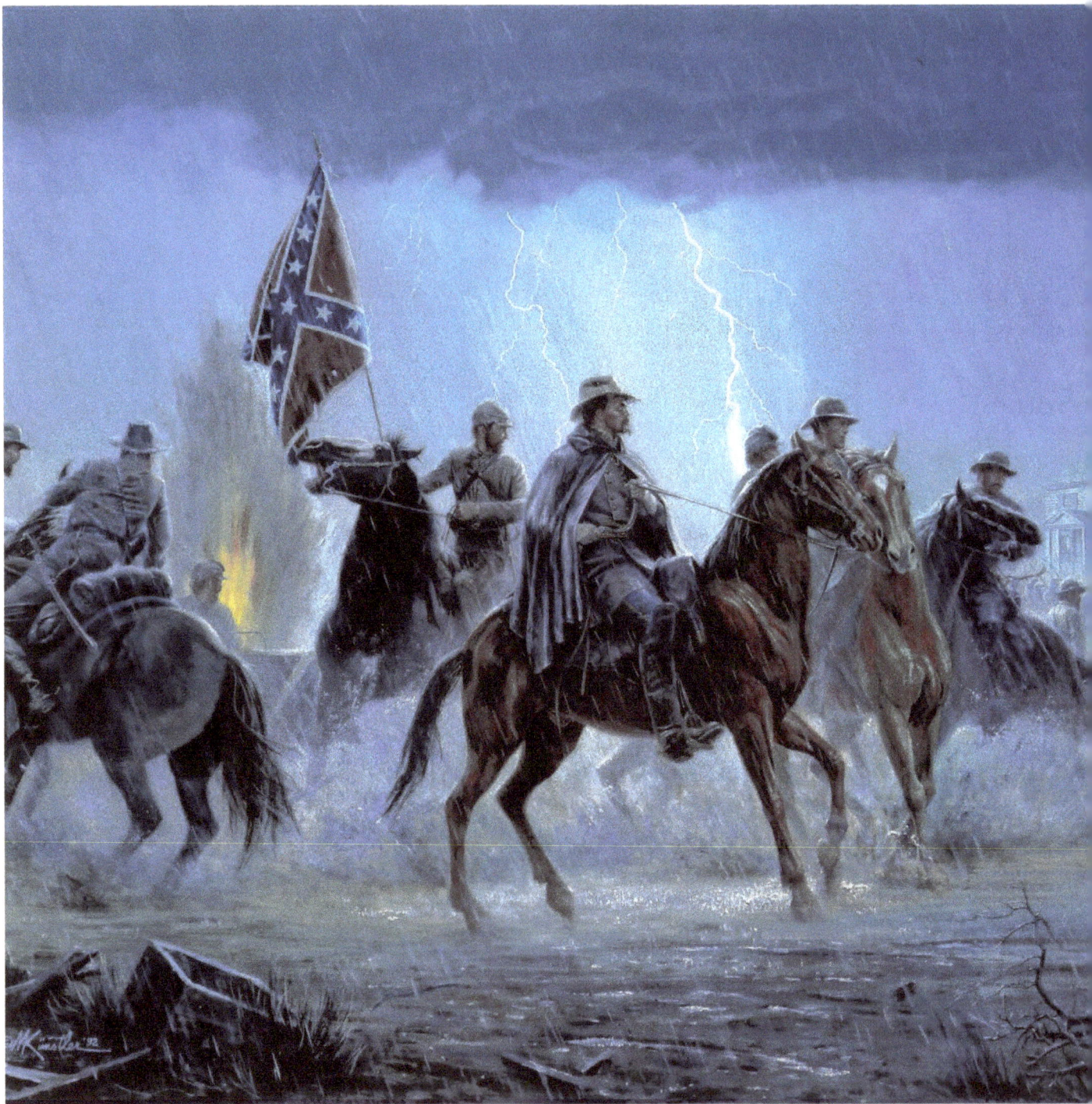

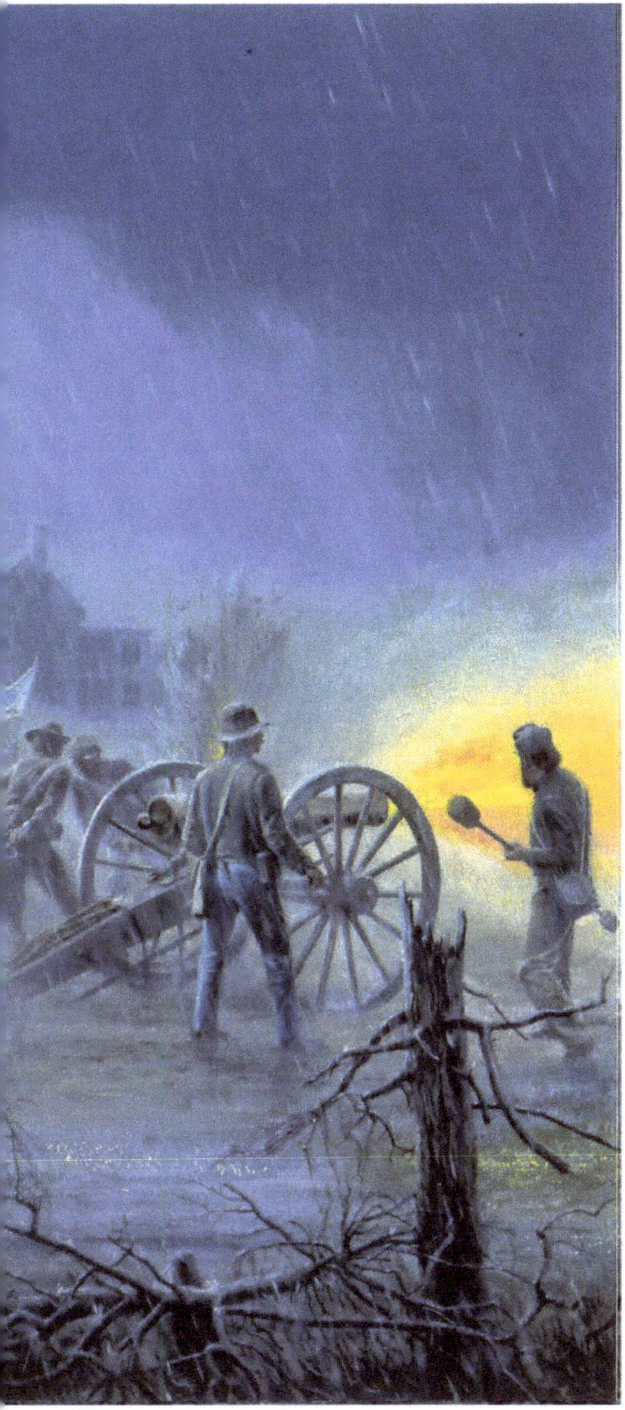

THUNDER IN THE VALLEY

BATTLE OF NEW MARKET, VIRGINIA
MAY 15, 1864

1992, oil, 26 x 40

WHEN I DECIDED TO paint the May 15, 1864, battle of New Market, Virginia, I knew I wanted to incorporate three visual elements: the thunderstorm that occurred during the battle, the two hundred cadets from the Virginia Military Institute who fought valiantly here, and John C. Breckinridge, a former U.S. vice president who commanded the Confederates on this field.

During my tour of the battlefield with park director Ed Merrill and curator Keith Gibson, I was struck by the charm and beauty of the Bushong house, which still stands at the center of the battlefield.

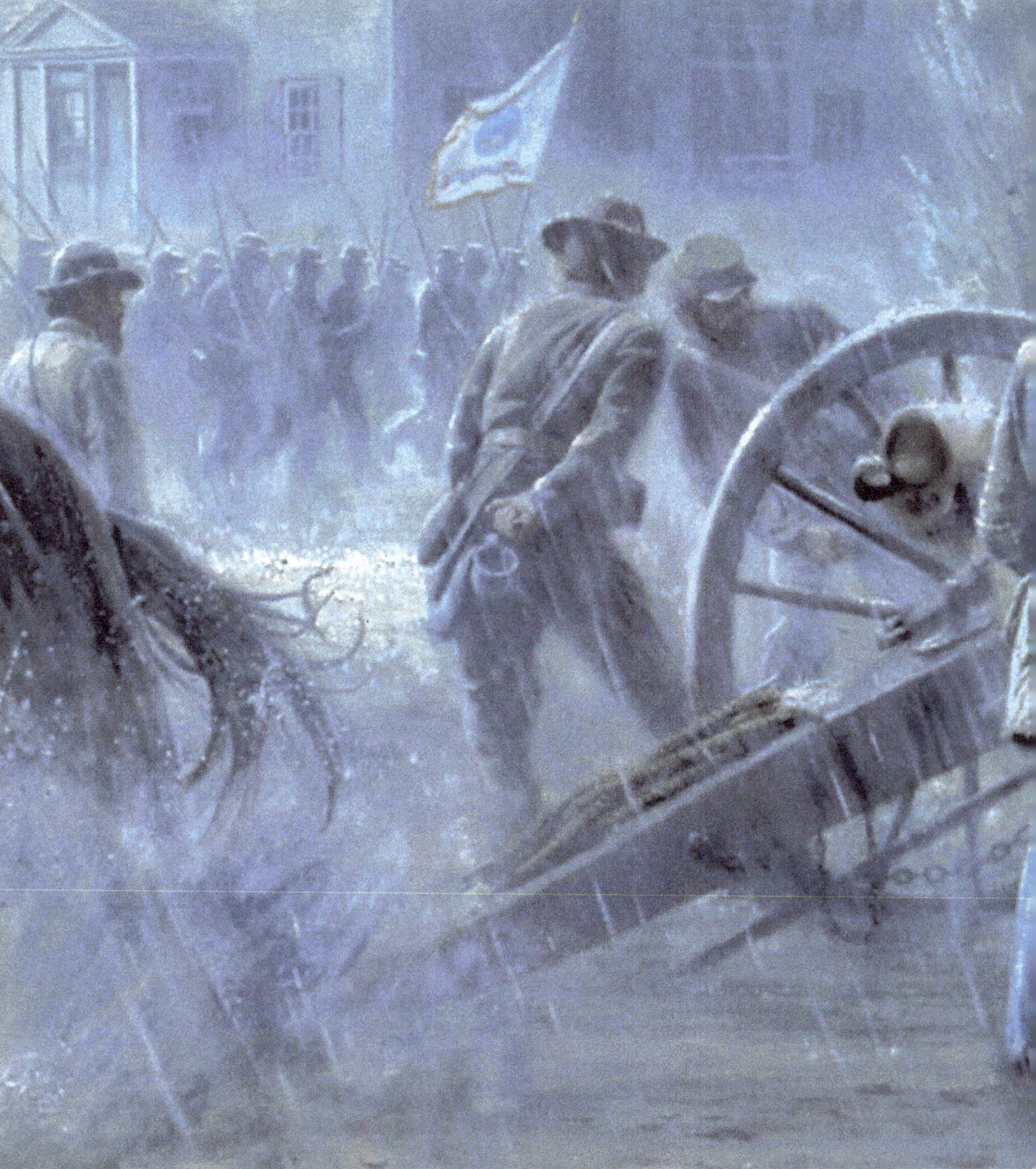

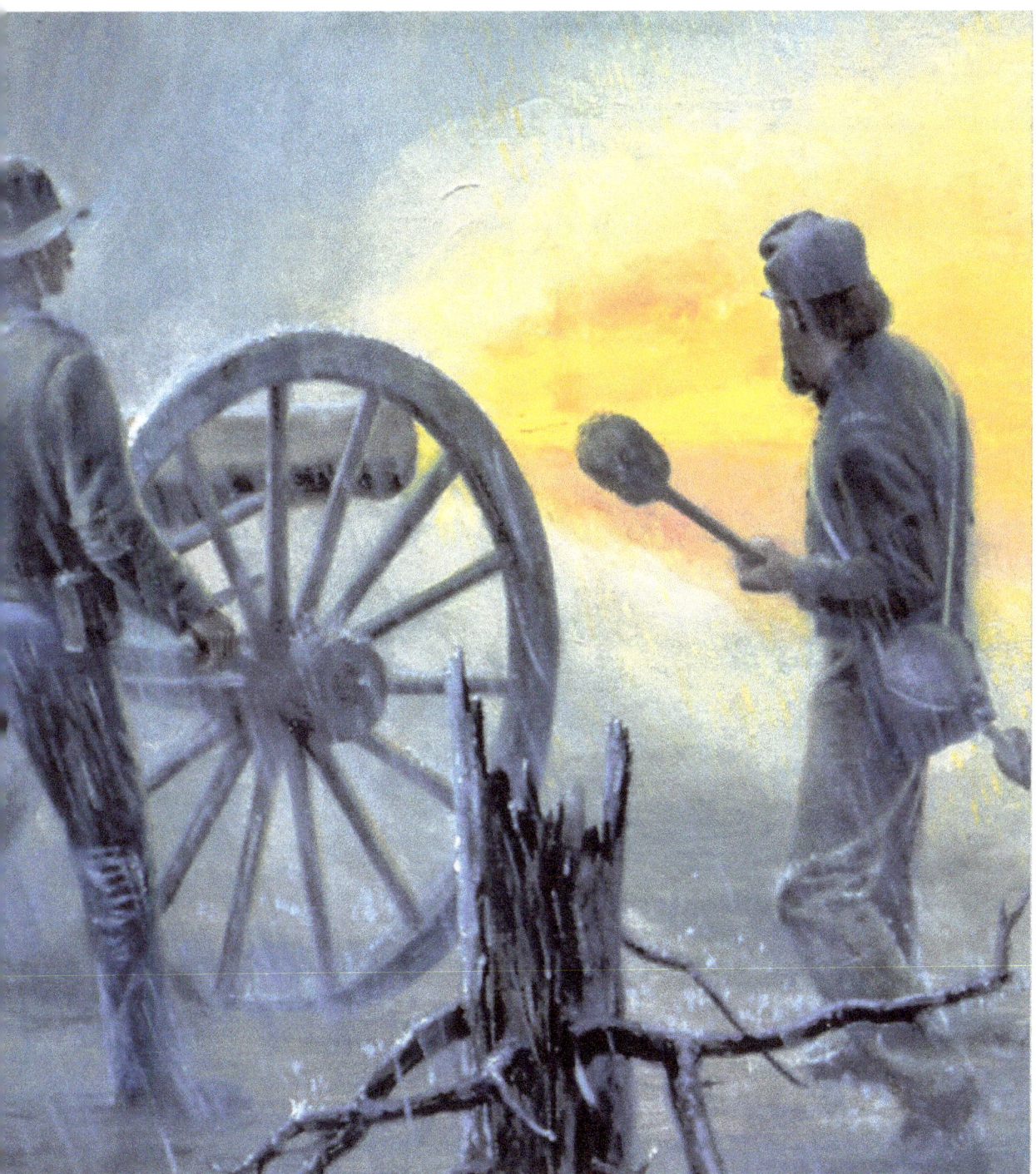

As I wandered around the battlefield where Breckinridge had set up his command post, I realized I could show him in conjunction with the VMI cadets and an artillery battery in action near the command position. I could utilize lightning as a light source and also feature the Bushong house.

With the battle occurring during a torrential downpour, the rain would wash the mud off men and horses as fast as they were being covered with it. I had never seen a painting of anyone in the rubberized blankets used at the time, so I decided to place one on Breckinridge.

Imagine trying to keep track of the enemy, keeping your powder dry and your weapon working, and also controlling your horse while lightning, thunder, and gunfire filled the air! Even more amazing is that despite these conditions and the fact that the Federals outnumbered them, Breckinridge and his men were victorious.

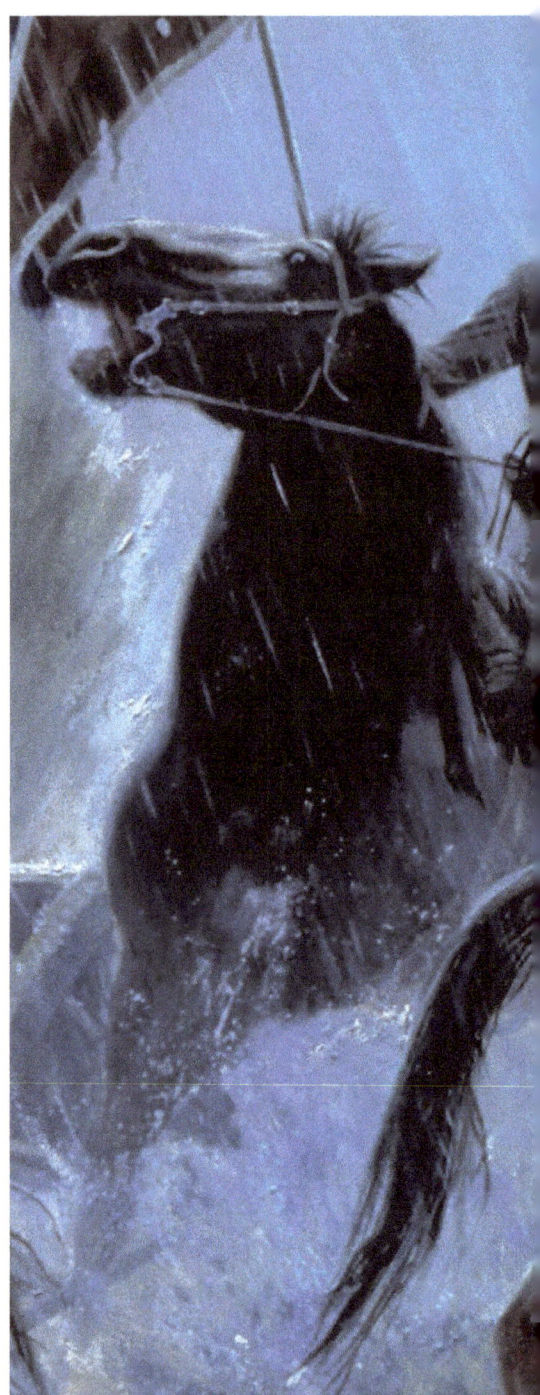

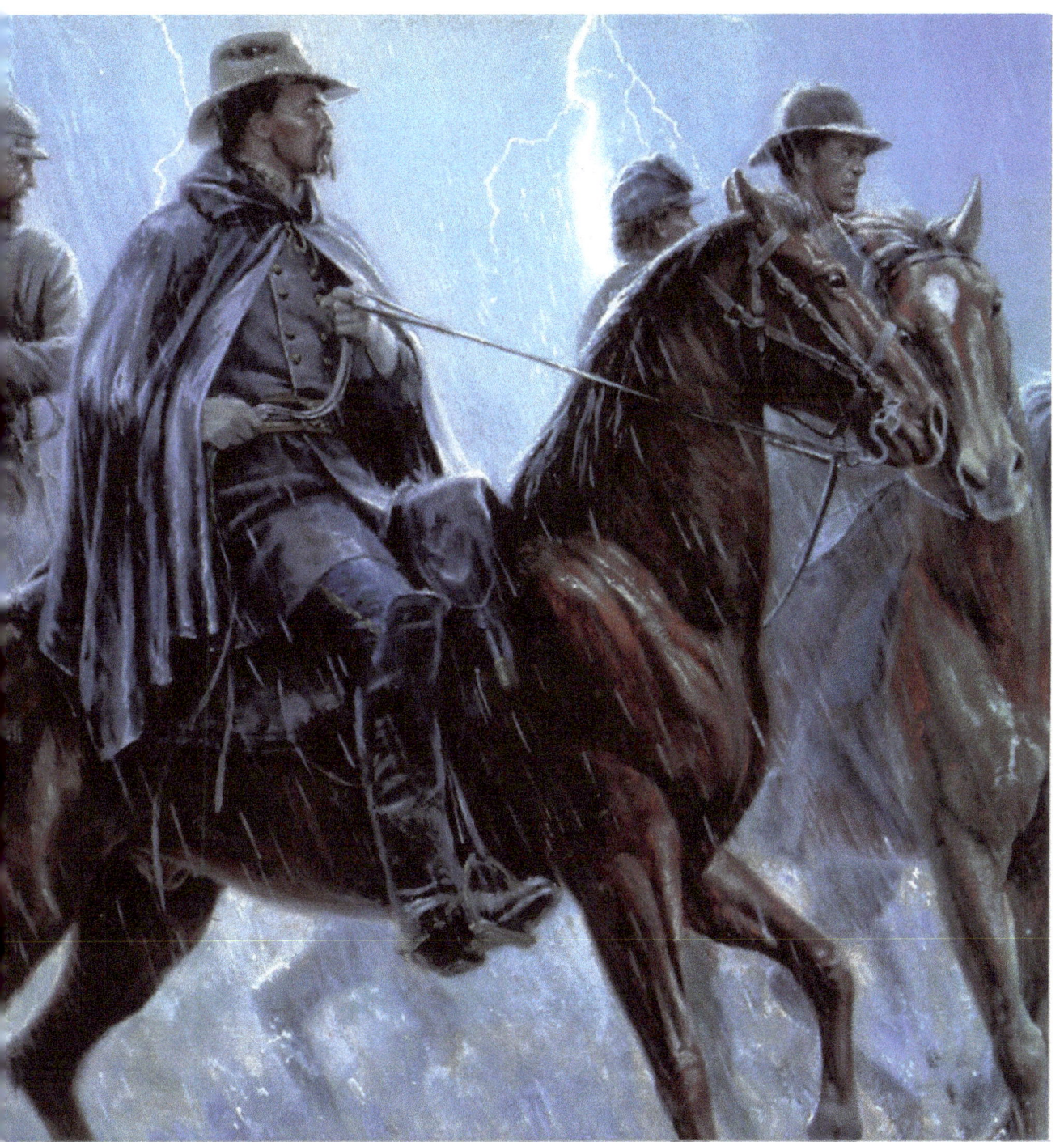

THE CHARGE AT TREVILIAN STATION

GEN. WADE HAMPTON AND THE CITADEL CADETS, JUNE 11, 1864   1996, oil, 8 x 40

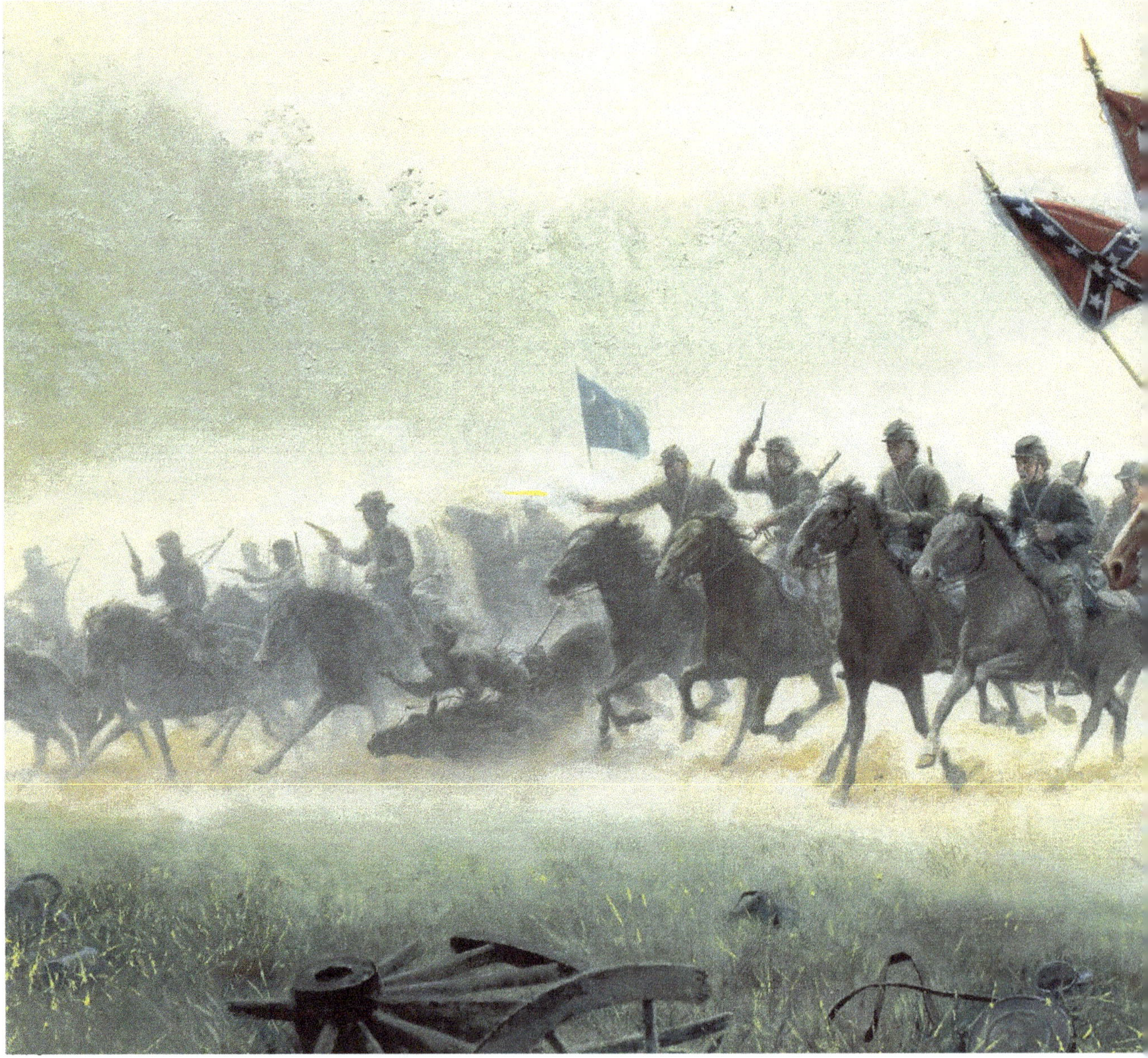

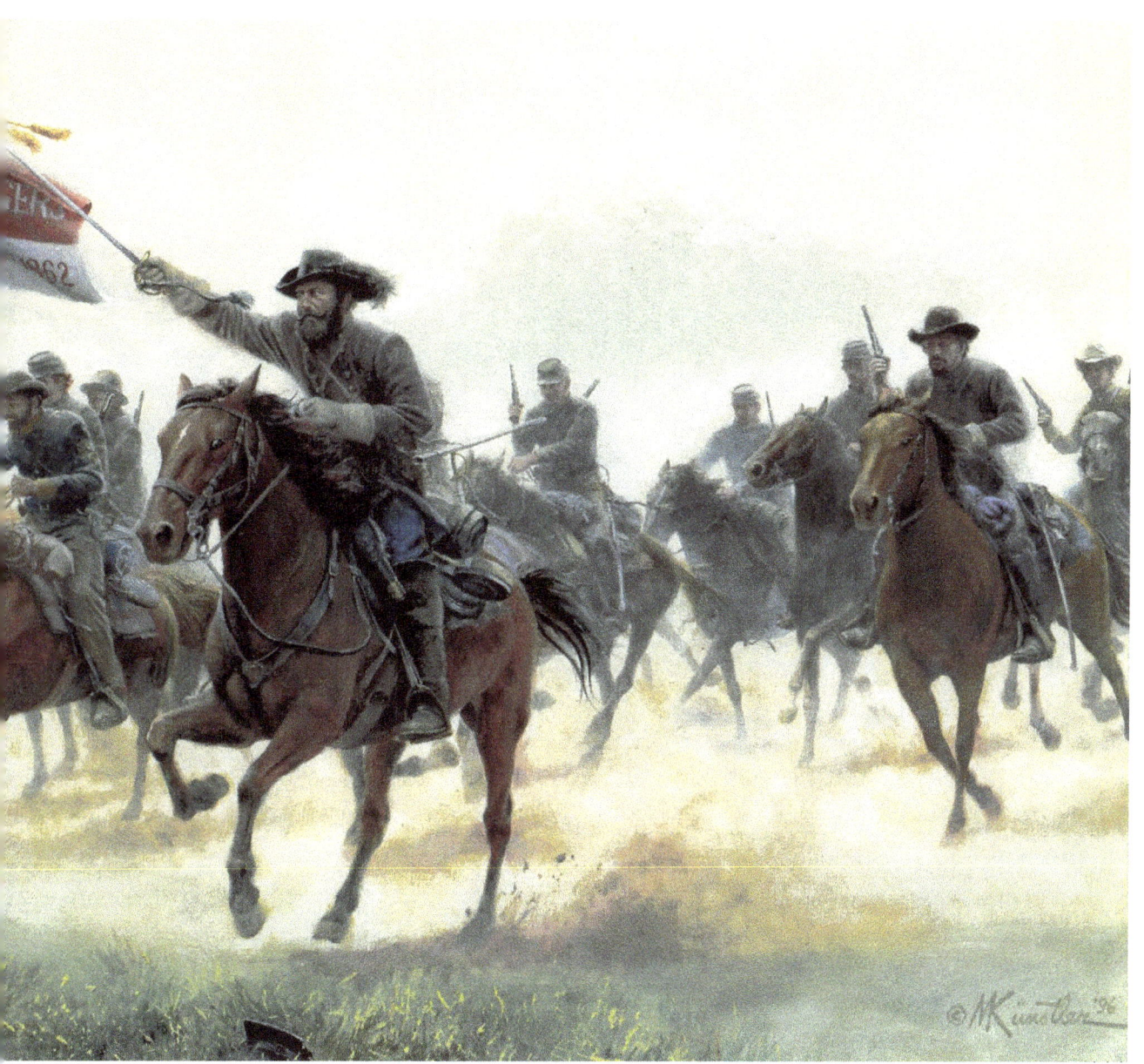

In EARLY JUNE 1864, Union Gen. Philip H. Sheridan led a cavalry force from Cold Harbor toward Trevilian Station, Virginia. His objective was to join forces with Gen. David Hunter, who was advancing from the Shenandoah Valley, and together they would destroy the Virginia Central Railroad and the James River Canal. While Sheridan's men advanced methodically toward their target, Confederate cavalry commander Wade Hampton hurried five thousand horsemen to thwart the Federal operation. The two cavalries collided around 5:00 a.m. on June 11, two miles northeast of the vital depot. The fighting lasted all day, ebbed that evening, and resumed the next day A stunning Confederate counterattack almost broke the Union line. Darkness ended the fighting, and Sheridan withdrew on June 13.

For my painting, I decided to depict Hampton's June 11 charge at Trevilian Station at the head of the Cadet Rangers, a recently arrived cavalry unit from the Citadel, to save a Confederate battery from capture. The cadets charged with pistols, because they were equipped as mounted infantry with Enfield rifles rather than carbines. To identify them, I added a flag based on a description in Gary Robert Baker's *Cadets in Gray*: "A very beautiful one of red and white silk. On one side is written the name of our company, 'Cadet Rangers' and beneath it on the white ground, 'Christmas 1862.'" The elate commemorated when the banner was presented to the cadets. The flag also contained a crescent embroidered in gold in the upper corner of each side.

Citadel museum curator Jane Yates and researcher Paul Fowler provided accounts of this very dramatic moment. Linking Hampton with the cadets depicts two extraordinary examples of Southern leadership on one canvas.

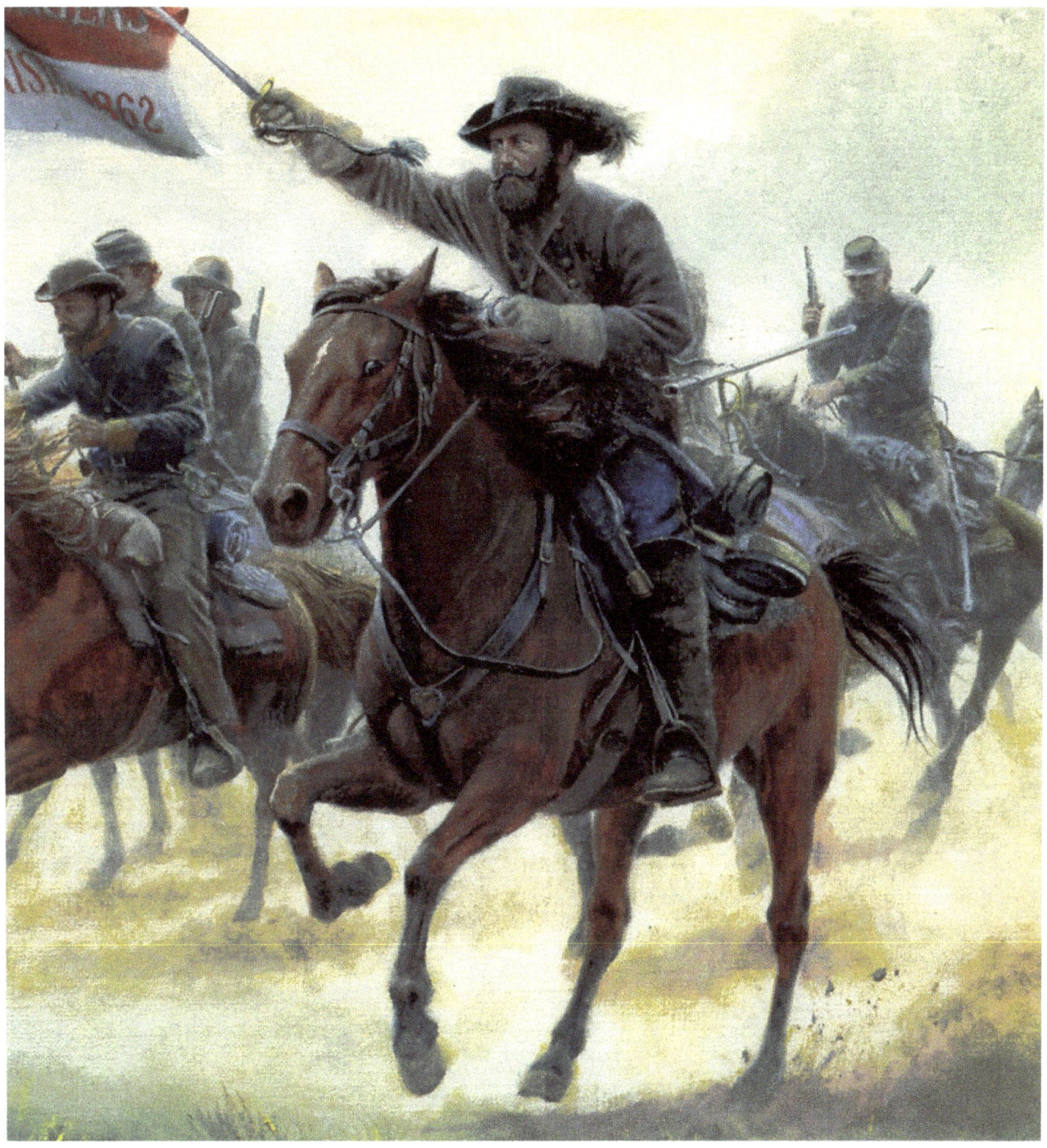

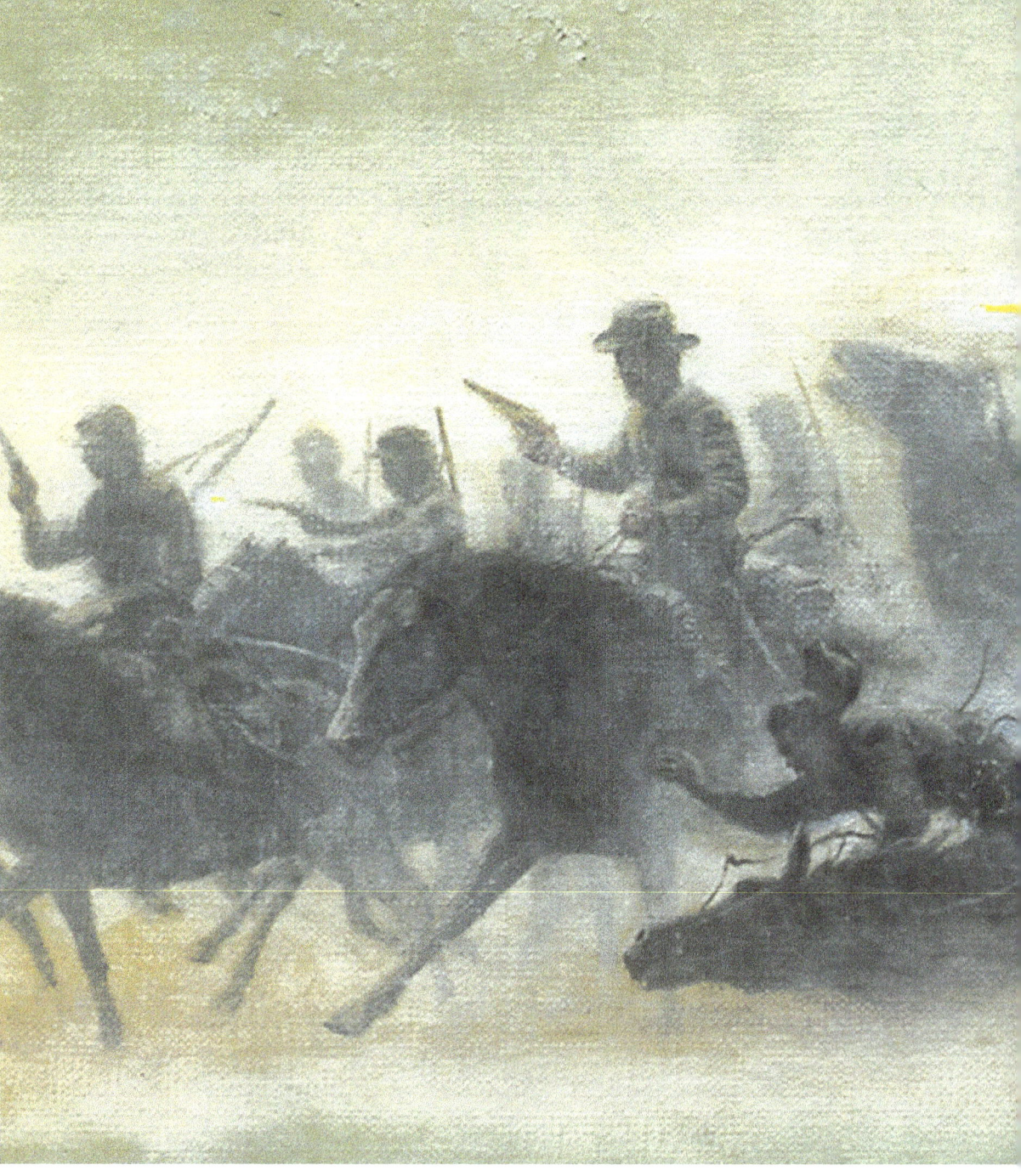

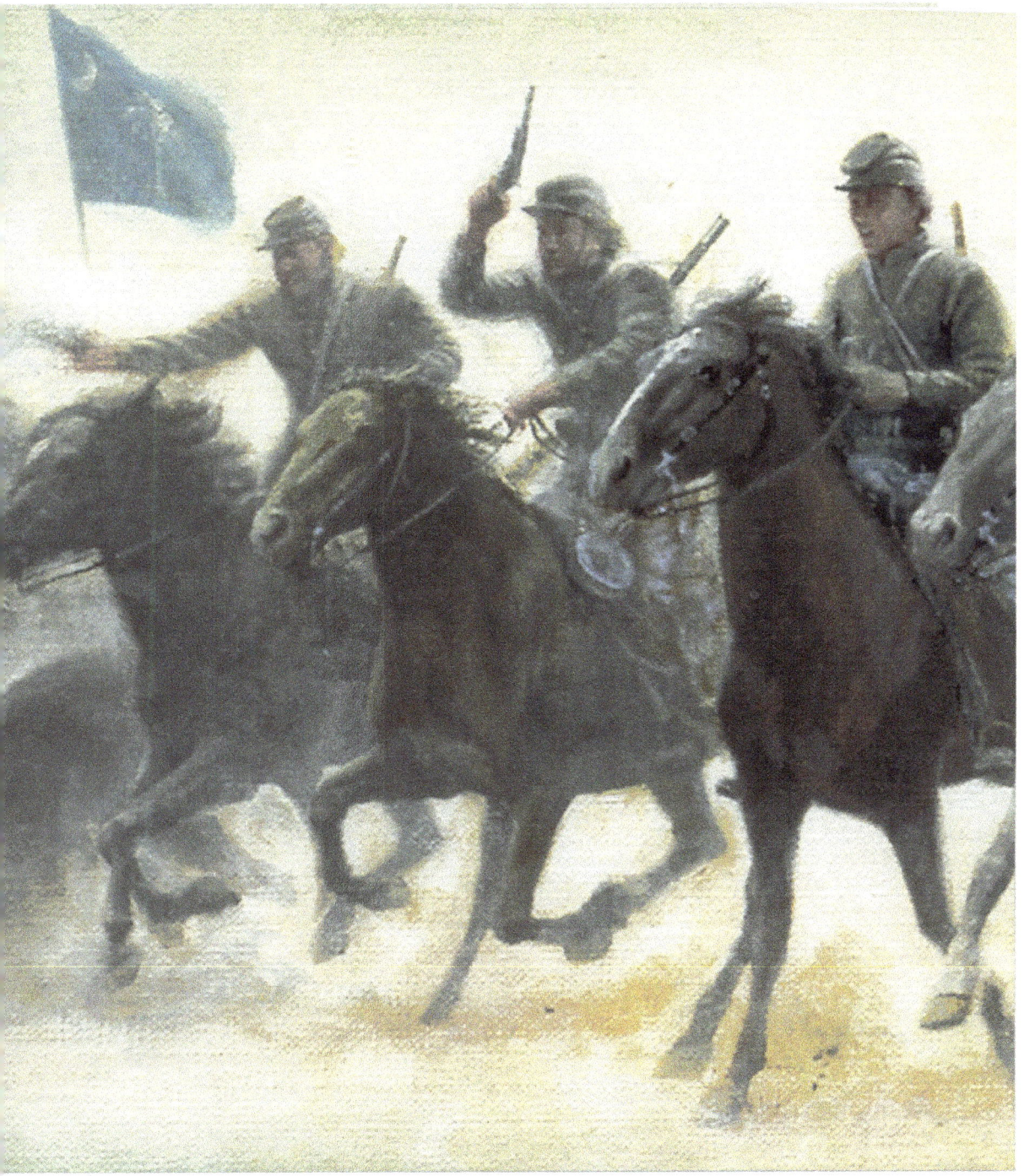

GEN. JOSHUA L. CHAMBERLAIN

1992, oil, 9⅝ x 10⅞

WHEN THE ARMY OF the Potomac arrived at Petersburg, Virginia, in the summer of 1864, Col. Joshua Lawrence Chamberlain—former commander of the Twentieth Maine and one of the heroic field commanders to have survived the battle of Gettysburg—was promoted to command the First Brigade of the First Division of the Fifth Corps. On June 18, he received orders to assault the Confederate line—alone. He was told that his brigade would initiate the attack and the rest of the army would follow.

The task was almost suicidal. Chamberlain not only followed orders but also led the attack. When a color bearer near him went down, Chamberlain took the flag and turned to urge his men forward. A bullet immediately passed through his hips. He propped himself up with his sword and kept the flag upright, knowing that if he fell, his men might falter and the charge would stall. After a while, he blacked out and collapsed.

Surgeons saw little hope for Chamberlain's survival, and two generals immediately recommended his promotion to brigadier general. George G. Meade promptly endorsed the request. Grant, with the authority to promote officers on the field for acts of gallantry, awarded Chamberlain a general's star—the only battlefield promotion he ever made.

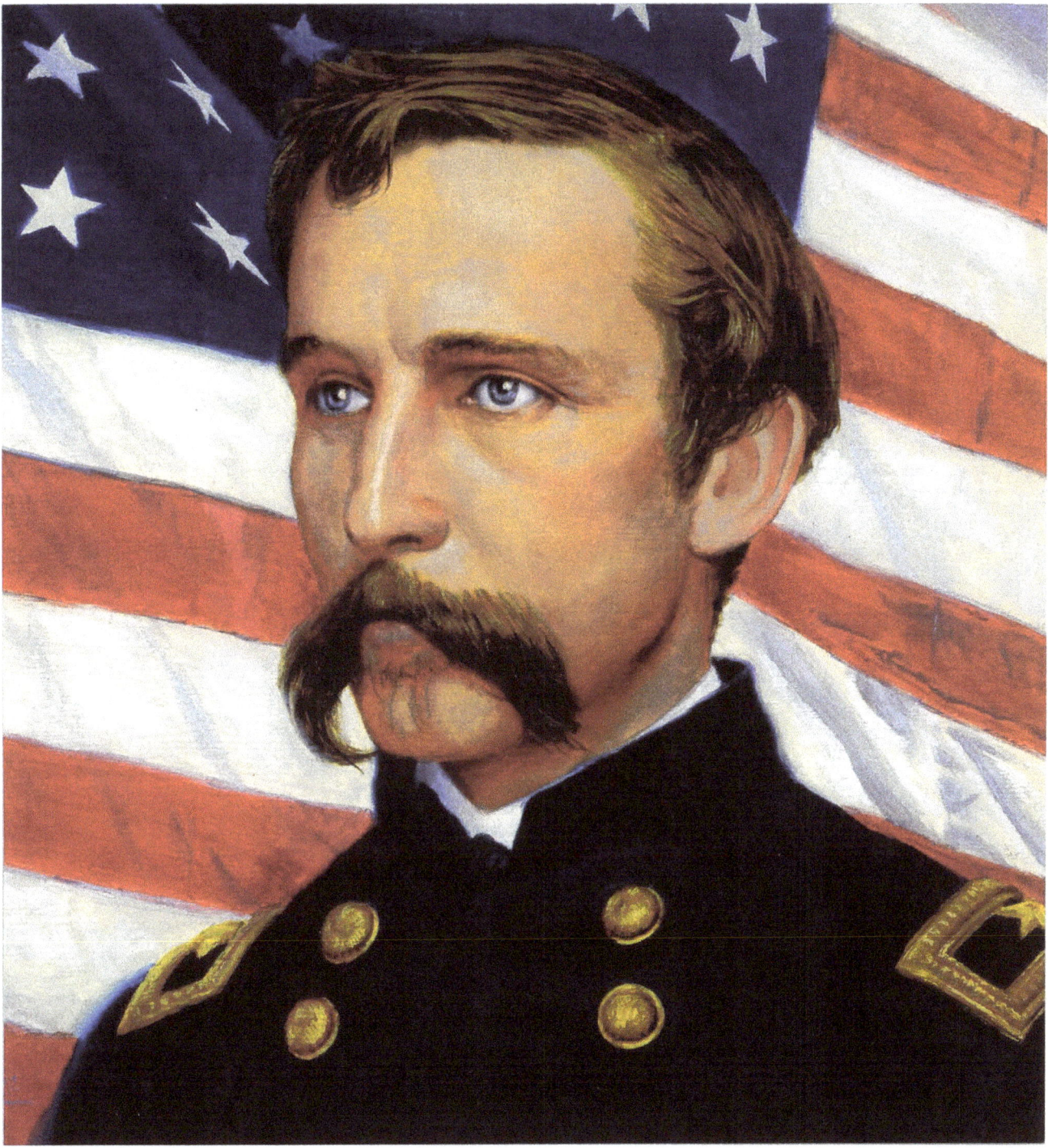

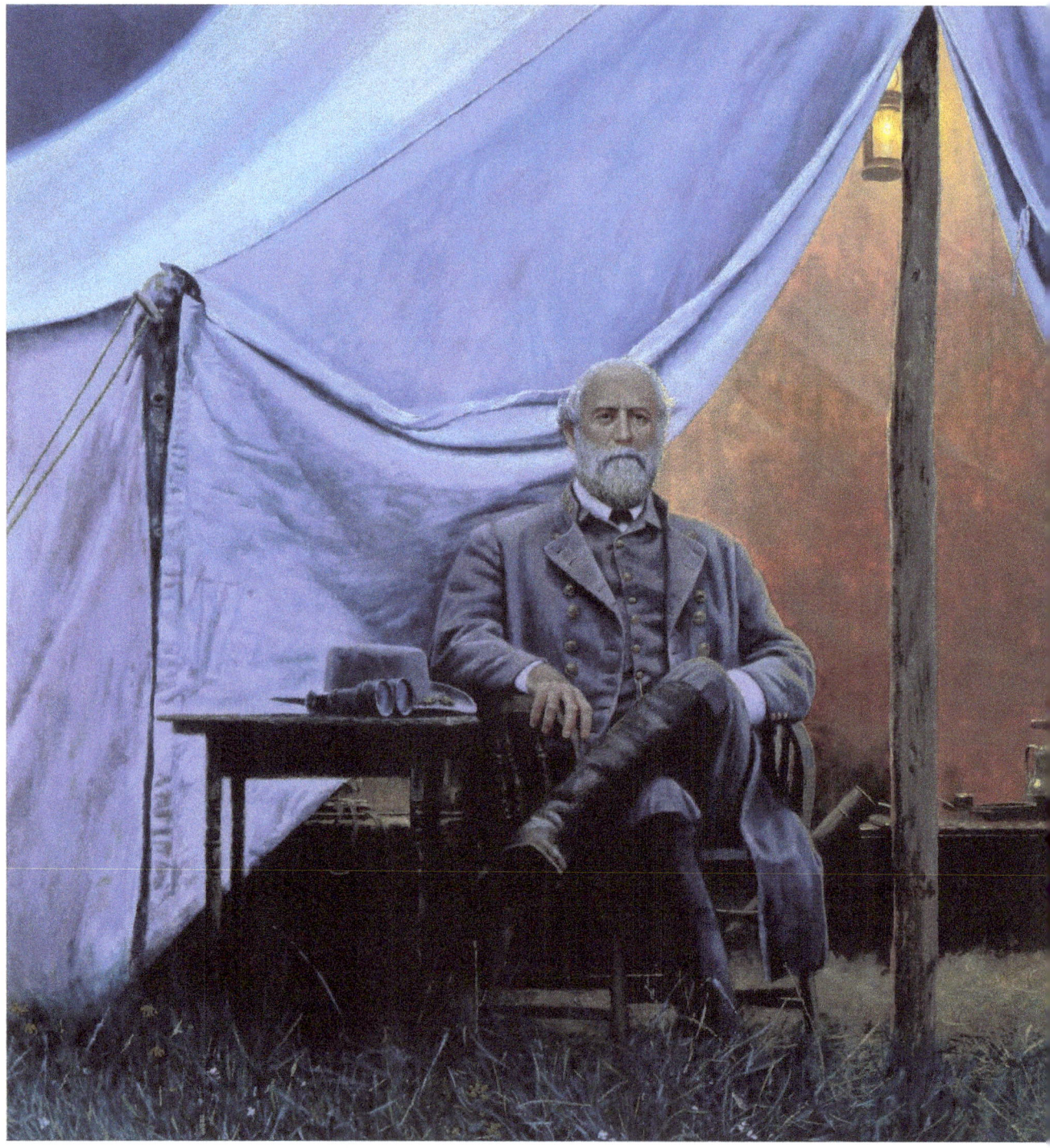

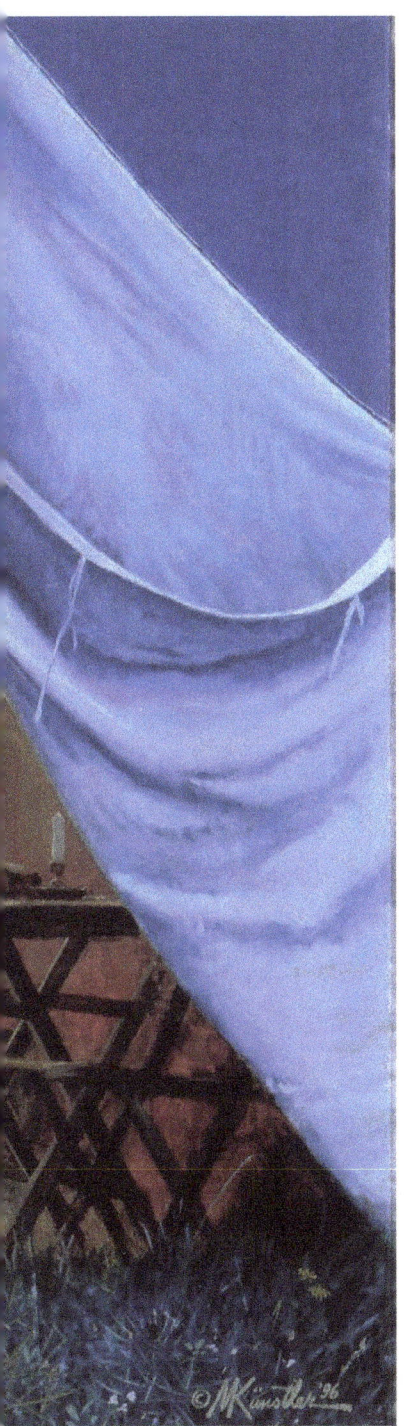

THE LONELINESS OF COMMAND

GEN. ROBERT E. LEE

1996, oil, 24 x 30

PERHAPS THE MOST FRUSTRATING time of the war for Robert E. Lee was when he found himself in the summer of 1864 confined to the area between Petersburg and Richmond. For the first time since he had been given command of the Army of Northern Virginia, he was at the mercy of an opponent who dictated where his forces could and could not go.

I have painted Lee many times, and the angle of his head or the lighting is different every time. In a character study such as this one, the pose of the figure is the most important element. Here it is designed to capture Lee's dignity at a time of brooding contemplation, reflecting the burden of command that the great general must have felt virtually at every waking moment during the entire war and especially at the Petersburg front.

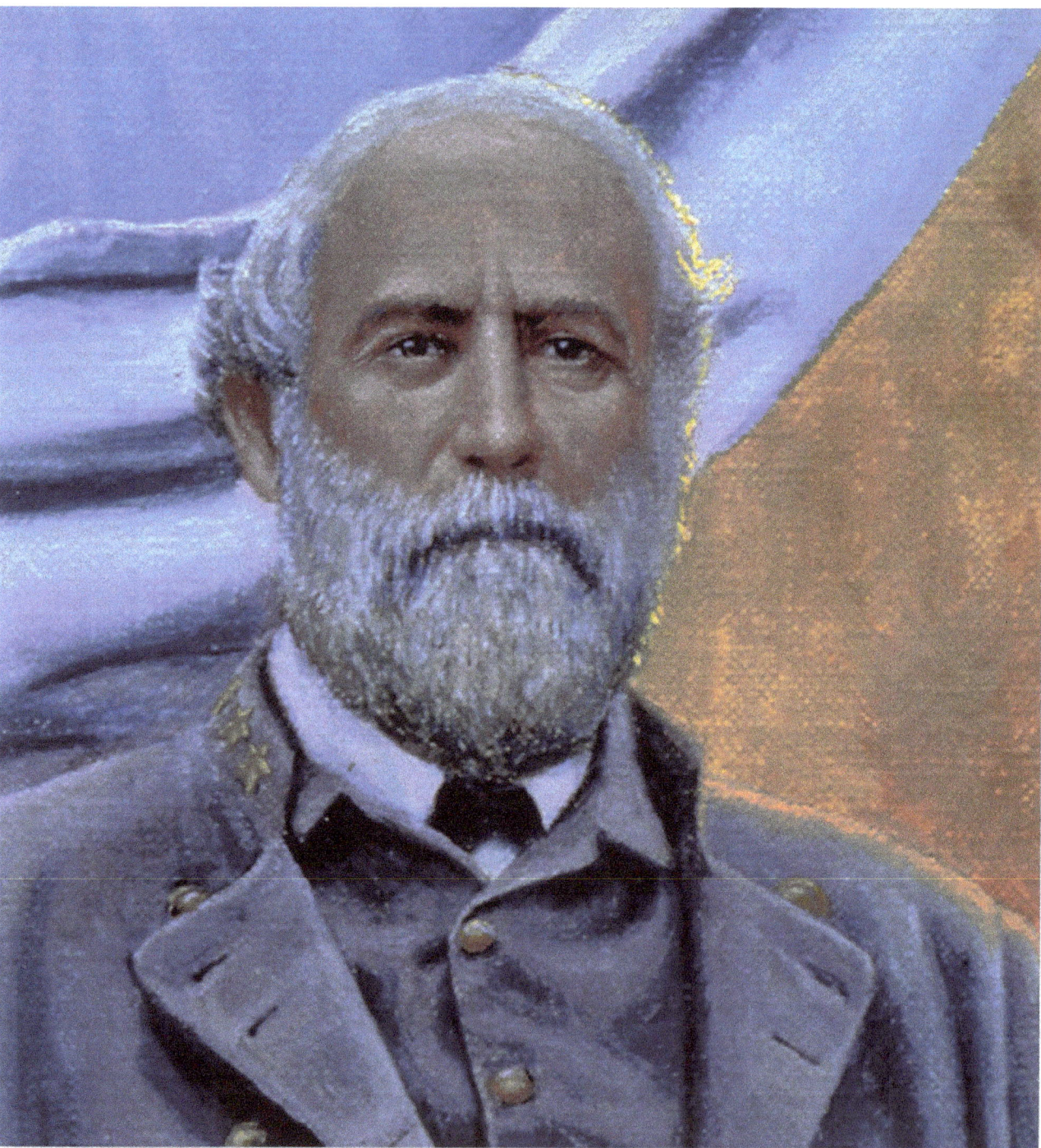

THE LONELINESS OF COMMAND (STUDY)

GEN. ROBERT E. LEE

1995, mixed media, 18½ x 22½

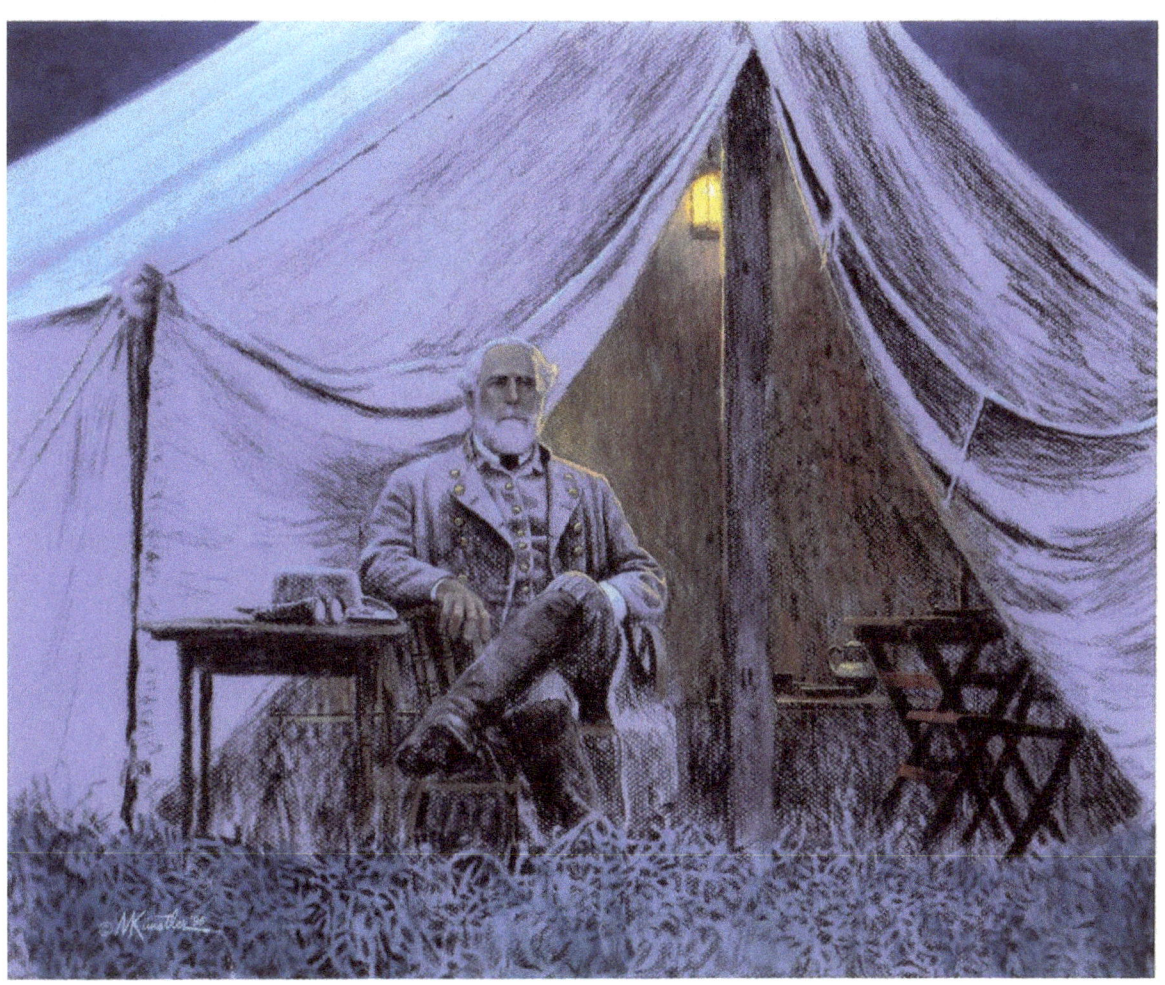

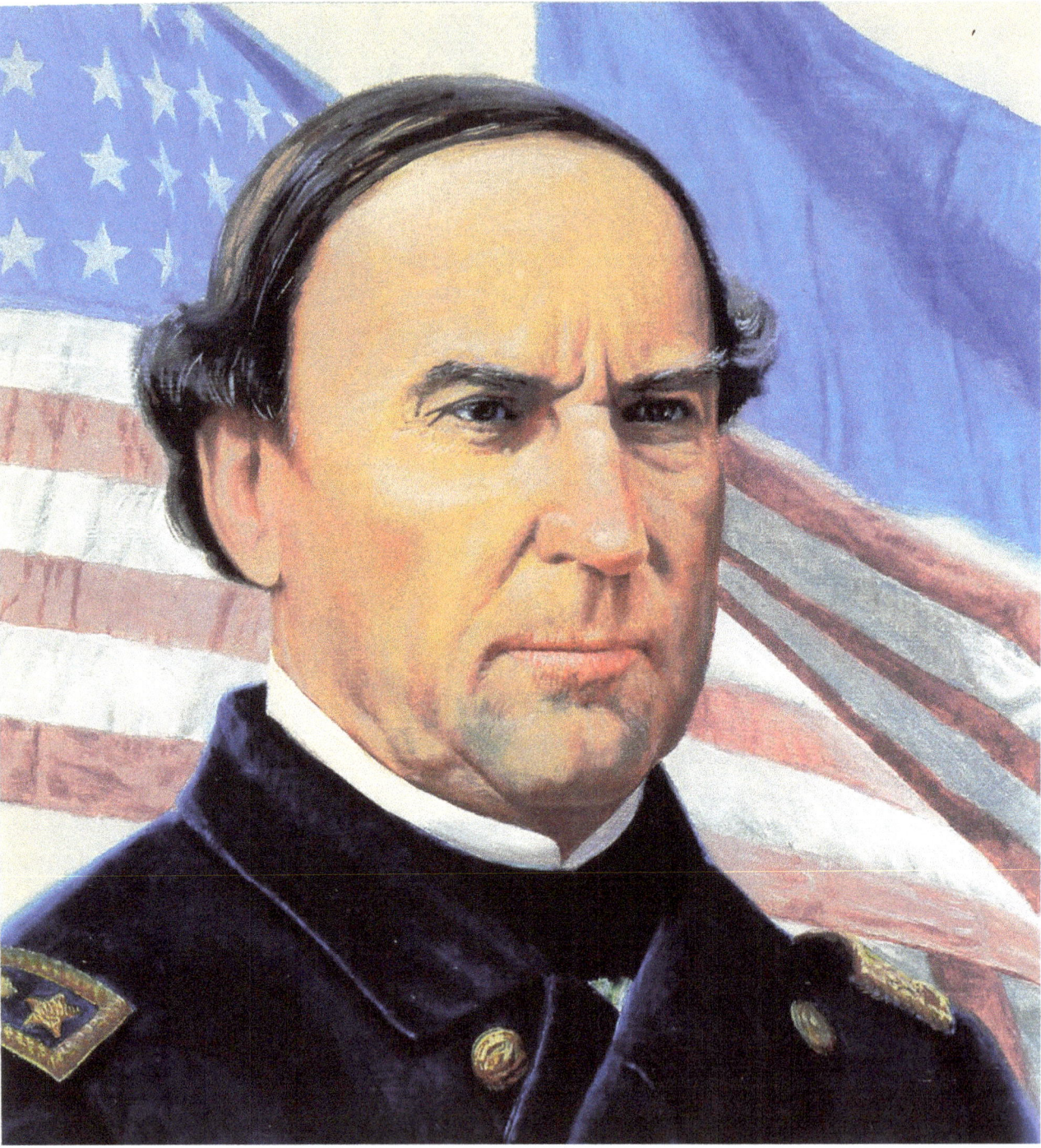

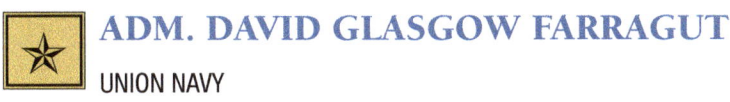

ADM. DAVID GLASGOW FARRAGUT

UNION NAVY

1990, oil, 10 x 11½

David Glasgow Farragut's naval career began at the age of eleven during the War of 1812 when his stepfather, Cmdr. David D. Porter, commissioned him as a midshipman. A Tennessean by birth, Farragut resided in Norfolk, Virginia, when the war came in 1861. His loyalty to the Union made him unwelcome there, but Northerners also questioned his allegiance. In late 1861, Secretary of the Navy Gideon Welles placed Farragut in charge of the West Gulf Blockading Squadron and gave him the task of capturing New Orleans.

On April 24, 1862, Farragut successfully guided his fleet past the forts guarding the Crescent City, and the city surrendered the next day He was awarded with promotion to rear admiral and the official Thanks of Congress. Farragut's greatest victory, however, was the August 5, 1864, battle of Mobile Bay When one of his ships was sunk by a mine near the fort guarding the bay, and the flotilla briefly halted, allowing the fort to rake the vessels, Farragut ordered his flagship to proceed through the heavily mined waters with the famous command: "Damn the torpedoes! Full steam ahead!" The Union ships occupied the bay, captured the remaining Confederate vessels, and compelled the fort's surrender. Afterward, Farragut was promoted to vice admiral. Ill health prevented him from any further action during the war.

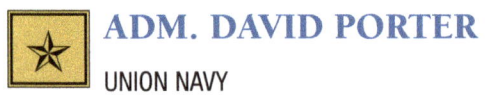

ADM. DAVID PORTER

UNION NAVY

1990, oil, 10 x 11¼

THE THIRD CHILD OF Cmdr. David Dixon Porter (and stepbrother of David G. Farragut), David Porter went to sea at the age of ten. He was a veteran naval officer when the Civil War began, and his first assignment was as the head of the naval arm of the relief effort for Fort Pickens at Pensacola, Florida.

In 1862, Porter commanded the mortar boats that supported Farragut's capture of New Orleans. Later that year, Porter commanded the Mississippi Squadron and supported the Union army's engagements at Arkansas Post and Vicksburg. His successes led to his promotion to rear admiral and responsibility for Union naval control of the Mississippi River north of New Orleans.

In the spring of 1864, Porter's ships supported the Red River campaign, after which he was given command of the North Atlantic Blockading Squadron. At the January 1865 battle of Fort Fisher, he commanded the largest American fleet ever assembled to that point in history There he directed the war's greatest naval bombardment and helped to capture Wilmington, North Carolina—the South's last open major seaport.

During the war, Congress sparingly issued citations to honor individual wartime accomplishments; only thirty were published in the *Congressional Record*. David Porter received three of these.

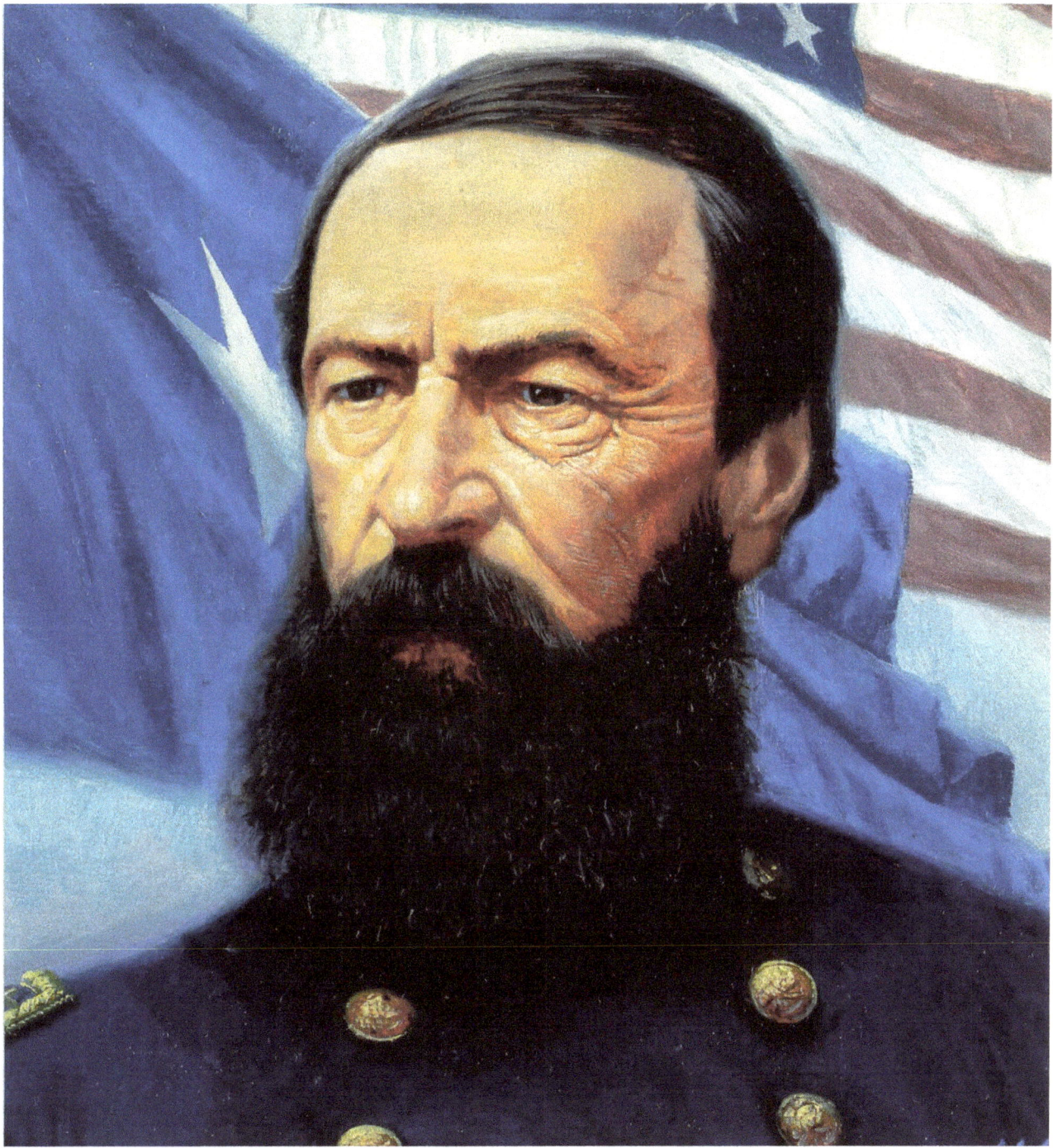

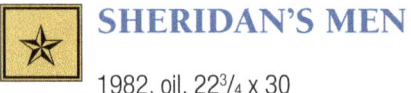

SHERIDAN'S MEN

1982, oil, 22¾ x 30

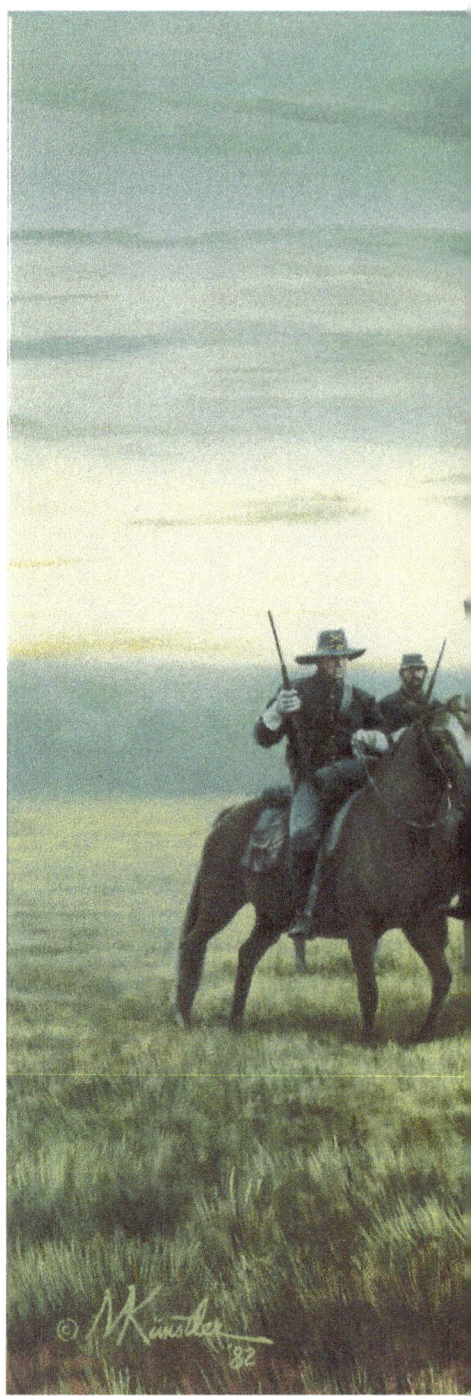

WHEN ULYSSES S. GRANT gave Philip H. Sheridan command of the Army of the Potomac's cavalry, Sheridan reshaped these horsemen into the Union's most effective weapon. Earlier in the war, the cavalry had been the weakest branch of the Federal services, and its Confederate counterpart had taunted and tortured the Northerners with speed and skill. Sheridan's goal in the Shenandoah was to use cavalry as a striking force rather than as mounted infantry During the summer of 1864, he demonstrated how to best use one's cavalry in the field and came close to achieving his goal of ridding the Shenandoah Valley of all Southern forces.

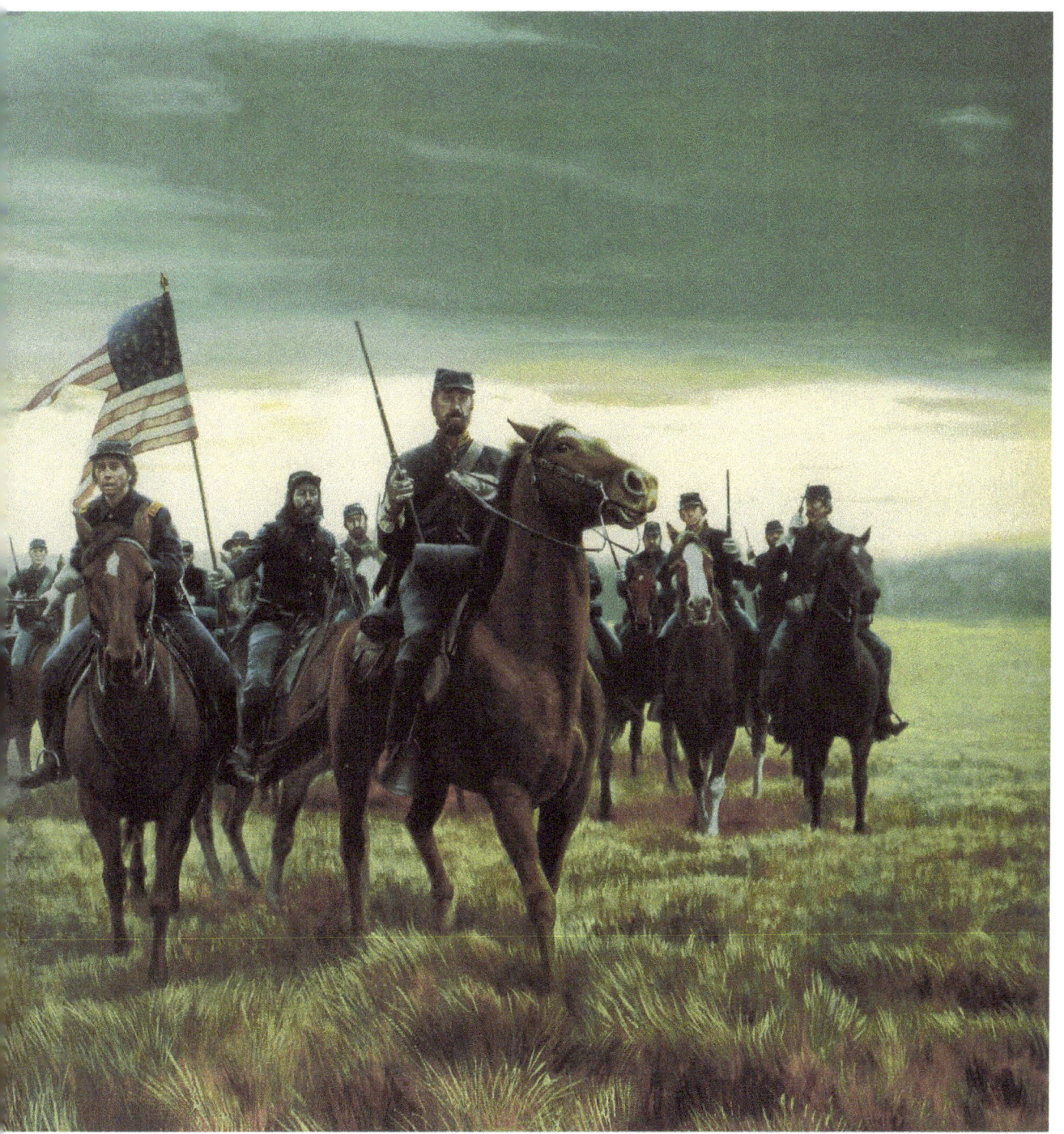

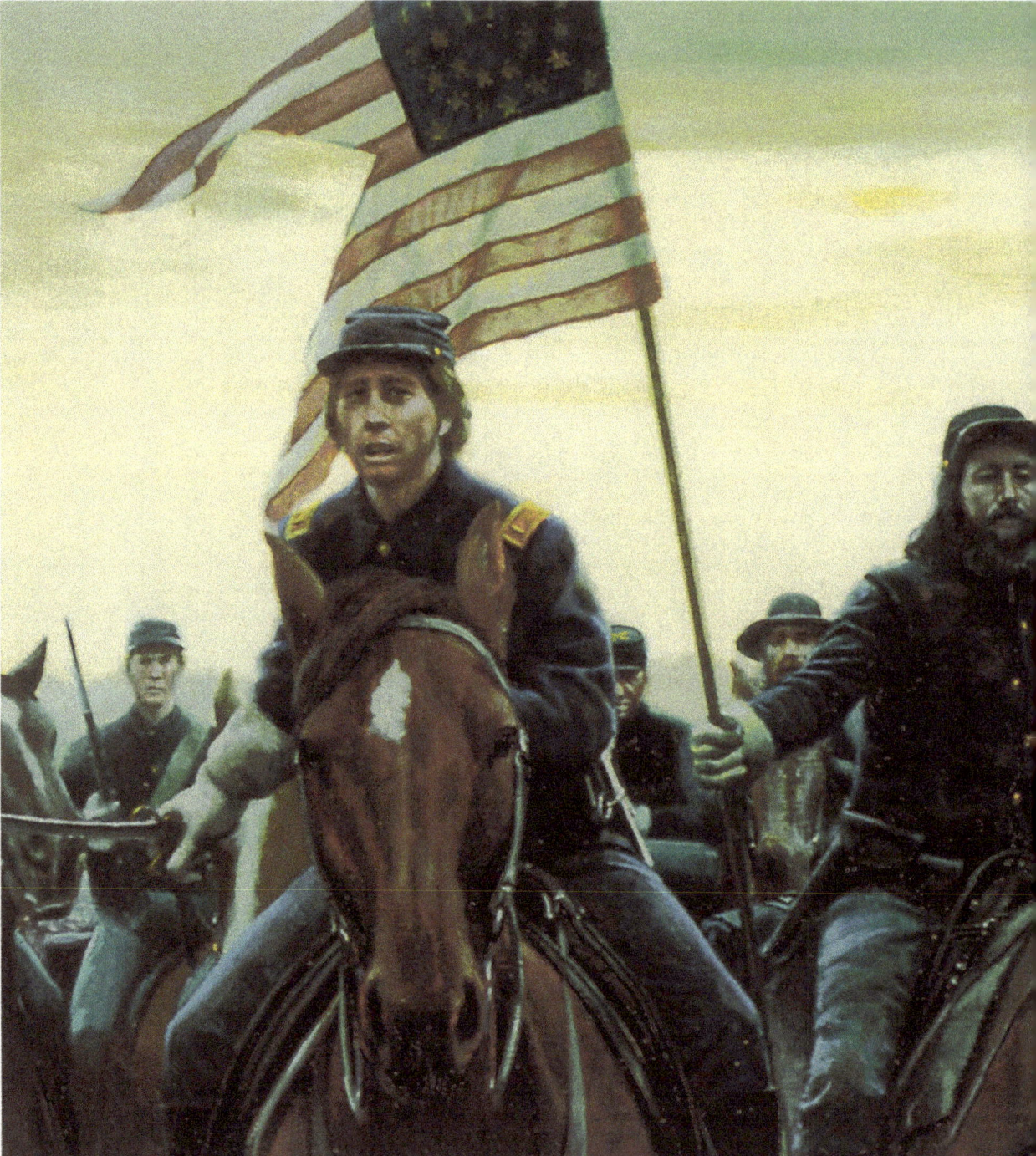

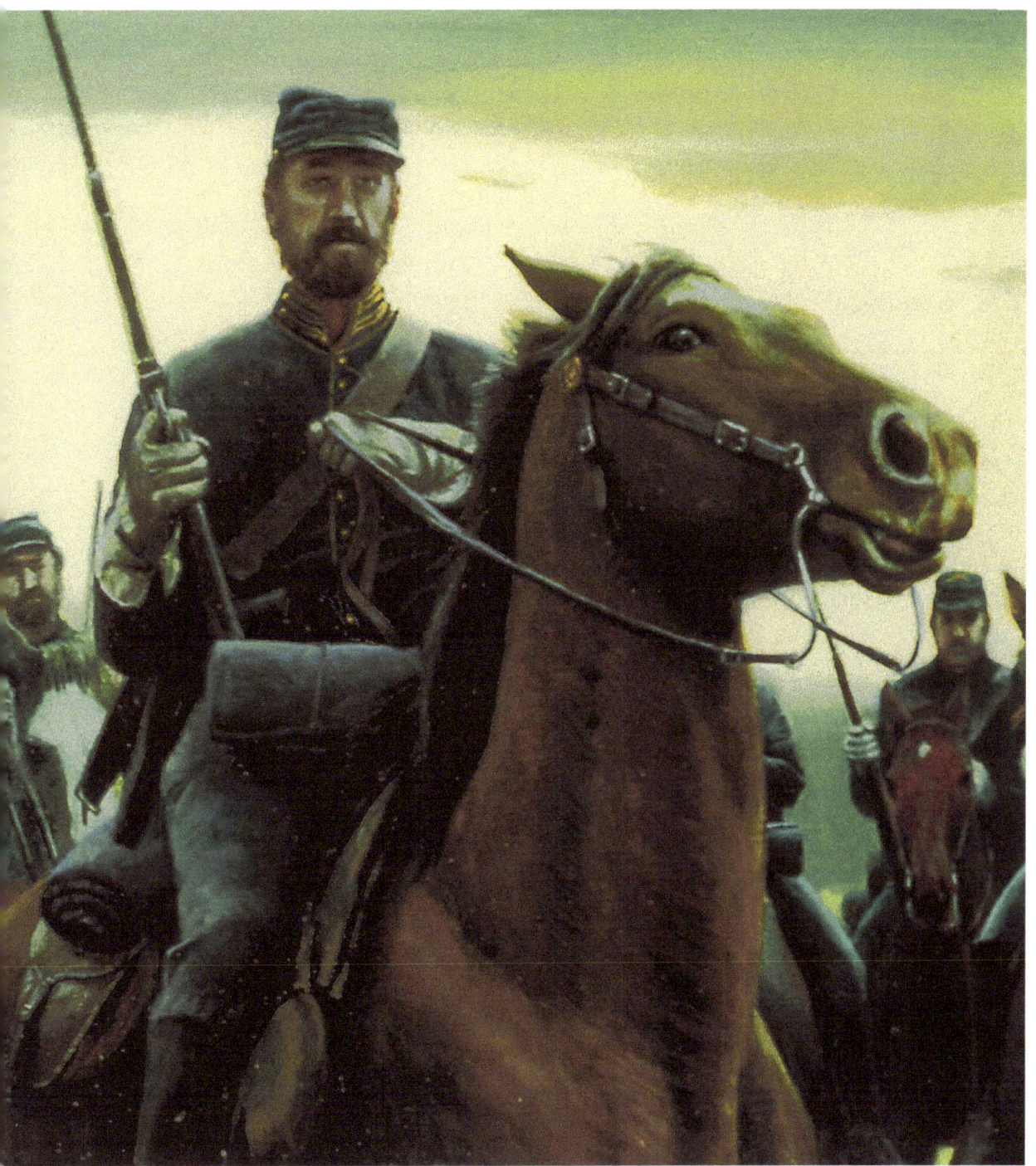

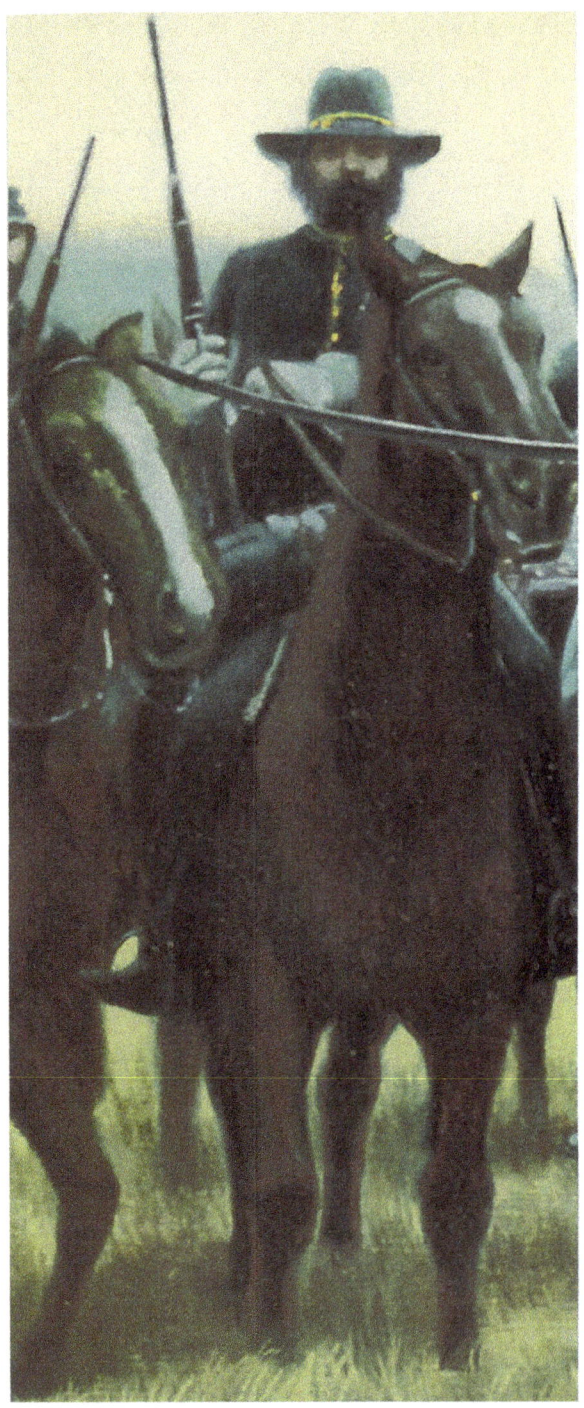

Sheridan was a short (five feet four inches tall), fiery man with a hot temper. His ability to wield infantry and cavalry together on a battlefield impressed all who witnessed those actions. Recollecting "Little Phil's" leadership during the last weeks of the war, Joshua Lawrence Chamberlain observed, "We had a taste of General Sheridan's fighting style, and we liked it. He transfuses into his subordinates the vitality and energy of his purpose, transforms them into part of his own mind and will. He shows the power of a commander."

Throughout the spring of 1864, Sheridan's horsemen wreaked havoc on Southern rails and supply wagons. In May, he mounted a raid near Richmond, seeking Jeb Stuart's cavalry. He found him near an abandoned stagecoach station at Yellow Tavern, and during the fighting Stuart was mortally wounded.

Grant gave Sheridan command

of the Army of the Shenandoah and instructed him to eliminate the region's role as the major food supplier for the South. As part of this conquest, Sheridan's men successfully engaged the Confederates at the third battle of Winchester (the first decisive Union victory in the Shenandoah), Fisher's Hill, Cedar Creek, and Waynesborough and pursued a "scorched-earth" policy until this objective was met.

In this painting, I keyed the colors to the troopers' dark blue uniforms. By making the sky dark with a light streak at the horizon, I added drama by contrasting the darkest dark of the cavalrymen's caps against the lightest light of the sky.

My goal was to emphasize the toughness, strength, and confidence of the Union cavalry. Well equipped and led by a lieutenant and a sergeant, this unit projects the image of a formidable foe as mobile infantry equipped with rapid-firing weapons.

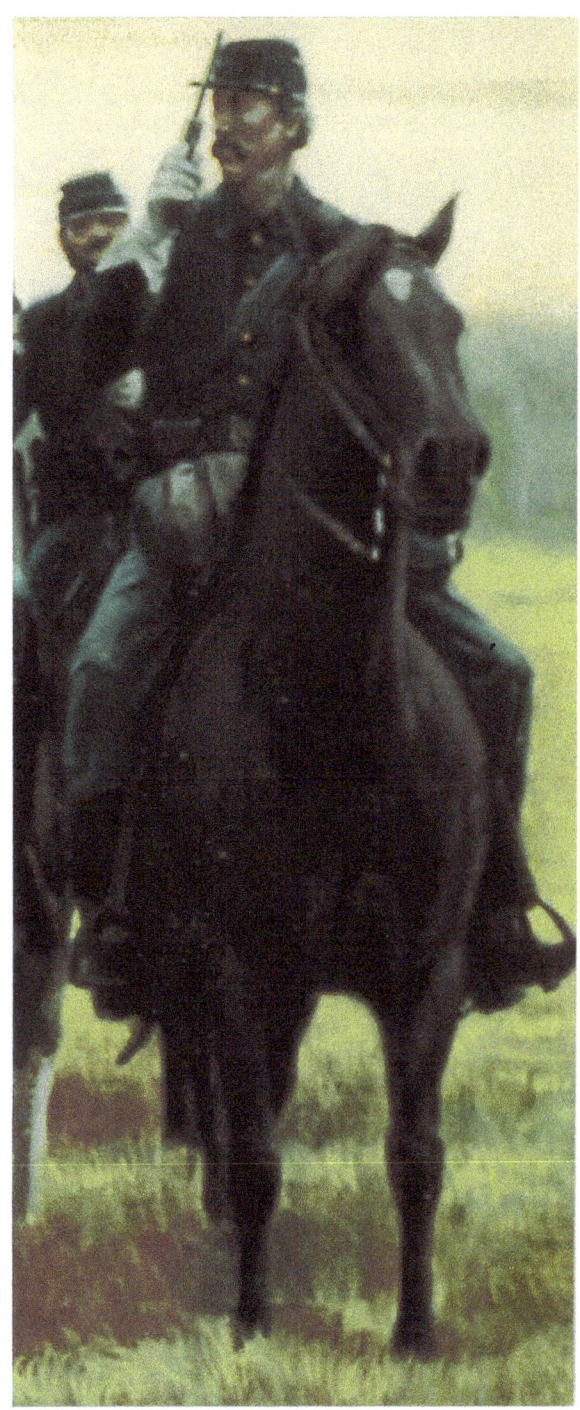

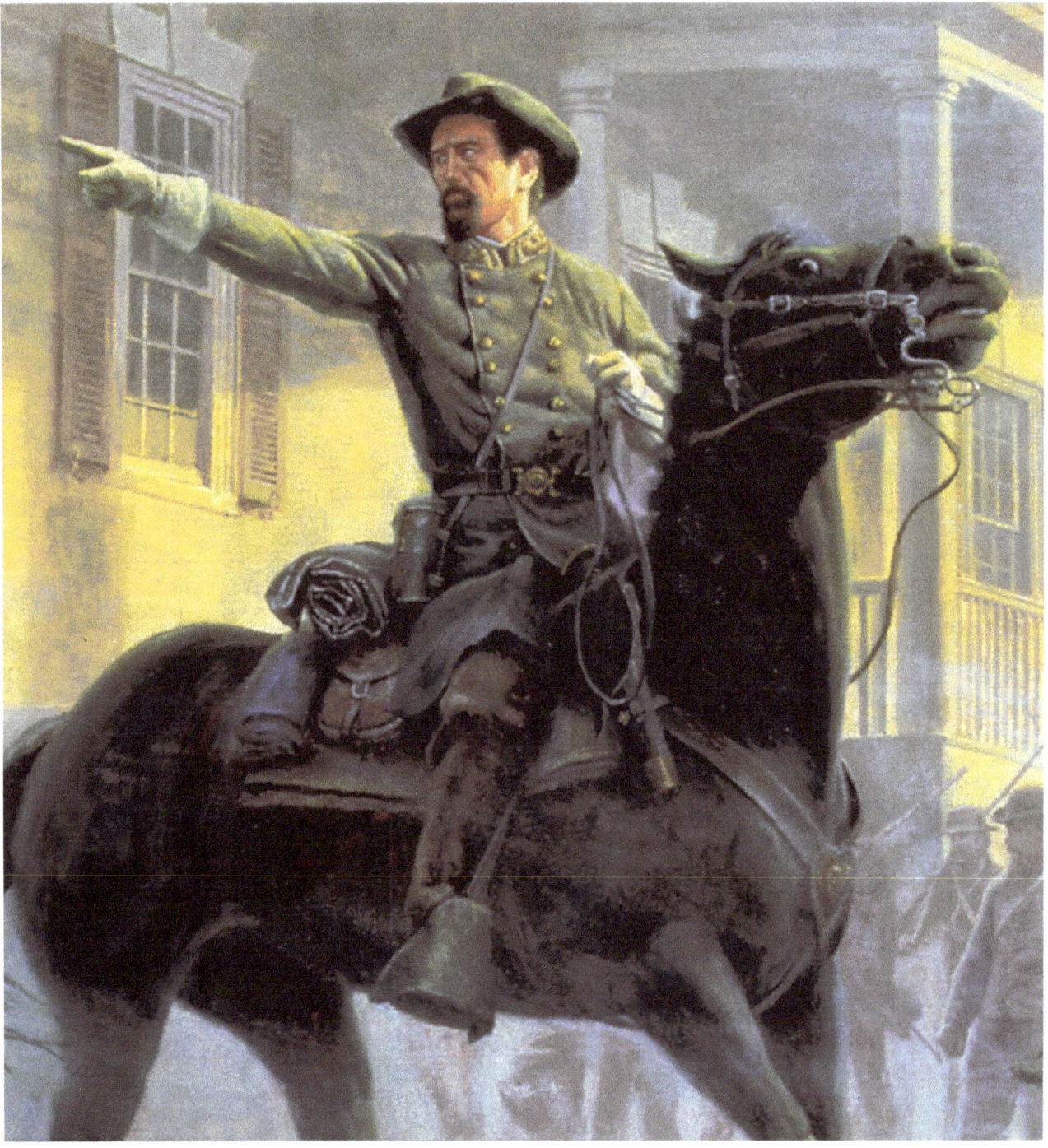

SHENANDOAH SUNRISE

GEN. JOHN B. GORDON AT CEDAR CREEK, VIRGINIA
OCTOBER 19, 1864

1993, oil, 28 x 46

IN EARLY OCTOBER 1864, Union Gen. Philip H. Sheridan's campaign to conquer and occupy the Shenandoah Valley seemed to reach a successful conclusion. All of the upper valley had borne the brunt of the fighting, including the torching of several farms and plantations. Union victories at Winchester, Fisher's Hill, and Tom's Brook had greatly reduced the fighting capacity of Confederate Gen. Jubal A. Early's command. At this point, Sheridan began making preparations to leave the Valley and join Grant's lines at Petersburg. He left his troops in camp near Cedar Creek while he journeyed to Washington for a strategy conference.

The Confederates, however, were not subdued and received reinforcements. After surveying the Federal positions on October 18, Gen. John B. Gordon and Maj. Jedediah Hotchkiss forwarded a daring attack plan (which was similar to Stonewall Jackson's flanking maneuver at Chancellorsville) to Early, who quickly approved it. They attacked with five infantry divisions just before daybreak on October 19, wrecking two of Sheridan's three corps. After their initial success, the Confederates bogged clown when hungry soldiers focused on plundering

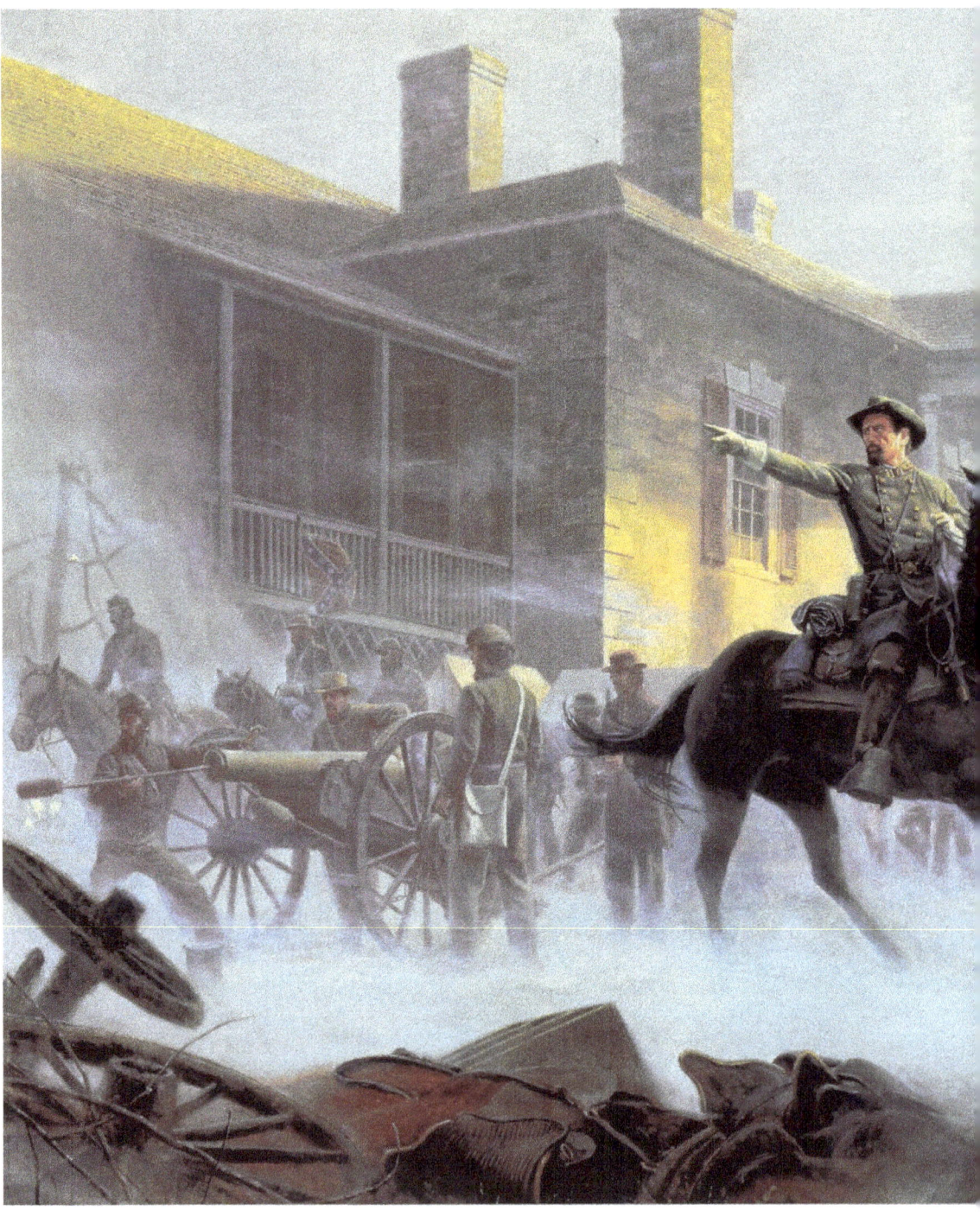

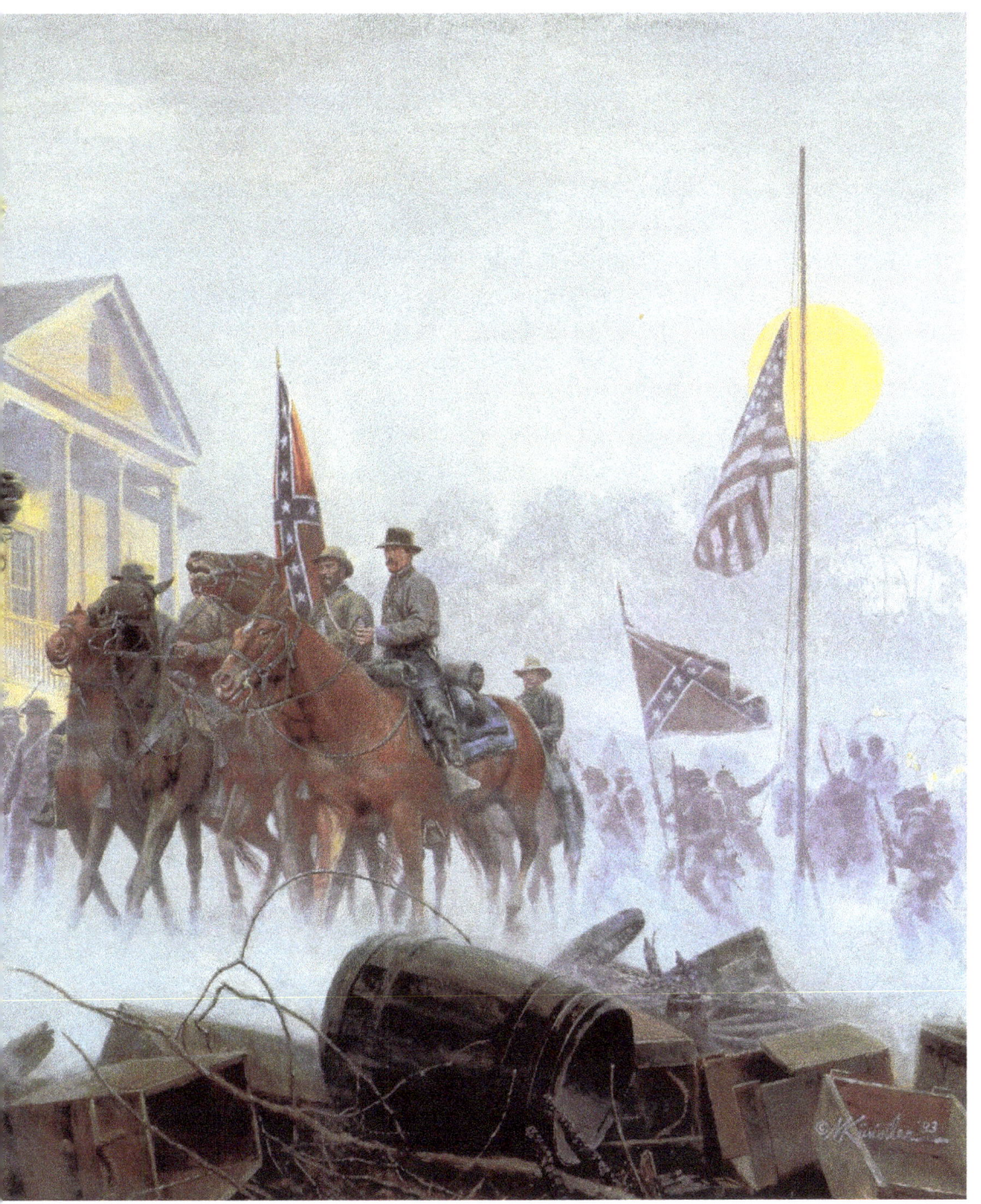

the Union camps, and the low-hanging fog that had aided the assault at first now hindered the pursuit of the fleeing Federals. Confederate caution allowed the Union units to regroup, and Early believed that his army had succeeded in ridding the field of the enemy. Within four hours his five divisions had driven off seven Federal divisions and taken more than thirteen hundred prisoners. When he encountered Gordon near the front, Early commented, "Well, Gordon, this is glory enough for one day." Gordon urged him to press on, but Early was convinced the Federals were abandoning the area.

In Winchester, Sheridan heard the unmistakable sounds of battle and rushed back to his army, rallying stragglers along the twelve-mile route to get back to the battle front. After he arrived at his reconstructed line, he saw an opportunity to counterattack in the face of Early's nonaction. At 4:00 p.m. he ordered an infantry corps to assault and followed that with his cavalry. Confederate units broke piece by piece, as Gordon commented, "like hard clods of clay under a pelting rain." Early's army crumpled and retreated. On October 20, he withdrew to New Market, leaving the Shenandoah entirely in Federal possession.

My first visit to the Cedar Creek battlefield and Belle Grove plantation was in the fall of 1992 as a guest of Wil Feltner of the F&M Bank–Winchester. When I saw Belle Grove, I realized it would make a wonderful backdrop for a painting of this historic clash in which the fate of the Shenandoah Valley was decided.

The action around Belle Grove on October 19, 1864, is a compelling story. Southern troops had just overrun the property, which was being used as Sheridan's headquarters. John B. Gordon arrived at the site to direct operations,

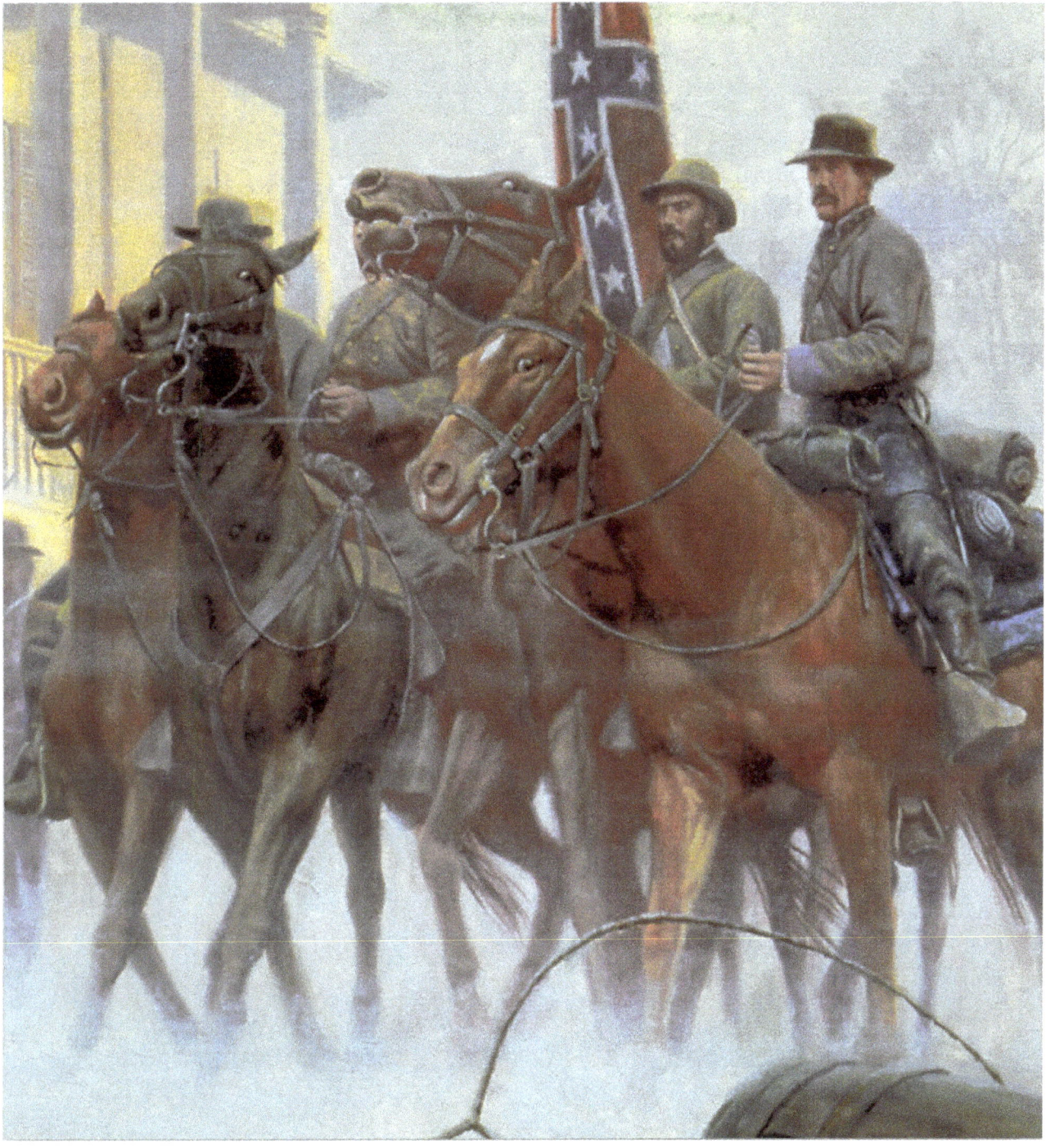

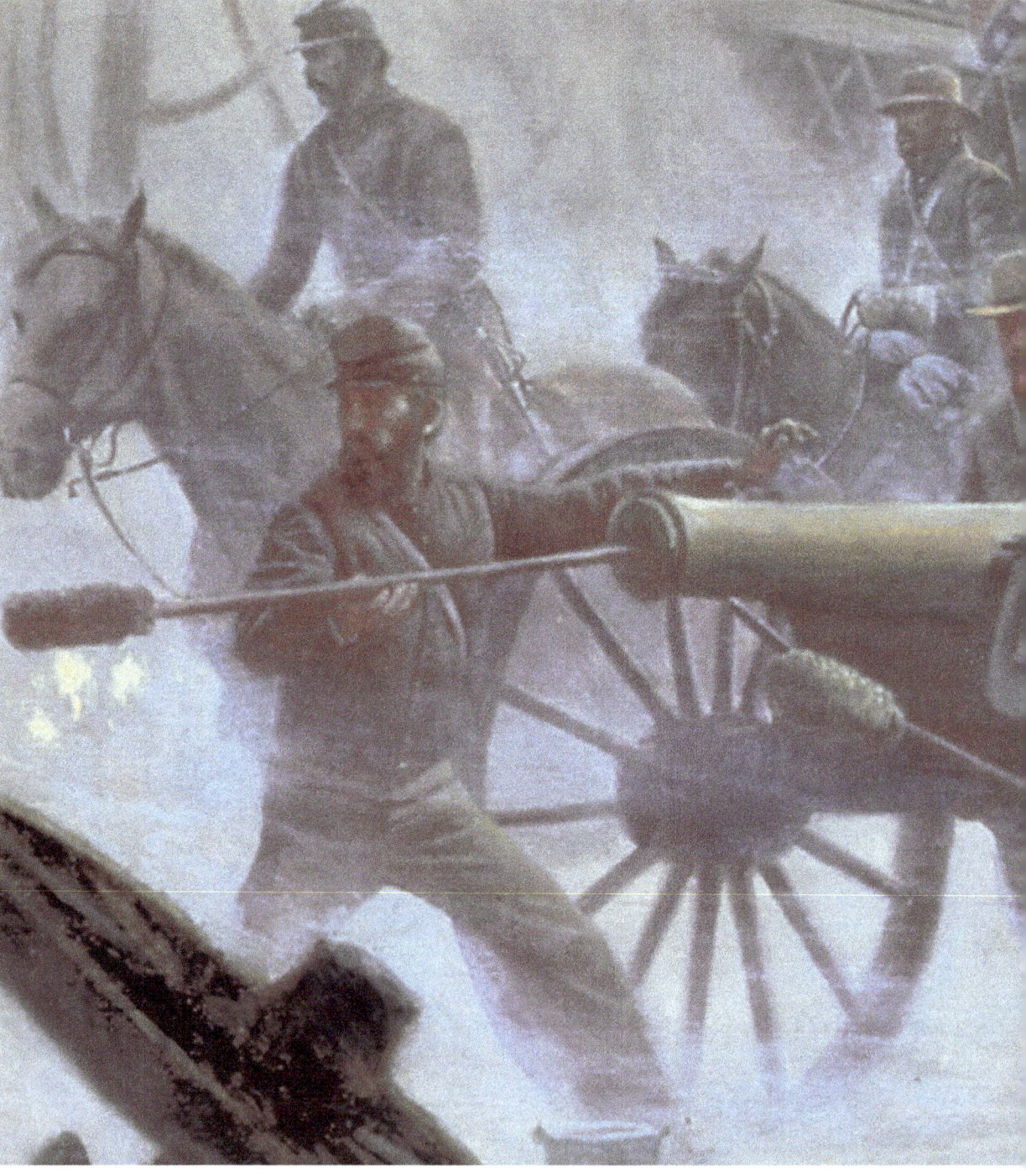

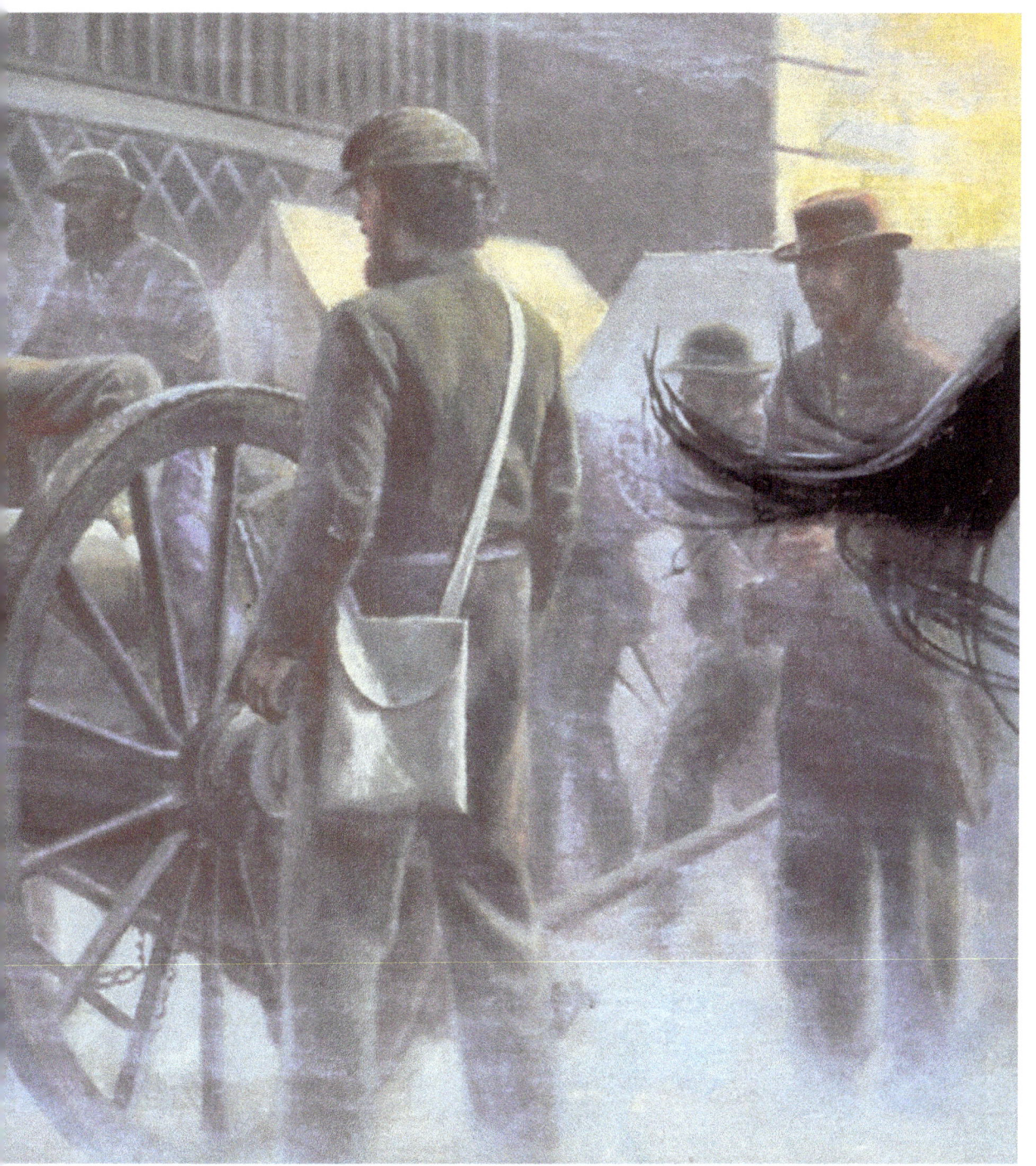

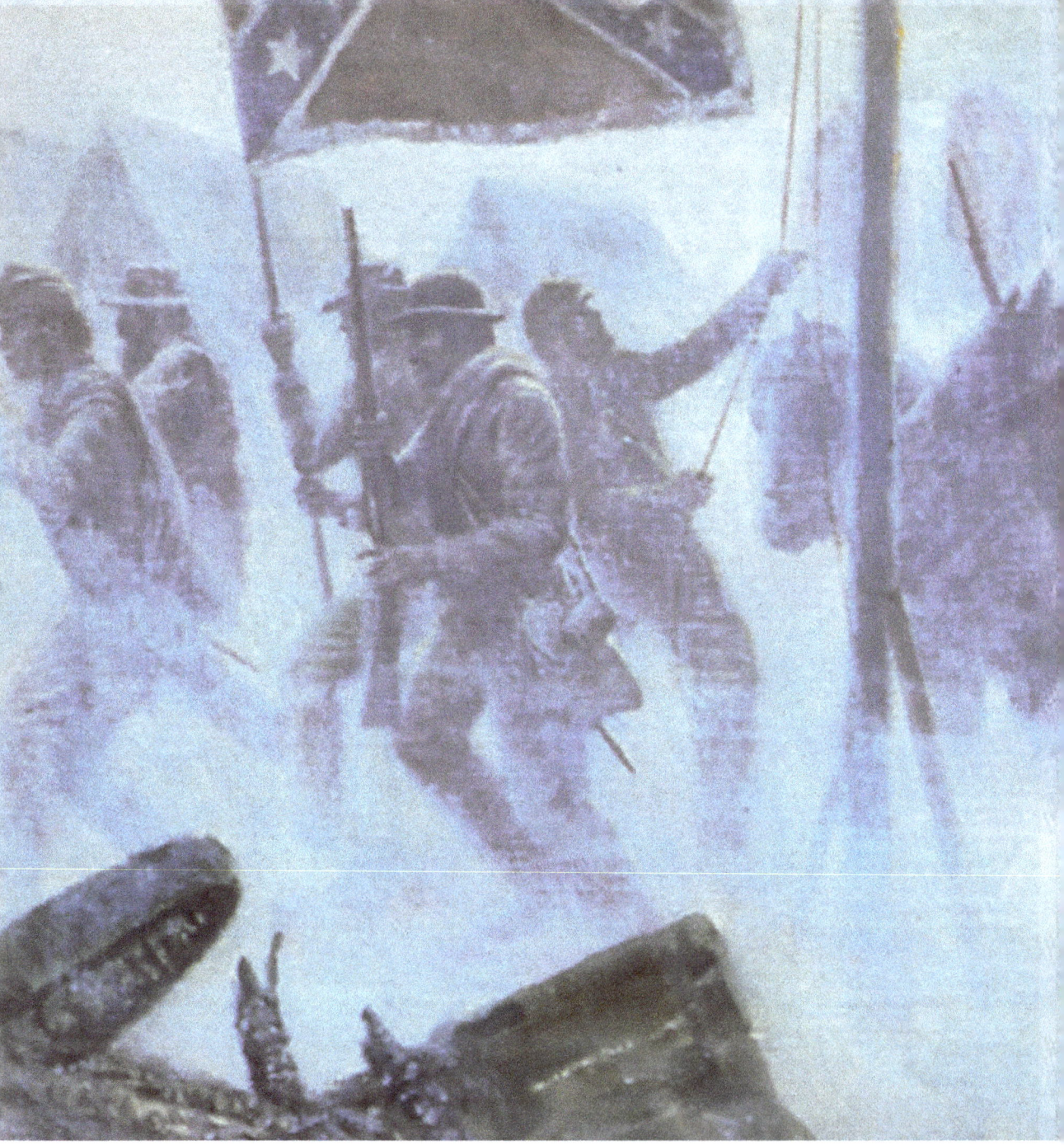

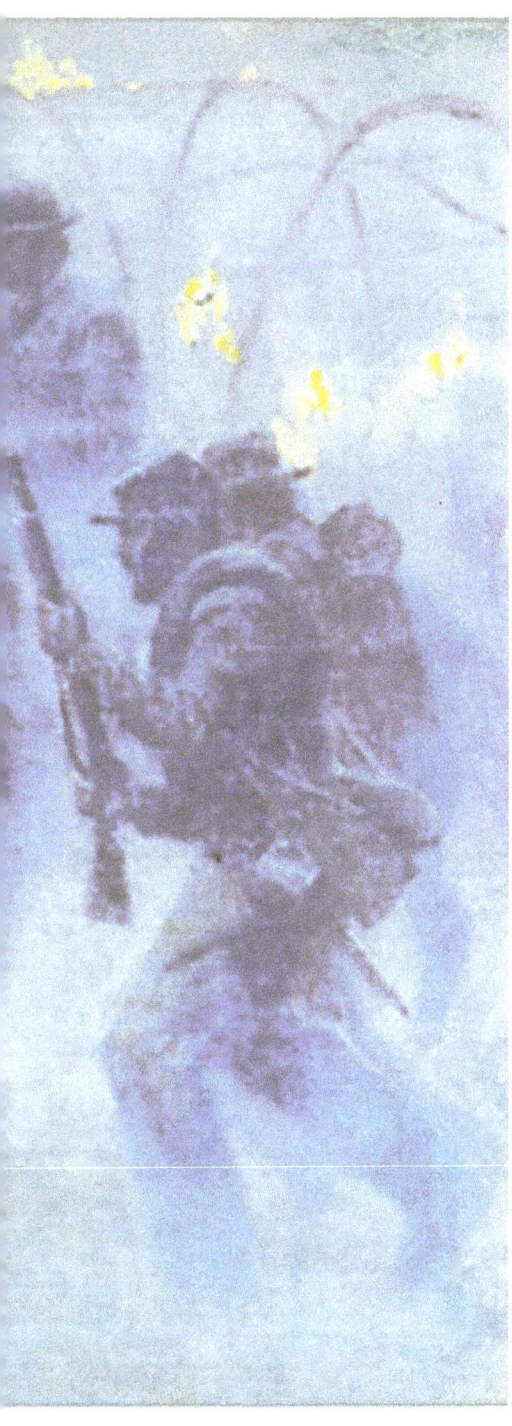

and I chose to recreate the scene of his arrival while his soldiers scrambled to possess the area. This afforded me a rare opportunity to show artillery, cavalry, infantry, and a command staff in action in front of the beautiful mansion, which I also learned had been designed by Thomas Jefferson.

By twilight, Sheridan had reclaimed the house for his headquarters. A bonfire in the front yard burned into the evening while artillery and wagons rolled up and stretcher-bearers brought in the wounded. Praise streamed into Belle Grove from Washington and Petersburg. Lincoln wrote: "Tender[ing] to you and your brave army the thanks of the nation, and my own personal admiration and gratitude, for the month's operations in the Shenandoah Valley; and especially for the splendid work of October 19, 1864."

"WAR IS HELL!"

GEN. WILLIAM TECUMSEH SHERMAN IN ATLANTA, GEORGIA

NOVEMBER 15, 1864

2001, oil, 54 x 88

No COLLECTION OF CIVIL War paintings would come close to being complete without an image of Gen. William Tecumseh Sherman. Along with Sheridan, he rounds out the circle of Union leadership initiated by Grant as general in chief. My only problem was determining how and when to portray him.

In a speech after the war, Sherman said, "There is many a boy here today who looks on war as all glory, but, boys, it is all hell." Over time that has been shortened to "War is hell." Few people would know better than Sherman, for it was he who brought the hellish torch to the Deep South in 1864.

Like Sheridan's scorched-earth policy in the Shenandoah Valley, Sherman's view of war dictated that the conqueror consume, burn, or destroy anything that might contribute to the enemy's ability to wage war. He realized that this included the destruction of civilian property as well as military assets, which would debilitate the South and facilitate a Union victory.

Because the burning of Atlanta has been immortalized for many people in the film version of *Gone with the Wind,* I was drawn to place this scene in that context. I began by placing Sherman on horseback, looking back at the city in

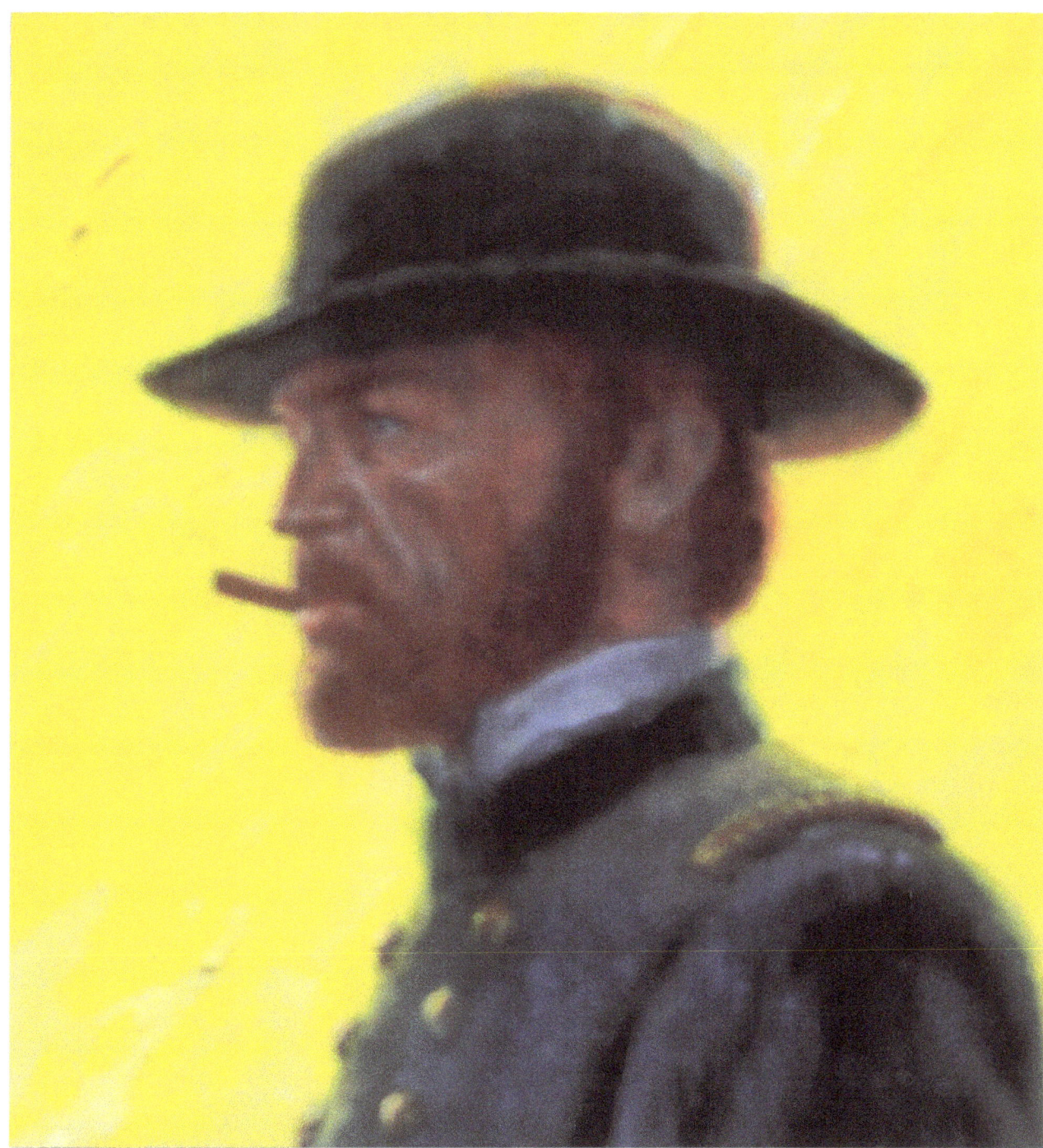

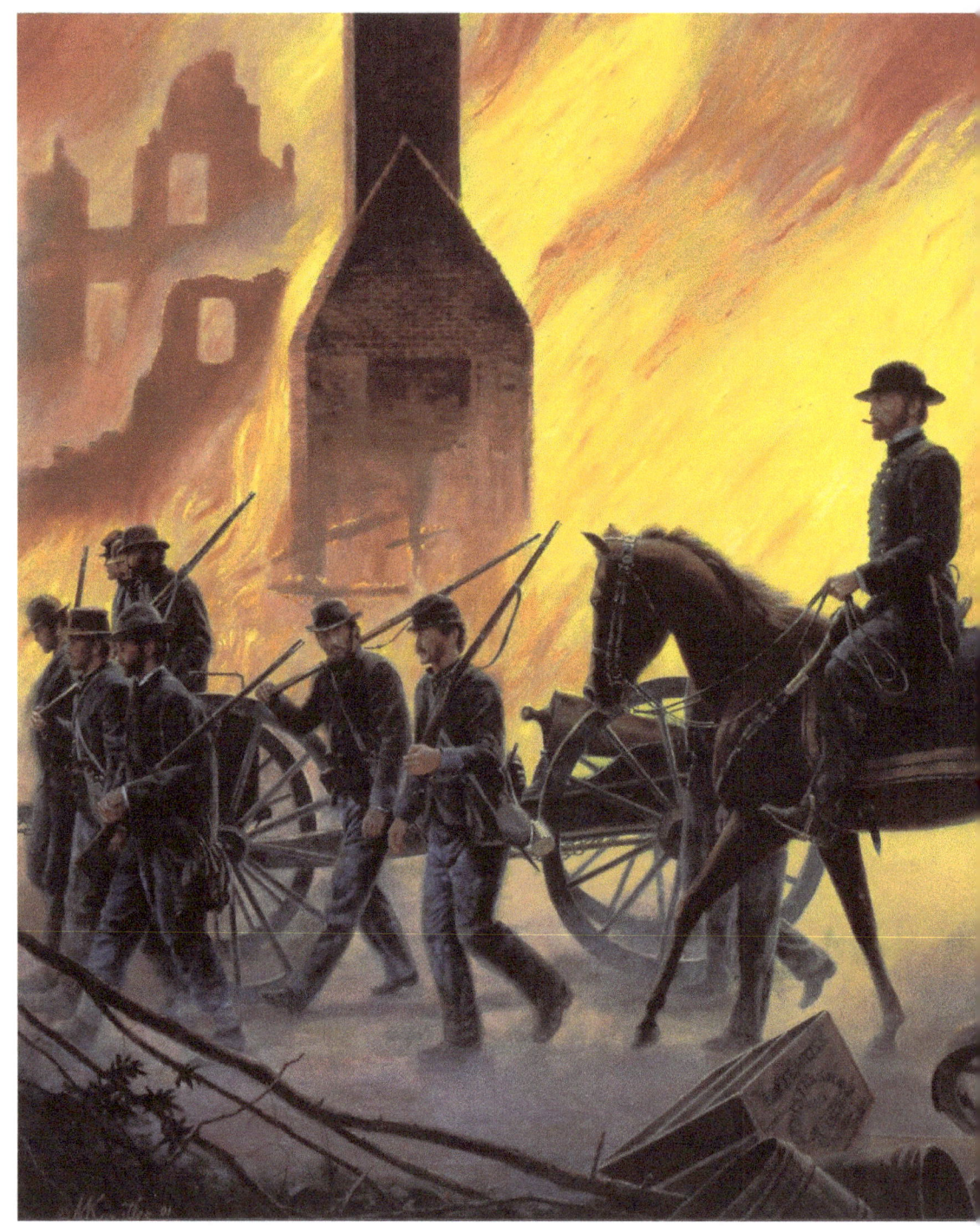

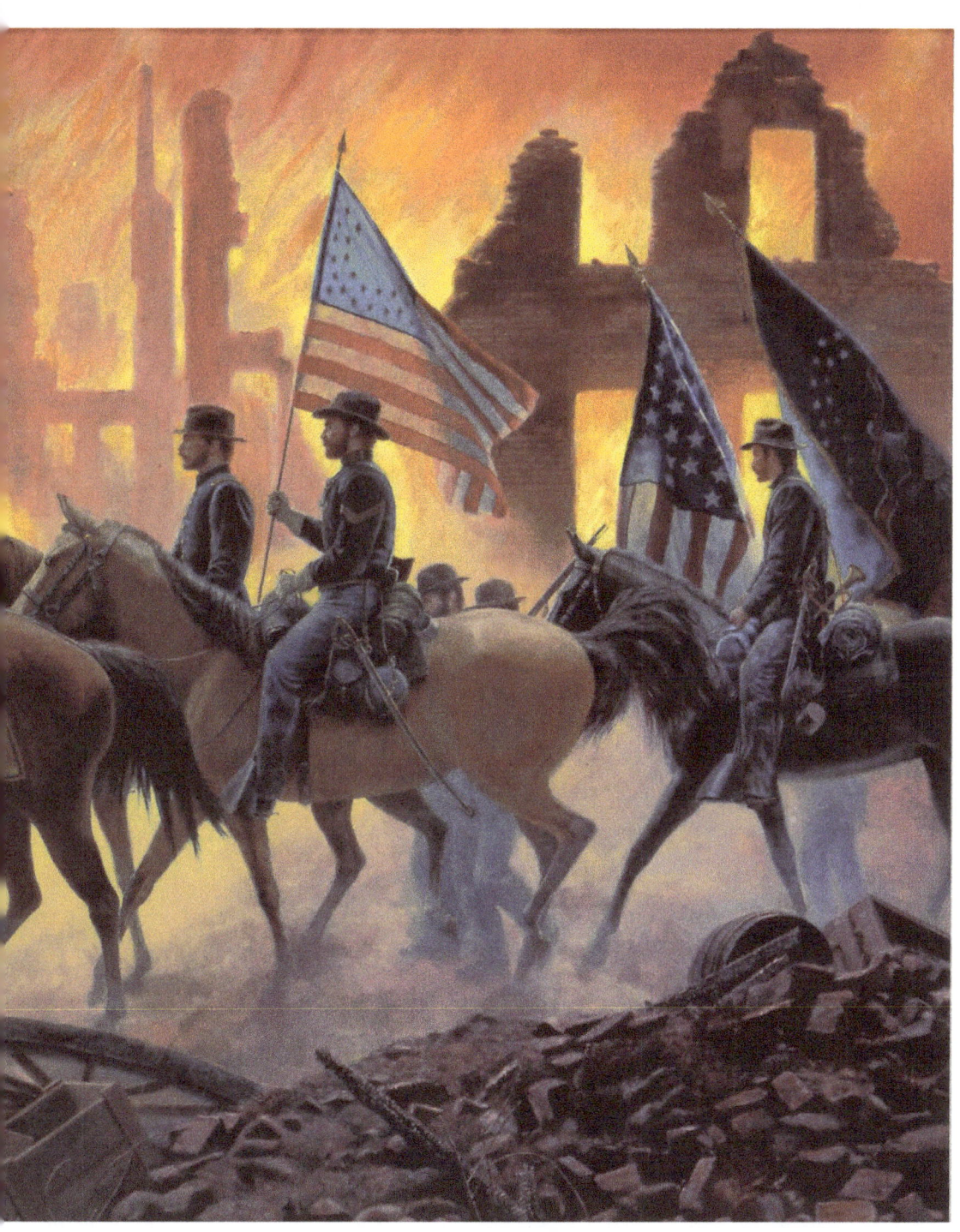

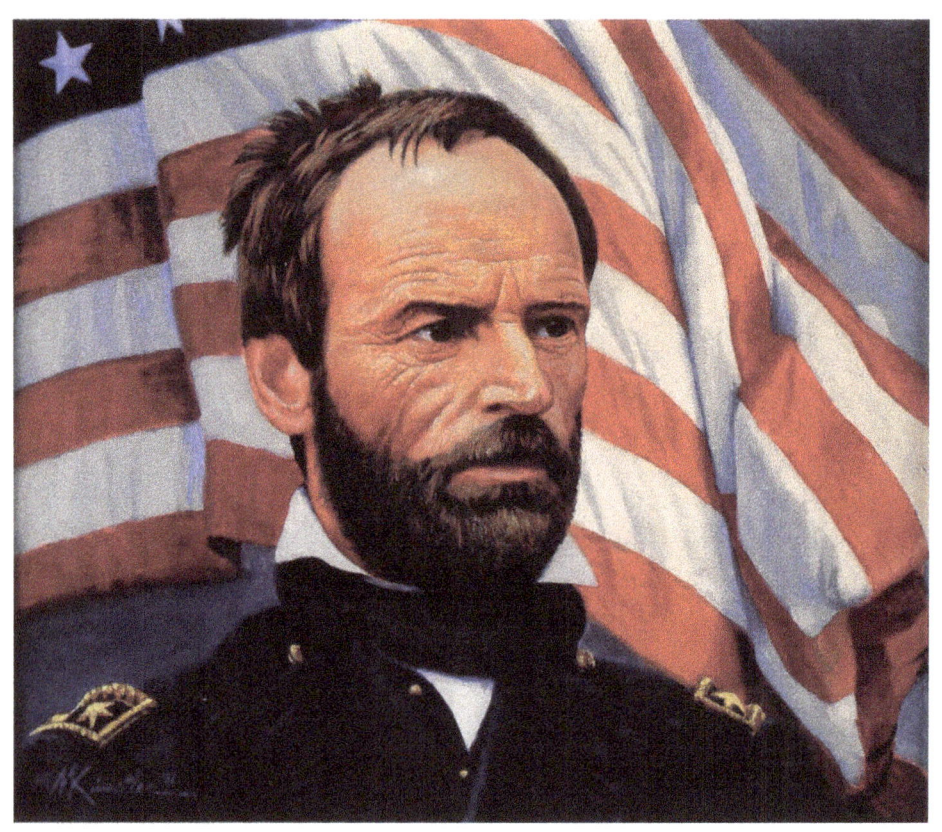

GEN. WILLIAM TECUMSEH SHERMAN

1991, oil, 10 x 11½

flames from a rise in the countryside. Then I remembered his famous quote and thought about hell and decided to dramatize the scene by making it fiery.

After many sketches, I decided to use the fire as my main light source. Still, I knew of no way to include Sherman. That is, until I took another look at Burke Davis's Sherman's *March to the Sea*.

I learned that on the night of November 15, while the fires raged, the Federals began leaving the city. How could I place Sherman in the picture when he did not leave until the next day? While some thought that he was watching the fire from his headquarters, further research indicated that he was in the streets, directing troops in extinguishing any fires that threatened private homes. With this information, I chose to depict Sherman with his troops in the city.

The raging fires provide drama and light while the scorched remains of chimneys, nicknamed Sherman's Sentinels, give mute testimony to the devastation.

The keys to this painting are, of course, the lighting effect in the background and Sherman in the center. The general's determined personality is suggested by the jaunty angle of his ever-present cigar. The final painting includes the elements of the burning of Atlanta, dramatic lighting, Sherman, and units of his army. It is as close as I could come to portraying "Uncle Billy's" most famous quote: "War is hell!"

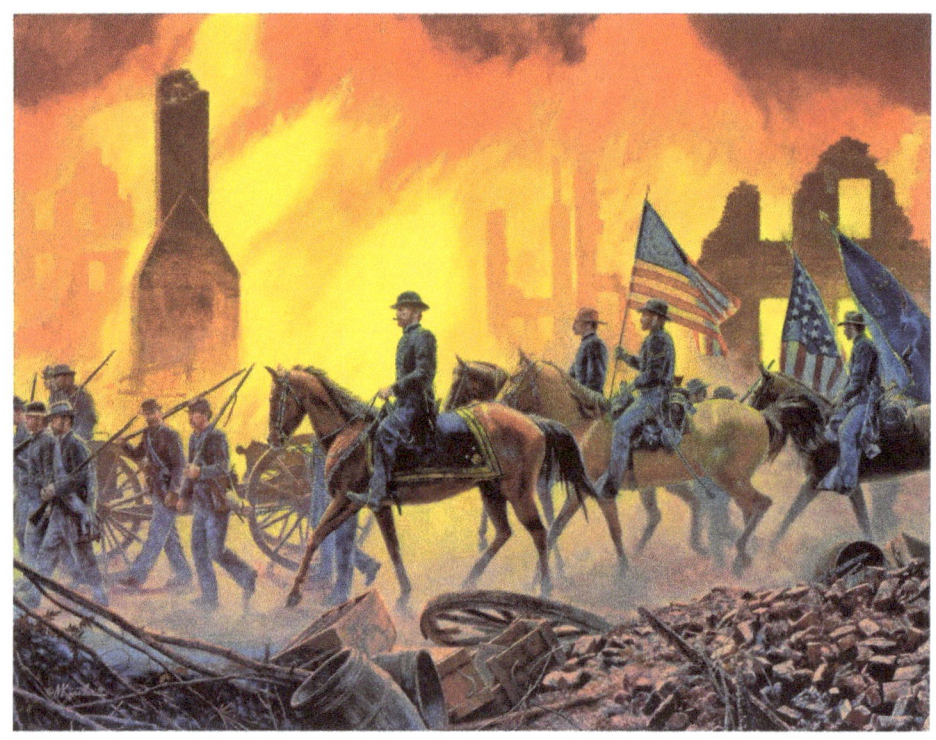

"WAR IS HELL!"

GEN. WILLIAM TECUMSEH SHERMAN, ATLANTA
NOVEMBER 15, 1864

1991, oil, 30 x 38

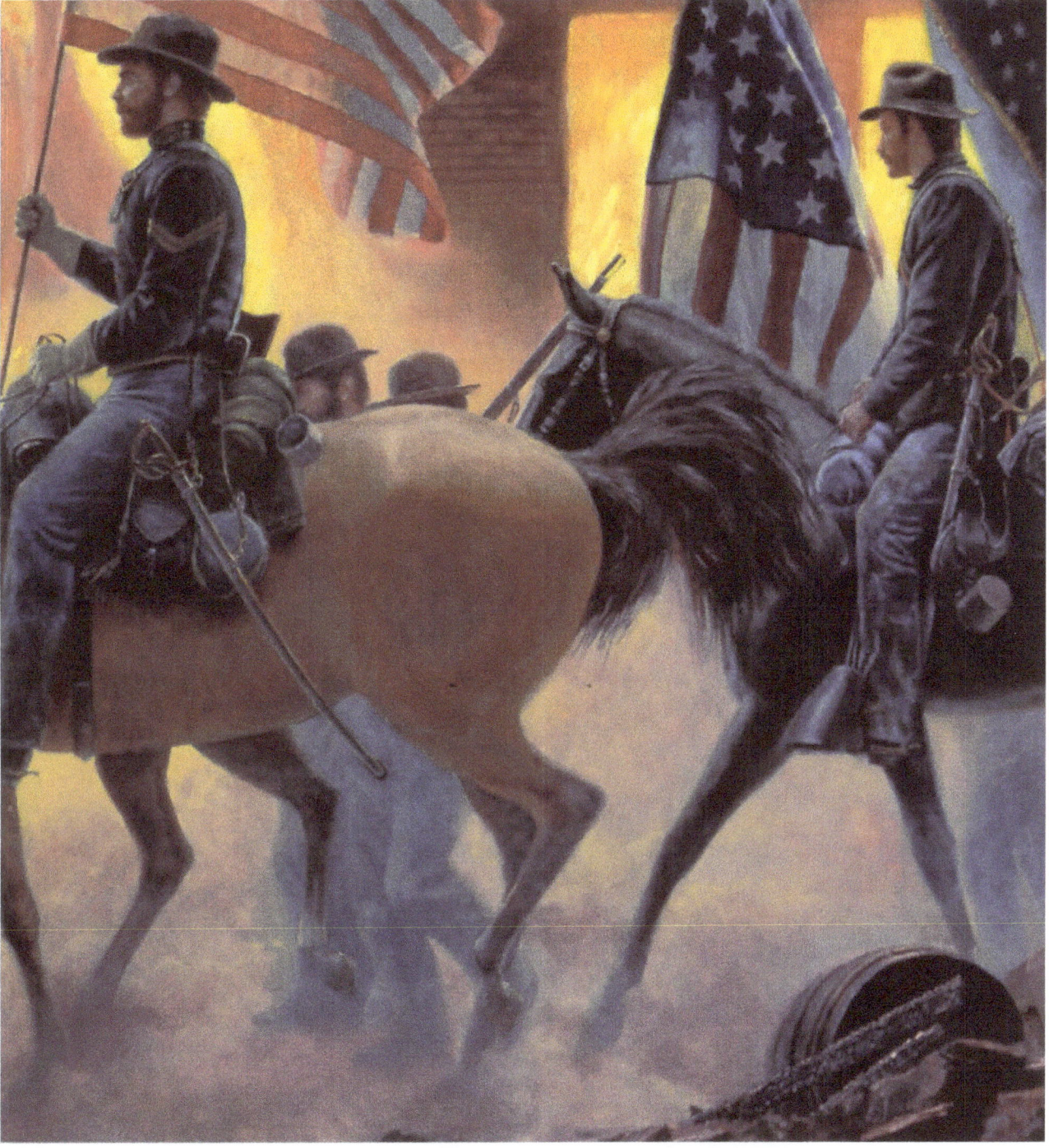

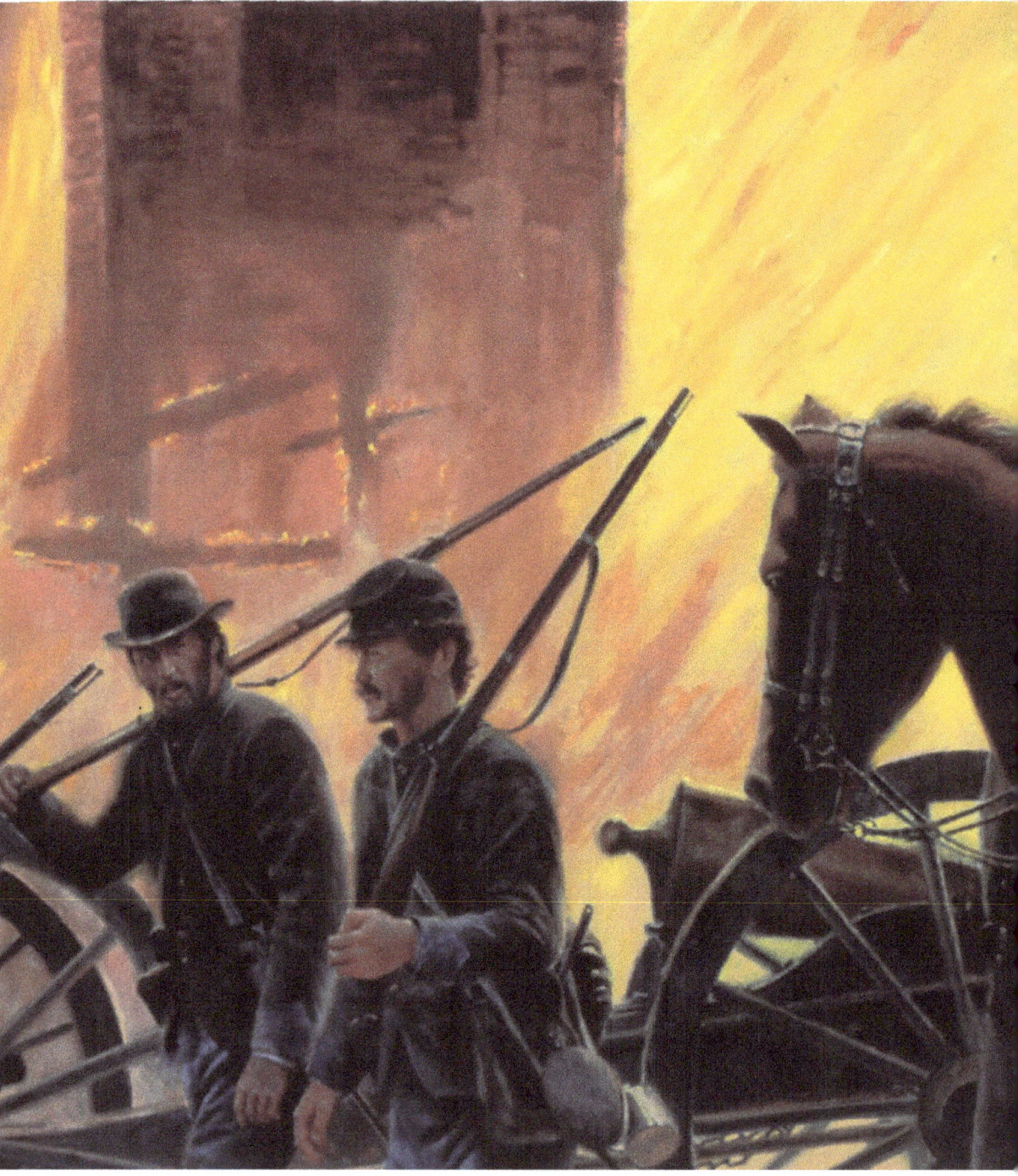

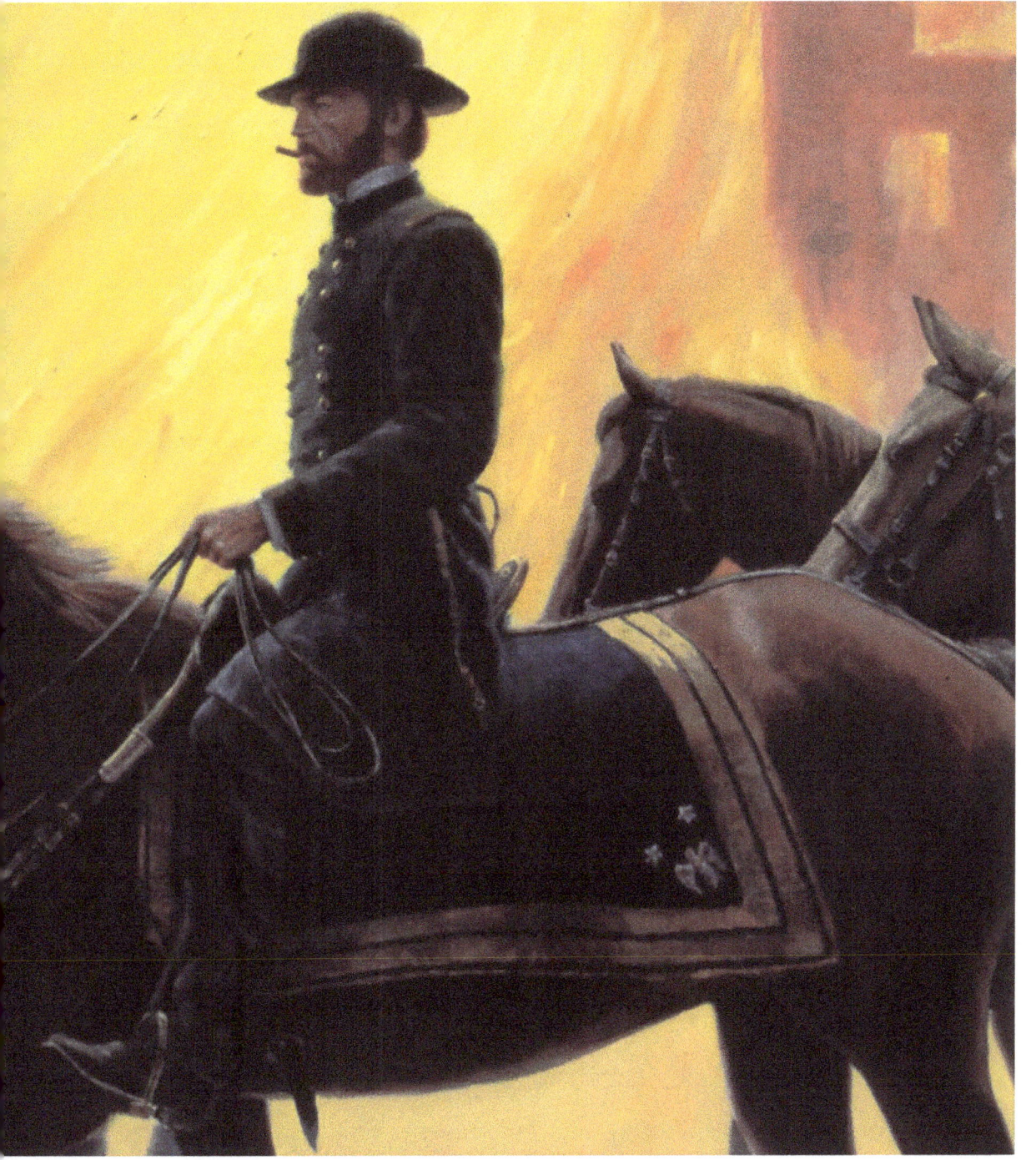

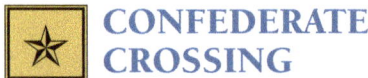

CONFEDERATE CROSSING

GEN. NATHAN BEDFORD FORREST
OWEN'S FORD
NOVEMBER 28, 1864

2004, oil, 24 x 38

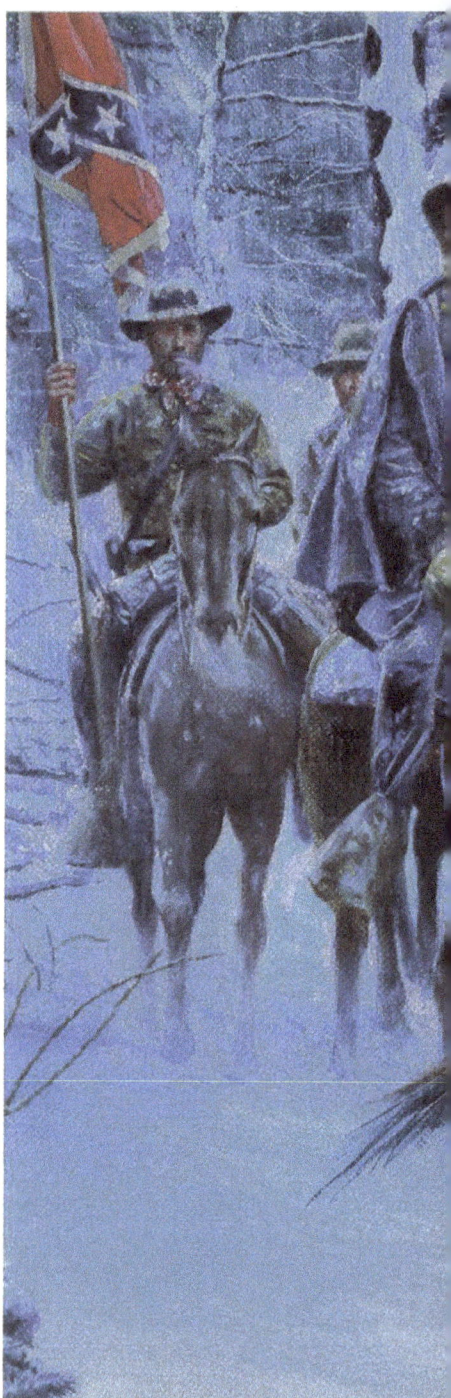

IN NOVEMBER 1864, Sherman prepared to lead a powerful army in a devastating March to the Sea across Georgia. In a desperate attempt to stall that campaign, Confederate Gen. John Bell Hood led his army from Georgia into the heart of Tennessee. Southerners hoped that Hood's advance would distract Sherman from further ravaging the Deep South—but it was not to be. Northern forces were strong enough to oppose Hood with other armies: troops under Gens. George H. Thomas and John M. Schofield. In late November, Hood attempted to envelop and destroy Schofield's force near Spring Hill, Tennessee. Leading the Confederate advance was

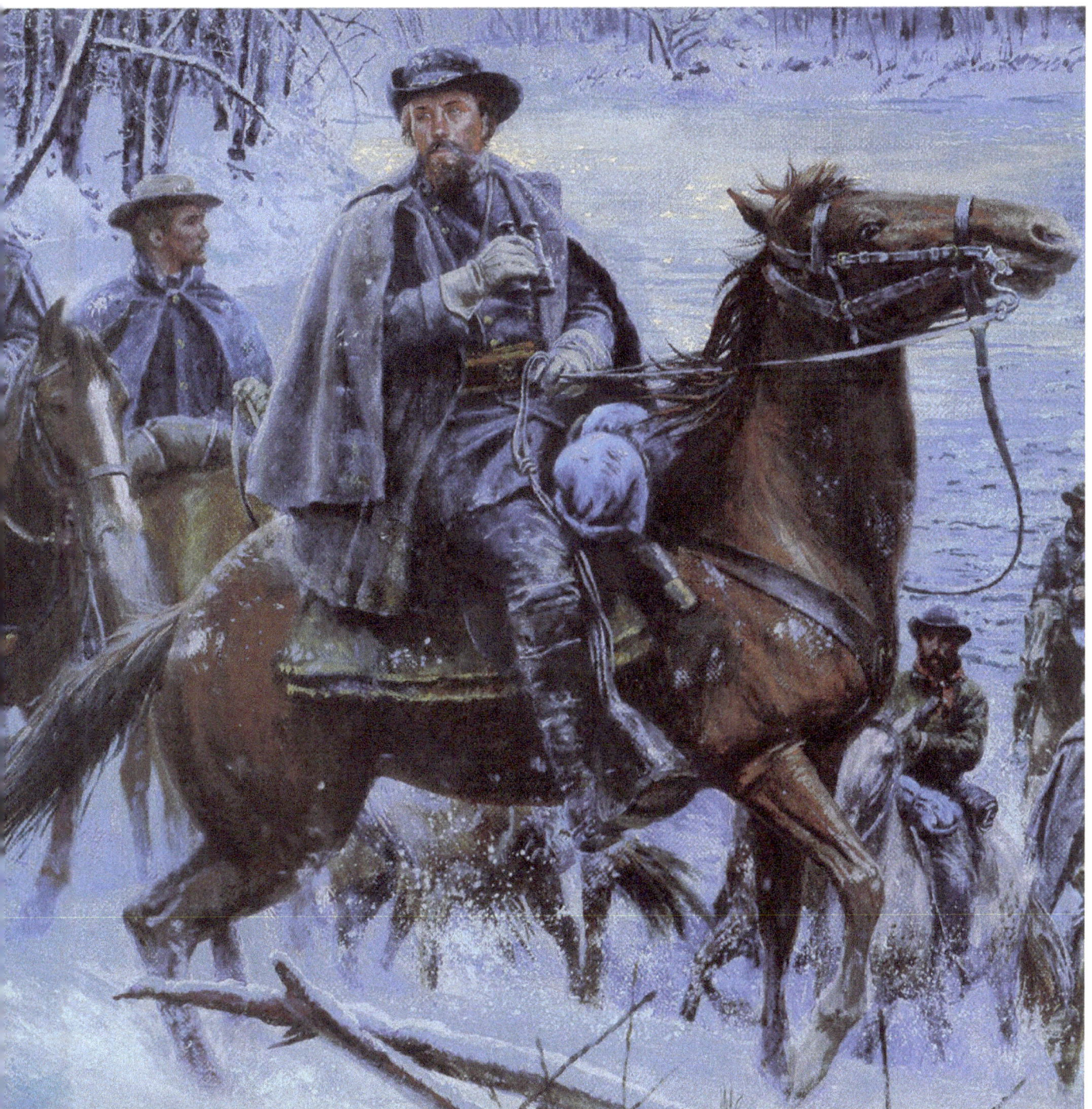

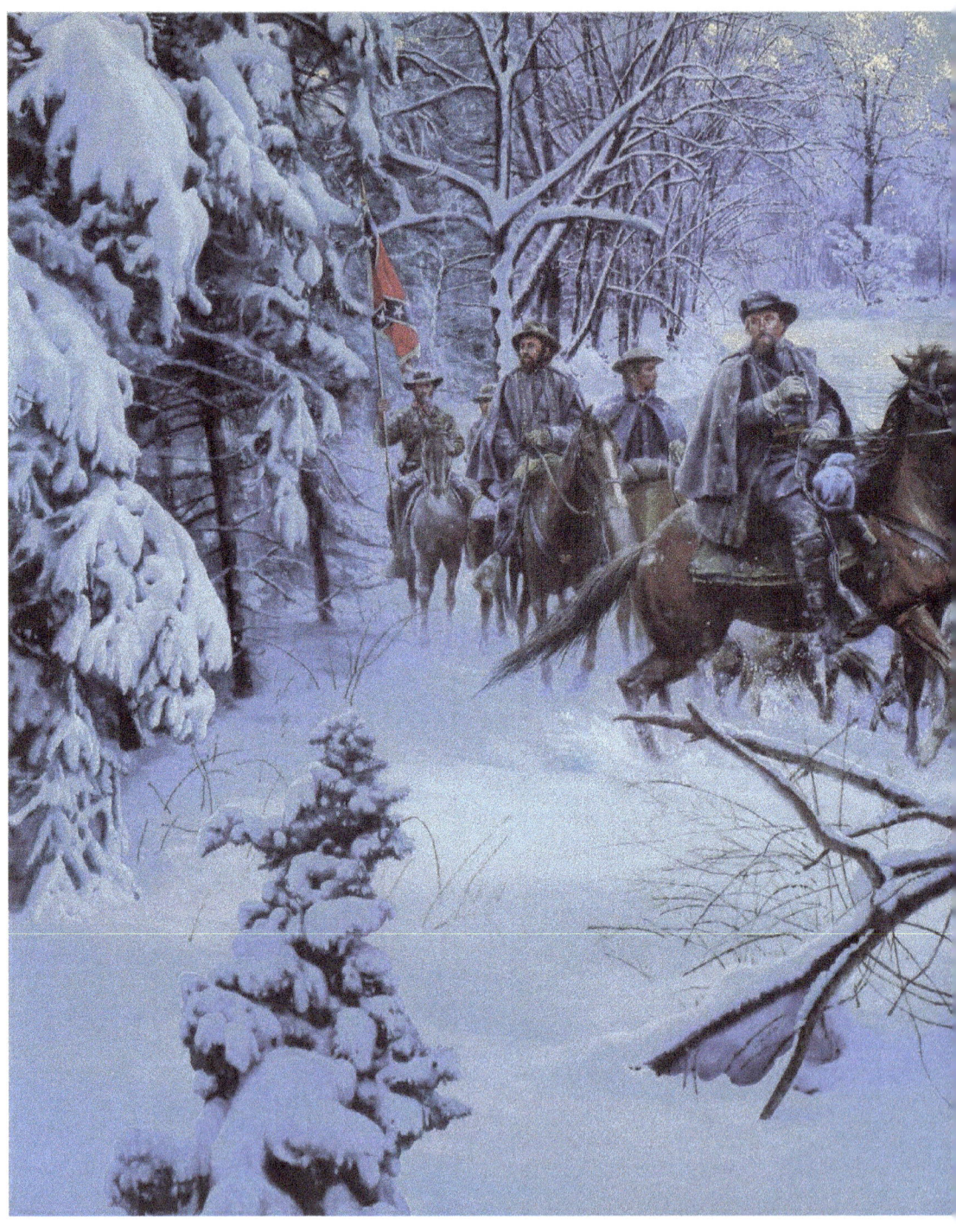

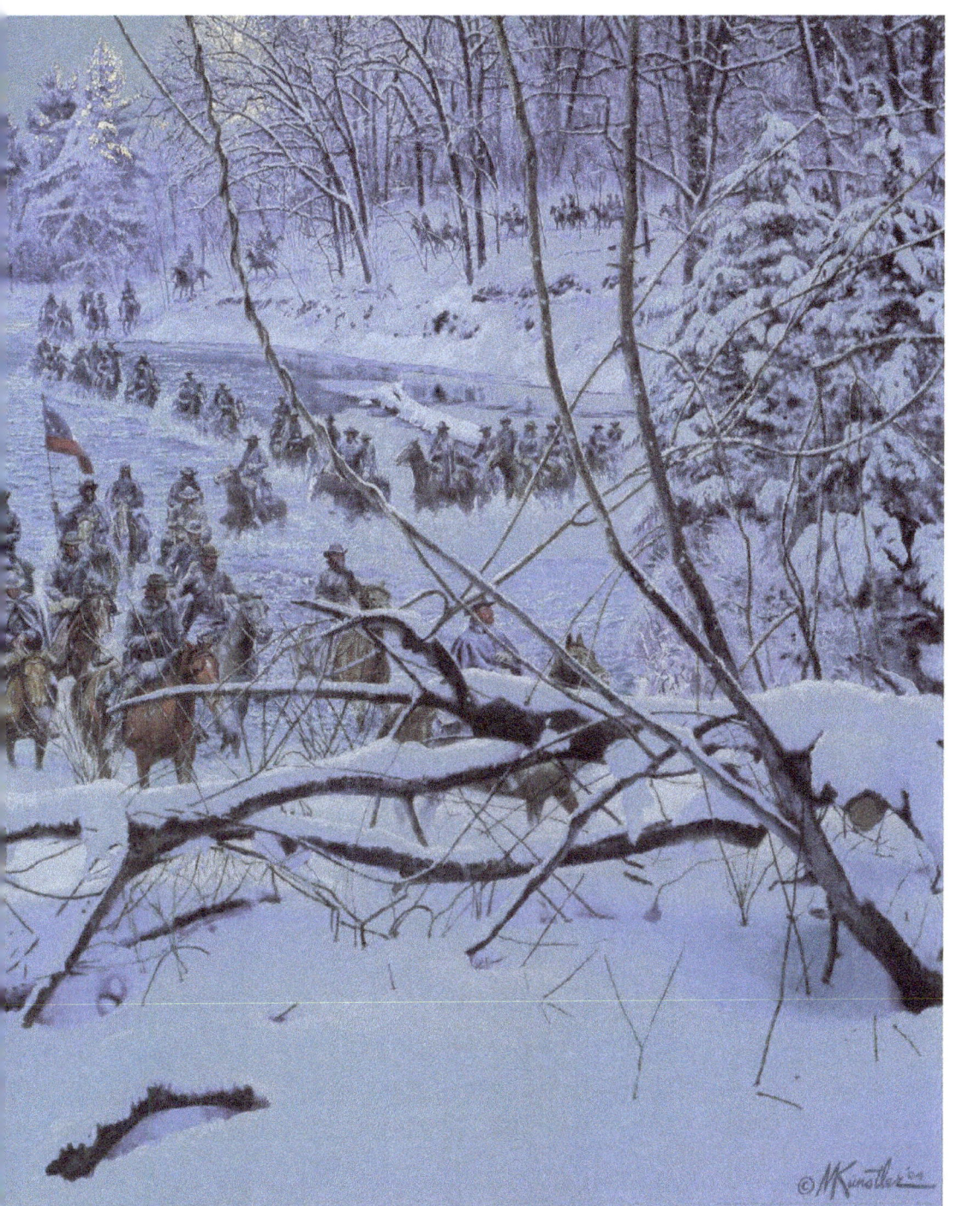

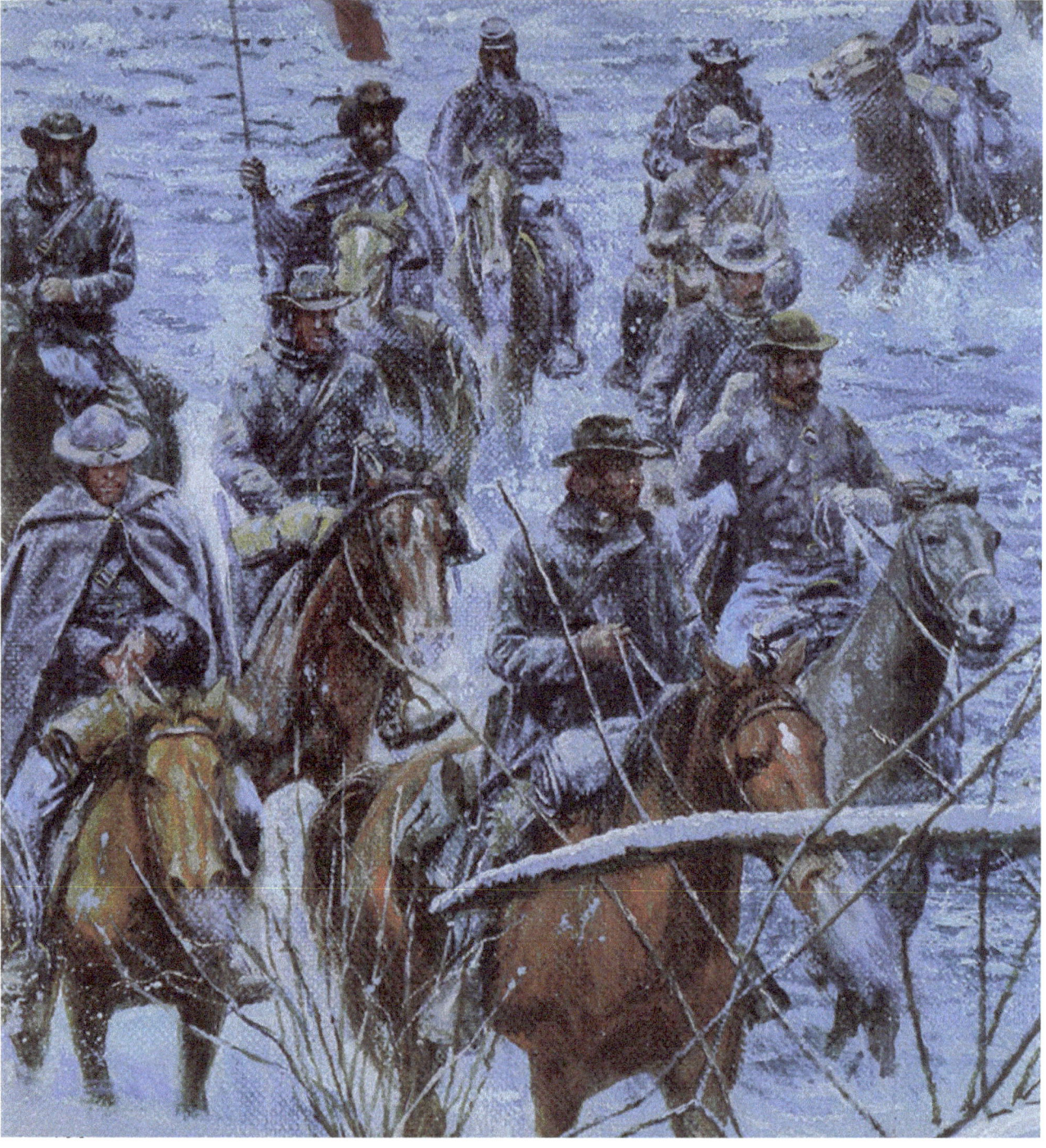

Gen. Nathan Bedford Forrest's cavalry, which forded the Duck River on November 28 and spearheaded the attack.

While ultimately having no effect on the outcome of the campaign, Forrest and his cavalry aggressively engaged the forces before them—driving back cavalry, pressing the infantry, and attacking supply trains.

This painting depicts an obscure event that was overshadowed by a disastrous military campaign. Brian Steel Wills's excellent biography of Forrest, *The Confederacy's Greatest Cavalryman,* observed that Forrest always moved quickly while always remaining alert to danger. That's the emotion I hope to convey in this picture. Here Forrest is seen advancing with troops commanded by Col. Jacob B. Biffle (pictured immediately behind Forrest) as they ford the river. It was undoubtedly a tense moment: Federals might have opened fire on them from a riverside ambush. Fortunately for the Southerners, they crossed unopposed—but the day was cold, the snow was thick, and the water was icy.

I positioned the viewpoint of the painting so that the sunlight draws the viewer's eye to Forrest, emphasizing his prominence and giving depth to the picture. By taking a high viewpoint, I was able to paint a more panoramic vista and get more than sixty horses and riders into the painting. By depicting the last rider coming into the picture in the extreme upper-right corner of the painting, I created a sense of flow that encourages viewers to feel what it would be like to glimpse the passing of a large body of cavalry

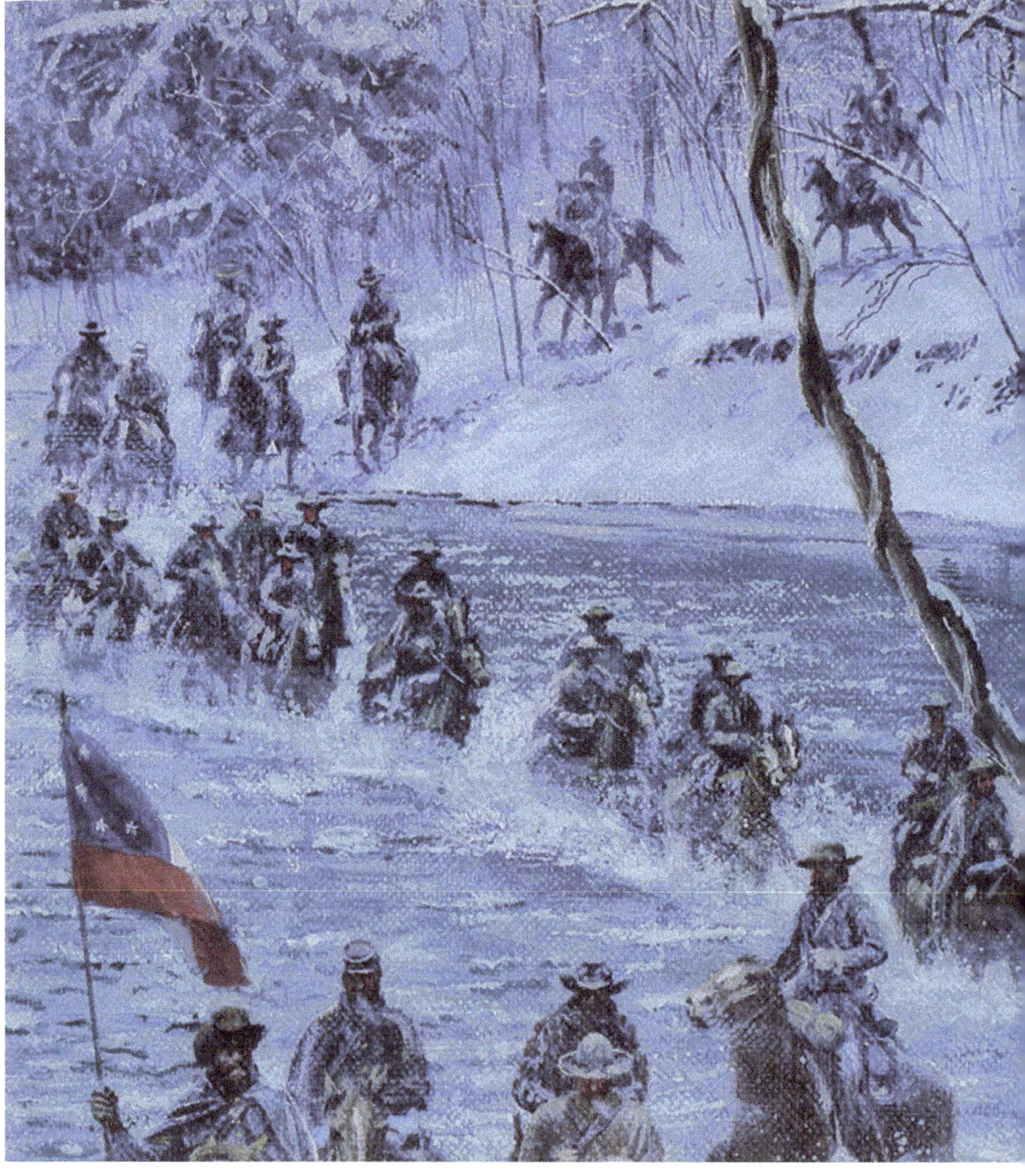

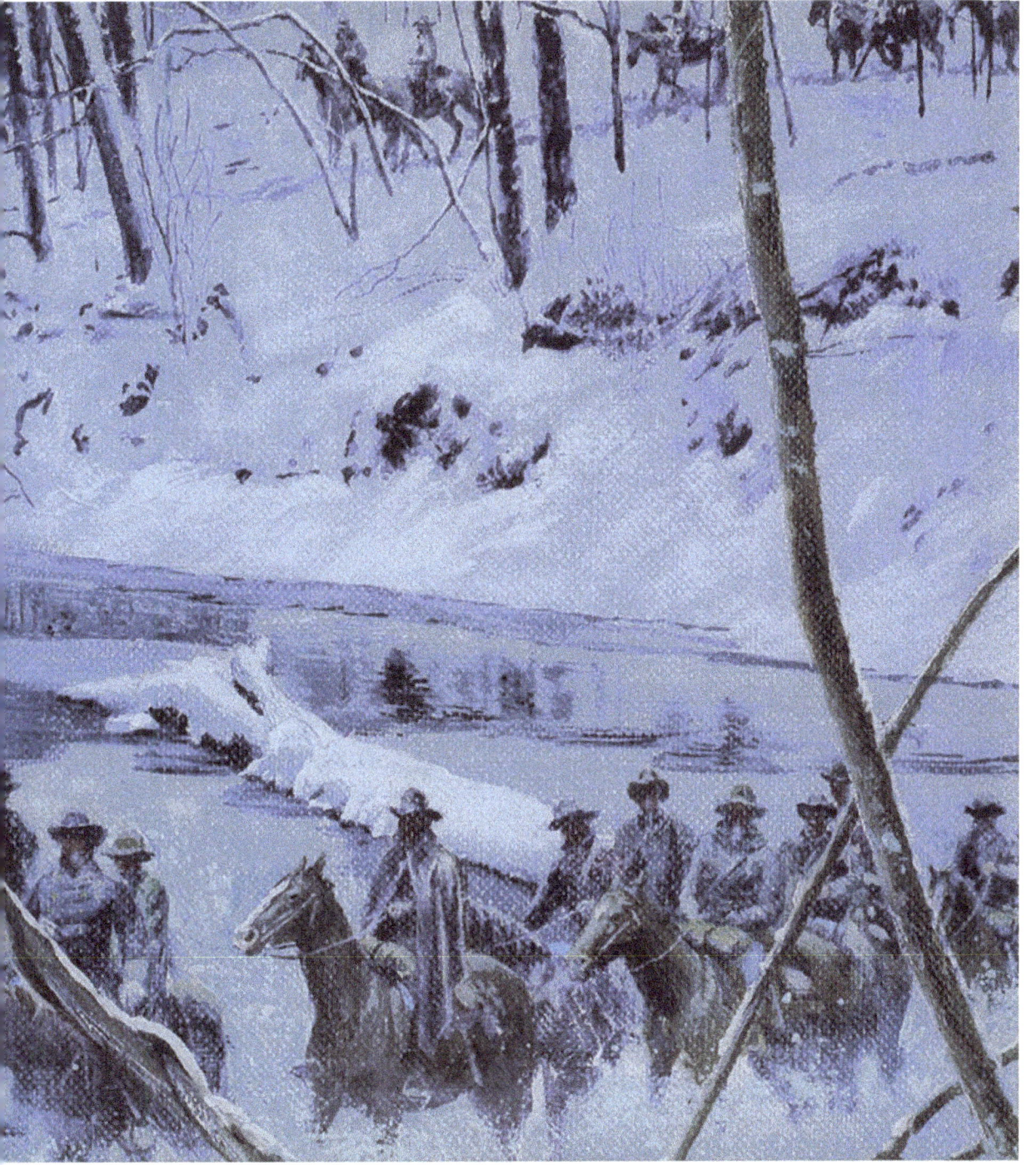

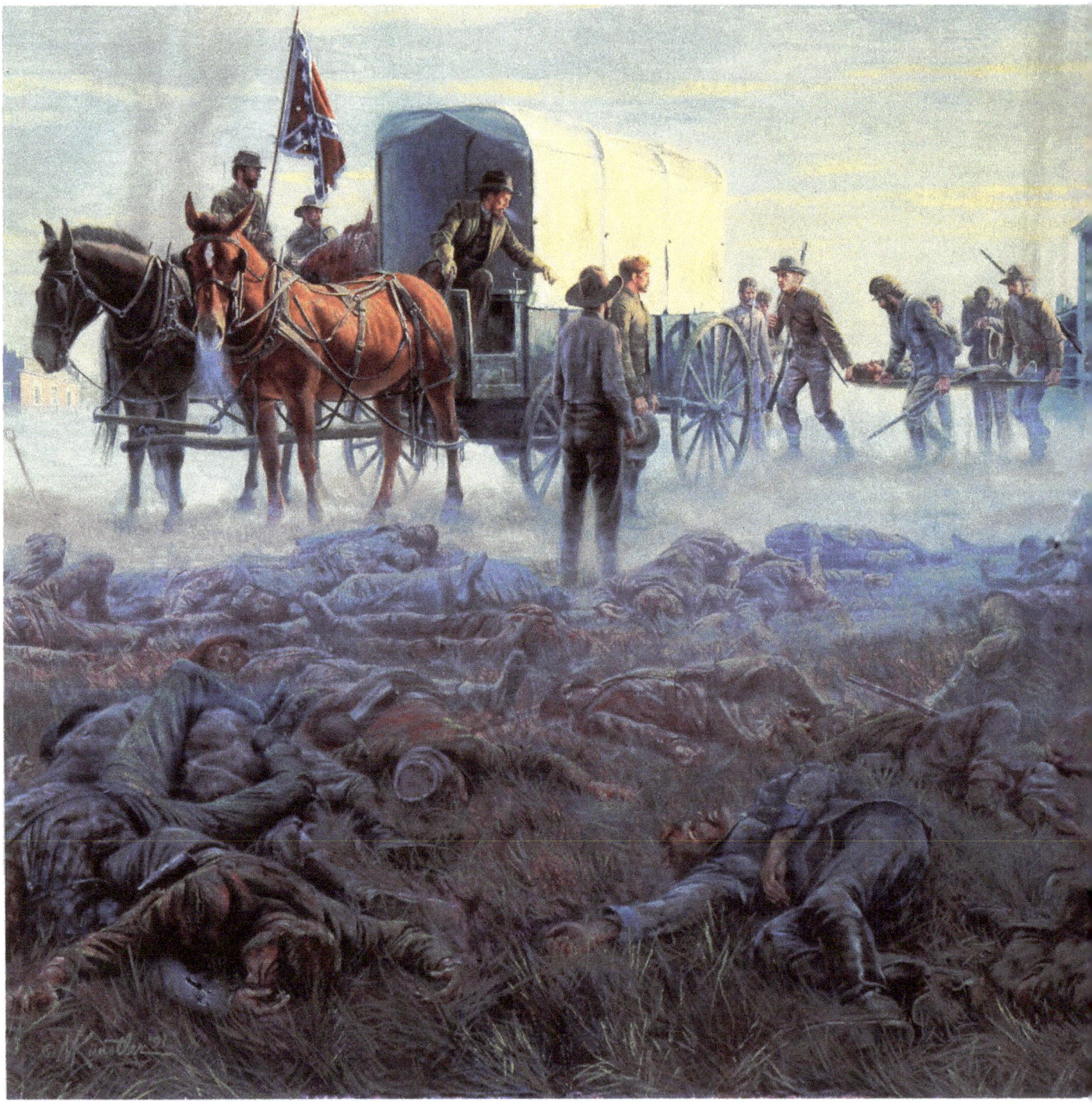

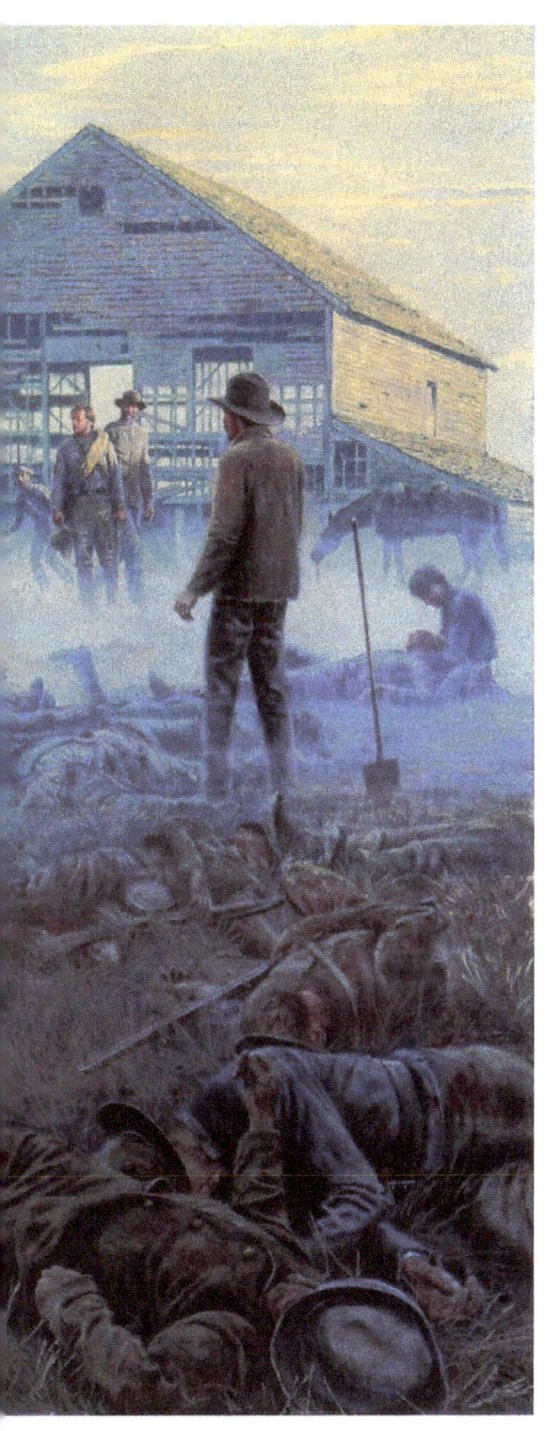

 ## BRINGING CLEBURNE IN

FRANKLIN, TENNESSEE

DECEMBER 1, 1864

1991, oil, 24 x 36

Iɴ ʟᴀᴛᴇ Nᴏᴠᴇᴍʙᴇʀ 1864, Hood's Army of Tennessee closed in on Schofield's smaller force near the town of Franklin, Tennessee. The night before, Hood believed he had trapped Schofield near Spring Hill, but confused orders and carelessness allowed the Federals not only to evade the trap but to march past the sleeping Confederate army Hood awoke the next morning enraged by the news that his prey had escaped. He rushed his army in pursuit of Schofield, but to do so, they moved in "light marching order," that is, without artillery and supply wagons.

When Schofield arrived in Franklin in the morning on November 30, he found the two

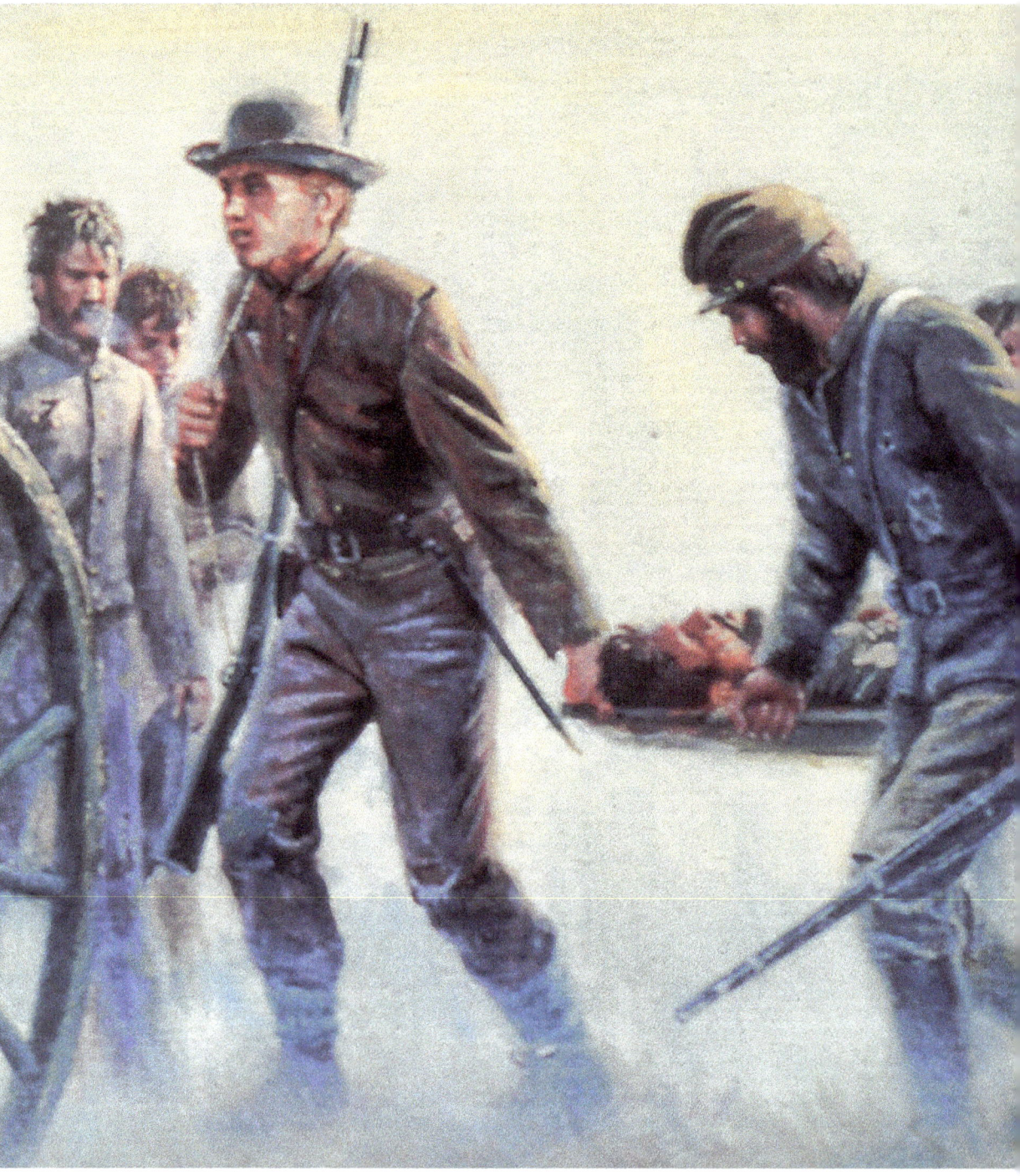

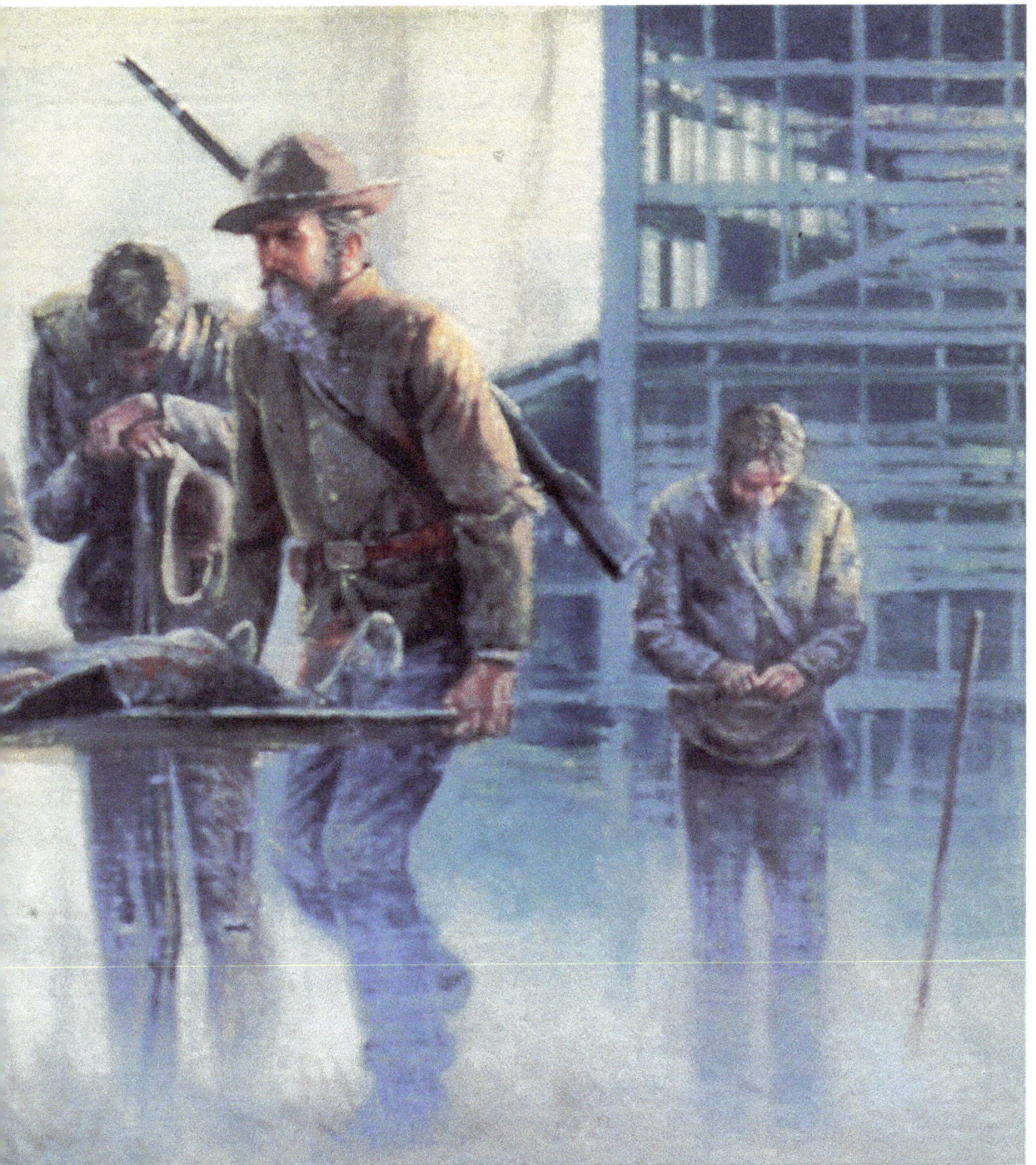

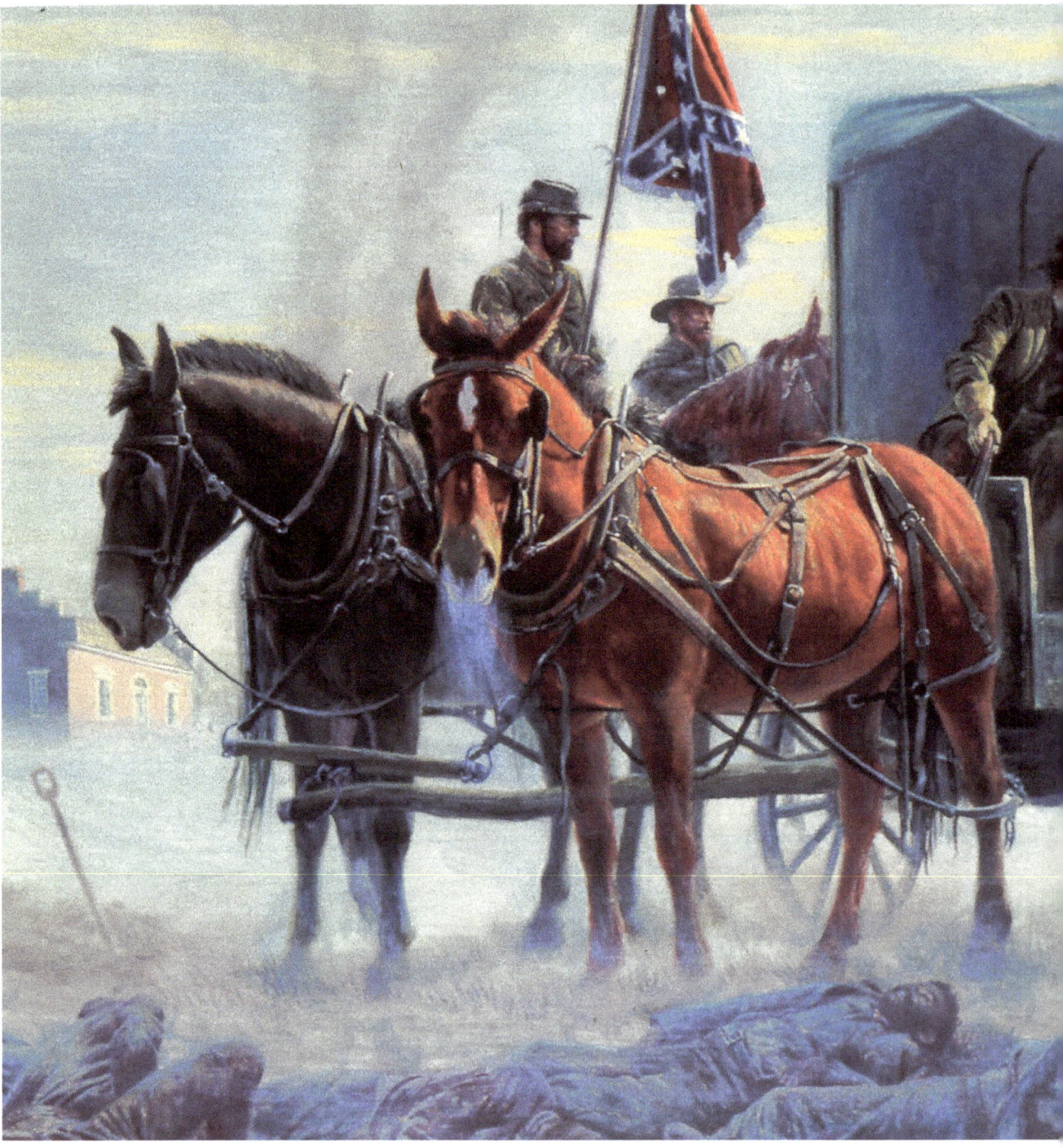

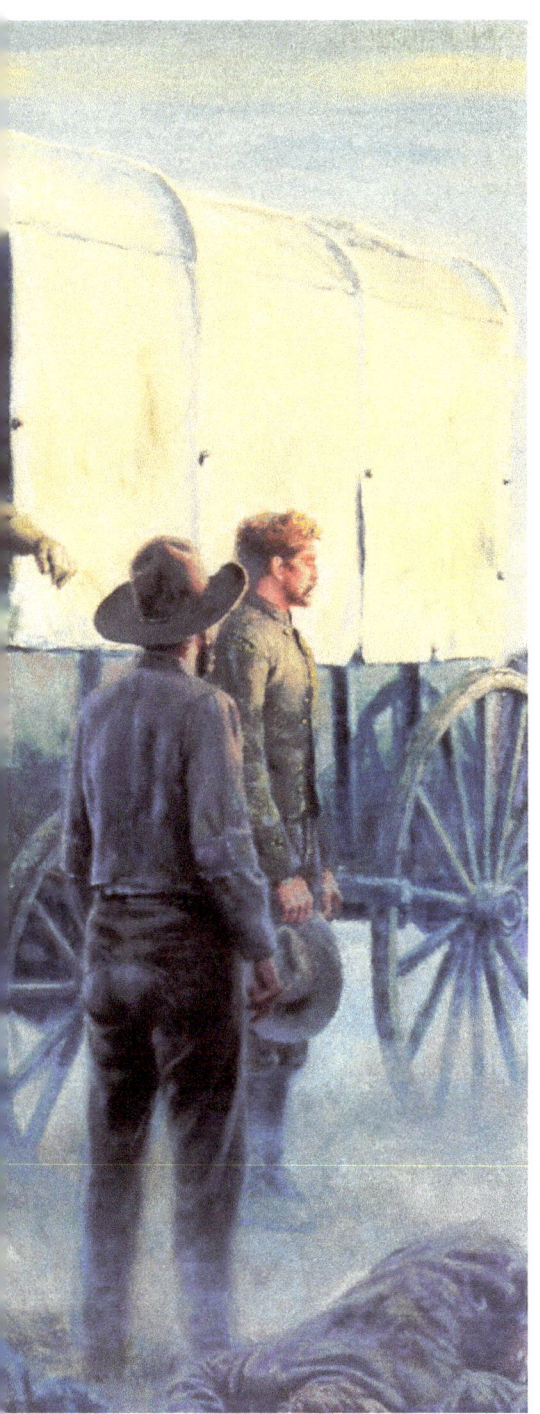

bridges across the Harpeth River unusable. While his engineers repaired them, his exhausted army repaired former breastworks around the city and rested. Hood's army appeared on the scene shortly after noon and began to form battle lines for a frontal assault across two miles of open ground. Despite objections from his subordinate commanders, Hood ordered the attack while there was little sunlight left to the day. During the next five hours of fighting, six Confederate generals were killed, five were wounded, and one was captured. When Hood's troops withdrew at 9:00 p.m., Schofield rushed his men across the river, fully abandoning the area by 2:00 a.m. and wrecking the bridges behind them.

Prior to dawn, Hood's artillery arrived and opened fire on the town, but there was no return Union fire. Scouts found the town abandoned, and Hood claimed the victory. But of the eighteen thousand Confederates who charged the Union line the previous night, more than six thousand became casualties, seventeen hundred of which were fatalities. Among them was Patrick Cleburne, the most promising general in Hood's army Cleburne's body was recovered near the cotton gin building of the Fountain Branch Carter farm.

In reality, the battle of Franklin was a devastating defeat for the Confederacy. After his third corps rejoined his army, Hood could only muster nineteen thousand men for his march on Nashville, where he would face seventy thousand waiting in the most fortified city on the continent. Hood's bravado at Franklin had gained nothing, and an army had been wasted when the South could ill afford to lose any potentially powerful force.

I tried to tell the story of Franklin in the most direct way possible—by showing the horrors of war with bodies strewn across the landscape. I used the early morning sun to focus attention on Cleburne as a work detail carries his body in front of the cotton gin building to an ambulance. All eyes are on him. But in the end, the viewer's eye finally comes to rest on the shadowy foreground and perceives the real message of the massive loss of life on this battlefield.

The Fountain Branch Carter House in Franklin

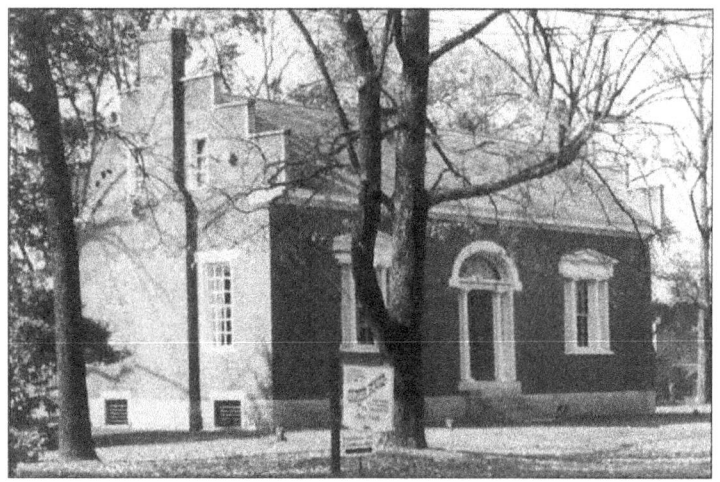

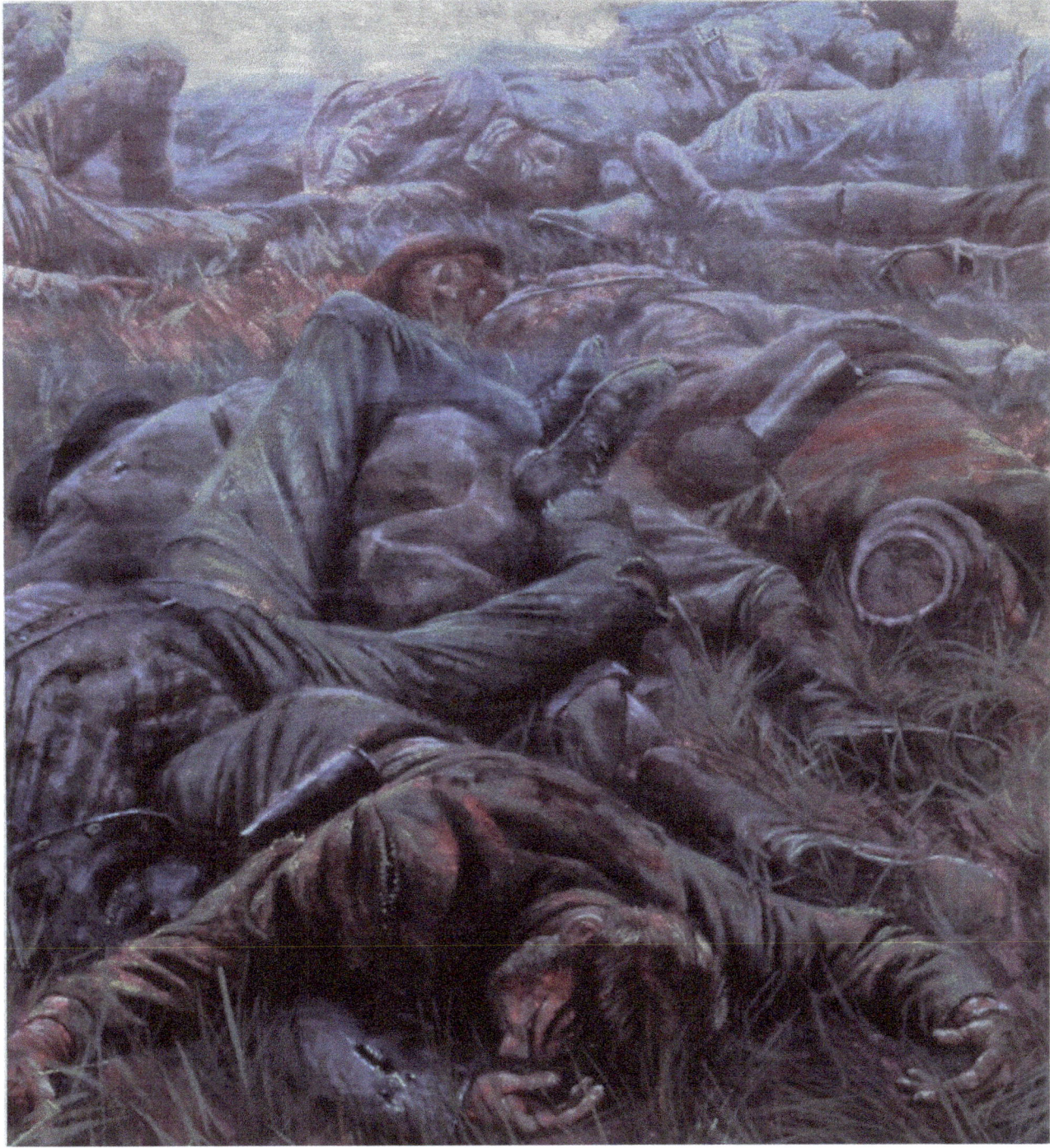

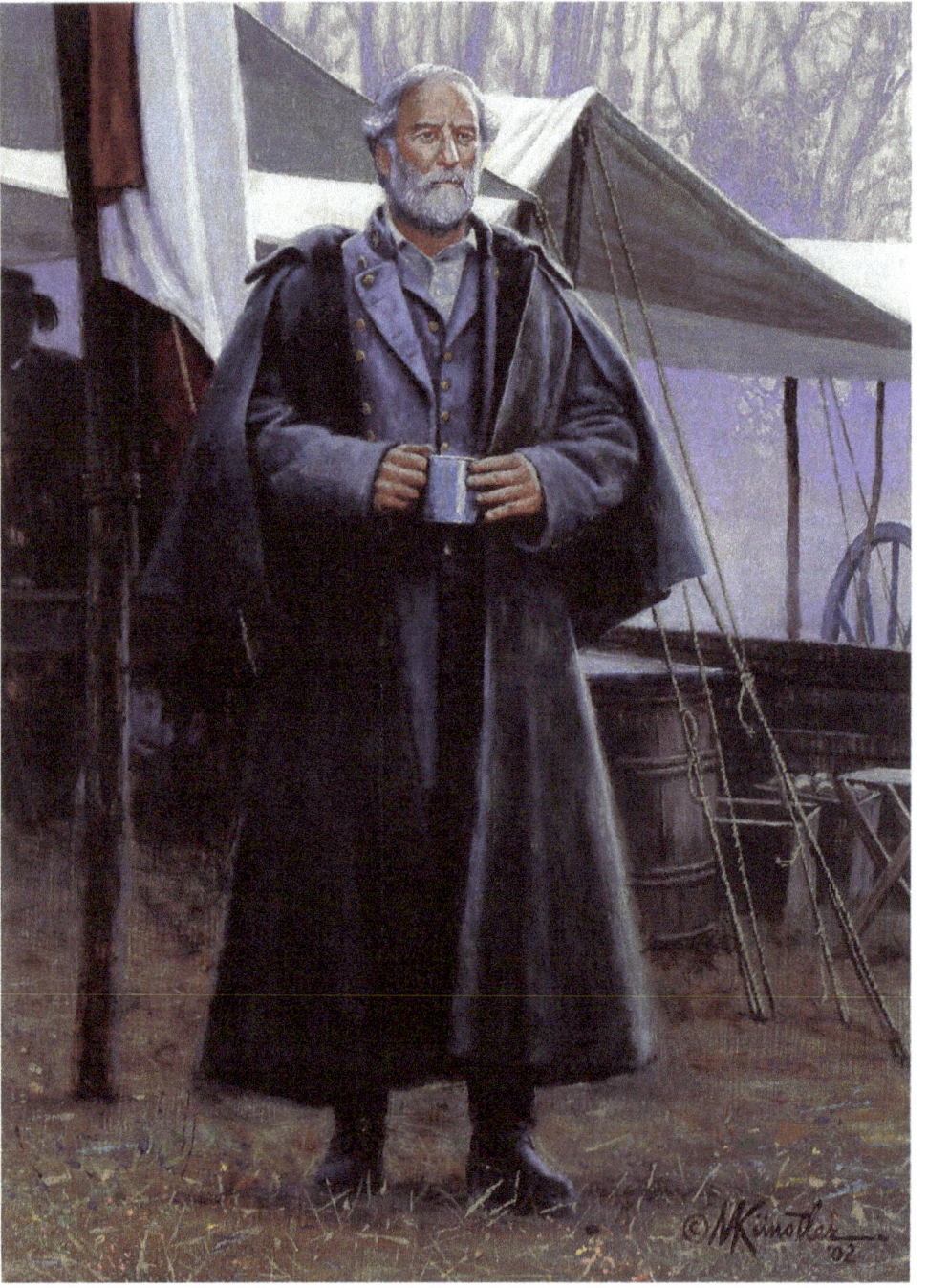

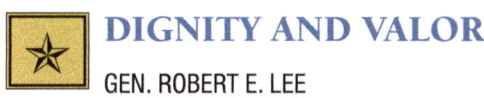

DIGNITY AND VALOR

GEN. ROBERT E. LEE

2002, oil, 11¼ x 8

AS FALL TURNED TO winter, all Lee could do was watch and react to whatever Grant's army did. Pinned down and besieged, he saw that the end was not far.

Lee would have preferred to keep his winter headquarters in camp, but others (including his wife and his staff) persuaded him to accept the invitation of a local family to spend the winter at their home two miles west of Petersburg. There, in addition to his duties to provide for the army, consult with the Davis administration, devise a bold move to break Grant's hold on the area, and resist the increasing pressure of the Union buildup in front of him, Lee found himself close enough to his family to visit them occasionally in Richmond, although he never stayed away from the army for more than a day at a time.

As Lee anticipated the spring, Douglas Southall Freeman noted, "All that [he] had learned in nearly four years of war, all that his quiet energy inspired, all that his associates could suggest or his official superiors devise—all was thrown into a last effort to organize and strengthen the thin, shivering, hungry Army of Northern Virginia for the last grapple with the well-fed, well-clad, ever-increasing host that crowded the countryside opposite Lee's lines."

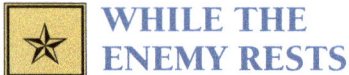

WHILE THE ENEMY RESTS

PARIS MOUNTAIN, VIRGINIA
DECEMBER 1, 1864

1997, oil, 24 x 38

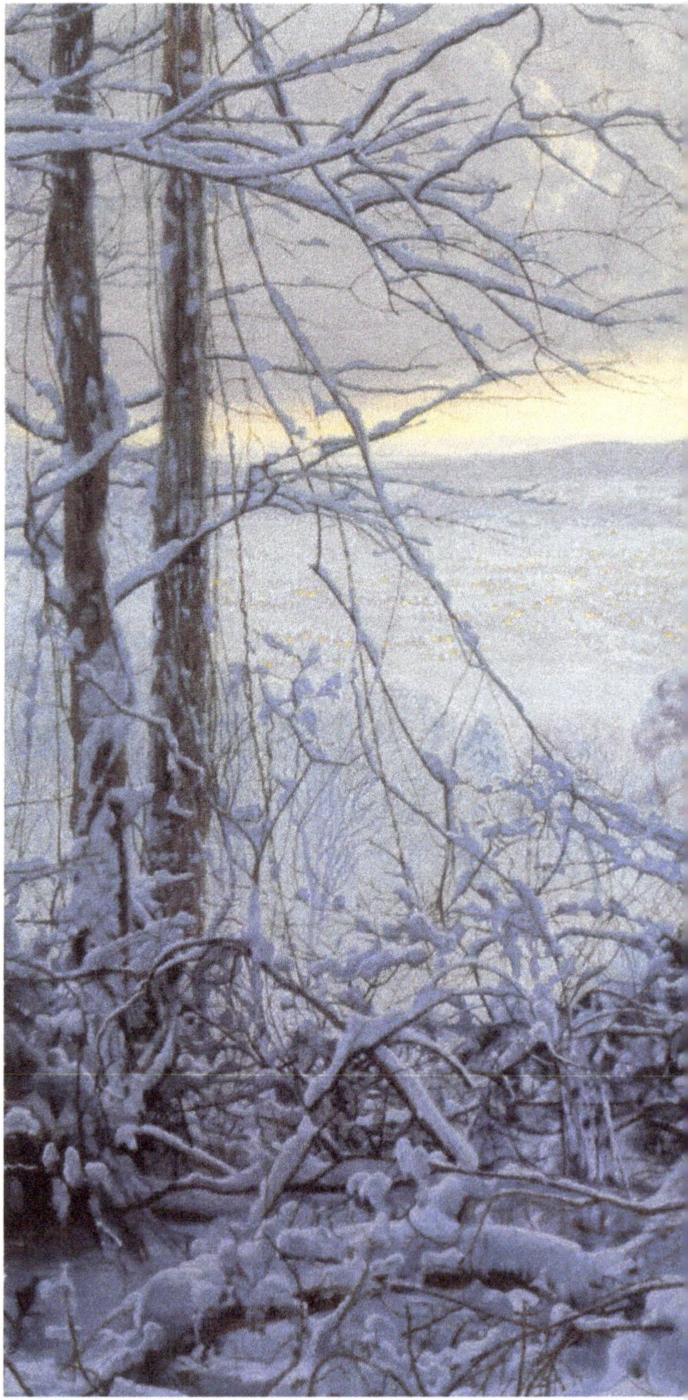

AFTER THE BATTLE OF Cedar Creek, the Confederate army withdrew from the Shenandoah Valley. Sheridan's army now turned its attention to Loudoun and Fauquier counties, where irregular troops such as Mosby's Rangers, a loosely organized but motivated force, had for almost two years successfully harassed Union troops and disrupted communication and supplies in the region. In late 1864, Maj. John S. Mosby's command consisted of about four hundred men.

Previous efforts to rid the area of partisans had been frustrated by

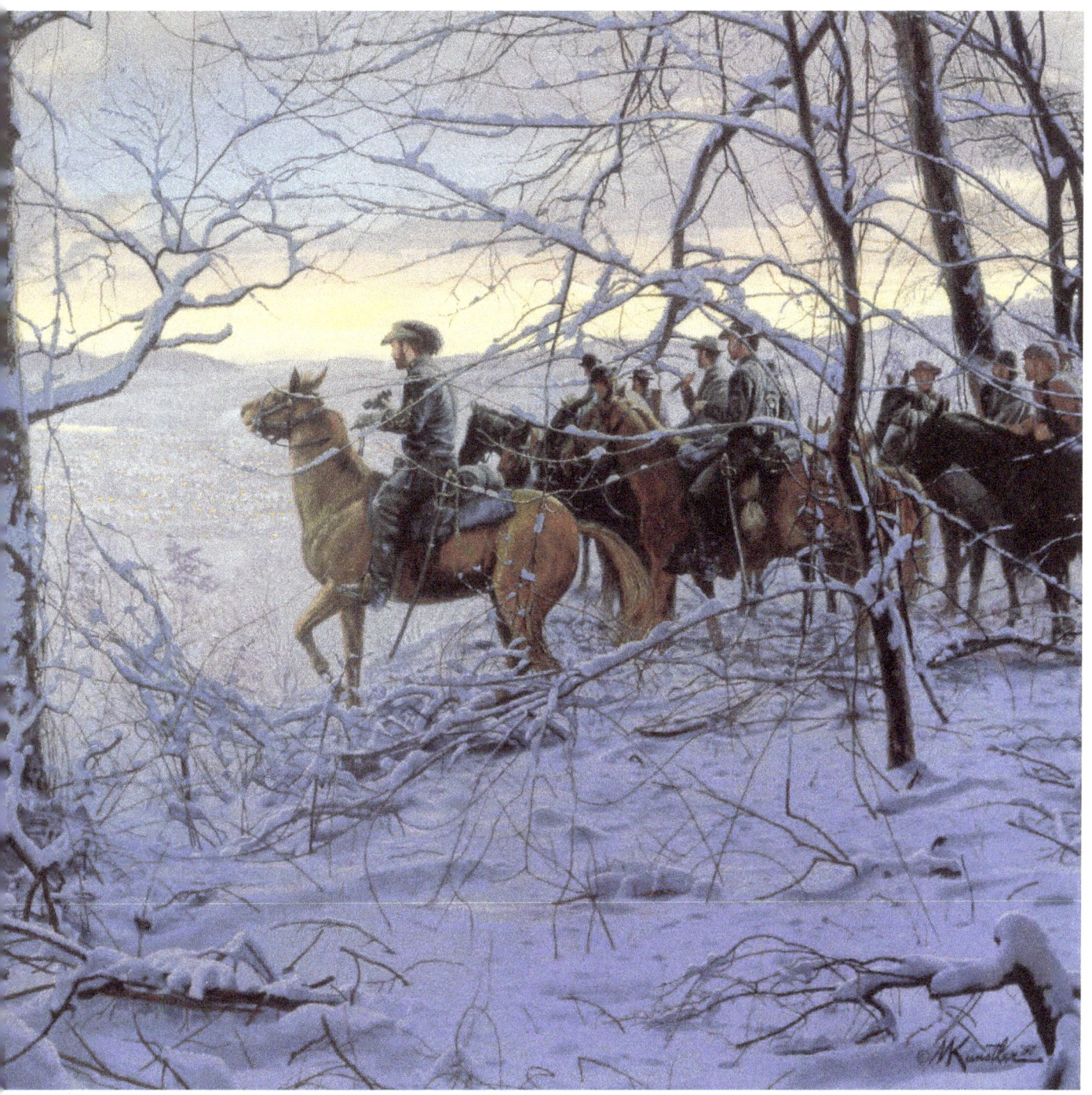

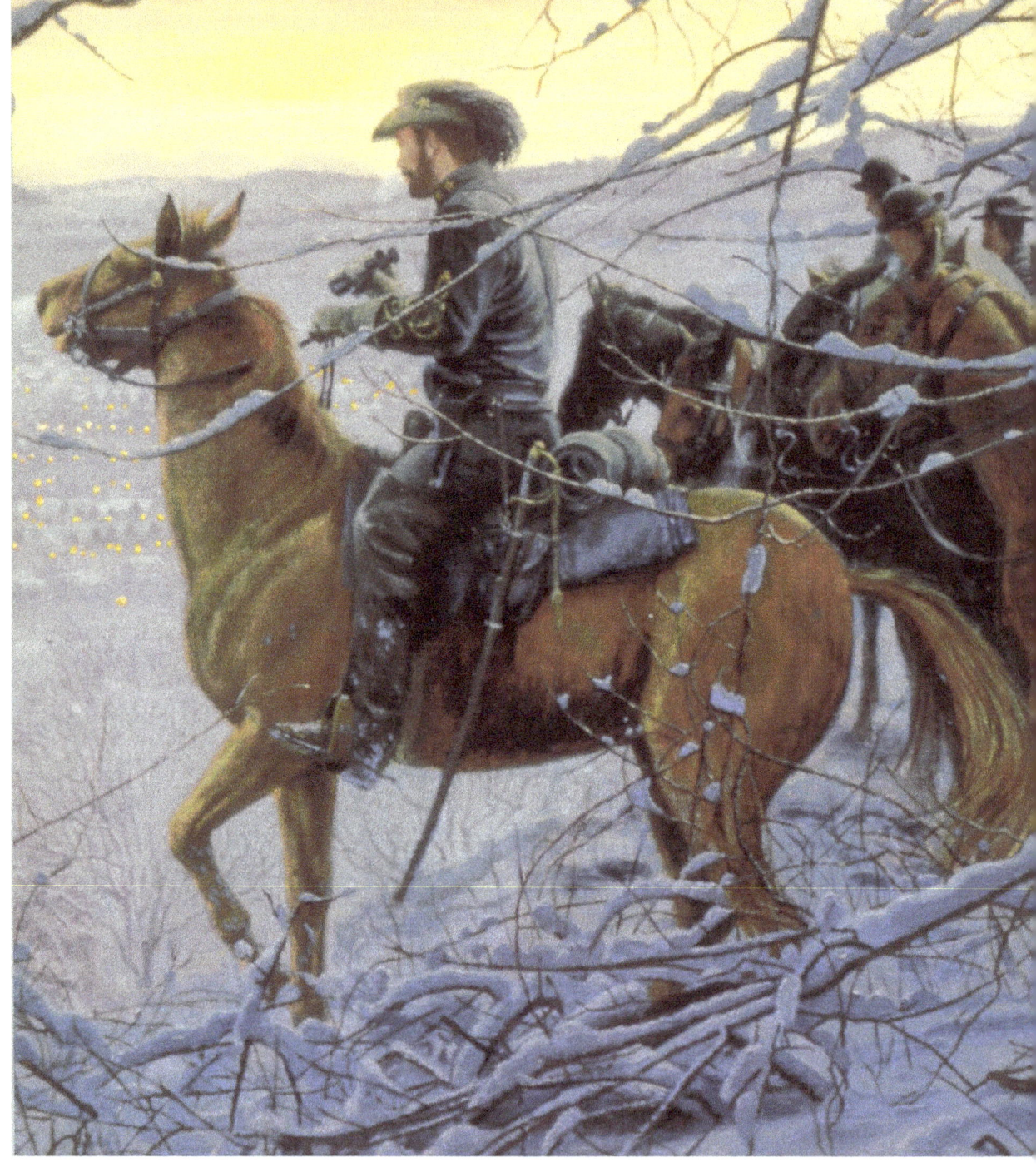

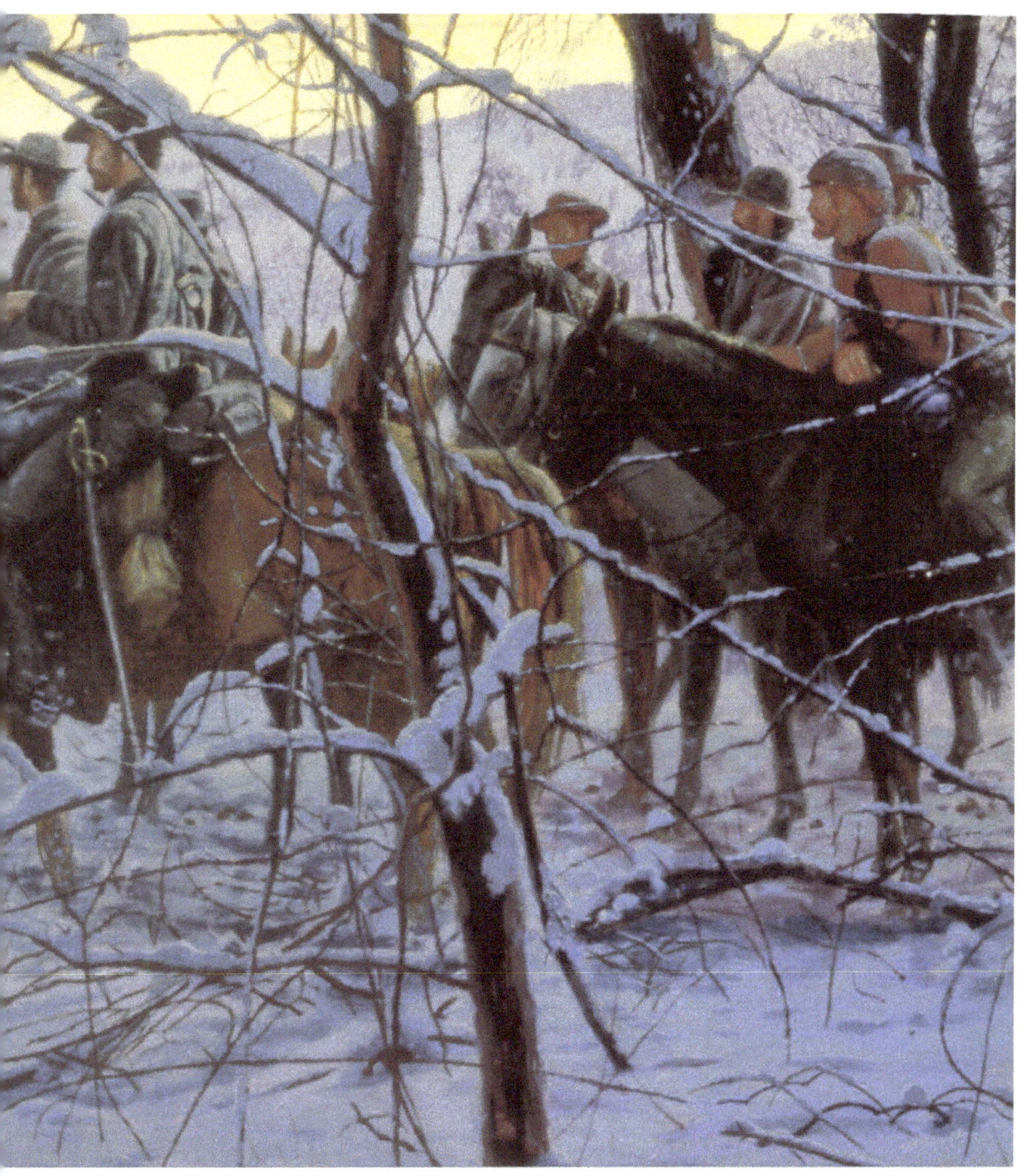

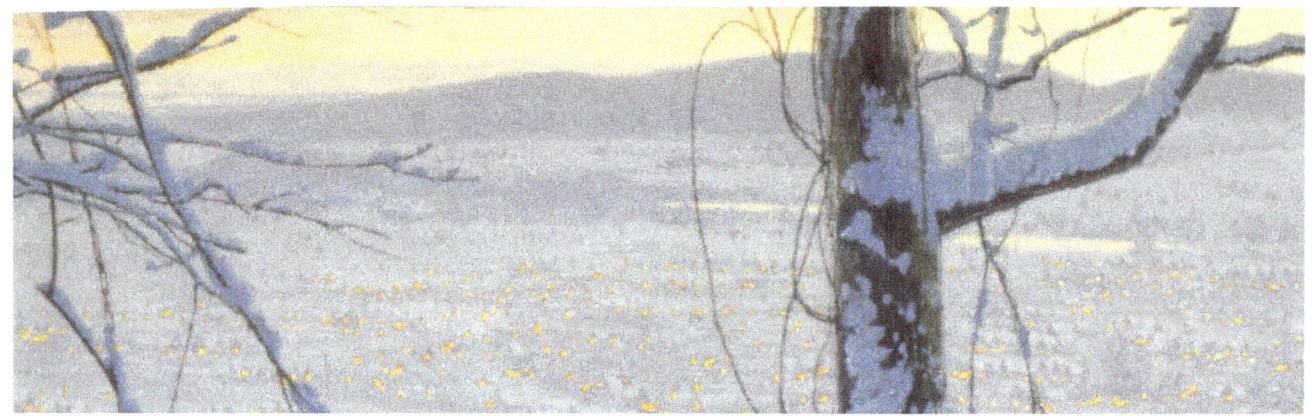

Mosby's guerrilla tactics. Now, Sheridan chose to attack Mosby's support system rather than exhaust his efforts on pointless pursuits of small groups of men who knew how to disappear easily into the woods and hills. Thus he initiated a scorched-earth policy to destroy crops, burn barns and mills and their contents, and drive off all livestock. On November 28, 1864, the campaign began; progress was easily charted by noting the advancing columns of black smoke and the spreading smell of burning hay, corn, and wheat.

Mosby recognized the handwriting on the wall. The destruction of forage meant that his men's horses could not be sustained. While the Union army engaged in the "Burning Raid," he ceased operations here and then traveled to meet with Lee at Petersburg. The time had come to divide his command and reallocate his resources to other areas to better serve the cause.

The idea for this painting came to me from David Falkenstein, a Civil War enthusiast in Strasburg, Virginia, who suggested a wintry Mosby image to me in a letter. Historian Jeffry Wert, author of *Mosby's Rangers,* recommended Paris Mountain to me as the background. In composing the image, I decided to time the setting at sunset for a dramatic lighting effect: nightfall contrasted with the striking streak of light at the horizon that marks the setting of the sun. Timing the piece at sunset also allowed me to show a panorama of glowing campfires with dramatic orange reflections on two of the three lakes in the Valley. This view, looking south, is recognizable from Route 50, which is also known as the John S. Mosby Highway.

The poses of the men and horses are also important. The field glasses and telescope show the men scouting the enemy camp, not riding into their own encampment. All of the horses are still—except Mosby's. The movement of his horse, along with the break in the horizon by his black-feathered hat, draws the viewer's eye toward Mosby. Somewhat subtly, the setting sun also conveys the passing of Mosby's Confederacy and the end of this era.

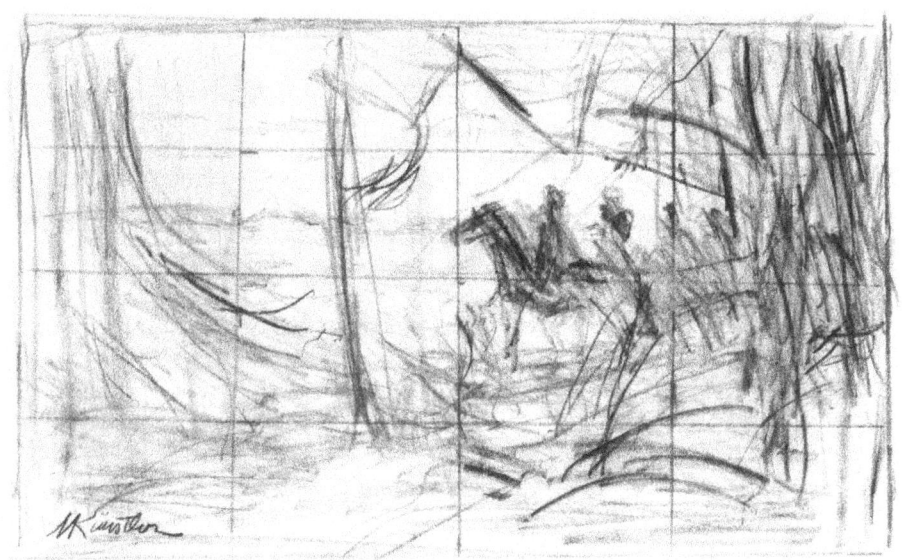

CONFEDERATE CHRISTMAS

1992, oil, 28 x 48

CHRISTMAS 1864 WAS NOT a particularly joyful time for the South, but for some time I had wanted to do a Christmas painting. The inspiration for *Confederate Christmas* came from a wartime etching discovered by Ted Sutphen of American Print Gallery in Gettysburg; at the time, he was my publisher of limited-edition prints.

After I studied the original etching, I began planning my own painting. Why not show the troops marching through the woods? Why not a snow scene? Why not set the scene at night and introduce torches to make the painting more dramatic? In addition to the artillery unit hauling the tree to its camp, why not add some infantry for variety?

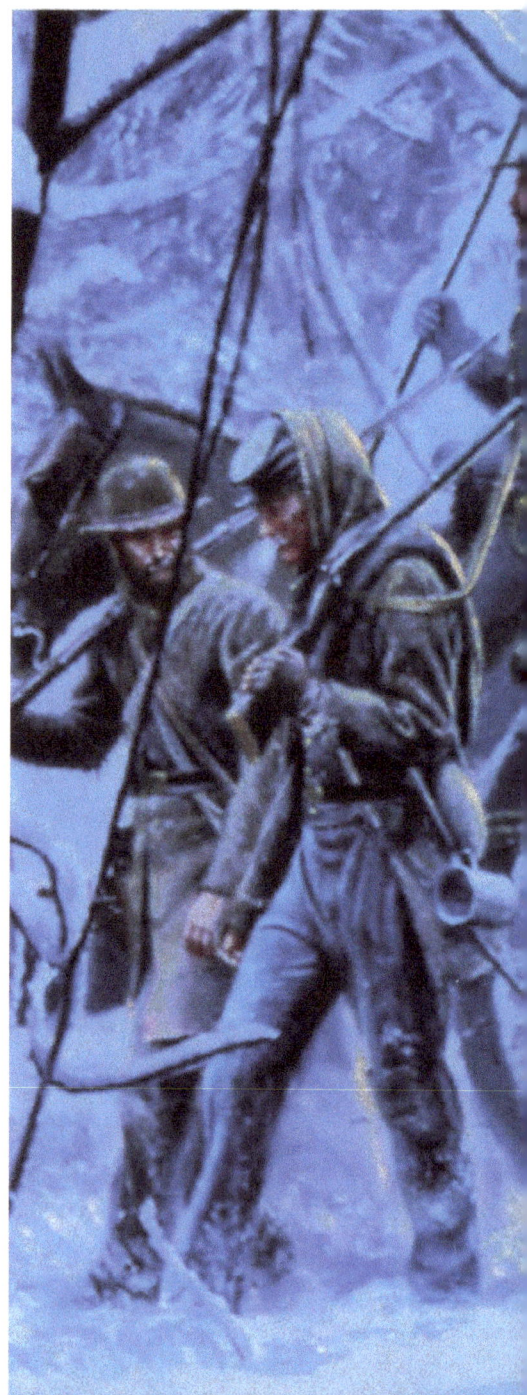

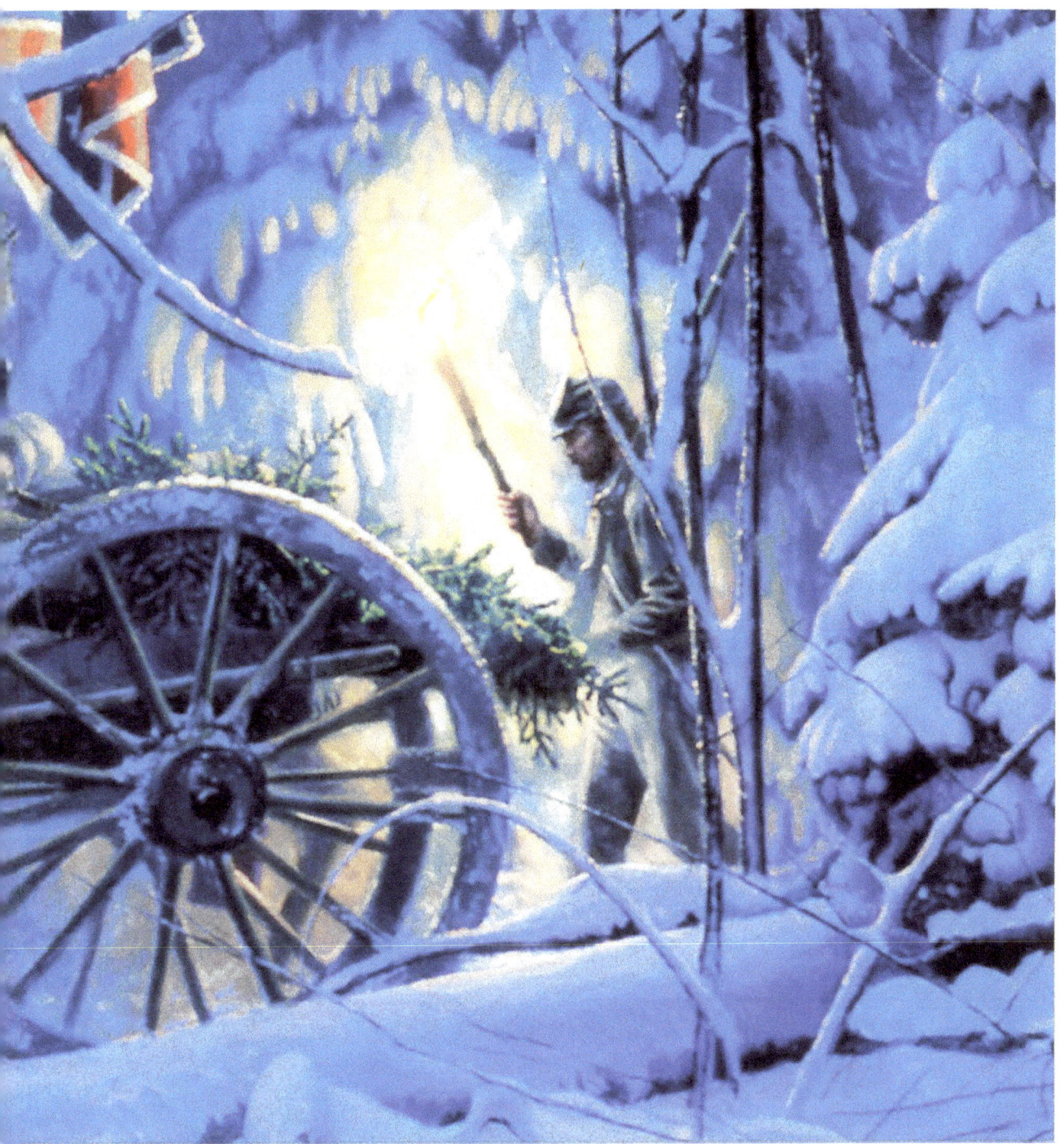

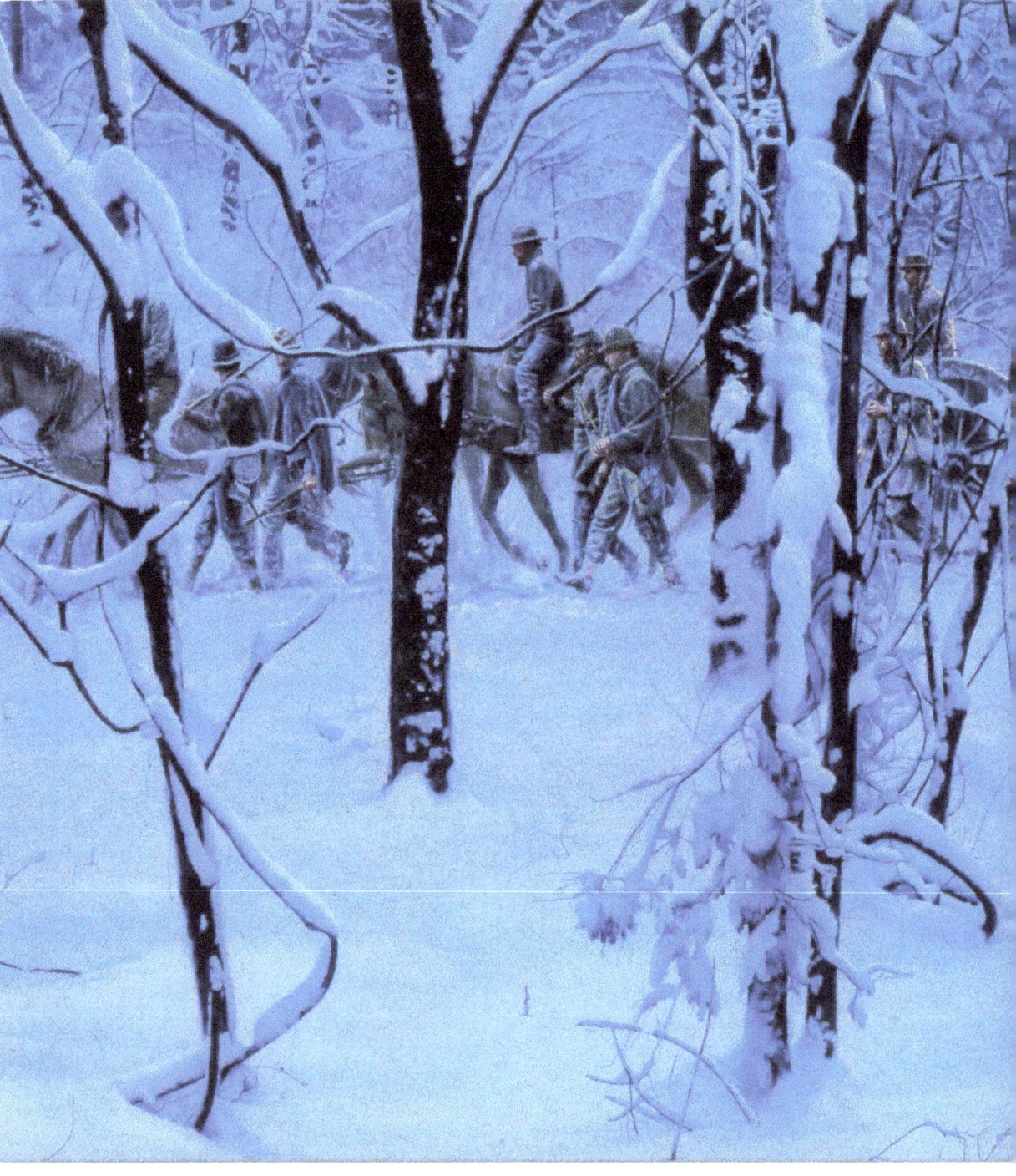

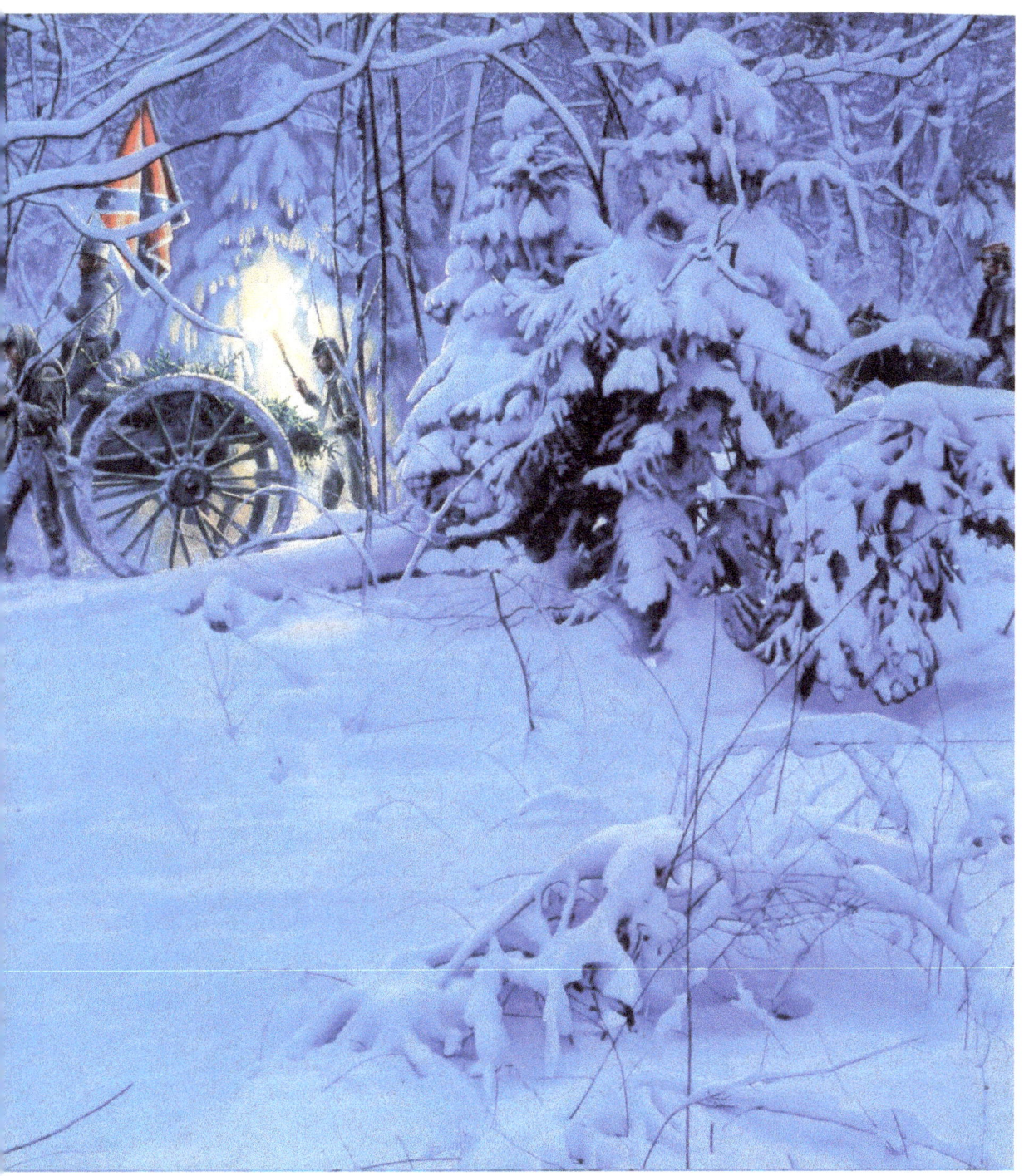

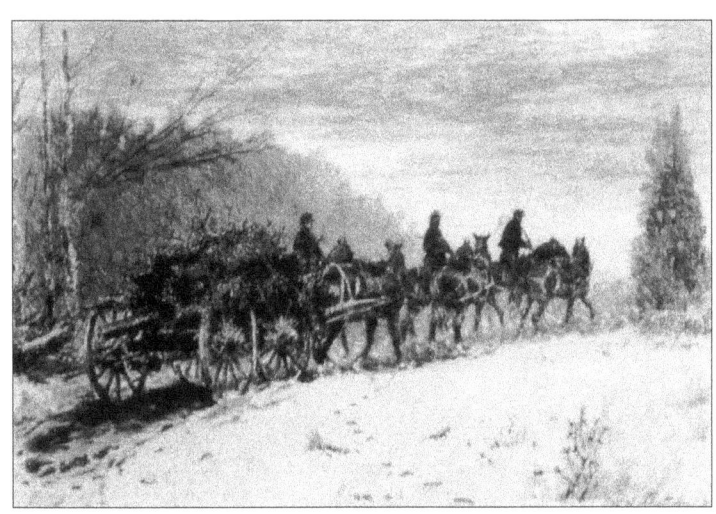

The nineteenth-century etching that inspired *Confederate Christmas*

Then I prepared some thumbnail sketches—small, crude scribbles—to explore these possibilities; I experimented with the soldiers. Should they be coming toward the viewer? heading away? march in profile? My thumbnail sketches became rough compositions and the basis for the final painting. The resulting scene is full of contrasts: the hint of war conveyed by the soldiers' uniforms and weapons and the white serenity of a snow-covered landscape at Christmastime. This time of year is a time of hope, and for many in Confederate gray and butternut, it was the last hopeful season they had before Sherman's army began its advance into South Carolina and the encircling Federals at Petersburg marched forward, toward Richmond.

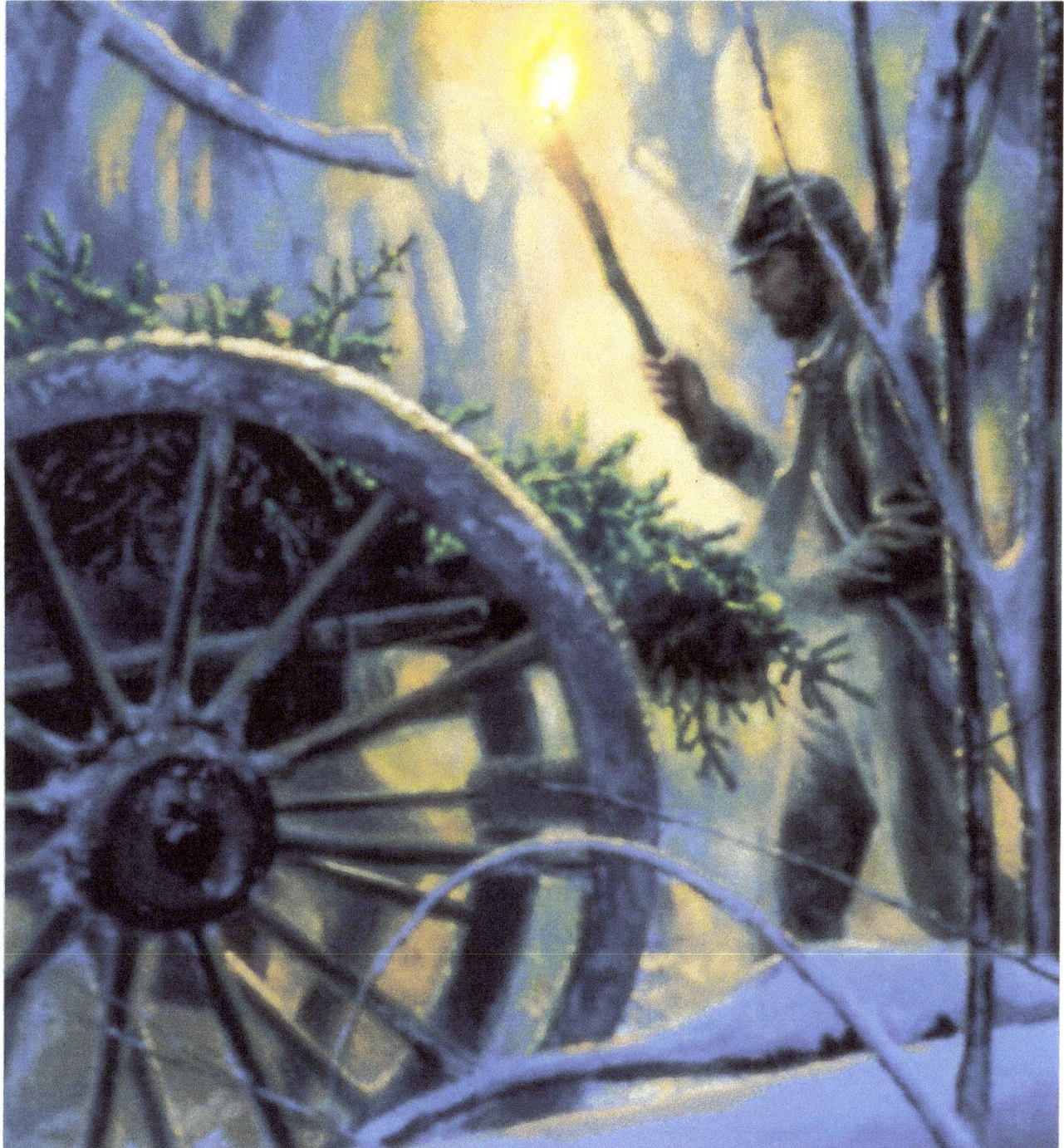

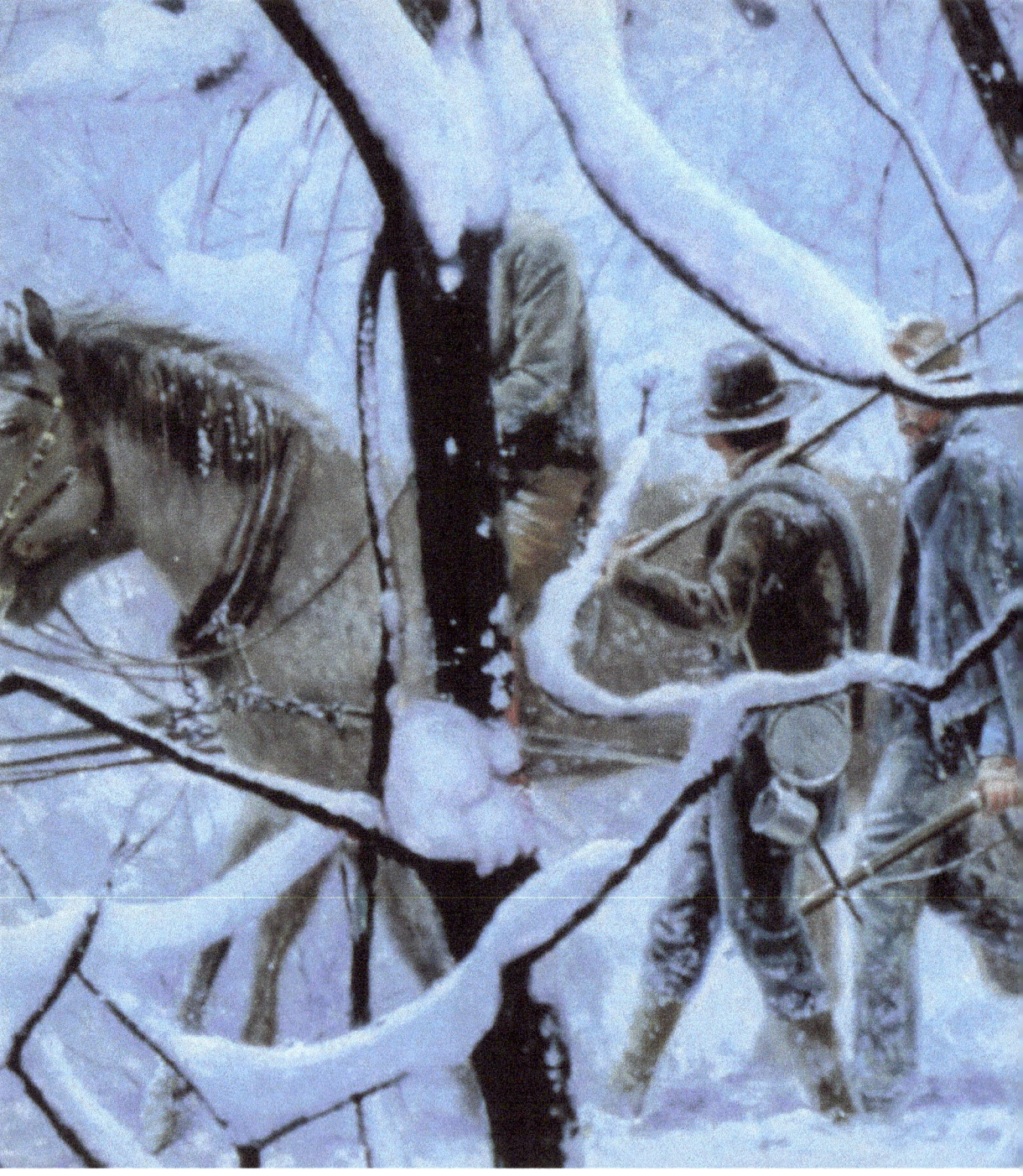

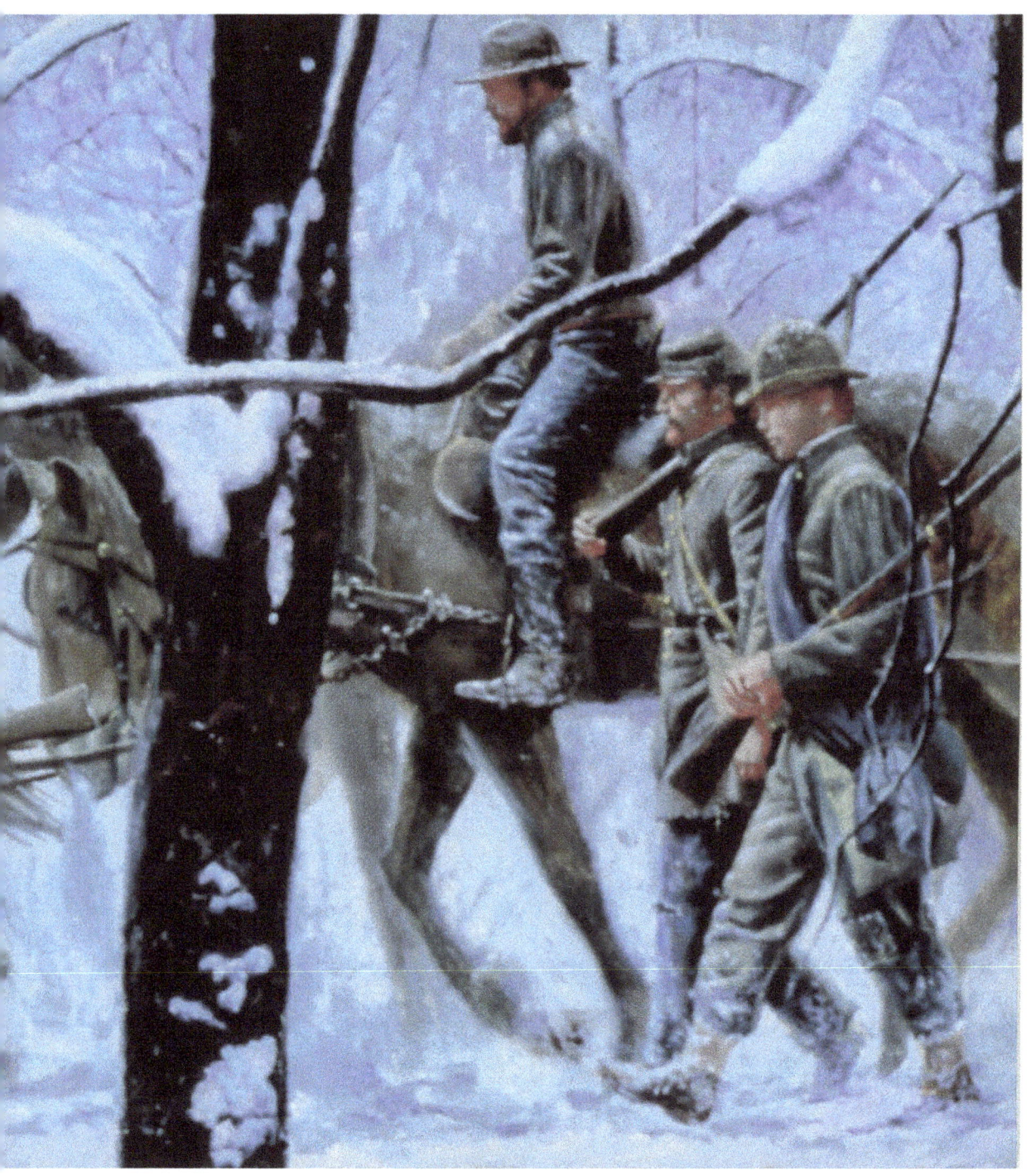

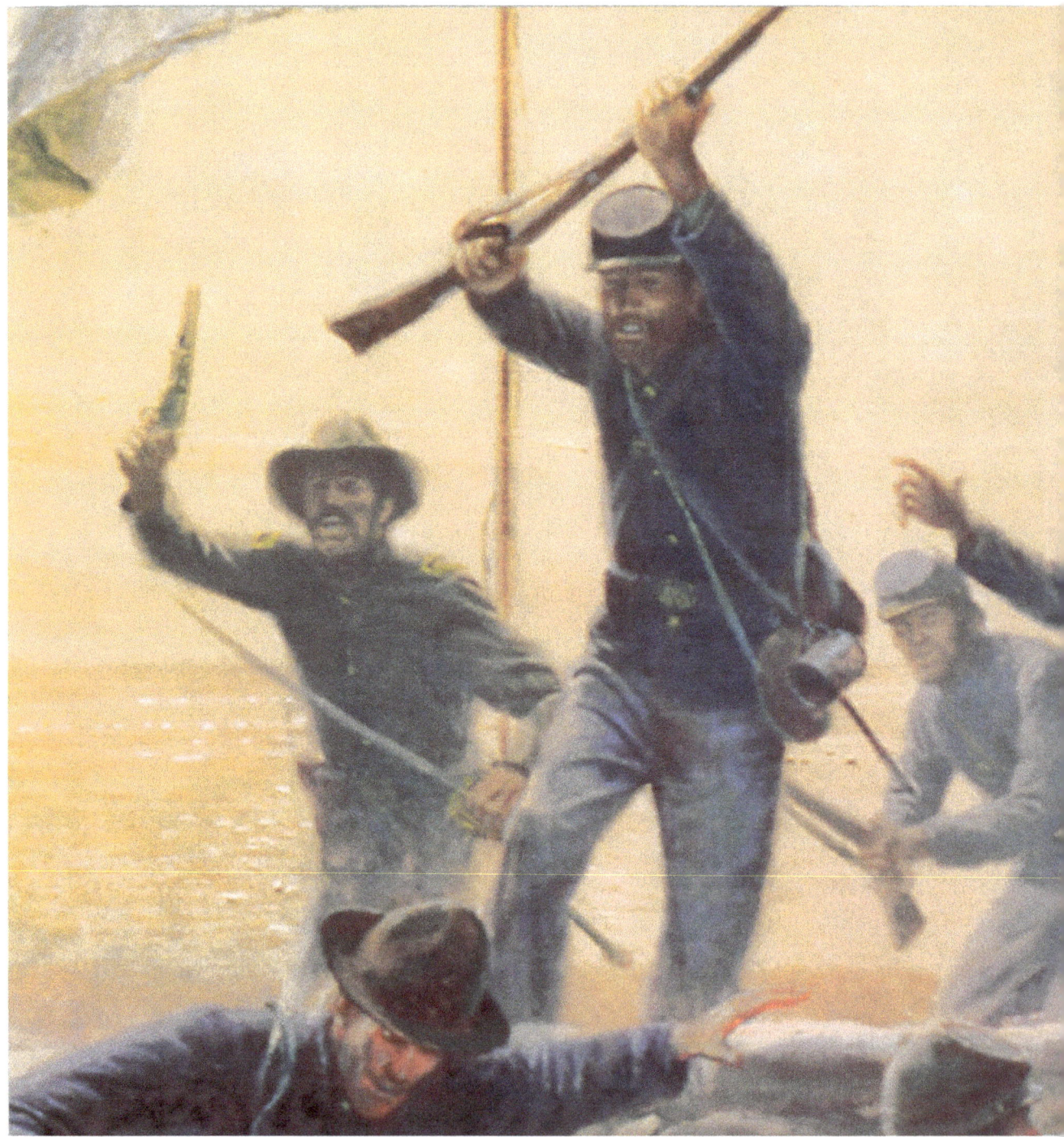

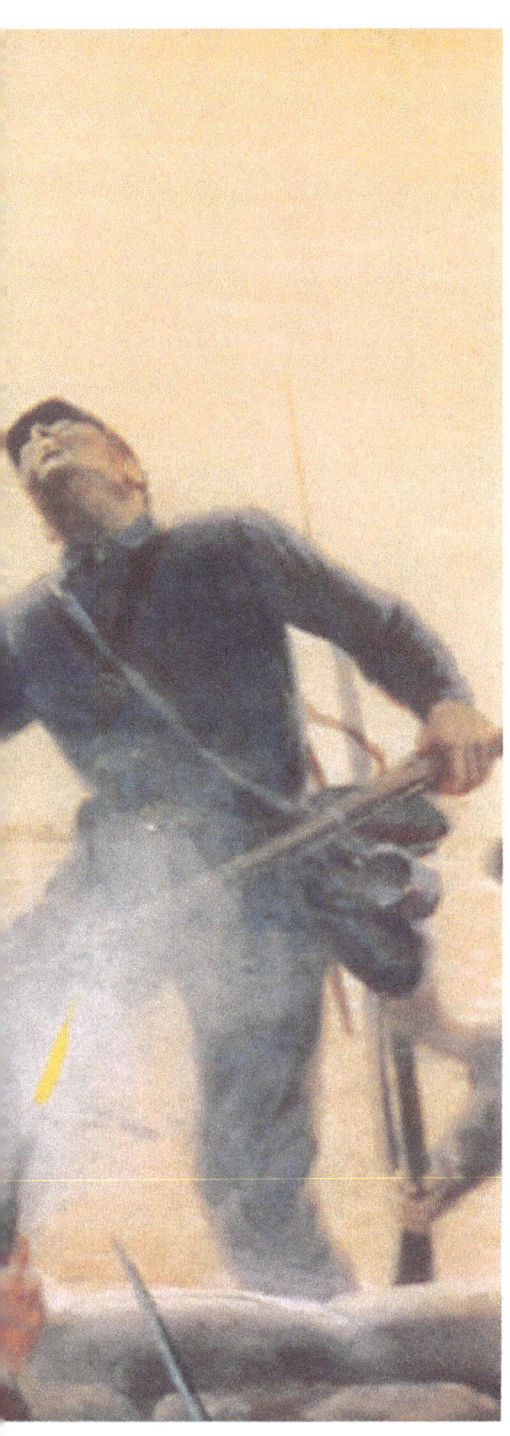

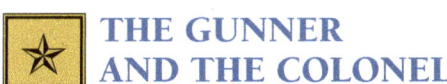

THE GUNNER
AND THE COLONEL

BATTLE OF FORT FISHER, NORTH CAROLINA
JANUARY 15, 1865

1992, oil, 24 x 42

AFTER READING ROD GRAGG's *Confederate Goliath,* I was so fascinated by his account of the battle of Fort Fisher that I felt compelled to paint it. When I called Rod, he told me that part of the fort still existed (three-quarters of it has been washed into the sea over the past century and a half) and had been preserved by the state of North Carolina. He also offered to meet me and act as my guide to the site. I arrived in Wilmington at the same time of year that the battle took place and with great luck was able to observe the lighting conditions and weather exactly the way it was in 1865. With

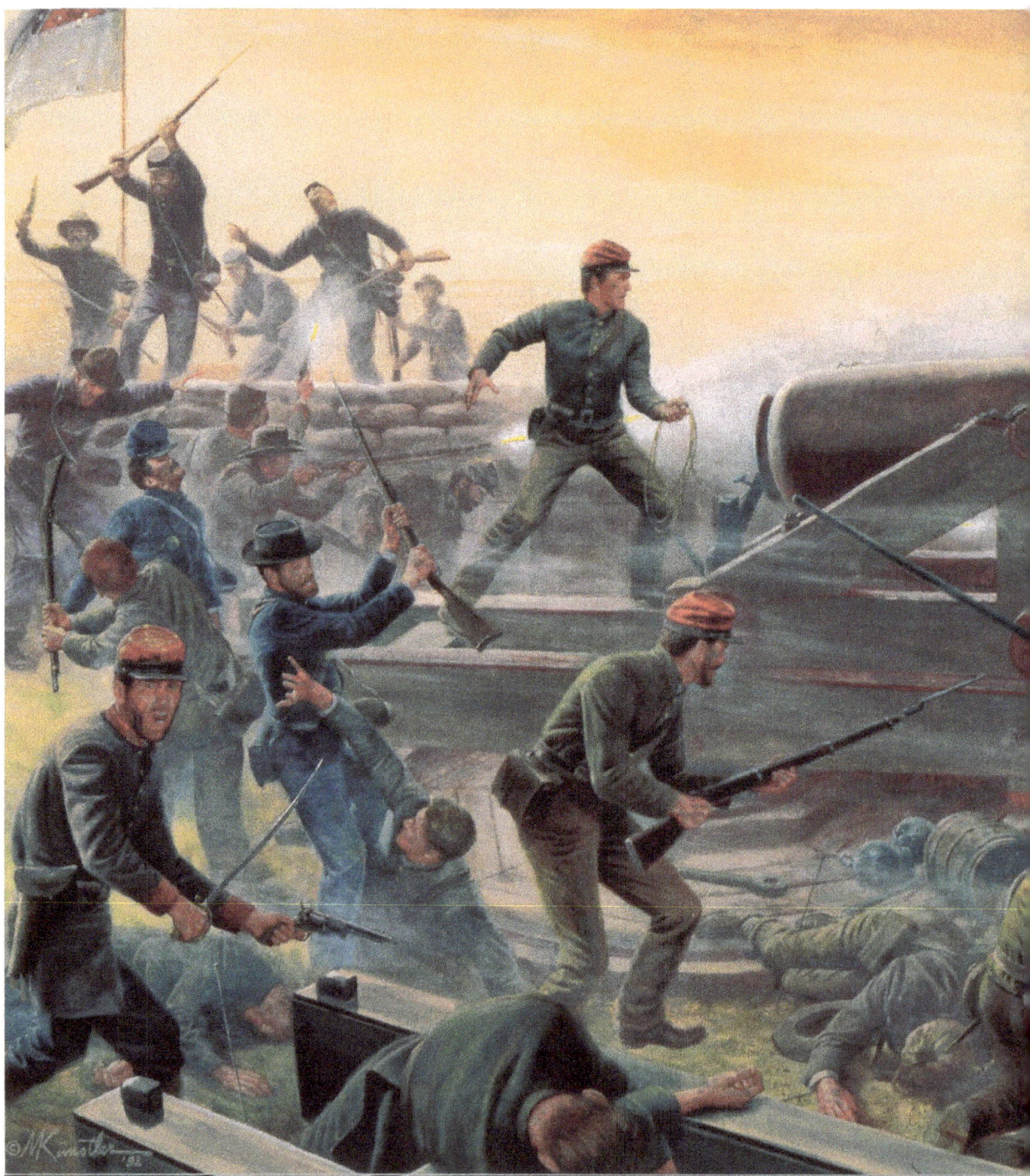

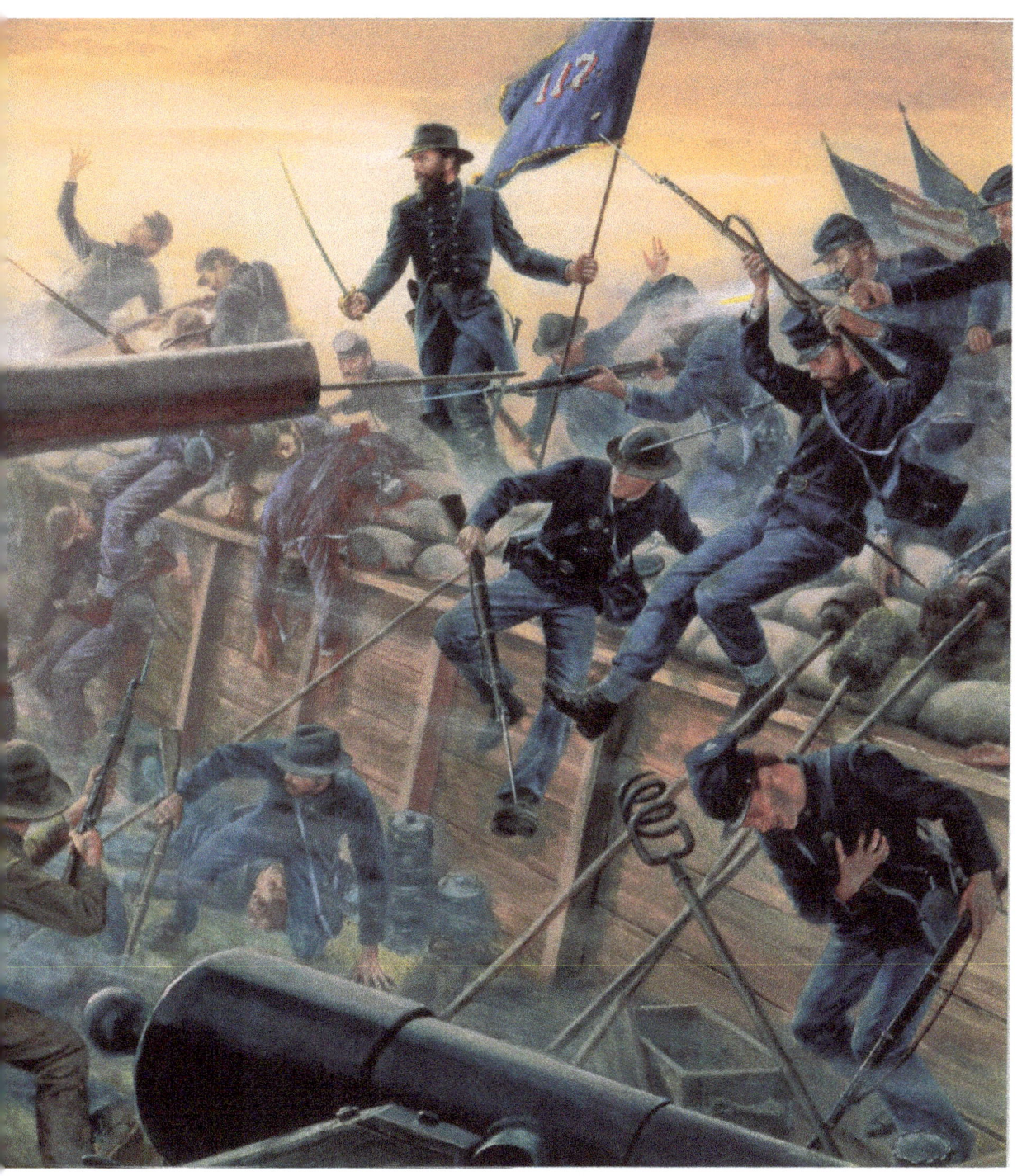

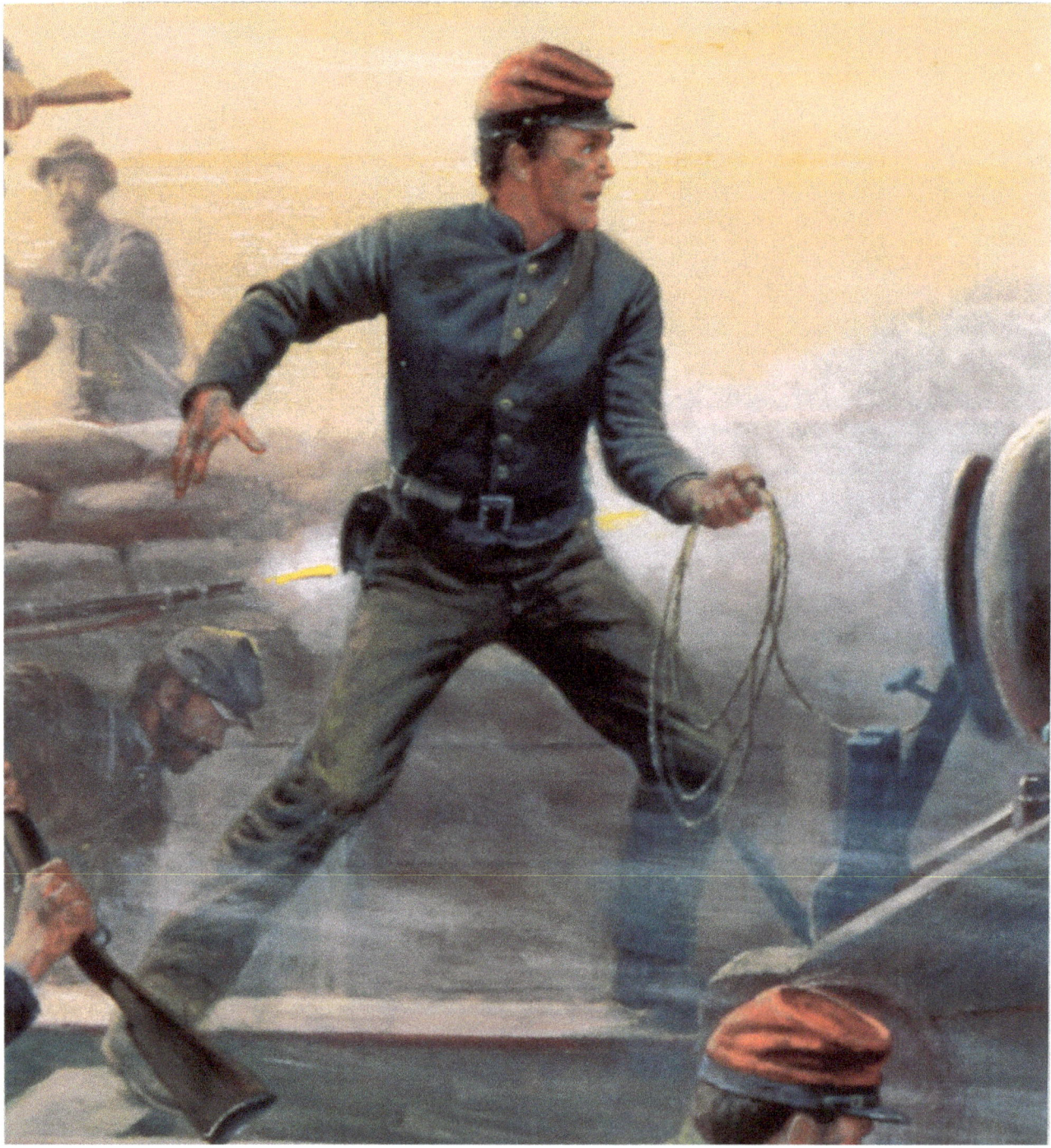

Rod Gragg and Gehrig Spencer, manager of the Fort Fisher State Historic Site, I surveyed the entire battlefield.

One of the most dramatic moments of the fighting occurred when the guns of Shepherd's Battery were overrun. Union Col. Newton Curtis led the charge with his sword in one hand and a guidon in the other. When the Federals reached the top of the steep embankment of the gun emplacement, there was vicious hand-to-hand combat. Curtis demanded the surrender of the gunner who stood on the gun carriage, trying to fire point blank into the massed Union troops. The unarmed gunner remained undaunted until he was struck down. This is the scene I tried to capture on my canvas, making the focal point of the painting the 10-inch Columbiad at this battery.

The wind was out of the northeast and the day was clear, thus the flags are flying toward the sun in the southwest. The clear weather gave me an opportunity to show the Cape Fear River in the background.

Among the elements of the painting are Capt. Kinchen Braddy, who commanded Second Company C of the Thirty-sixth North Carolina, which was in charge of defending Shepherd's Battery. He is seen in the left foreground, holding a pistol and sword. The flag in the upper left corner is the Second National Flag of the Confederacy, and the guidon carried by Curtis is that of the 117th New York, the regiment that was among the first to break into the fort. The damaged cannon in the foreground is a rifled and banded 32-pounder on a center-pintle barbette carriage.

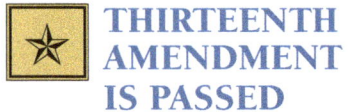

THIRTEENTH AMENDMENT IS PASSED

JANUARY 31, 1865

1991, mixed media, 10 x 11½

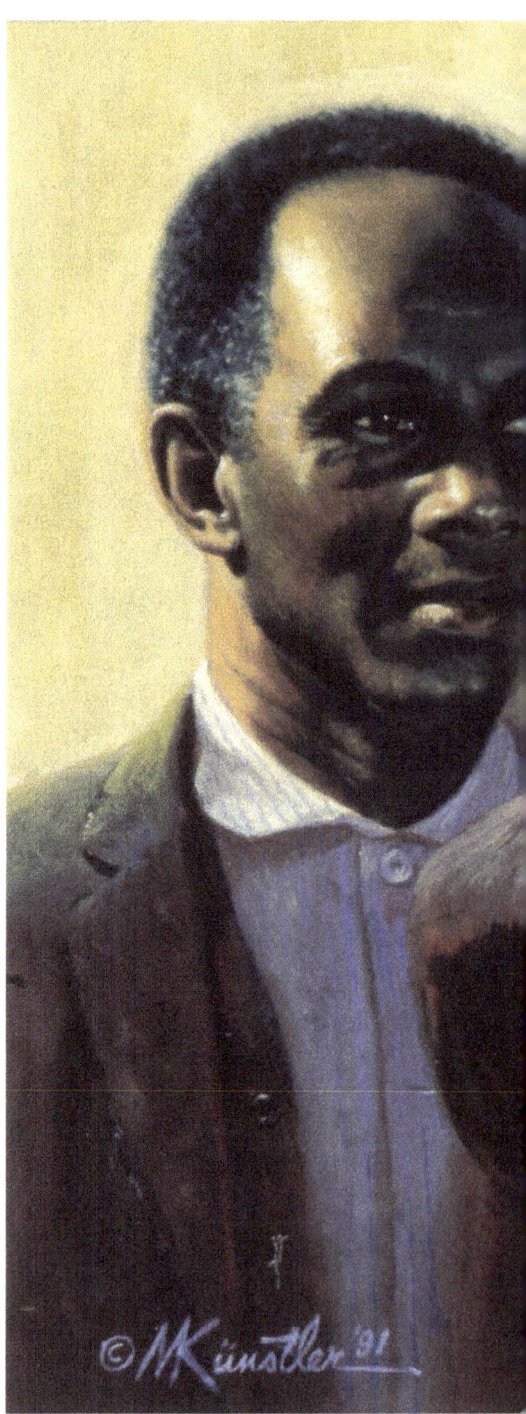

O N April 8, 1864, the U.S. Congress considered a constitutional amendment to the effect that "neither slavery nor involuntary servitude . . . shall exist within the United States, or any place subject to their jurisdiction." The Senate quickly passed the measure, but it failed in the House until after a summer of Union victories and Lincoln's reelection. The second vote was successful on January 31, 1865.

Ratification by the states followed quickly Although the president, Congress, and the states could not agree on what rights the amendment guaranteed the former slaves, the Union would never again be half slave and half free.

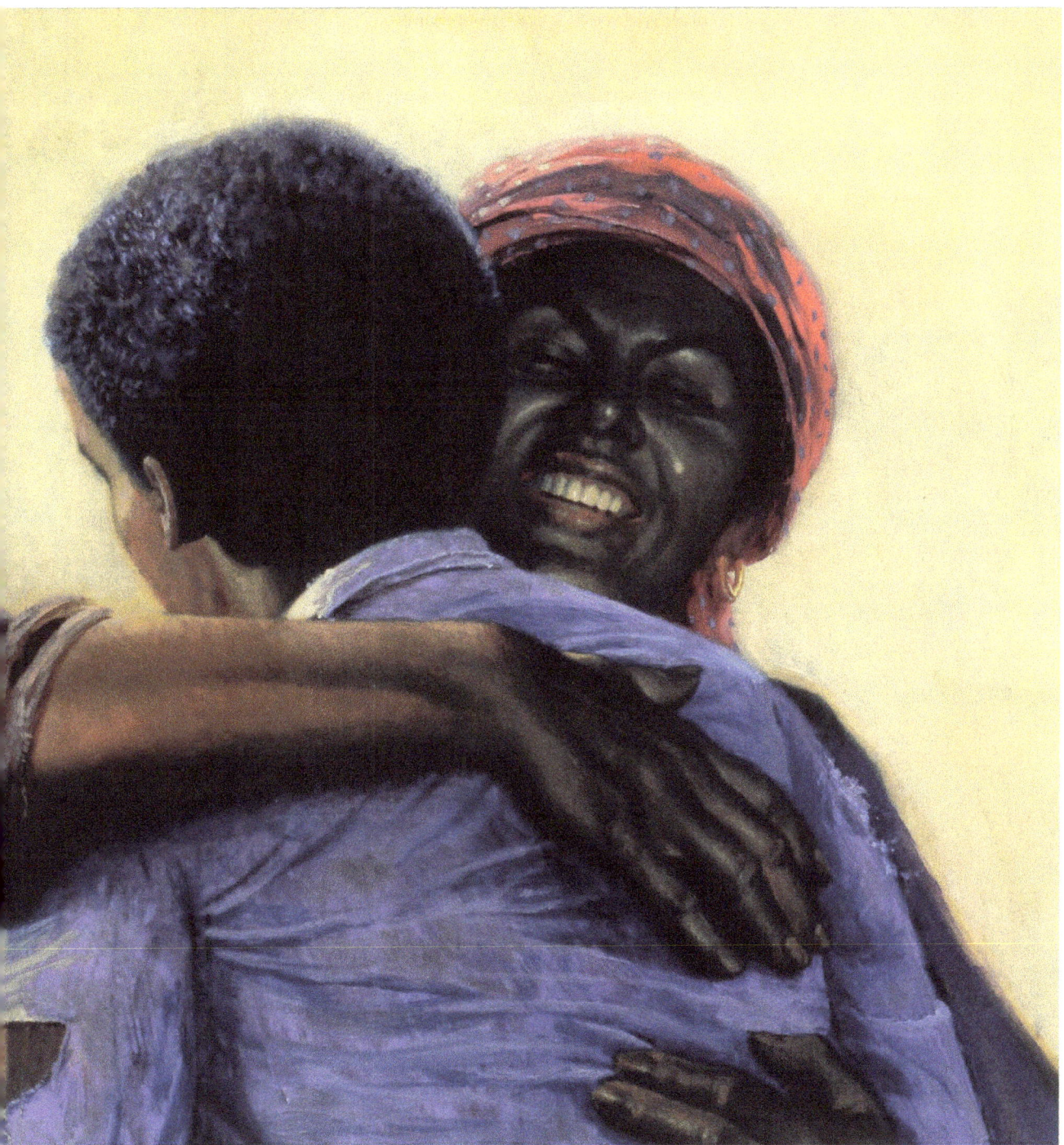

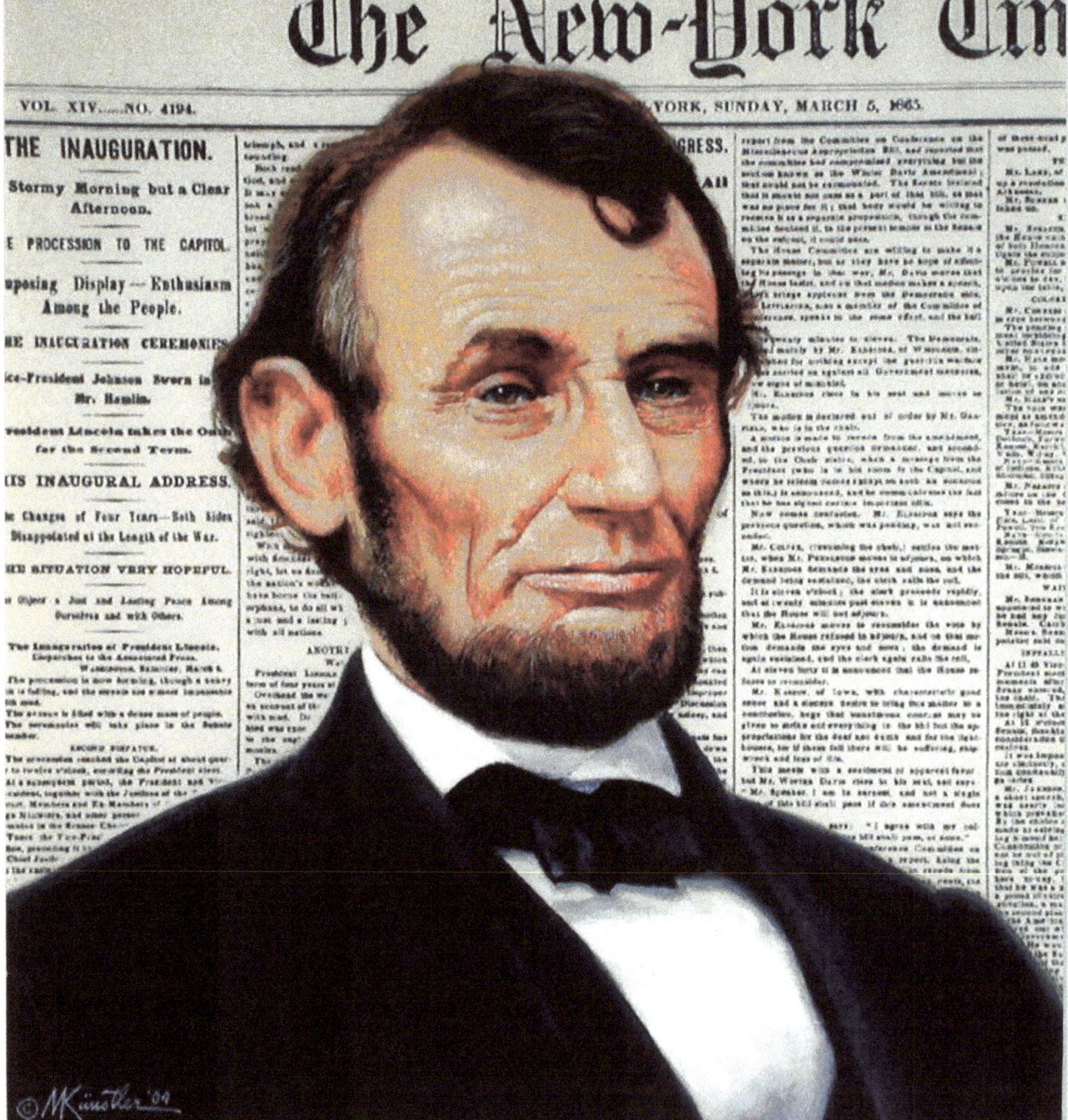

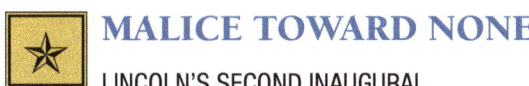

MALICE TOWARD NONE

LINCOLN'S SECOND INAUGURAL
MARCH 4, 1865

2005, mixed media, 10³/₄ x 9³/₄

MARCH 4, 1865, WAS a wet and windy day in Washington. But the dark clouds of war that had menacingly colored Abraham Lincoln's first inauguration in 1861 were dissipating when he went to the Capitol to take the oath of office for a second time. When the time came for him to step forward on the platform erected at the east front of the Capitol, the sun dramatically broke through the clouds and brightened the drenched crowd.

There Lincoln offered the briefest inaugural address by any president—703 words. While the topic of the war dominated these words, absent from them were accusations, blame, or arrogance. Instead, he presented the war as a struggle over slavery—"the cause of the war." He could not proclaim victory or even assert that the war was over: "Fondly do we hope—fervently do we pray—that this mighty scourge of war may pass away." But he concluded with the most eloquent words he ever composed: "With malice toward none; with charity for all; with firmness in the right, as God gives us to see the right, let us strive on to finish the work we are in; to bind up the nation's wounds; to care for him who shall have borne the battle, and for his widow, and his orphan—to do all which may achieve and cherish a just, and a lasting peace, among ourselves, and with all nations."

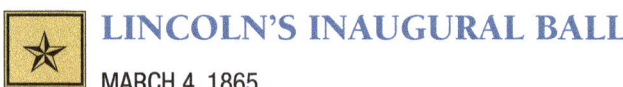

LINCOLN'S INAUGURAL BALL

MARCH 4, 1865

1997, oil, 30 x 30

I BASED THIS PAINTING of Lincoln's second inaugural ball on a Major and Knapp lithograph that was published by Frank Leslie in 1865. After the inaugural ceremonies at the Capitol, where he and Vice President Andrew Johnson were sworn in by Chief Justice Salmon P Chase, an escort of cavalry, bands, and spectators led the presidential party back to the Executive Mansion.

Newspapers reported that Lincoln shook hands with more than six thousand people at the reception that followed. In the painting he is accompanied by his wife, Mary, as he makes his way to the main ballroom where so many people wait to congratulate him. Vice President Johnson is directly behind him, and to the right are Gen. George Gordon Meade, Secretary of State William Henry Seward, and Attorney General Edward Bates. The uniformed figure to the left of the president is Gen. Ulysses S. Grant.

The mantle, clock, and candelabra are based on items that were in the White House at the time. I portrayed the president with tired eyes but slightly smiling. Perhaps he knew his work would soon come to an end. Within a month's time, Lincoln would sit at Jefferson Davis's desk in the Confederate White House in Richmond and Lee would surrender at Appomattox Court House.

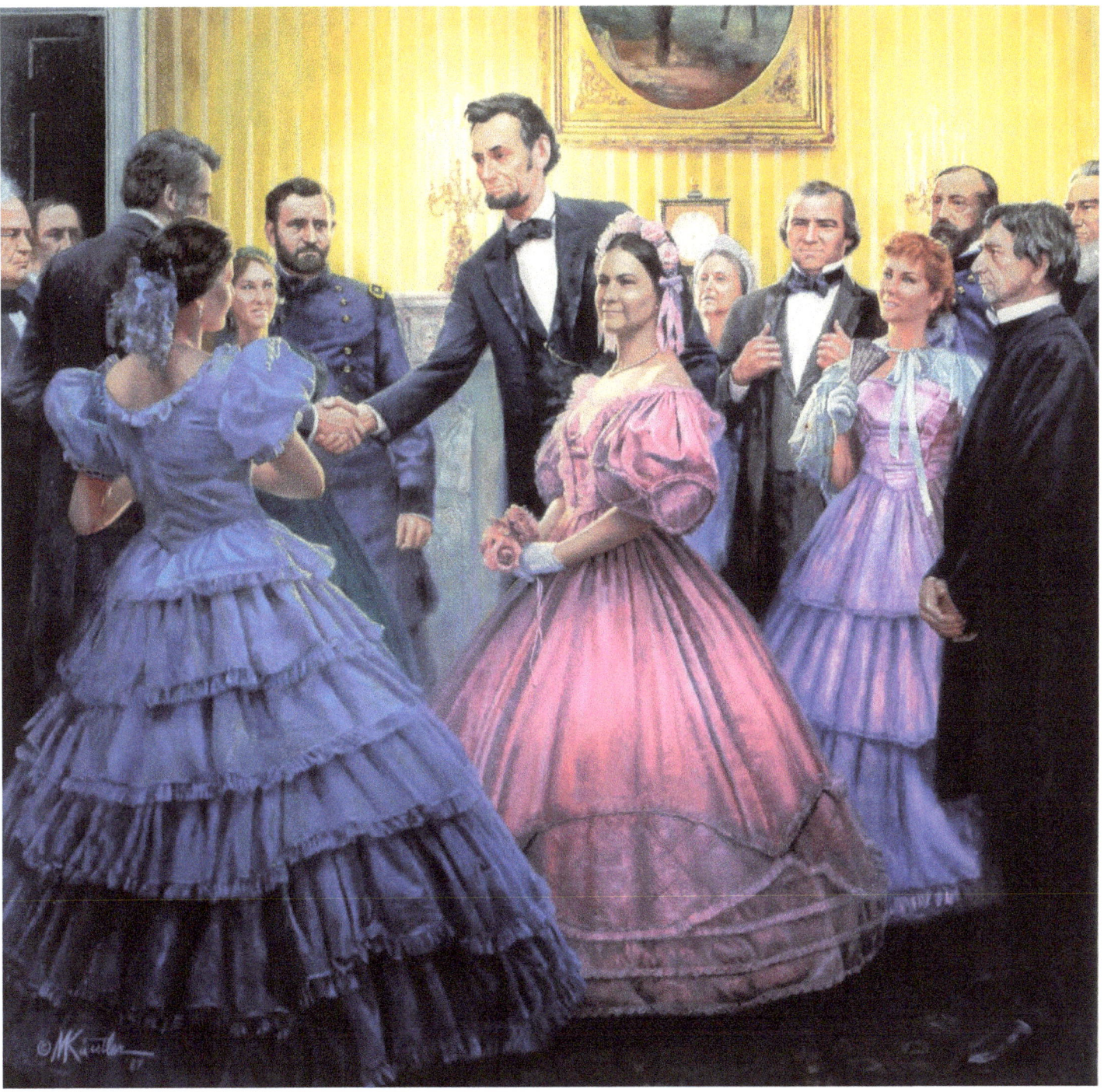

THE LAST RALLY

SAYLER'S CREEK, VIRGINIA

APRIL 6, 1865

1991, oil, 22 x 34

AT SAYLER'S CREEK ON April 6, 1865, during the retreat from Petersburg and Richmond, Robert E. Lee lost a quarter of his army. Stunned by what he saw, Lee rode among the battle's survivors and then, somehow, picked up a battle flag. The image of the gray general on a gray horse under the crimson banner electrified most of the men. "Where's the man who won't follow Uncle Robert?" they cried. He urged them on to re-form their line, and they withdrew behind the upcoming rear guard.

After reading Douglas Southall Freeman's four-volume biography of Robert E. Lee, I was captivated by this

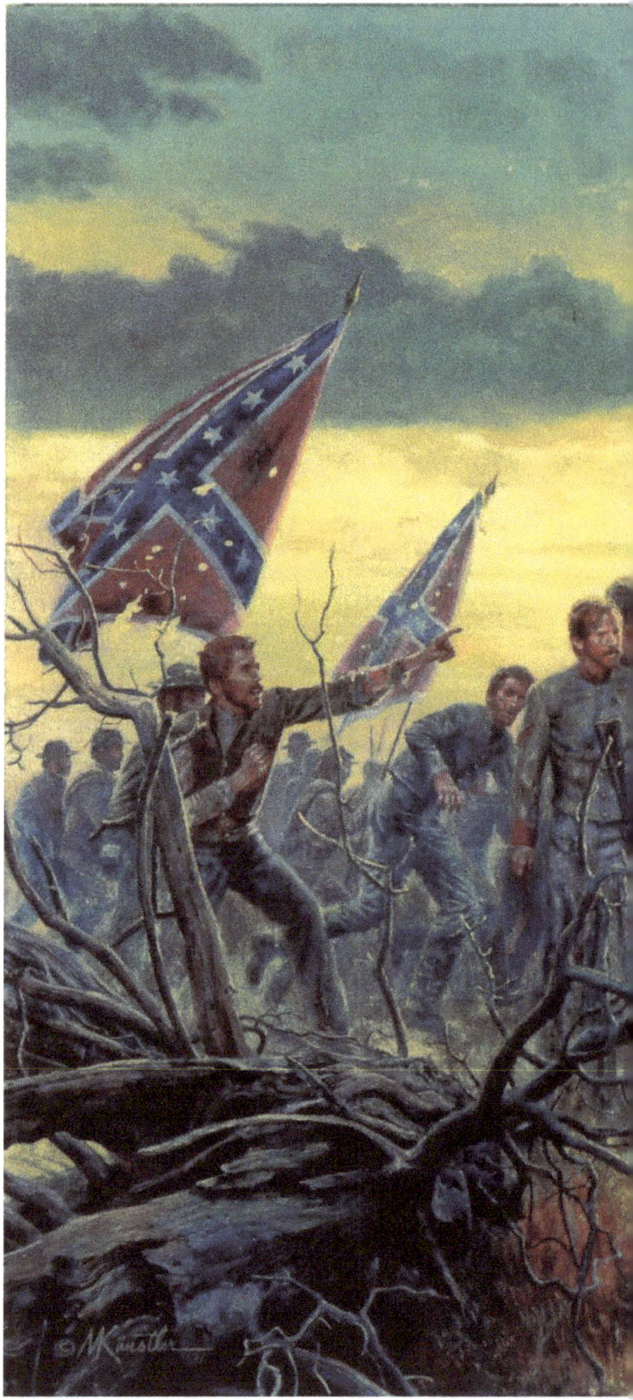

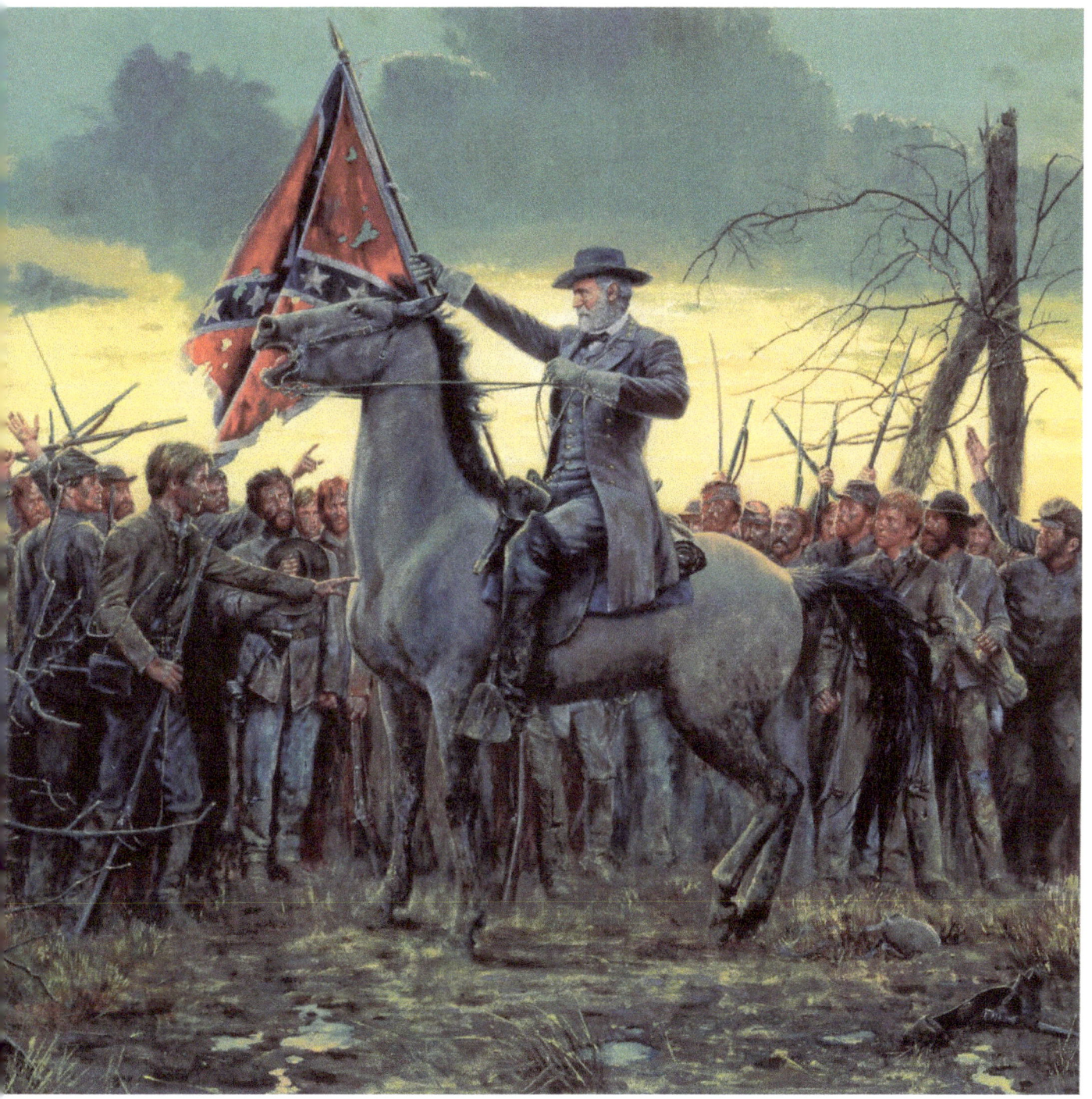

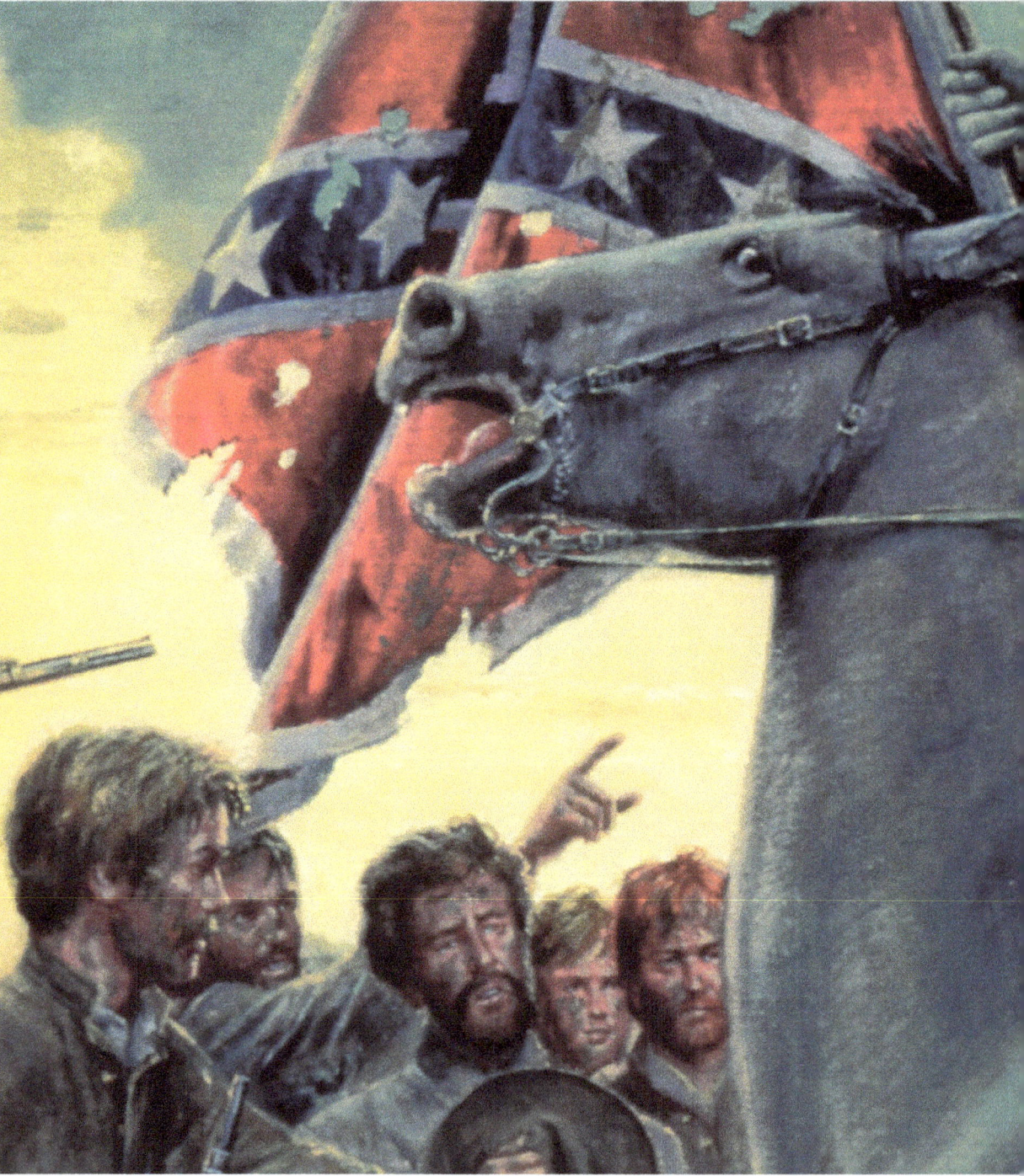

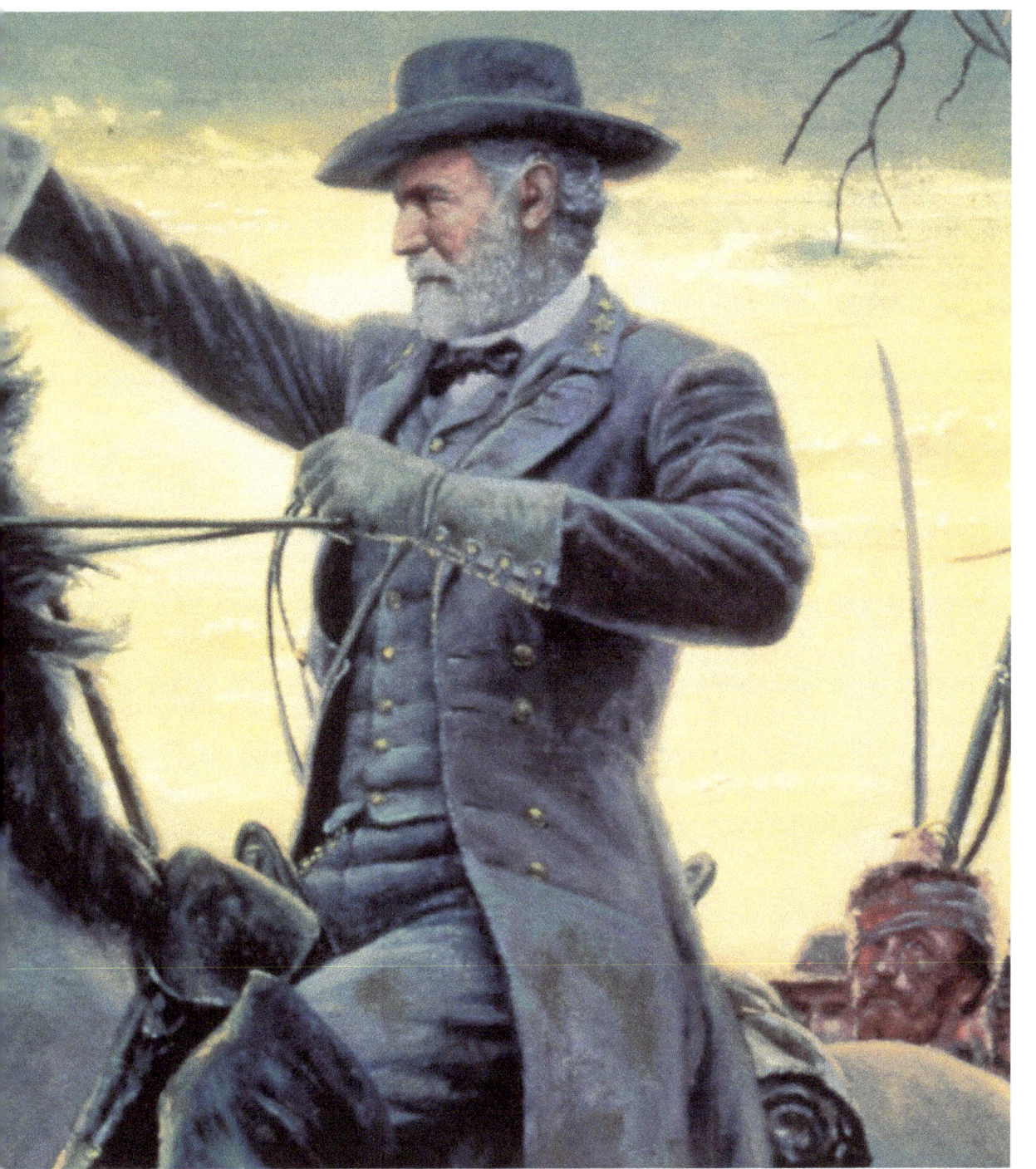

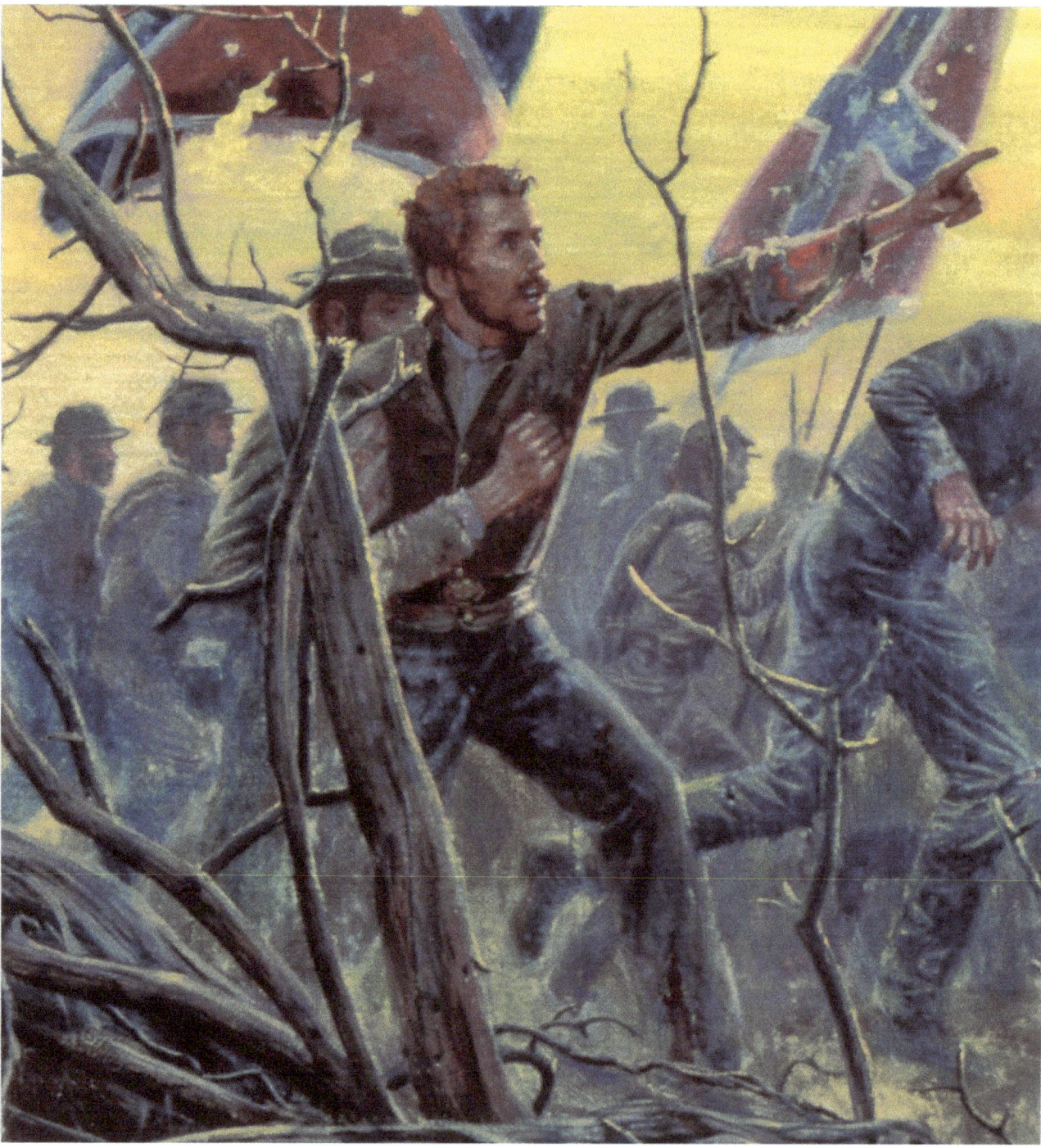

incident at Sayler's Creek. It was the only time during the four years of fighting that Lee actually held up a battle flag and rallied troops around him to prevent the rout of his army. It was a scene I felt obliged to paint.

By placing Lee facing to the left and the army retreating to the right, the opposing elements of the painting tell the story. From this viewpoint, the viewer looks to the southwest, where the sun was setting. With Lee in front of the sun, creating a bright spot around him, the painting has a remarkable focal point against a dramatic sunset sky.

The soldiers recognize Lee and swing around to see the great man up close. One reaches out to touch his horse, as they often did when he was near. Each pose comes from my putting myself in that position and weighing what an infantryman might be thinking, doing, or saying at that moment.

The dead limbs of the trees convey an atmosphere of death and destruction and also act as pointers to the center of interest: Lee. The mud and dirt and the discarded accoutrements impart a feeling of despair, even desperation. In the face of that setting, Lee imparts nothing less than his sheer willpower and determination to transform a retreating mob into the emboldened army that he had known since taking command in 1862 and had led from unlikely victory to unlikely victory, surviving disastrous failures against overwhelming odds. To lose heart would be to lose the war.

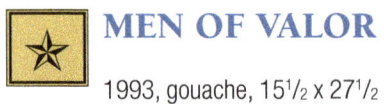

MEN OF VALOR

1993, gouache, 15½ x 27½

LEE MARCHED HIS REMAINING thirty thousand men across the Appomattox River and toward Lynchburg, but Ulysses S. Grant, with four times as many men at his command, sent his cavalry ahead to seize the railroad in the Confederates' line of march. Subsequent probes along the Union line found that Lee had few options other than to broker his surrender, and the two commanders began an exchange of letters on that topic. But Lee was not determined to surrender, and in an evening conference with his generals made plans for a predawn breakout on April 9.

In the early lightless hours of that Palm Sunday, Lee dressed in his finest uniform and rode out to watch his army attempt to break the Union line. Ground fog and smoke obscured his view, but the twelve thousand men in the line performed like the combat veterans who had served him so well for three years, routing the Federals in front of them. Exultant with their success, they paused only when a morning wind began to blow away the fog—revealing thickening ranks of Union troops, almost thirty thousand men. The Confederates had no choice but to pull back.

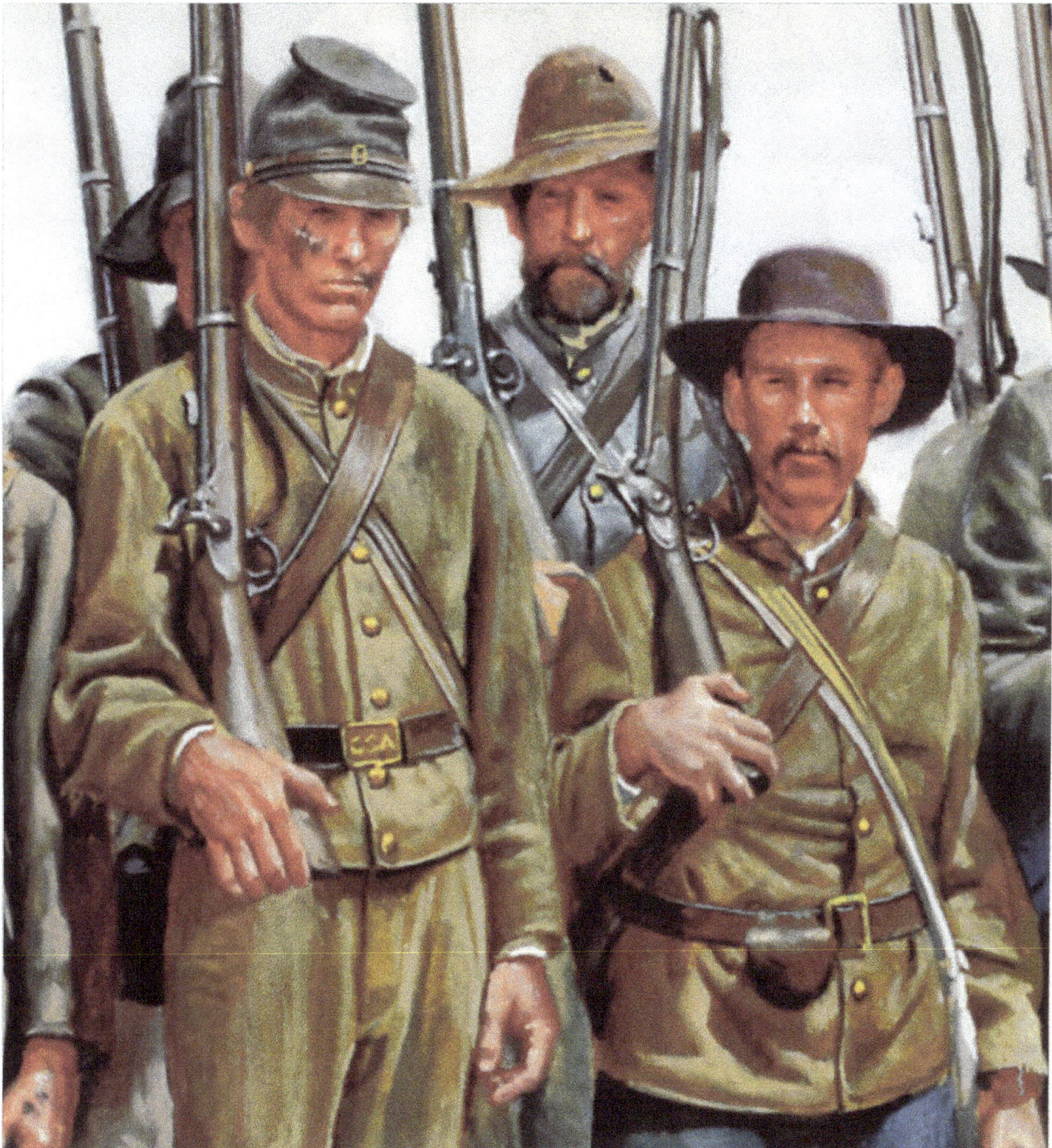

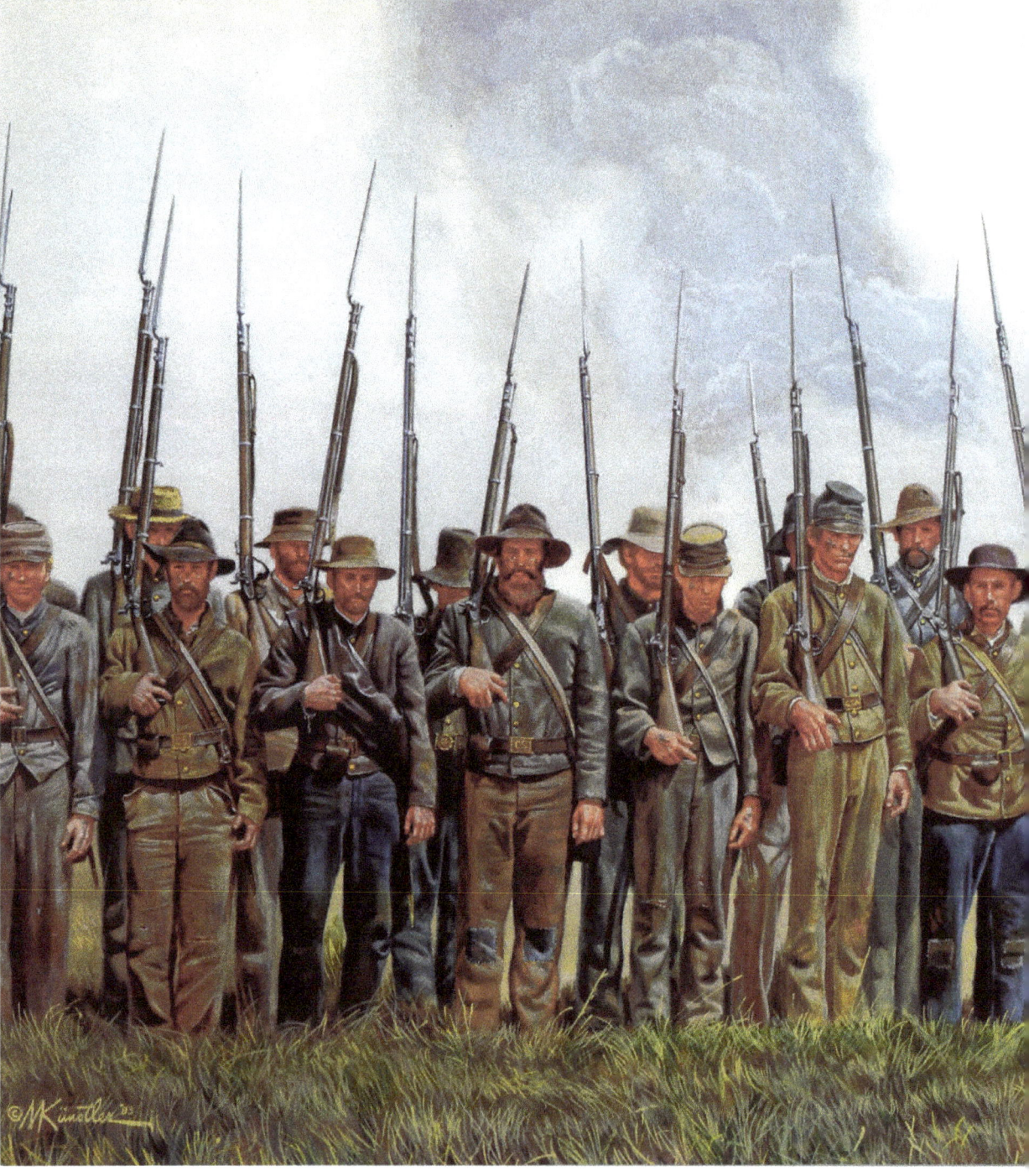

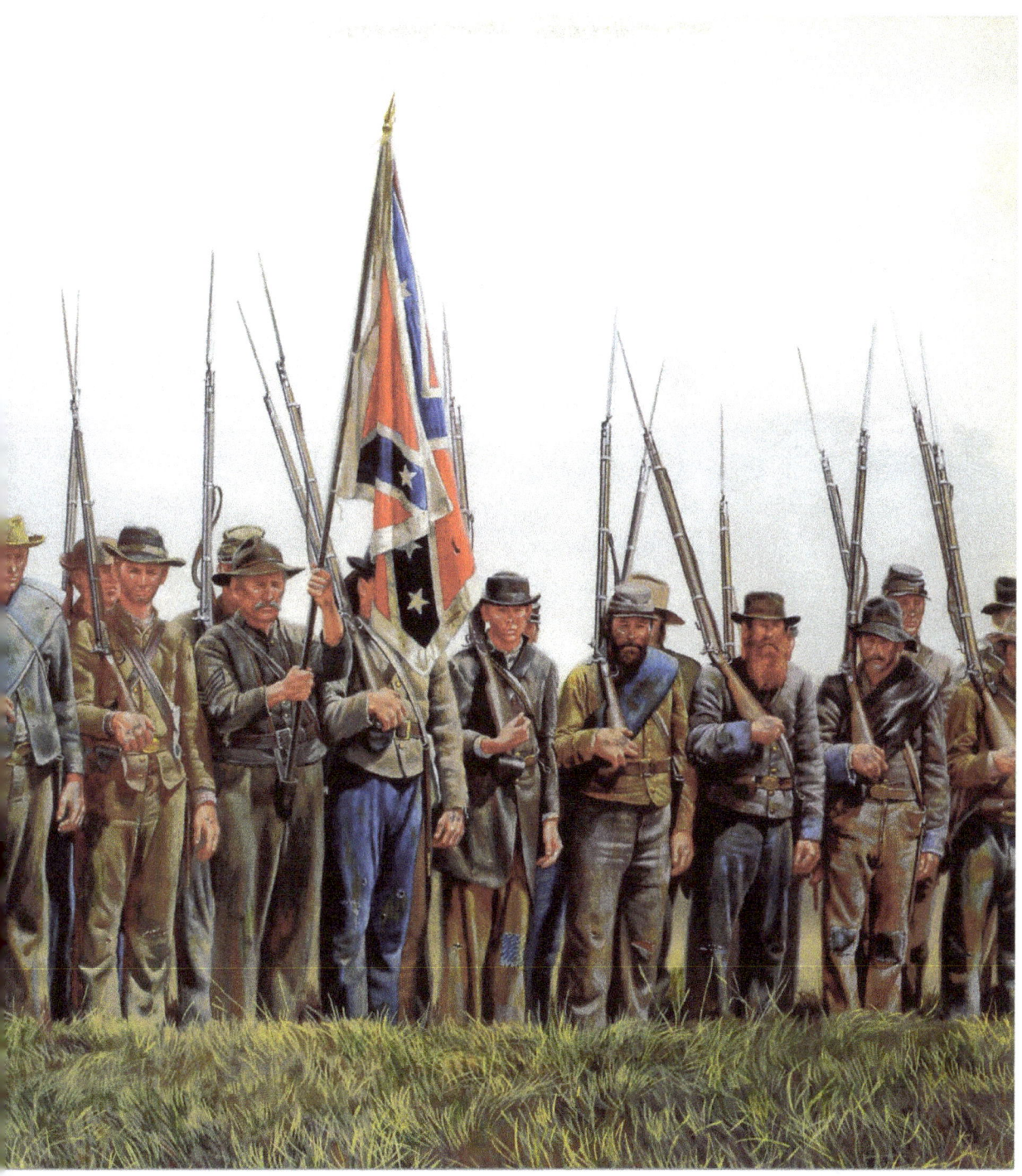

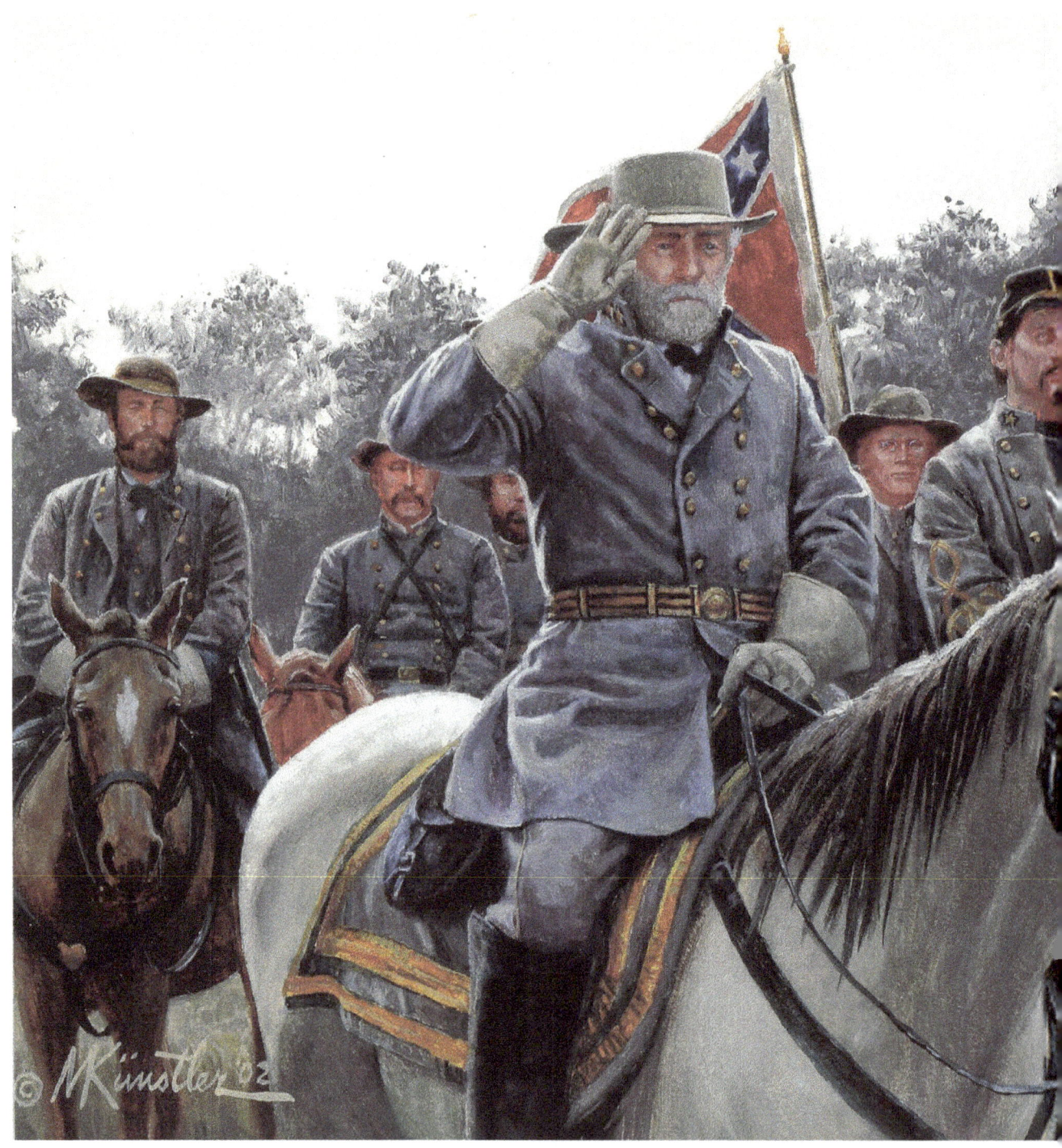

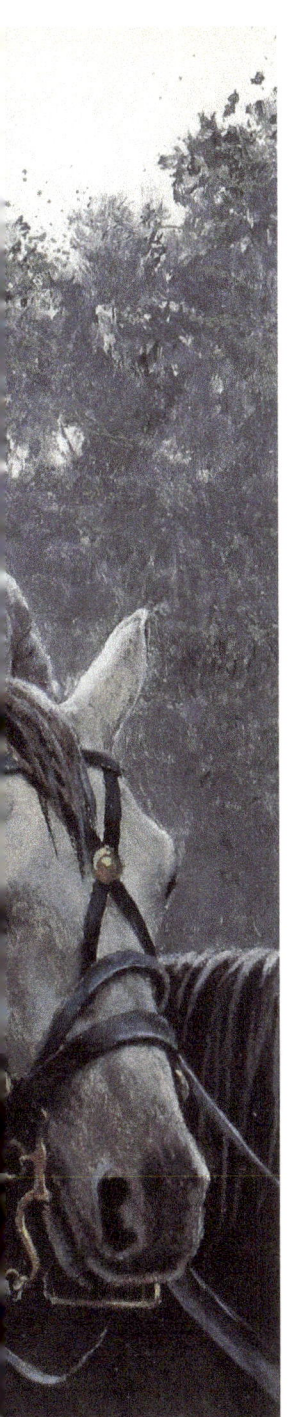

THERE WERE NEVER SUCH MEN

LEE AND STAFF

2002, oil, 9¼ x 11

AT HIS VANTAGE POINT overlooking the aborted breakout, Lee received messages from his generals of the gathering of innumerable Federals around them. To his staff who had accompanied him, he said, "There is nothing left me to do but go and see General Grant, and I would rather die a thousand deaths."

At the appropriate time, Lee rode to the meeting place with adjutant Walter Taylor, military secretary Charles Marshall, and Sgt. George Tucker, who bore a flag of truce. The small party advanced to the Confederate picket line, requested a cease-fire, and waited to hear from Grant. Lee withdrew to the shade of a tree, and James Longstreet joined him there. When a Union officer arrived to escort Lee to the meeting, Longstreet said, "Unless he offers us honorable terms, come back and let us fight it out." The words seemed to lift Lee's spirits a little, and he departed toward the village of Appomattox Court House.

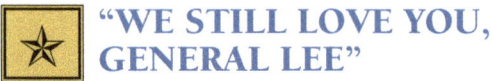

"WE STILL LOVE YOU, GENERAL LEE"

APPOMATTOX COURT HOUSE, VIRGINIA
APRIL 9, 1865

1992, oil, 54 x 88

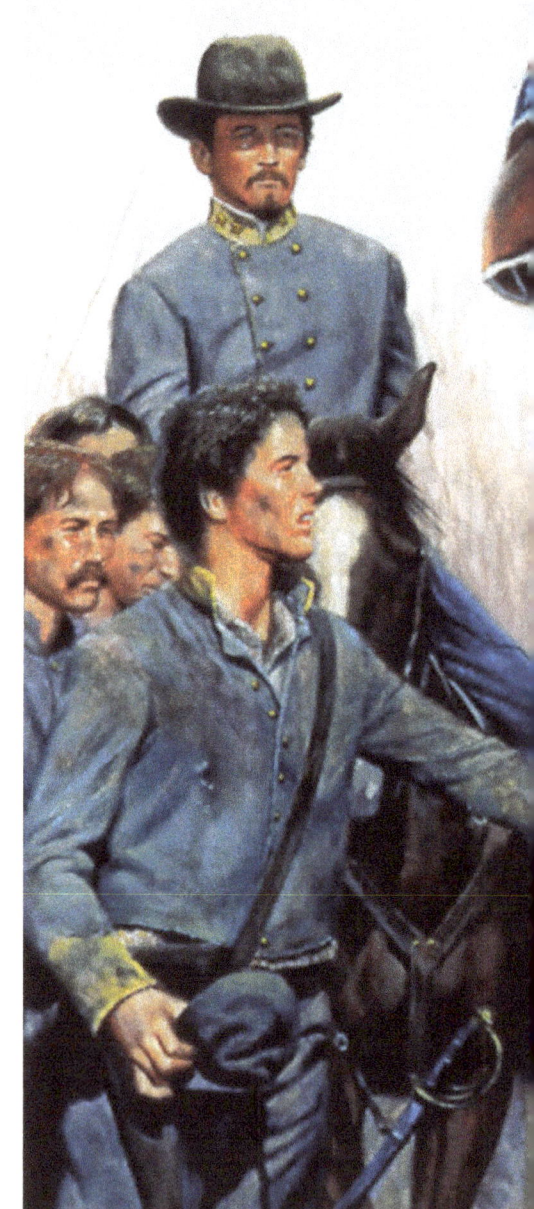

RETURNING TO HIS CAMP after meeting with Grant at Appomattox Court House, Lee rides his beloved Traveller through the Southern lines. He wears a full-dress uniform, sash, and ceremonial sword. He had wanted to look his best for the encounter with Grant, which he had faced with characteristic dignity.

Although defeated, Lee had negotiated generous terms that paroled his men and allowed them to keep their horses. As he rides past them, the soldiers, many with tears in their eyes, cheer and press toward him, touching his leg or his horse out of affection.

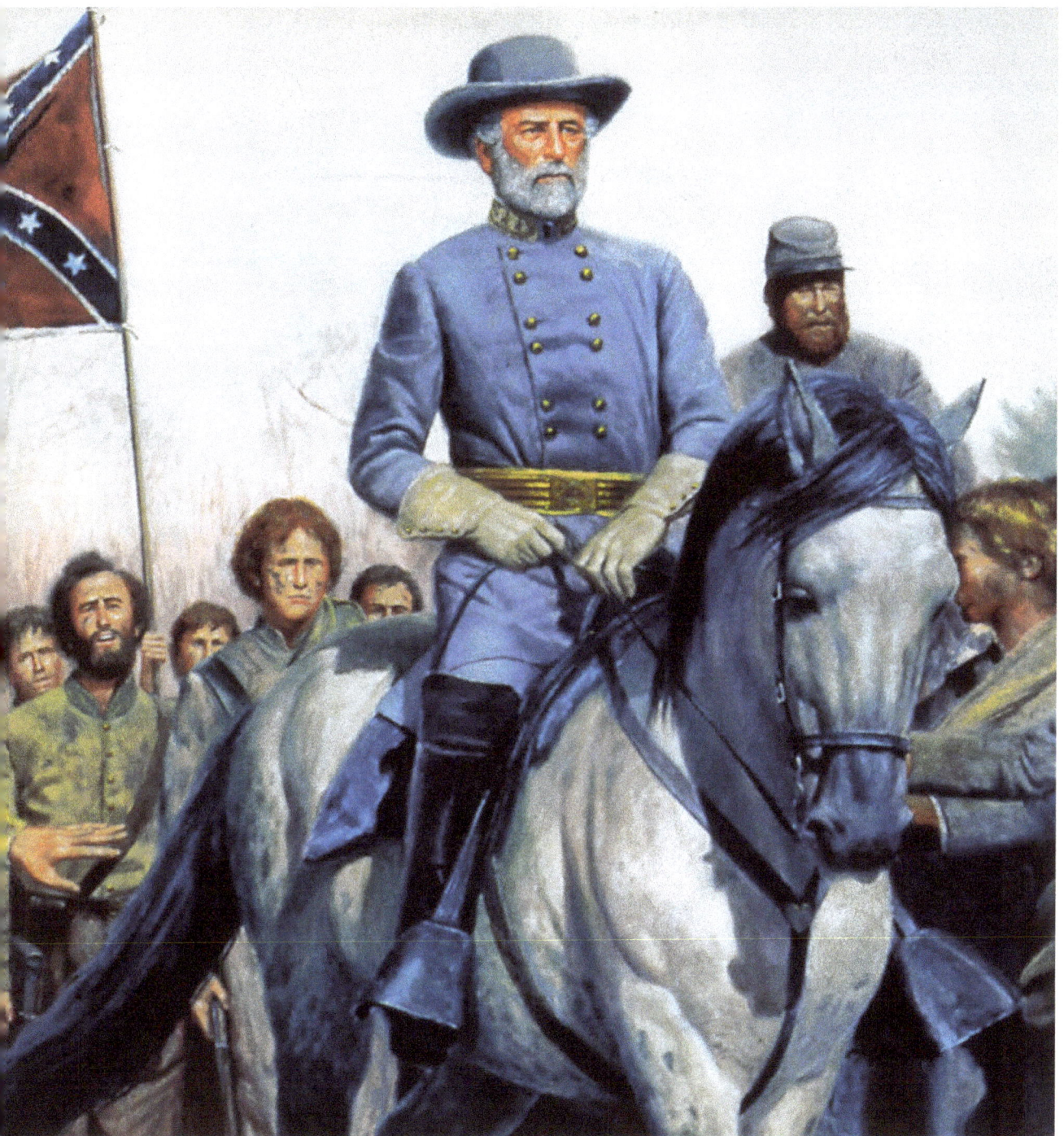

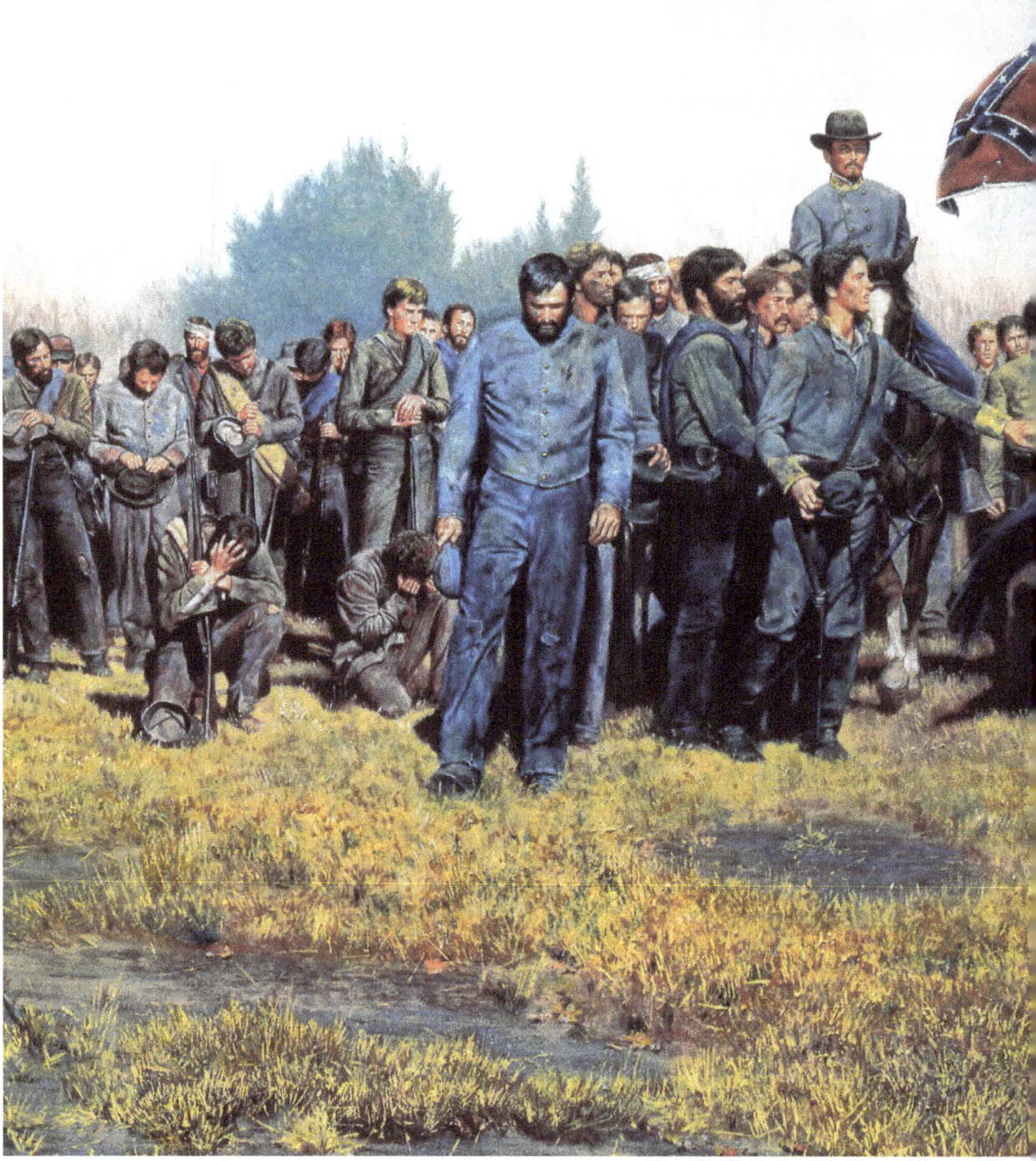

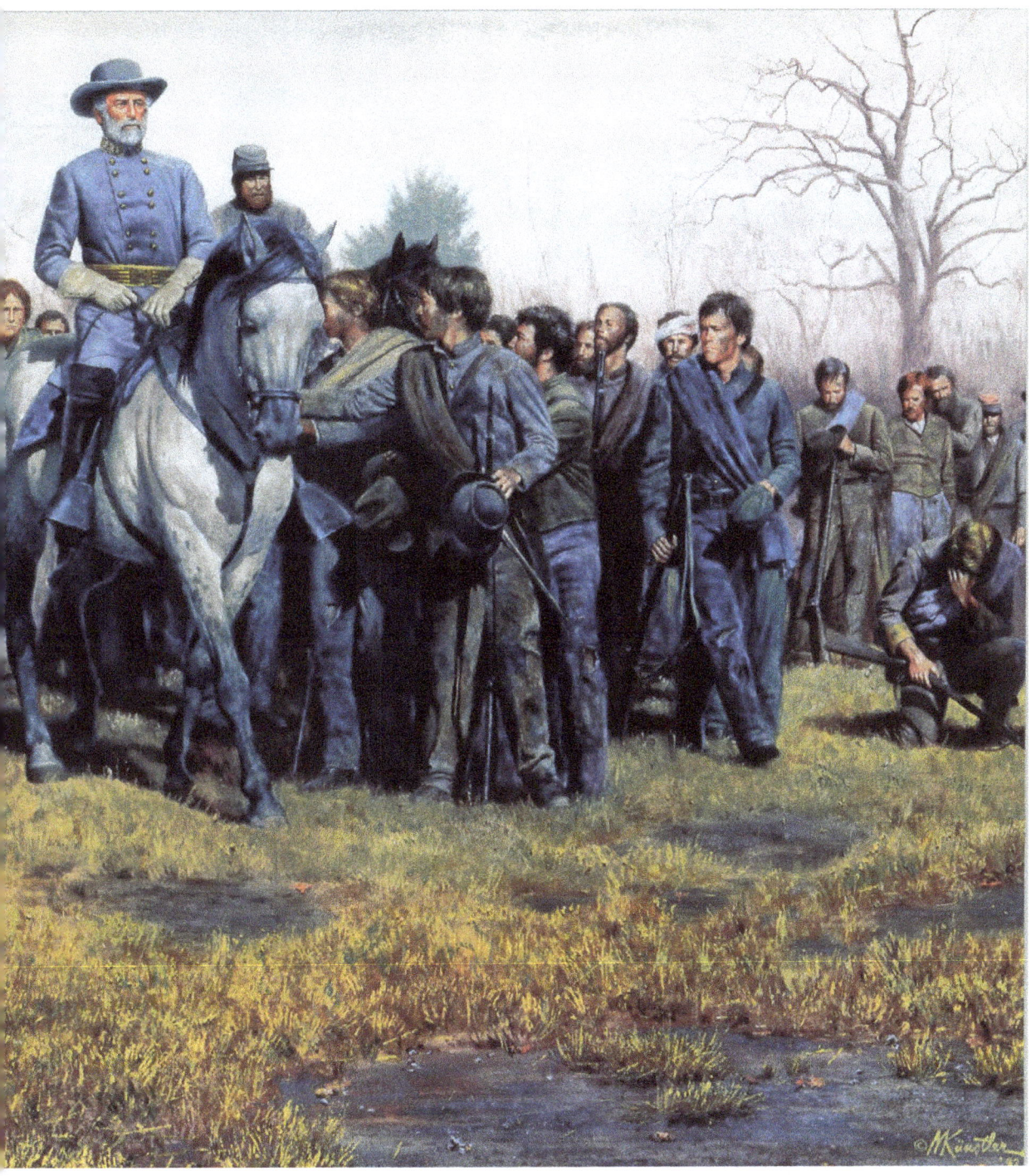

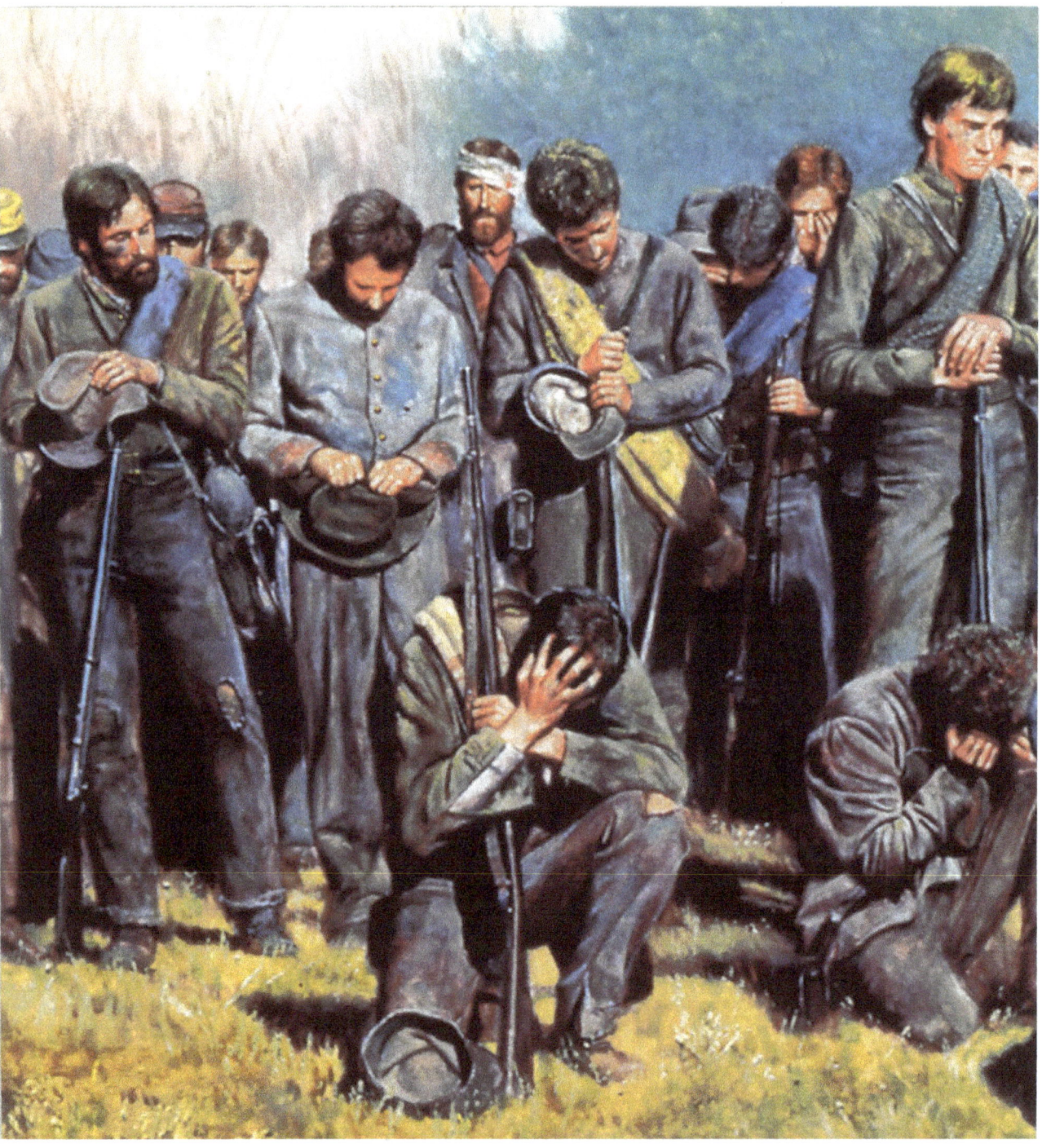

Pausing, Lee told his army, "Men, we have fought the war together, and I have done the best I could for you." He then doffed his hat, uttered a heartfelt good-bye, and returned to his tent. A tattered soldier turned in the ranks and shouted, "We still love you, General Lee!" Even now, almost 150 years later, the legacy of the man still evokes strong sentiments from those who study the war.

In 1960, I read Burke Davis's *To Appomattox*. At the time, I was not particularly interested in the Civil War, but I found his descriptions of the surrender and Lee's return to his headquarters very poignant. More than twenty

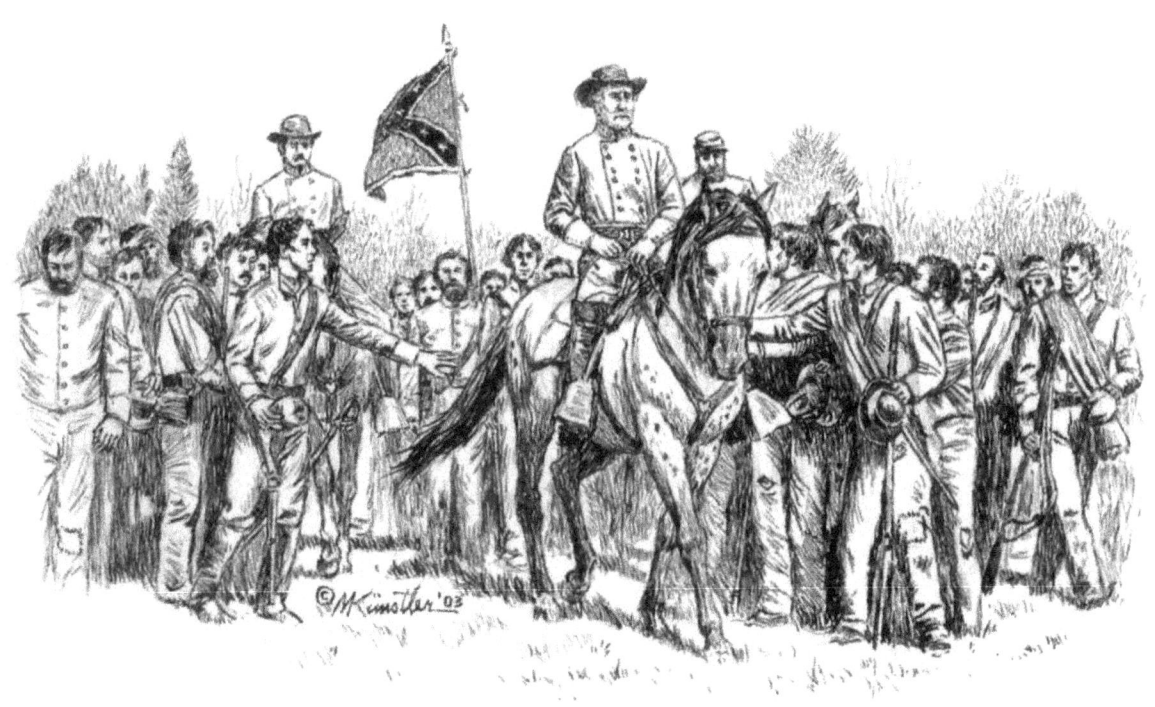

years later I was commissioned to do a painting that would become the logo for the television miniseries *The Blue and the Gray.* I became inspired and did a series of paintings on the Civil War that were exhibited in 1982 at a one-man show at Hammer Galleries in New York City One of those paintings was *"We Still Love You just as Much as Ever, General Lee."*

After the show, I moved on to mostly western and Americana themes. Finally, I embarked on a series of epic events in American history, such as the fall of the Alamo, Custer's Last Stand, and the battle of Gettysburg. While I was in Gettysburg, researching the painting that became *The High Water Mark,* I met Ted Sutphen of American Print Gallery. He later published my work as limited-edition prints, including the paintings in these books.

To make a print of *"We Still Love You, General Lee,"* I borrowed the original painting from the owner, and I made a number of minor changes to the painting that

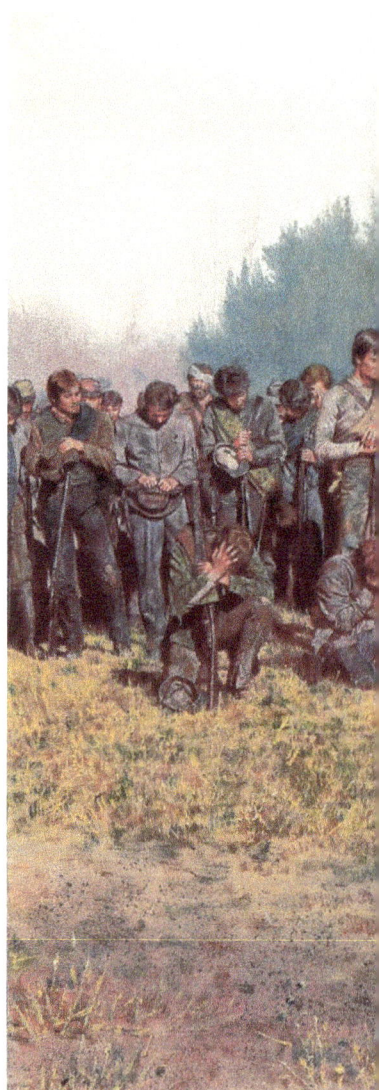

"WE STILL LOVE YOU, JUST AS MUCH AS EVER, GENERAL LEE"

APPOMATTOX COURT HOUSE, VIRGINIA

APRIL 9, 1865

1989, oil, 26 x 42

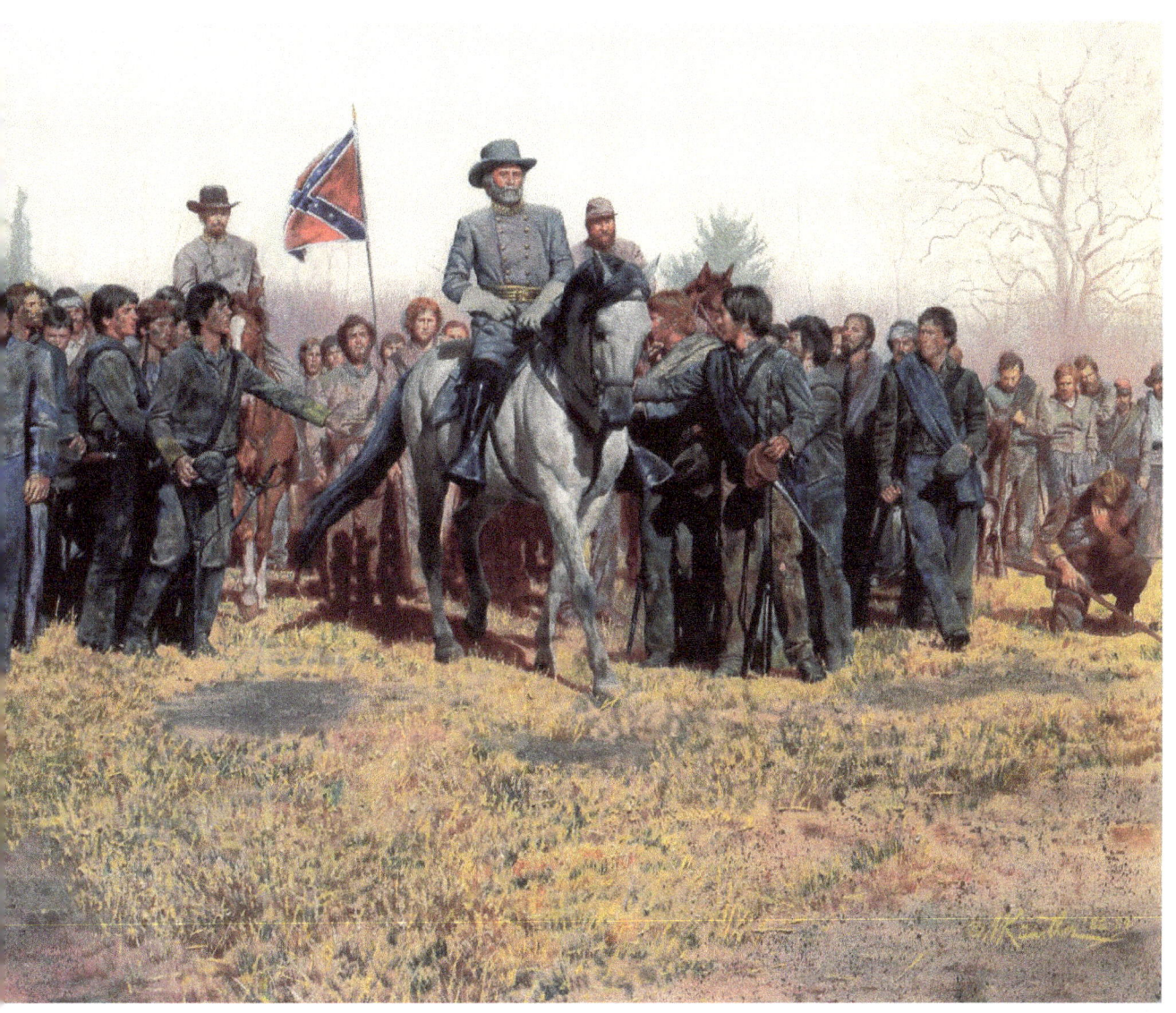

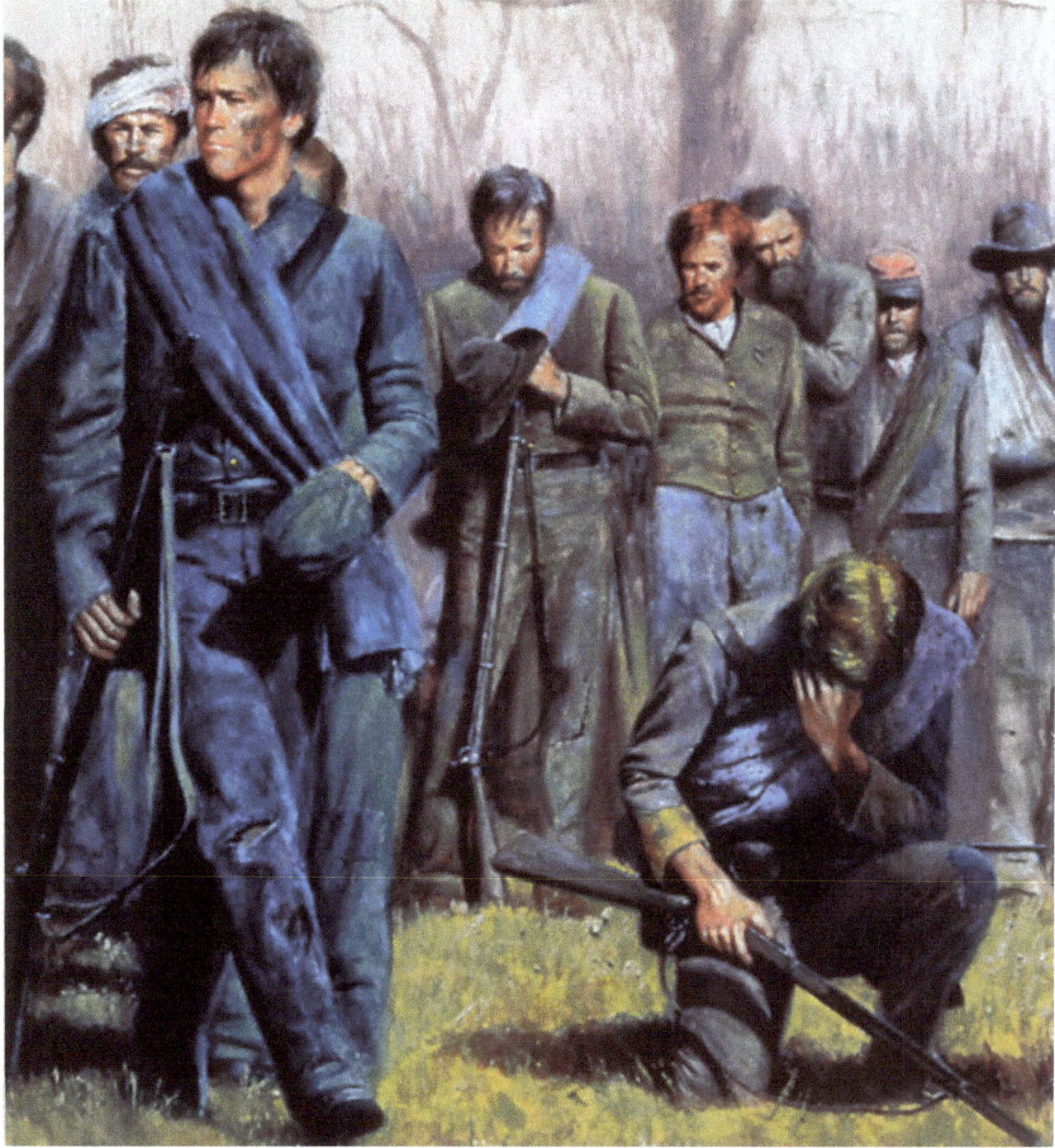

I felt would improve it. Most artists love to have an opportunity to work on a painting years after they have "finished" it. The print was well received, but I was not satisfied.

I have always wanted to paint a mural. To embark on a very large painting, however, it is necessary to have a finished smaller painting. I chose *"We Still Love You, General Lee"* for this huge undertaking because I felt it had all the ingredients of composition, color, emotion, and an event of epic proportion. Again I made changes. Thus, I have two finished paintings of Lee at Appomattox. It all goes back to 1960 and *To Appomattox* . . . and I still have the book!

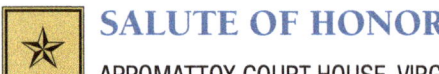

SALUTE OF HONOR

APPOMATTOX COURT HOUSE, VIRGINIA

APRIL 12, 1865

2001, oil, 22 x 44

THEY FACED EACH OTHER in two long straight lines—just as they had so many times before on so many bloody battlefields. This time was different, though. Three clays earlier, Lee had surrendered the skeletal remnants of his hard-fighting Army of Northern Virginia to Grant in farmer Wilmer McLean's parlor. Now it was time for the sons of the South to lay clown their arms and give up their bloodied battle flags. As enemies, these men in blue and gray had faced each other at Petersburg and Cold Harbor, at Gettysburg and Chancellorsville, at Fredericksburg and Antietam, at Second Manassas and Malvern Hill. Now they again stood in great ranks opposite each other—one the victor, the other the vanquished.

Placed in command of receiving the Southern surrender was Brig. Gen. Joshua Lawrence Chamberlain, a Northern war hero who bore four battle wounds inflicted by these men in gray and butternut now assembled before him. Absent in Chamberlain, however, was any animosity toward these former foes; present instead was a sense of respect for his countrymen who had given their all in the grip of war.

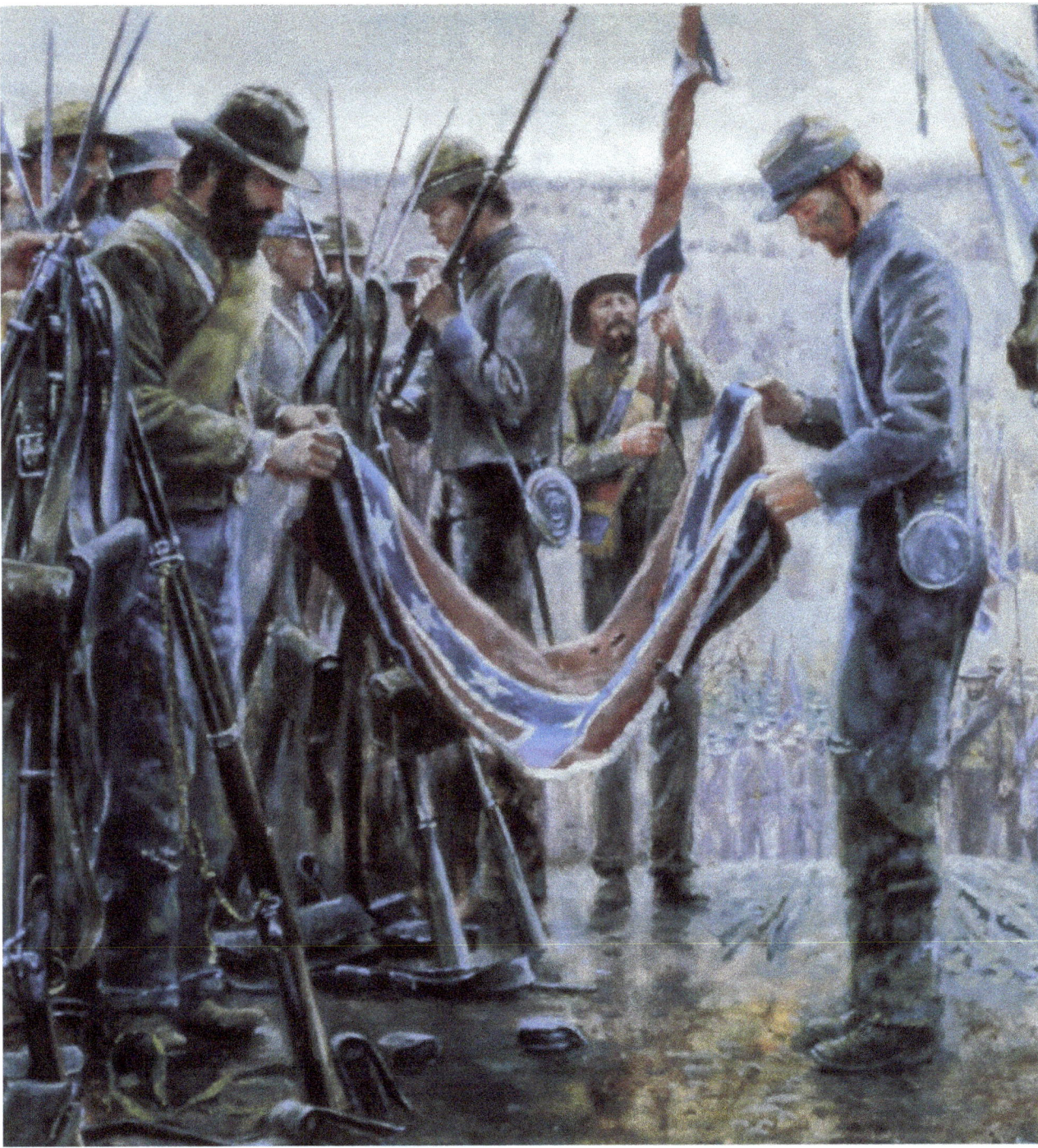

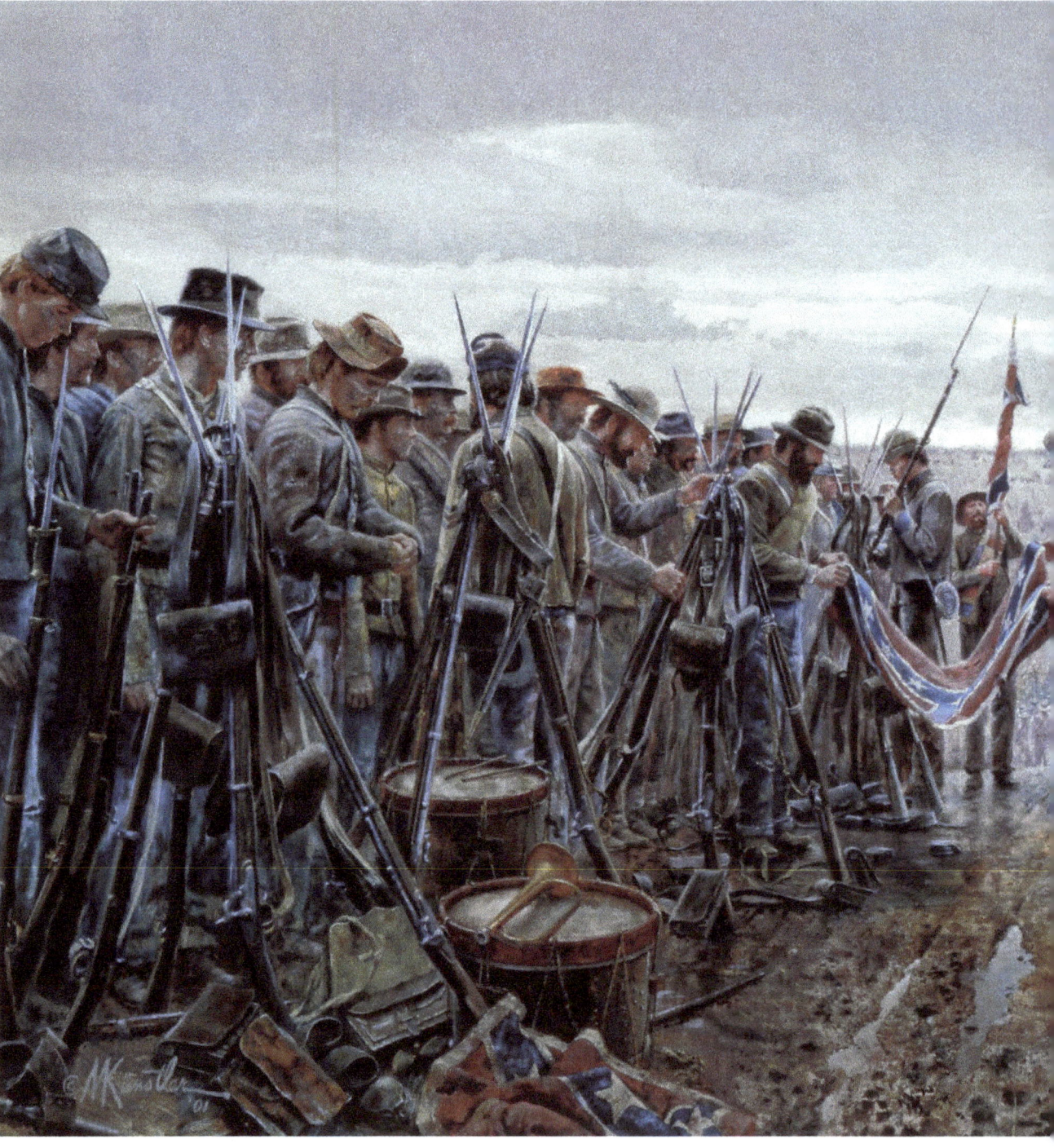

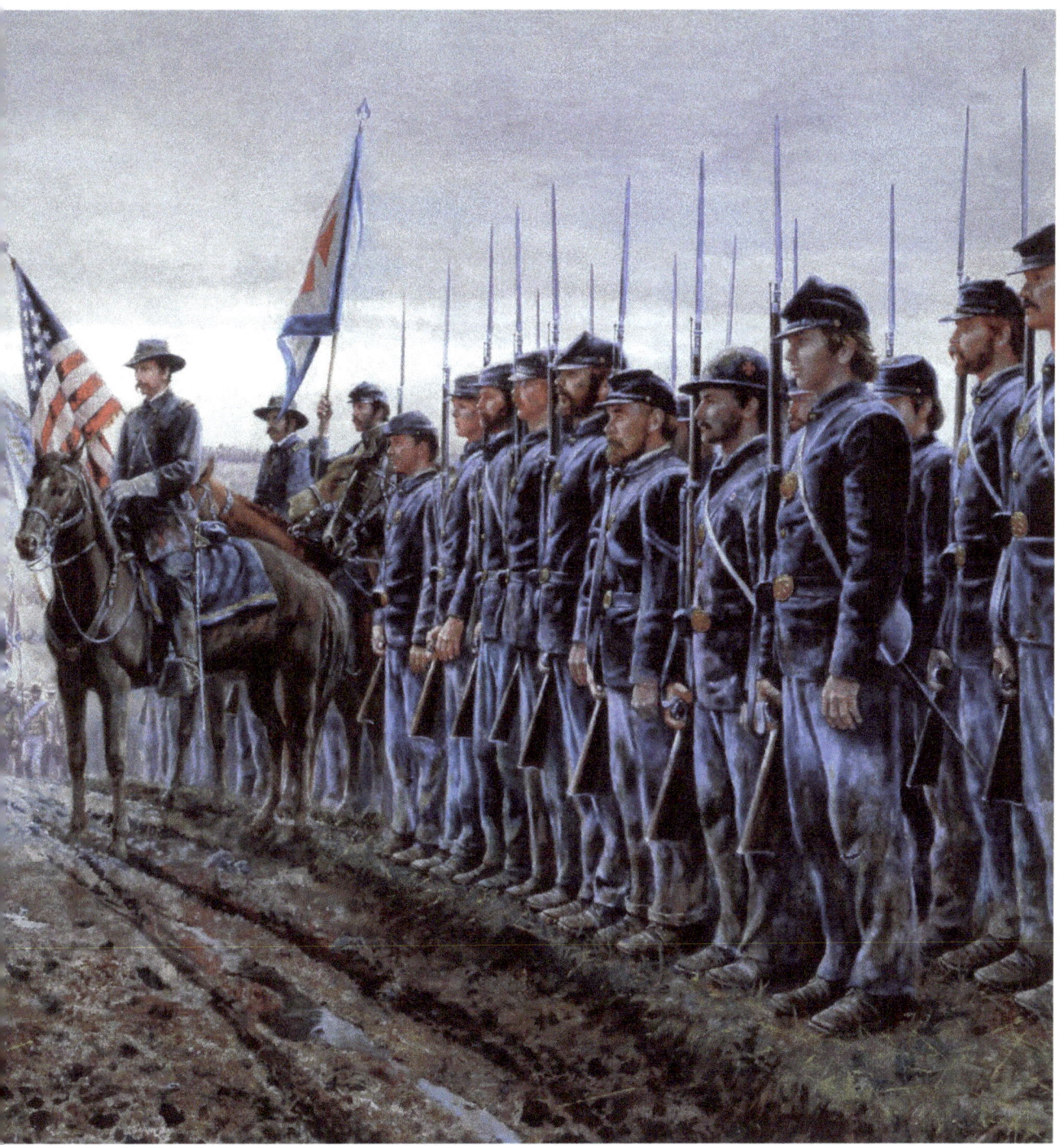

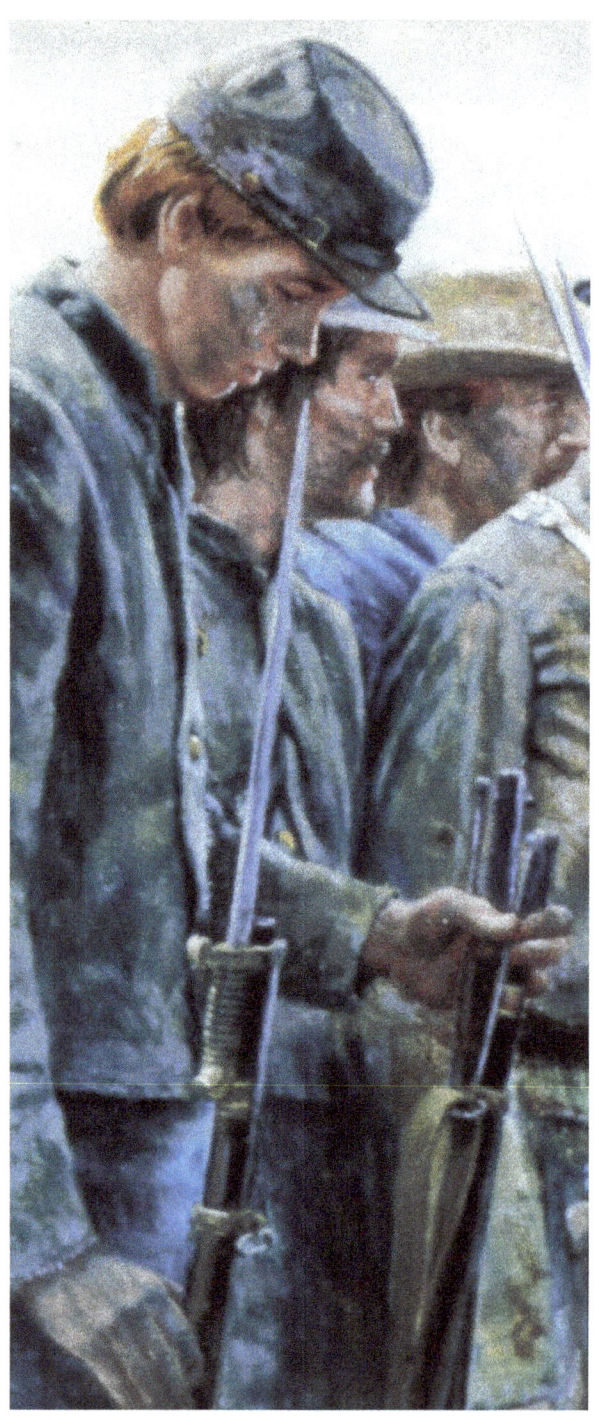

At Chamberlain's order, there was no jeering from the Federal troops. No beating of drums, no chorus of cheers, no other unseemly celebration in the face of a fallen foe. "Before us in proud humiliation," Chamberlain later recalled, "stood the embodiment of manhood: men whom neither toils and sufferings, nor the fact of death, nor disaster, nor hopelessness could bend from their resolve; standing before us now, thin, worn, and famished, but erect, and with eyes looking level into ours, waking memories that bound us together as no other bond. Was not such manhood to be welcomed back into a Union so tested and assured?"

At Chamberlain's command, his troops shifted their weapons to "carry arms"—a soldier's salute, delivered in respect to the Southerners standing before them. Confederate Gen. John B. Gordon immediately recognized this remarkable, generous gesture and responded with a like salute: honor answering honor. The ceremony concluded and a new day began, built on this salute of honor on the fields near Appomattox Court House. Former foes—showing mutual respect and mutual toleration—now faced the future together as Americans.

The surrender at Appomattox is a tempting scene for any artist. When I decided to do this work, I did not want to paint Lee and Grant inside the McLean house. The late Tom Lovell, a dear friend and a master artist, had already painted that scene to perfection. Instead, I thought about the days that followed the surrender and realized that the formal surrender of arms, which occurred three days later, was an incredibly dramatic and poignant moment in the conclusion of the war. Professor James I. Robertson Jr. of Virginia Tech agreed to meet me at Appomattox, and we studied the field and discussed the events of those crucial days with Joe Williams, the curator and chief

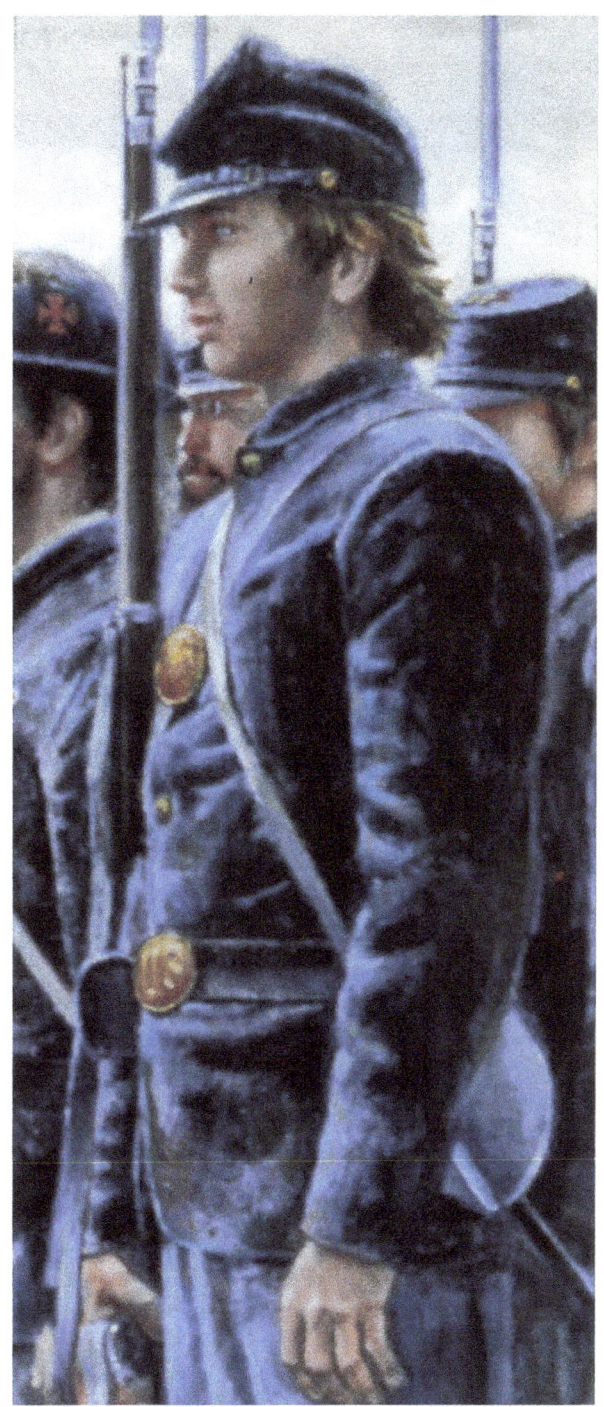

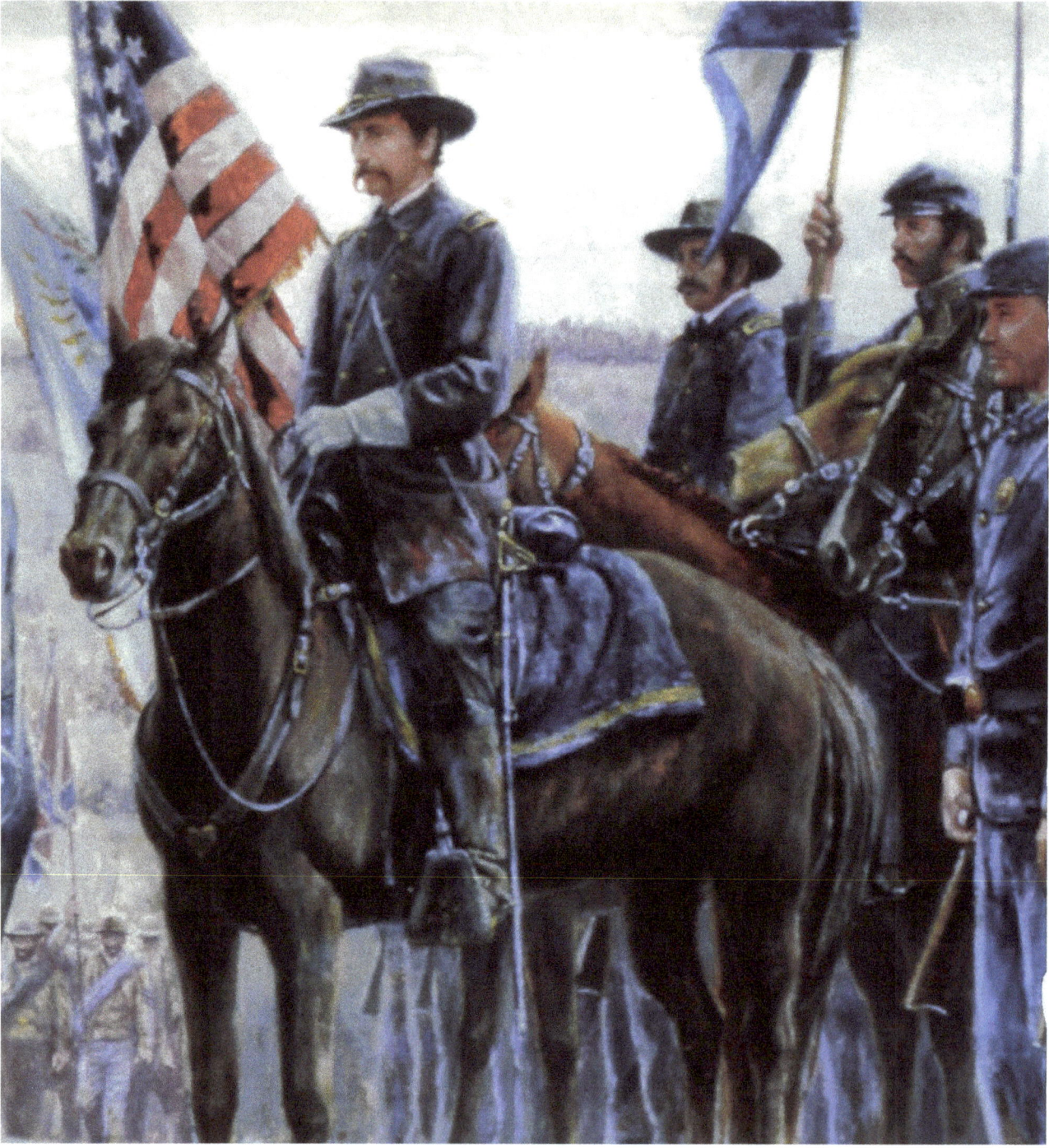

of the Division of Museum Services at Appomattox Court House, and with Appomattox historian Ron Wilson. All three men offered their insights on this subject. Also helpful were Tom Desjardin, an expert on Joshua L. Chamberlain; Col. Keith Gibson of the VMI Museum; and Michael J. McAfee, the curator of history at the West Point Museum.

Chamberlain holds a place of honor near the center of the painting, because it was his gracious gesture that helped establish the spirit of reconciliation that eventually reunited the North and the South as one nation. I painted the regimental colors of the Thirty-second Massachusetts, the regiment that was positioned at the far right of the Union line with Chamberlain. By adding Chamberlain's old brigade flag to the right, I surrounded him with flags in order to move the viewer's eye directly to him. The Confederate soldier furling the battle flag occupies the exact center of the painting, creating, between him and Chamberlain, a solid center of interest.

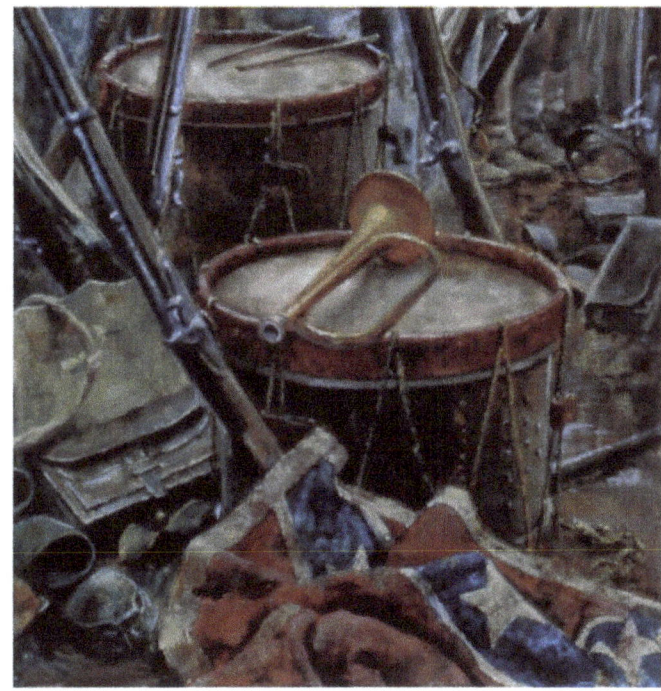

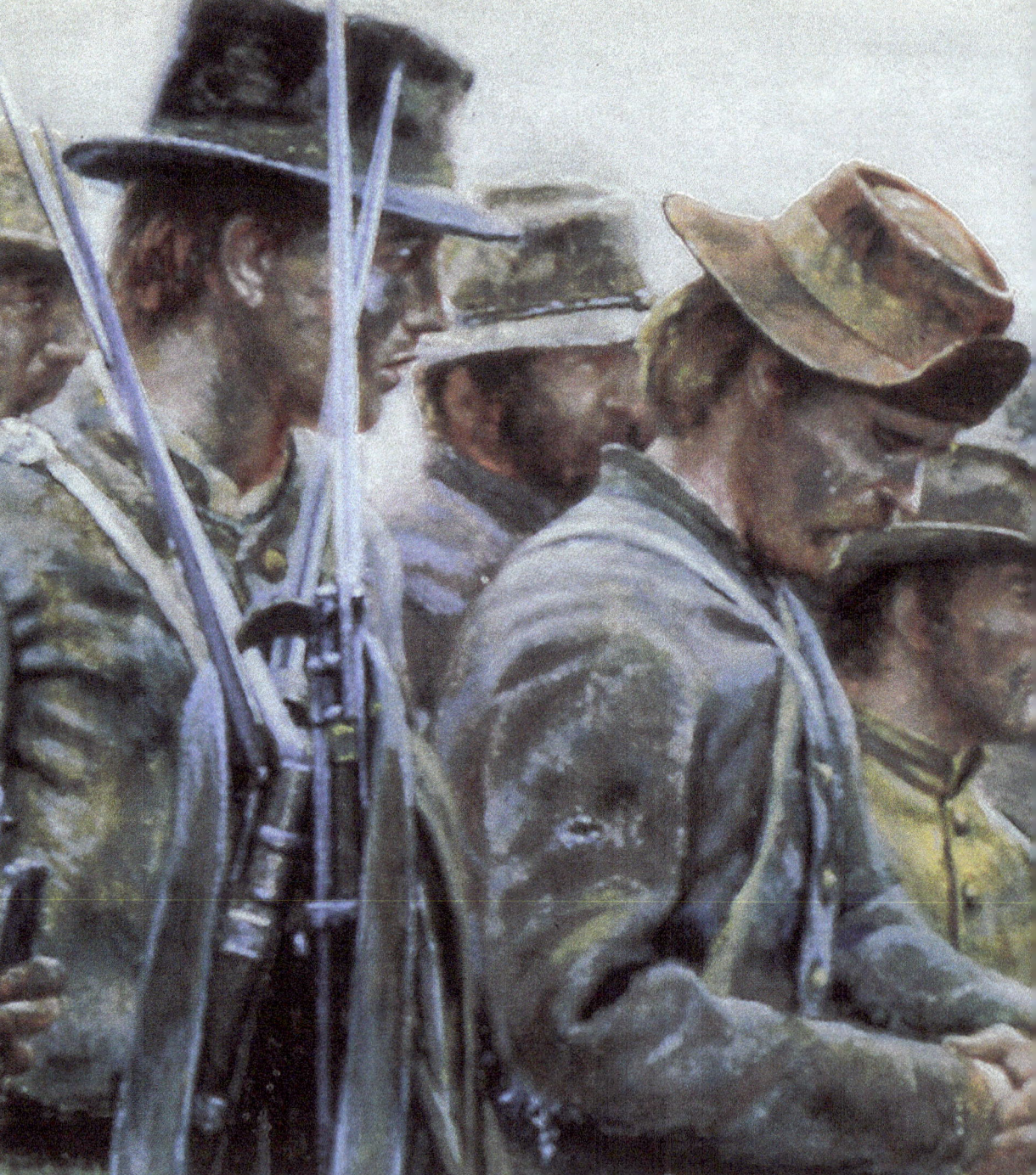

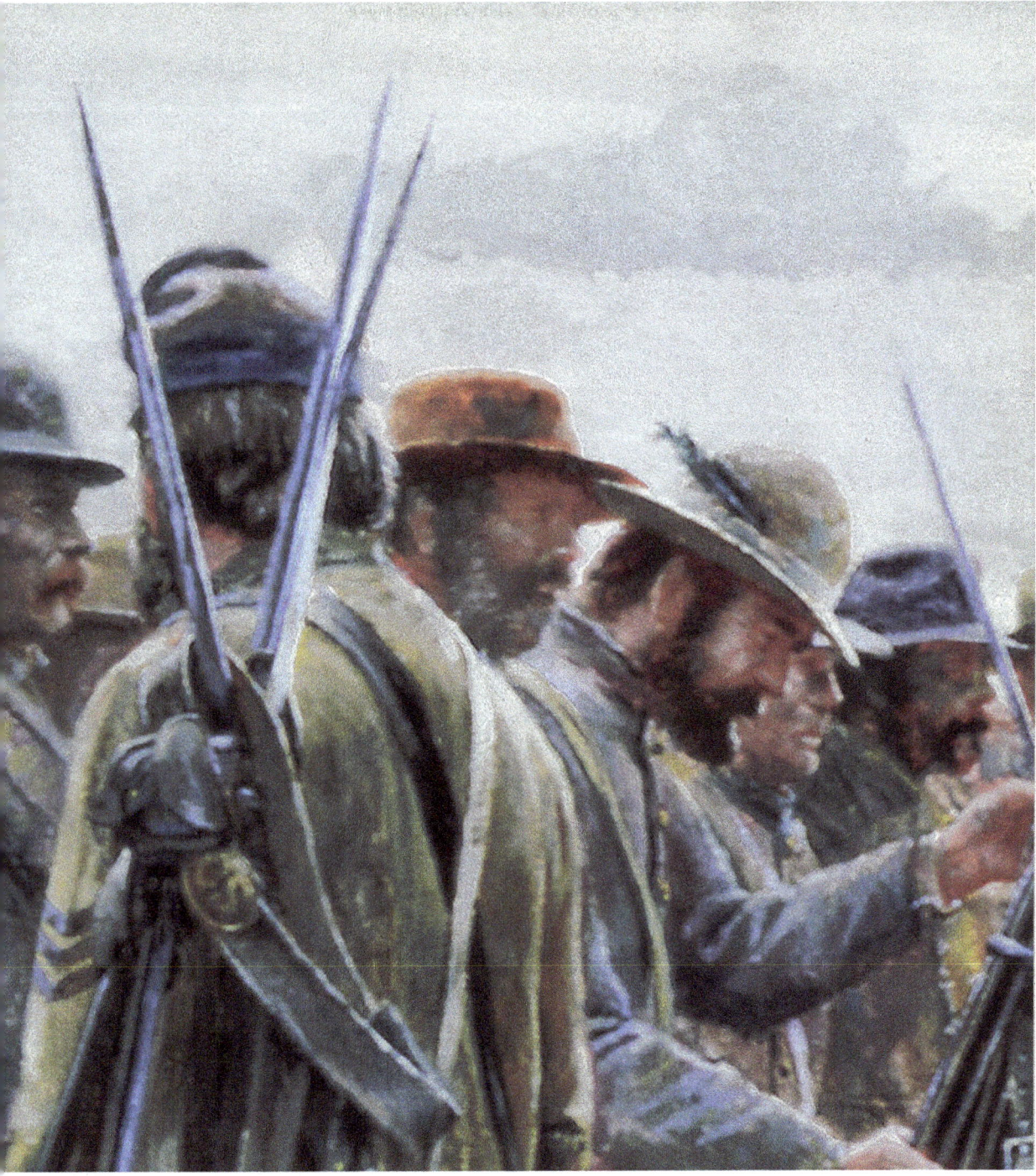

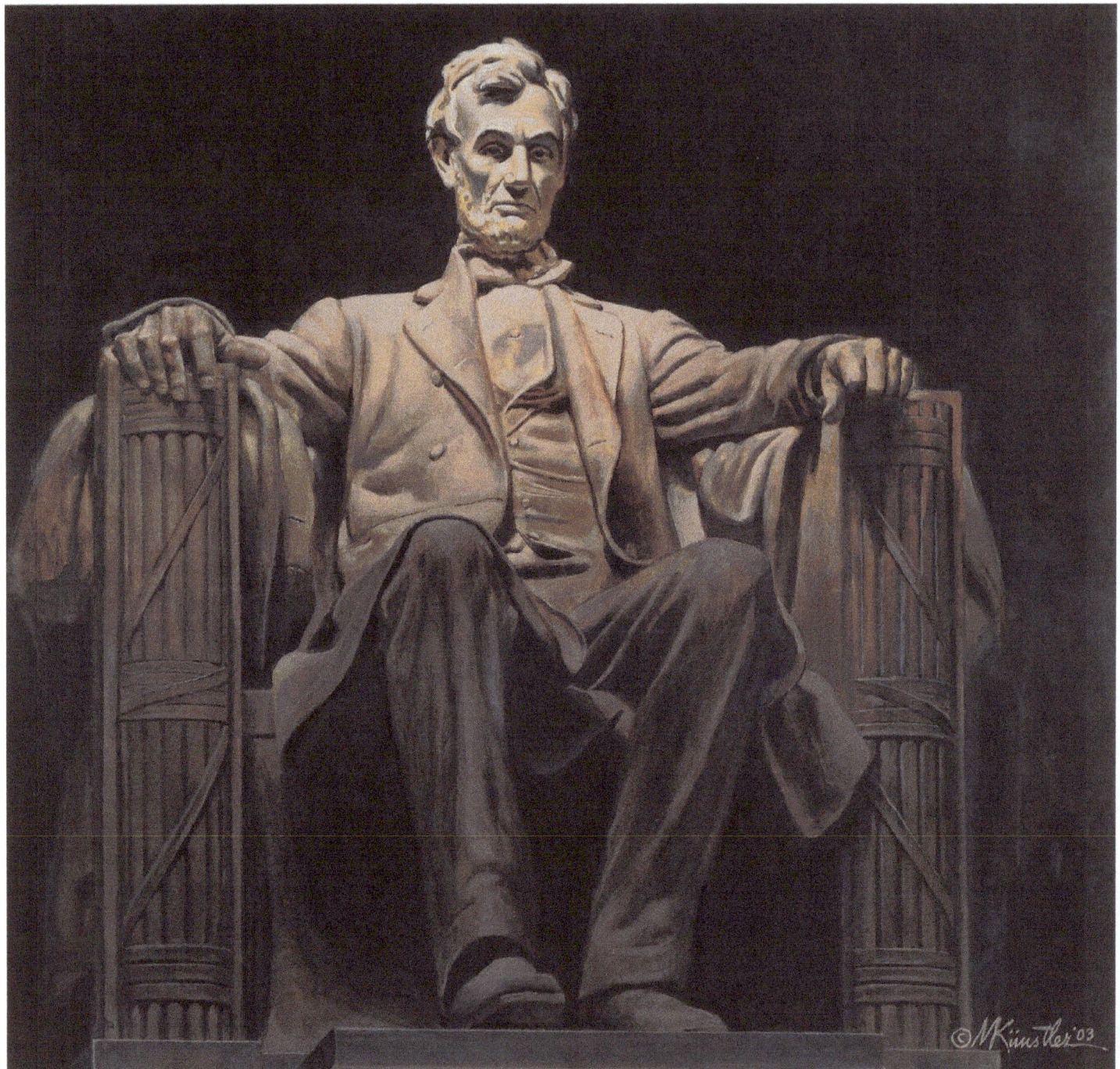

©MKünstler '03

LINCOLN MEMORIAL

2003, mixed media, 12 x 12

THE CELEBRATION IN WASHINGTON, D.C., that followed the news of Lee's surrender at Appomattox Court House was shattered around 10:30 p.m. on April 14 when actor John Wilkes Booth shot Abraham Lincoln at Ford's Theatre. Also targeted to die that night were Vice President Andrew Johnson and Secretary of State William H. Seward, but the former was never threatened and the latter was only wounded.

The unconscious president was carried to a boardinghouse across the street from the theater, and a vigil was kept throughout the night as Washington dignitaries paid their respects. Lincoln died at 7:22 a.m. on April 15. Mary Lincoln was so distraught at witnessing her husband's murder, she could not accompany the body when it returned to Springfield, Illinois, by the reverse route Lincoln had taken as president elect in 1861.

Two weeks later, Booth was killed during his apprehension. Of his eight co-conspirators, four were sentenced to hang—including the first woman to be executed by the federal government—and four were imprisoned. A ninth conspirator was apprehended a year later, but a jury acquitted him.

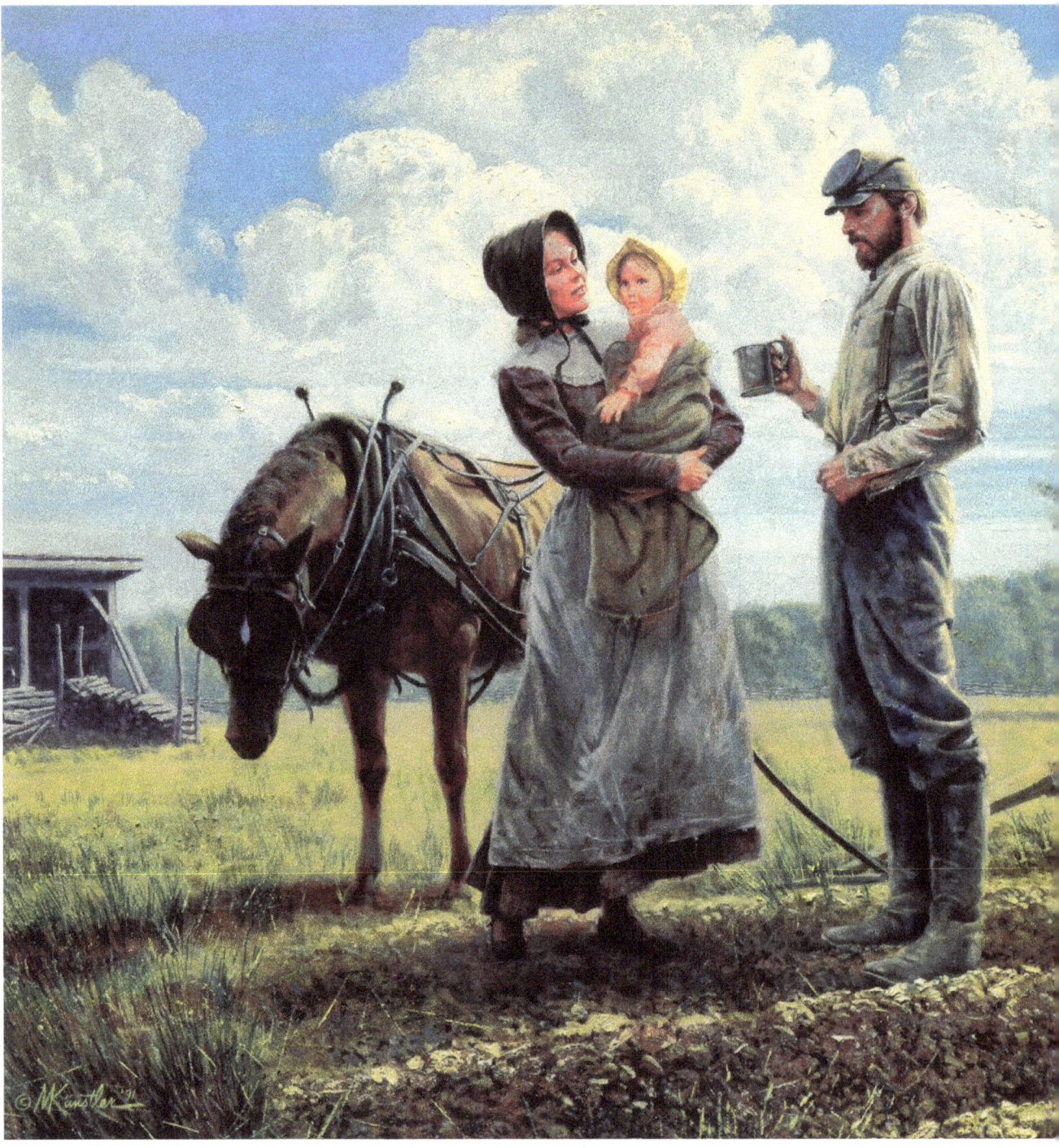

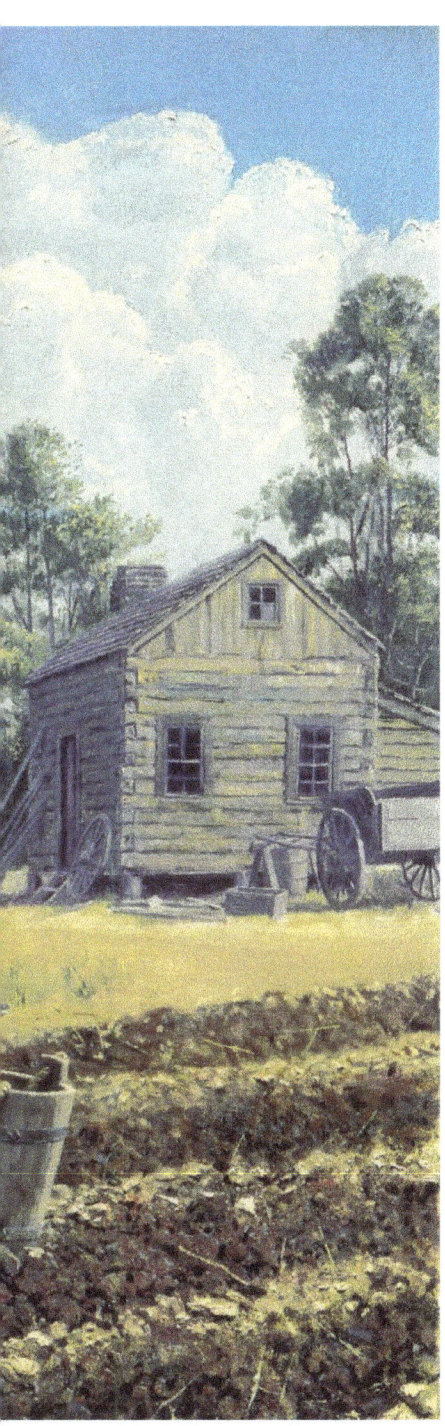

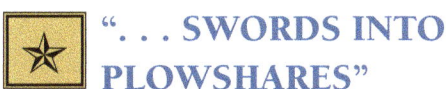 **". . . SWORDS INTO PLOWSHARES"**

1991, oil, 20 x 26

Two WEEKS BEFORE THE surrender at Appomattox Court House, Lincoln stated that all he wanted, when the time came, was "to get the men composing the Confederate armies back to their homes, at work on their farms or in their shops." Returning planters and their progeny came home to poverty instead of plantations. Yeoman farmers came home to patches of land barely kept going by the hard work and sacrifices of wives and children.

Secession had cost the South one-fourth of its white men between eighteen and thirty-five years of age, two-fifths of its livestock, half of its farm equipment, and two-thirds of its total property. Yet the survivors went to work, cheerless but determined, to salvage as much as possible from the wreckage and to build a better future.

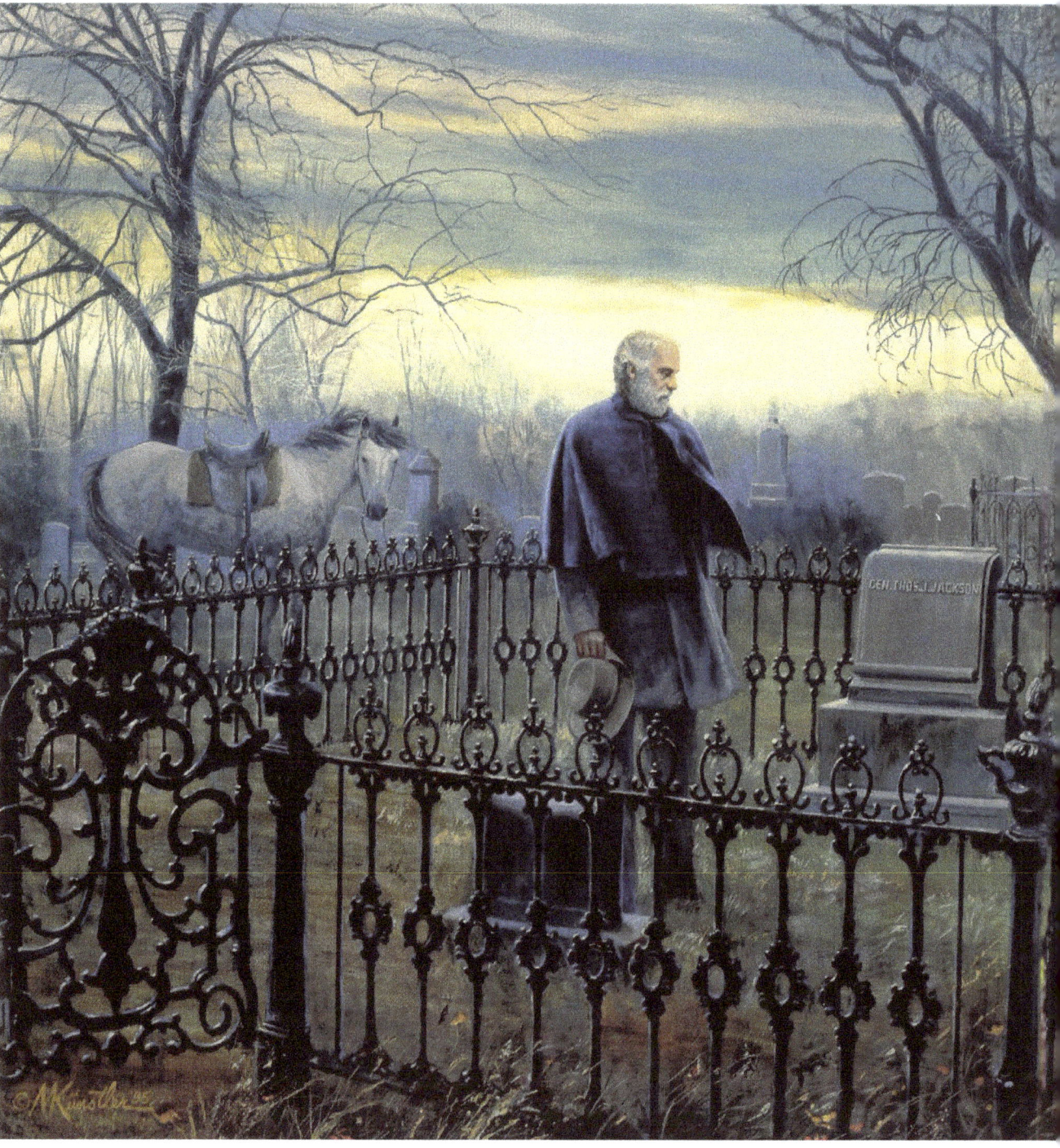

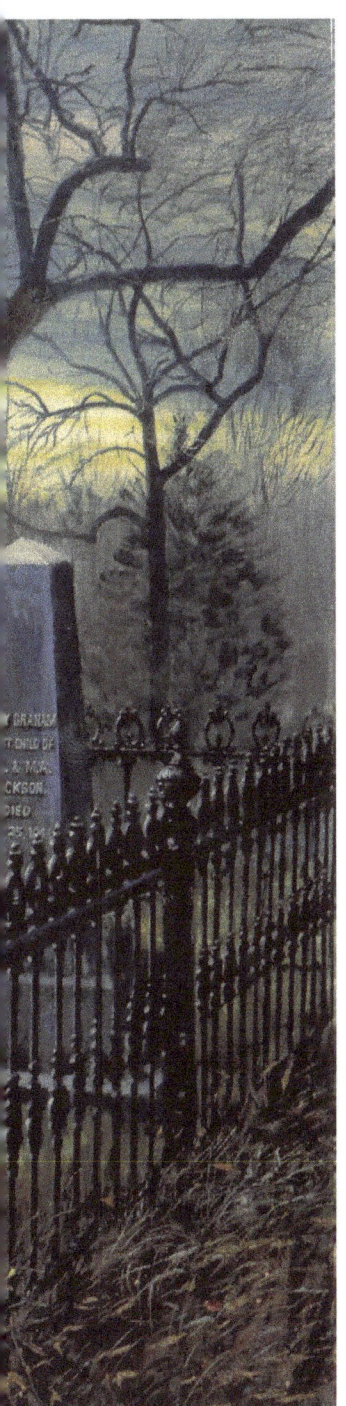

THE FINAL VISIT

ROBERT E. LEE
LEXINGTON, VIRGINIA

1995, oil, 16 x 2

I BELIEVE THERE WAS probably never a time when Lee wondered what might have been if his most faithful lieutenant, Thomas J. "Stonewall" Jackson, had remained with him throughout the war. I am sure he believed that Jackson's death was an act of Providence. Lee's attitude in his last years—and the fact that his life ended in the same town where Jackson was buried—intrigue me.

For *The Final Visit,* I chose a winter setting with gray colors to heighten the drama of a visit to Jackson's grave. The wind whipping at Lee's cloak and Traveller's mane adds poignancy to the moment, symbolizing a sense of loss while also representing the brief time the two men spent together, forging their strong alliance. This is a unique subject for me, and I believe this painting conveys a positive and appropriate way to remember two of the South's most beloved generals.

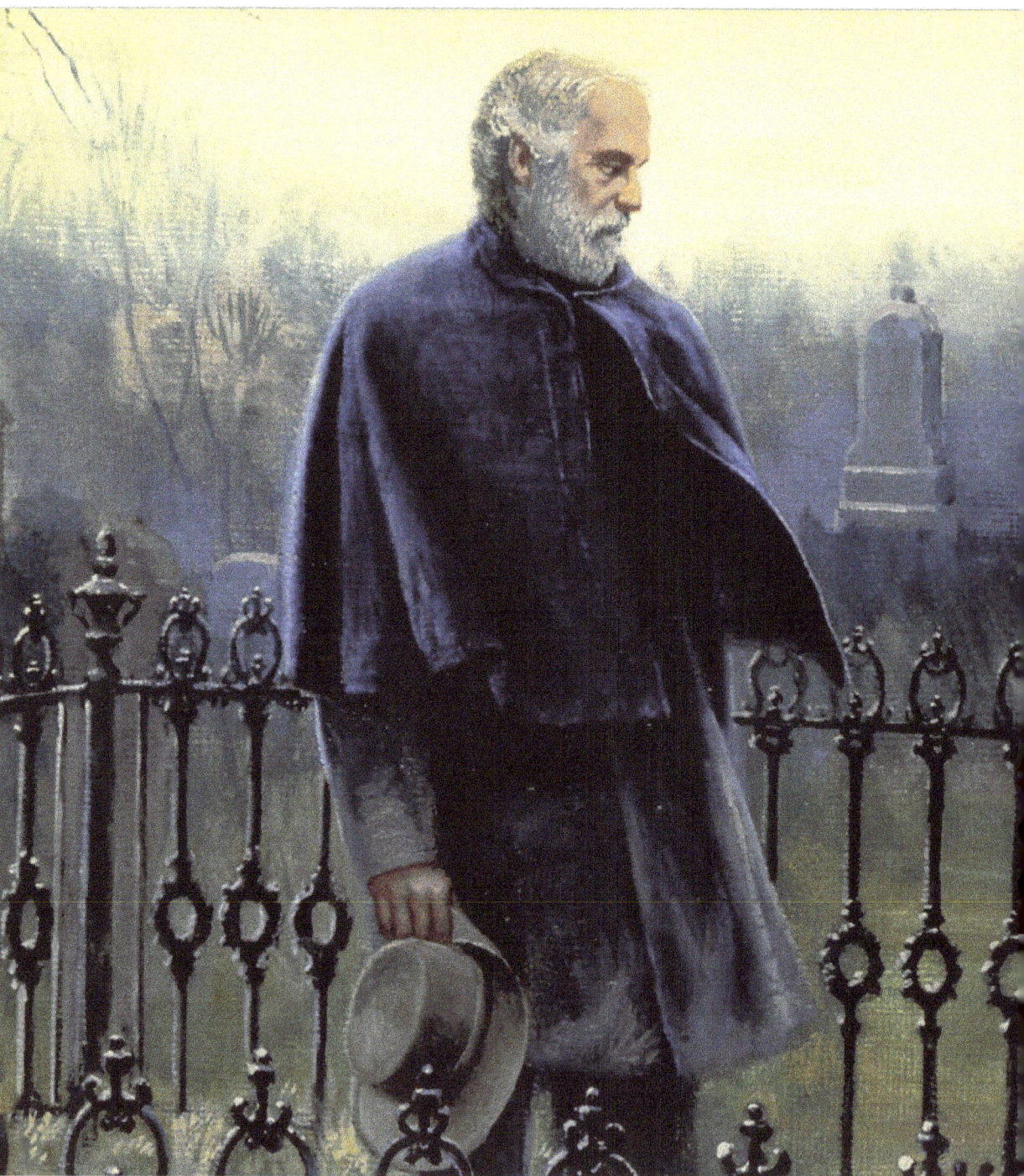

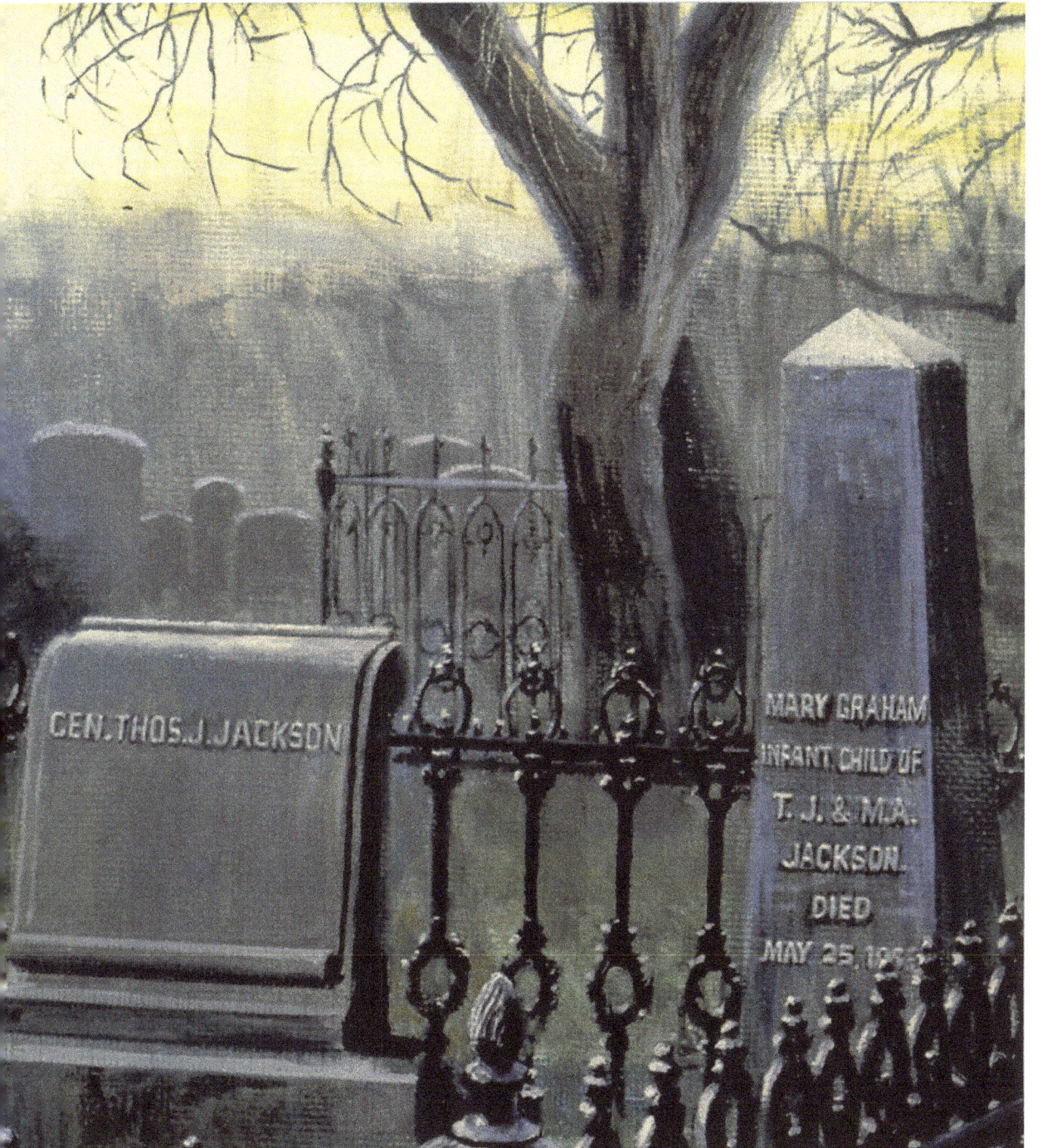

INDEX

ABOUT THE ARTIST

Mort Künstler is now known as America's foremost historical artist, but over the course of his fifty-year career he achieved that and many other distinctions. His name is well known to the publishers of illustrated books and magazines and to the art directors of advertising agencies because Künstler first made his mark as an outstanding illustrator. His paintings appeared on the covers of *Newsweek* and *Sports Afield,* in promotions for many motion pictures, and in countless advertisements and editorial features in national trade and consumer magazines.

Since 1977, when his paintings were first shown in major gallery and museum exhibitions, Künstler has been recognized as a distinguished fine artist. His paintings were exhibited in fifteen solo shows at the prestigious Hammer Galleries in New York City and numerous one-man exhibitions in museums around the country.

Künstler's career as an illustrator began in the 1950s, a time when the market had been reduced by the demise of many publications and the increased use of photographs in advertisements. His paintings appeared in some of the best-known publications of the day: *True, Argosy, The Saturday Evening Post, Sports Afield, Outdoor Life,* and *American Weekly.* In 1963 he began creating the kinds of historical paintings for which he is so well known today Assignments from magazines like *National Geographic* and *Newsweek* and for movies such as *The Hindenburg* gave him a chance to research his subjects and use that information to compose dramatic depictions of important historic events.

Beginning in 1985 there was an explosion of interest in Künstler's work from television and movie producers, book publishers, art buyers, and military buffs. Several books on his paintings were published, including companion books to epic films such as *Gettysburg* and *Gods and Generals.*

Künstler was the subject of a number of television programs. In October 1993, the Arts & Entertainment Network aired a one-hour segment on his Civil War paintings, showing the artist in his studio with many of these paintings in progress.

There is no other artist in the nation's history who has recorded so many events in American history, and certainly no one has painted them with the extraordinary authenticity and drama as Künstler. In a catalog for a 1998 exhibition of Künstler's Civil War paintings at the Nassau County Museum of Art, museum director Constance Schwartz observed that "Künstler is an heir to the European academic tradition" and compared his works to those of Thomas Eakins, Gilbert Stuart, Winslow Homer, Frederic Remington, and Charles Russell.

Professor James I. Robertson Jr. applauded Künstler's work by noting: "He is the foremost Civil War artist of our time (if not of all time) because of his devotion to the truth and detail in history. No one has better captured on canvas the sights, the feelings, the encompassing drama that formed the conflict of the 1860s. Many gifted wielders of the brush have given us scores of Civil War illustrations, but only Künstler has carried that skill to a level approaching perfection."

ACKNOWLEDGMENTS

I would like to thank Ron Pitkin, president of Cumberland House, and Ed Curtis, my editor, for their vision and creation of this series of Civil War books.

Dr. James I. Robertson Jr., historian and Alumni Distinguished Professor at Virginia Tech, has once again graced a book of mine with a superbly written foreword. I thank him for his contribution, but more important, the friendship we have shared over the years.

Rod Gragg, historian and author of numerous books on American history, has been a valued colleague and friend for many years, and I appreciate all his wise counsel.

Richard Lynch, president of Hammer Galleries, has encouraged and advised me for more than thirty years. I appreciate all his efforts on my behalf, as well as those of Howard Shaw, vice president of Hammer Galleries, and the rest of the staff.

My daughter, Jane Künstler Broffman, has been the head of this project. I can't thank her enough for all the time and expertise she has contributed to ensure not only the historical accuracy of these volumes but their beautiful appearance.

American Spirit Publishing, my publisher of fine-art prints, has flourished with her guidance and vision.

Paula McEvoy and Lissette Portillo of Künstler Enterprises have assisted in the production of this volume while handling the operation of my busy studio. I am thankful for all their hard work and effort.

My wife, Deborah, has supported and encouraged me, both personally and professionally for so many years, and I could not have done this without her. Painting is only my second love.

—Mort Künstler

www.ingramcontent.com/pod-product-compliance
Lightning Source LLC
Chambersburg PA
CBHW052134170526
45162CB00003B/13